THE A-Z OF THE MILLENNIUM

THE A-Z OF THE MILLENNIUM

Edited by Phil McNeill and Deanne Pearson

Designed by Linda Baritski and Phil McNeill
Jacket design by Paul Sudbury

Main text by Fred Dellar, Dan Fielder, Ray Setterfield and Mitchell Symons
Illustrations by Tom Hughes
Picture research and production by Eve Cossins
Research by Mark Crossland and Caroline Warde

With thanks to Terry Green, Hugh Bradley, Richard Campbell,
Sasha Willox, Alison Ives and Joseph Crowe
Special thanks to Neil Armstrong and Vivian White

Published by David Crowe and Mark Peacock
The Debenhams A-Z Of The Millennium book is an original concept by Peter Kaursland

First published in Great Britain in 1999 by Generation Publications Ltd
9 Holyrood Street, London SE1 2EL
genpub@btinternet.com

ISBN 1 903009 27 8

Production by Mike Powell & Associates (01494 676891)
Origination by Colour Systems Ltd, London
Printed and bound in Italy by Giunti Industrie Grafiche

***Pictured above:* Earth seen from the Moon by the Apollo 11 astronauts.**
***Previous page:* A Millennial meeting of the giants as The Beatles feel the force of Cassius Clay (later Muhammad Ali) on February 22, 1964, during their first trip to America. They had just gone to No 1 in the USA for the first time. Three days later, he won the world heavyweight title for the first time by beating champion Sonny Liston**

THE A-Z OF THE

MILLENNIUM

CONTENTS

From Apollo to Zoos, this is our complete *Illustrated Alphabet of the Millennium* created by young British artist Tom Hughes

FOREWORD

The 1,000-year journey to tomorrow's world

BY NEIL ARMSTRONG

In ancient times, the concept of a day was easy to understand: the time from one dawn to the next dawn or from one high noon to the following high noon. Longer periods of time were derived from the heavens: the number of days from one full moon to the next (about 29½ days) or from one summer solstice to the next (about 365¼ days). These numbers were untidy and did not easily lend themselves to being assembled into a logical arrangement.

Diverse societies around the Earth devised various kinds of calendars, attempting to put a measure of order in the recording of the days and the seasons. Calendar-making was frustrating; there was the inevitable need to periodically add days or months to account for the fractional inconveniences. Much of the world now uses the calendar devised by Julius Caesar (the Julian Calendar) as modified in the 16th century by Pope Gregory XIII (the Gregorian Calendar). Under this calendar, intended (but probably not correctly implemented) to define its first year as the year of the birth of Christ, 1AD (Anno Domini), we now near the end of the second Millennium. It is not surprising that experts have differing opinions as to when, precisely, that Millennium end occurs.

Among the many notable achievements of the second Millennium, history will prominently note the beginning of man's ability to travel away from Earth. Certain historical contributions to that achievement stand above the rest. In the early 16th century, Nicolas Copernicus concluded that the Earth was not the centre of the Universe, but rather rotated around the Sun. A century later, Johannes Kepler, drawing from the astronomical measurements of Tycho Brahe, devised the laws of planetary motion.

In the early 17th century, Galileo Galilei developed the law of the pendulum and the law of falling bodies. He used the new invention, the telescope, to observe the heavens and discovered that Earth's moon was a spherical body which reflected sunlight, that there were also four moons orbiting Jupiter.

Near the end of the 17th century, Sir Isaac Newton, drawing from Kepler's Laws, developed the more general Laws of Motion. Newton wrote to Robert Hooke: "If I have seen further, it is by standing on the shoulders of giants." Newton's Laws made possible the machines which produced the Industrial Revolution. The progress those machines provided was, in large measure, responsible for the increases in living standards we enjoy today.

The intellectual power of Copernicus, Kepler, Galileo and Newton, combined with the invention of the liquid rocket and the electronic computer in the last century of the second Millennium, shattered the chains of gravity that had heretofore constrained homo sapiens to the surface of Earth. And so it happened that a few of us, near the end of the second Millennium, ventured forth away from Earth and outward into space.

It was a beginning.

NEIL ARMSTRONG
JULY 20, 1999

Apollo 11 astronauts Neil Armstrong and Edwin 'Buzz' Aldrin plant the United States flag on the surface of the Moon on July 20, 1969. The picture was taken by a 16mm movie camera in the lunar module, Eagle

The Millennium at a glance...

	ART	MUSIC	LITERATURE	ENTERTAINMENT
1000s	**Bayeux Tapestry** *This work of embroidery depicting action in the Battle of Hastings is 224 feet long.*	**Sacred Music** *Chant hymns – responses to a priest's invocations – are the only known music of this period.*	**Book of Lore** *The Leech Book, a compendium of medical advice, folklore and superstition, was issued in 1010.*	**Birth of Modern Chess** *Chess was rediscovered in India and developed into the present 64 squares system.*
1100s	**Art in Chains** *The Orthodox Church enforced strict constraints on religious scenes.*	**The Highest Praise** *A hymn composed by French St Bernard of Clairvaux (1090-1153) has 2,966 lines.*	**Winchester Bible** *The Winchester Bible, lavishly and beautifully illustrated, was produced 1160-80.*	**The King Takes All** *Hunting was so popular, Henry I claimed all hunting land for himself.*
1200s	**New Perspective** *Italian artist Cimabué, founder of naturalist art, was born in 1240.*	**The Oldest Song** *'Sumer is Icumen', written c.1240, is the world's oldest song.*	**Book of Knowledge** *Bartolomew Anglicus, a popular encyclopaedia, was written about 1230.*	**Same Again, Landlord** *Distilling techniques were refined, increasing the popularity of taverns.*
1300s	**The Real Thing** *Jan Van Eyck (1390 -1441) produced realism masterpieces.*	**Composer's Triumph** *India's Amir Khusrau was renowned for fusing Hindu and Muslim spiritual themes.*	**The Teller of Tales** *Geoffrey Chaucer, right, conjured up The Canterbury Tales.*	**Pass The Swan, Please** *Feasting was great fun for the rich, and roast swan one of the popular dishes.*
1400s	**Birth of Surrealism** *Hieronymus Bosch (1450-1516) is still considered the best painter of fantasy.*	**Magic Of The Minstrels** *Music became popular as minstrels toured manor houses, castles and fairs.*	**Caxton's First Book** *Printing press inventor Caxton published his first book, The Sayings Of The Philosophers.*	**Time For A Good Read** *William Caxton's revolutionary presses brought literature to the masses for the first time.*
1500s	**Michelangelo Masterwork** *Michelangelo's sculpture of David, right, was completed in 1504.*	**The First Opera** *Italian Claudio Monteverdi wrote the first opera.*	**Literature's Glory Days** *A golden era for English literature, led by Shakespeare, Ben Jonson and Marlowe.*	**Applause For The Bard** *The theatres were hugely popular. Shakespeare, as an actor, performed at the Globe.*
1600s	**Portrait of Perfection** *Rembrandt van Rijn (1606-69), noted for his portraiture, painted his way into history.*	**Ballet is Born** *Ballet originated in the formal dances at the French Court under Louis XIV (1638-1715).*	**The King James Bible** *King James I ordered an English translation of the Bible. His Authorised Version is still in use.*	**Spoilsport Puritans** *Puritans banned theatres, betting and dancing, and burned unauthorised books.*
1700s	**Art Becomes Fun** *Rococo art, a light and frivolous style of painting, was popular in Europe until about 1760.*	**Best of Baroque** *J S Bach (1685-1750), right, was a leading light in baroque music.*	**Johnson Spells It Out** *Dr Johnson's Dictionary of the English Language was published in 1755.*	**Censorship Arrives** *A 1737 law meant all plays were to be officially censored.*
1800s	**Creating a Good Impression** *Impressionism was the big attraction of the 1800s, the stars being Monet, Degas and Renoir.*	**Land of Hope and Glory** *A tune composed by Sir Edward Elgar (1857-1934) was to become 'Land of Hope and Glory'.*	**Dickens By Instalment** *The work of novelist Charles Dickens was first serialised in magazines to eager readers.*	**The Big Kick-off** *The Football Association began in England in 1863.*
1900s	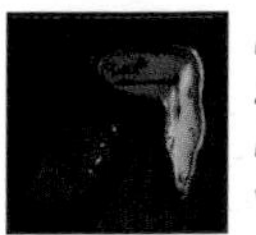 **Dali The Master** *Surrealism reached its highest form with Salvador Dali.*	**The Fab Four** *The Beatles stand as the most successful and influential pop music band of all time.*	**Stalin Takes The Record** *A record-shattering 672 million copies of the works of Josef Stalin were sold or distributed.*	**Lights, Camera, Action!** *Cinema made actresses such as Marilyn Monroe, right, into world stars.*

the key events of every century

WAR

Battle Of Hastings
William the Conqueror defeats King Harold at Hastings in 1066.

Holy Wars
Richard the Lionheart set off on the Second Crusade.

Start of an Empire
Genghis Khan's Mongolian armies swept across Asia and created a huge empire.

Hundred Years' War
The Hundred Years' War between England and France began in 1337.

The War Of The Roses
Thirty-year struggle between the Houses of Lancaster and York to wrest the Crown.

The Spanish Armada
Phillip II of Spain sent an armada of 130 ships against England. It was defeated.

England Divided
Civil War in England between Parliamentarians (Roundheads) and the Royalists (Cavaliers).

French Revolution
The Revolution and Reign of Terror began in 1789.

Napoleon's Waterloo
Britain's war with France ended with the defeat of Bonaparte at the 1815 Battle of Waterloo.

Second World War
The Second World War, the bloodiest conflict in history, caused nearly 55 million deaths.

POLITICS

Tax For Peace
King Ethelred II raised taxes to pay off invading Danes. Called 'Danegeld', it didn't work.

Keeping It In The Family
Henry I ordered his barons to accept his daughter as their future queen.

Magna Carta
King John was forced by his barons to sign the Magna Carta, the basis of British constitution.

Dick's Turn Again
Dick Whittington became Mayor of London four times.

Marriage Brings Peace
Lancastrian King Henry VII married Elizabeth of York and so put an end to the Civil War.

Henry Takes Control
A new law passed in 1535 made King Henry VIII supreme head of the Church of England.

Cromwell Rules
From 1653-58, England was ruled by military dictator Oliver Cromwell as Lord Protector.

Act of Union
The 1707 Act of Union ended the separate Scottish and English parliaments.

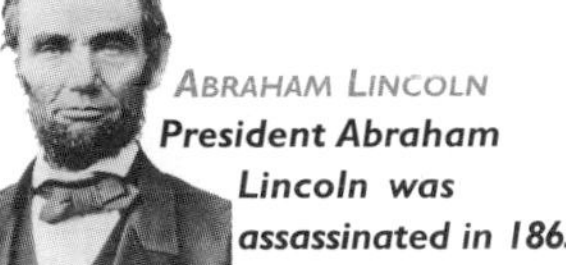

Abraham Lincoln
President Abraham Lincoln was assassinated in 1865.

Labour's Century
The Labour Party, in power at the start of the new Millennium, was formed in 1900.

ROYALTY

Ethelred's Bloodbath
Ethelred, already unpopular, ordered the deaths of thousands of Danish settlers in 1002.

Anguish of Henry I
Henry was deprived of his heir when his only son drowned.

Enter 'The Hammer'
King Henry III died in 1272 and was succeeded by his son, Edward I, 'Hammer of the Scots'.

Farewell, King
King Edward II was deposed in 1327 and agreed to abdicate. His son took over as Edward III.

Murder Of The Princes
The Princes in the Tower were murdered and their assumed killer became King Richard III.

Good Queen Bess
Elizabeth, daughter of Henry VIII, became Queen.

Charles Loses His Head
Charles I was put on trial for treason. He was found guilty and beheaded at Whitehall.

Home-Grown King
King George III (1760-1820) was the first English-born monarch since 1714.

The Victorian Era
In 1837, Victoria succeeded William IV to the throne. She reigned until 1901.

Death Of A Princess
In 1997, the world mourned the death of Princess Diana.

SCIENCE

Gunpowder Plotted
The Chinese made gunpowder, using charcoal, sulphur and potassium nitrate.

Wind Power Harnessed
Windmills were invented and spread across Europe. The production of silk began.

Clear Aims Established
The longbow was developed, the wheelbarrow invented, and spectacles first appeared.

The First Steel Crossbow
The steel crossbow appeared on battlefields for the first time. Fortunately, so did plate armour.

Mastery Of The Sea
Navigational techniques and vessels were greatly improved as exploration boomed.

Timely Invention
Clocks became common in the 1500s. And the first guns were fired.

Penny Drops For Newton
Sir Isaac Newton, right, discovered laws for mechanics, gravitation and calculus.

Industrial Revolution
The steam engine and other inventions ushered in Britain's industrial revolution.

Computer Breakthrough
English mathematician Charles Babbage designed an early computer in 1834.

The Space Age
The century of the Space Age, microchips and the Internet.

EXPLORATION

North America Discovered
Norwegian explorer Leif Eriksson is thought to have sailed to North America.

Trek Across Europe
Thousands joined the crusading trek across Europe to the Holy Lands. Many perished.

The Wonders of China
Italy's Marco Polo went to China and saw wonders of civilisation that were unknown in the West.

Canary Islands Discovered
A French ship, exploring the Atlantic Ocean, landed at the Canary Islands in 1312.

Conquering The World
This was the era of great explorers with Columbus, Cabot and Prince Henry of Portugal.

Drake's Circumnavigation
Sir Francis Drake went round the world, looting £1.5 million from the Spanish as he went.

Puritans Set Sail
The 102 Pilgrim Fathers set sail aboard the Mayflower from Plymouth for North America.

Captain Cook
Explorer Captain Cook crossed the Antarctic Circle.

Livingstone in Africa
Dr David Livingstone, the missionary and explorer, began working in the African interior.

Man On The Moon
Neil Armstrong became the first man to step on to the surface of the Moon in 1969.

ARCHITECTURE

1867 ***Sir Charles Barry's Palace of Westminster – a true world landmark and still the pride of London today***

1999 ***Sir Richard Rogers' Millennium Dome prepares for take-off downriver. But will we still love it in 2099?***

ART

The history of art through the Millennium sometimes seems like a retreat. From the beauty of Michelangelo's Sistine Chapel ceiling (below) to the 1960s comicbook Pop Art of Roy Lichtenstein (right) ... can that be progress? From *King Lear* to *Trainspotting*. From Mozart to Blur. Surely the world's going backwards...

At times, 20th-century art seems paralysed by self-consciousness, as if all the Great Art has been done, and all that's left is in-jokes and commercial stunts. Often, artists appear to create for other artists; you need to have been to art college to understand it.

But the best art still makes a connection without explanation – just like Lichtenstein, *Trainspotting* and Blur. For, as Shakespeare, Michelangelo and Mozart would no doubt agree, it's a happy artist whose audience says: "I don't know if it's art, but I like it..."

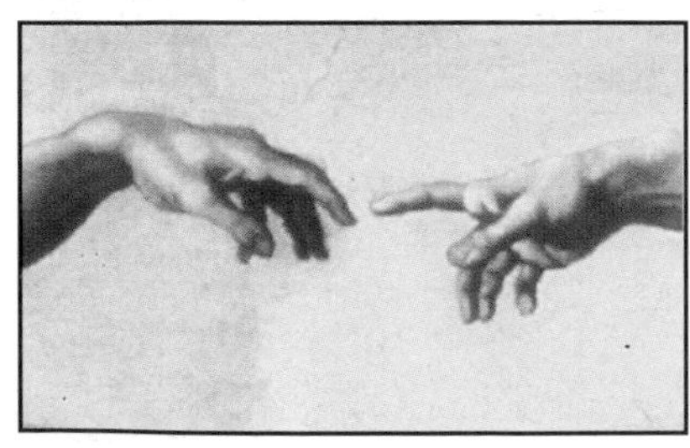

1000
VIKINGS DISCOVER AMERICA
The Viking Leif Ericson, not Christopher Columbus, was the first European to set foot in North America. Ericson named the area he discovered, on the northeast coast of Canada, Vinland (now believed to be Nova Scotia) because of the wild grapes growing there.

1010
FIRST NOVEL
The Tale of Genji by Shikibu Murasaki, lady-in-waiting to the empress of Japan, may be the world's first novel. It tells of Prince Genji's life and loves and has an underlying Buddhist philosophy.

1013
ENGLAND CONQUERED
Danish King Sweyn (Forkbeard) conquered England in 1013 forcing Ethelred the Unready (meaning ill-advised) to flee to Normandy. Within two years both kings were dead, leaving their sons, Canute and Edmund, to battle it out for the English throne. Edmund was murdered in 1016 and Canute became the undisputed ruler. And a good one at that.

NEIL ARMSTRONG AND APOLLO 11

Commander Neil Armstrong in Apollo 11, and Buzz Aldrin returning to the lunar module, Eagle. The two men spent two-and-a-half hours walking on the Moon

The greatest adventure of the Millennium began on July 16, 1969, when *Apollo 11* blasted off from the Kennedy Space Center, Florida, to the cheers of a million people on the ground – and watched by hundreds of millions more on television. But for Neil Alden Armstrong, the adventure had begun 31 years before that, when he took his first plane ride at the age of six. From that day on, he was hooked on flight.

Armstrong took flying lessons at the age of 15 in Wapakoneta, Ohio, and qualified to be a pilot at 16. His studies for an aeronautical engineering degree were interrupted by the Korean War, where he flew Navy Panther jets.

He became an astronaut in 1962, and made his first space flight aboard *Gemini 8* in 1966, piloting it to the first docking with another spacecraft. The docking was successful; what happened next was not. As the two craft orbited, locked together, they began to rock wildly, and Armstrong had to take emergency measures to get safely back to Earth.

That experience no doubt set him in good stead on July 20, 1969, as he brought *Apollo 11*'s lunar module – *Eagle* – in to land on the Moon, and found that "the auto targeting was taking us right into a football-sized crater with a large number of big boulders, and it required flying manually over the rock field to find a reasonably good area". With less than 30 seconds' worth of fuel left, Commander Armstrong calmly selected his spot in the Sea of Tranquility, then sent Houston the message: "The Eagle has landed."

A few hours later, Armstrong made the tricky descent down the ladder – with a metre drop from the last step – before delivering his famous line: "That's one small step for a man, one giant leap for mankind." Buzz Aldrin joined him, while their *Apollo 11* colleague Michael Collins stayed in orbit, and for two-and-a-half hours Armstrong and Aldrin experienced something that still makes the imagination reel: life on the Moon.

The lighter gravity was not a problem to the two astronauts, Armstrong has said. "It was, in fact, preferable both to weightlessness and to the Earth's gravity. We had much less trouble than expected on the surface. The primary difficulty was just far too little time to do the variety of things we would have liked. We had the problem of the five-year-old boy in a candy store."

After 21 hours on the Moon, and eight days away from Earth, the astronauts returned to a heroes' welcome – and a fortnight in quarantine…

Apollo 11 was the first of six *Apollo* missions to land on the Moon – not forgetting *Apollo 13*, which returned without landing due to a malfunction and was the subject of the film starring Tom Hanks. The last people on the Moon were astronaut Eugene Cernan and geologist Harrison Schmitt, with *Apollo 17* in 1972.

Back in 1969, many people thought there would be a permanent lunar base by the start of the new Millennium; it hasn't happened. But, as *Apollo 15* astronaut Dave Scott pointed out: "We could have run more missions, but in historical perspective – gosh, it's only been 30 years. That isn't long. When you look at the major explorations in history, there are 100, 200 years between the major events. So we're just regrouping now."

What they said about Apollo 11

"If I could have climbed into the TV set then I would have done so. I'm willing to predict that 500 years from now, 10,000 years from now, the people of the future will look back and say this was the greatest day in the history of mankind. We've been clinging here on this planet for millions of years, hoping some day to reach the Moon. And finally we broke free and the spirit of mankind soared into space on that night, and it will never stop soaring."
– Author Ray Bradbury

"It would have been nice to have changed the roles, where I could have been looking out the window all the time and controlling the spacecraft to land. That's just not the way it was scheduled to be. But if I did have the chance to do it again, I would try to sneak a look out the window just to be able to keep that in my mind for the rest of my life."
– Buzz Aldrin

A

1027
Girls For Sale
While King Canute was gaining kudos as a wise ruler of England, his sister was enjoying the proceeds of a lucrative white slave trade that she had set up, selling English girls to Scandinavia.

1032
Man Who Sold Papal Throne
Benedict IX became Pope for the first time. A corrupt figure, in 1044 he was declared unfit to rule by powerful Roman cardinals and was driven out of office. The following year he reinstated himself but within 12 months sold the papacy to his godfather. Benedict regained the office in 1047, only to be driven out again in 1048.

1040
Murder Most Foul
Macbeth murdered Duncan, King of Scotland, and took over as ruler. He died peacefully 17 years later and was succeeded by his stepson Lulach. Which only goes to prove that you cannot believe all you read in Shakespeare.

British fight fans watch in awe as the young American heavyweight Cassius Clay limbers up for his match with Henry Cooper at the Empire Stadium, Wembley, in 1963. Cooper knocked him down and nearly out, but was then cut so badly that the fight was stopped in the fifth

MUHAMMAD ALI

In 1996, the world watched as a trembling Muhammad Ali, stricken with Parkinson's disease, put the Olympic torch to the cauldron in a symbolic gesture to start the Atlanta summer games. It was another extraordinary moment in the life of the world's most famous sportsman.

Born Cassius Clay in Louisville, Kentucky, in 1942, he began boxing at 12 and broke through in 1960 when he won light-heavyweight gold at the Rome Olympics. He had exceptional speed for his build, and a relentless instinct for self-promotion. Calling himself The Greatest, he took to predicting in rhyme the round in which he would score his next KO.

'Float like a butterfly, sting like a bee'

ALI'S CORNERMAN BUNDINI BROWN, ADVISING HIM HOW TO BEAT SONNY LISTON IN 1964

In 1964 he pulled off a major upset by unseating world heavyweight champion Sonny Liston. But then he converted to the Nation of Islam, becoming a Black Muslim – and the popularity of the newly-named Muhammad Ali plummeted. Three years later, he antagonised Middle America by refusing to fight in the Vietnam war. "I ain't got no quarrel with them Viet Congs," he said.

Stripped of his title, Ali was threatened with prison. But, as public opinion turned against the war, support for him grew. Finally, after Ali had lost three of his best years of boxing, the Supreme Court ruled in his favour. It was, perhaps, his bravest fight of all.

In 1971 Ali lost his title to Smokin' Joe Frazier, but won it back in 1974. Next he faced the unbeaten George Foreman in the legendary Rumble In The Jungle. Ali, a 7-1 outsider, stood covered against the ropes and absorbed all the giant Foreman could throw at him – then scored an incredible knockout in the eighth. In 1978, he lost to Leon Spinks on a split decision, but then beat him to become the only man to win the title three times.

As illness set in, Ali's public appearances dwindled, but his humanitarian work and legendary deeds make him still one of the best-loved people on the planet.

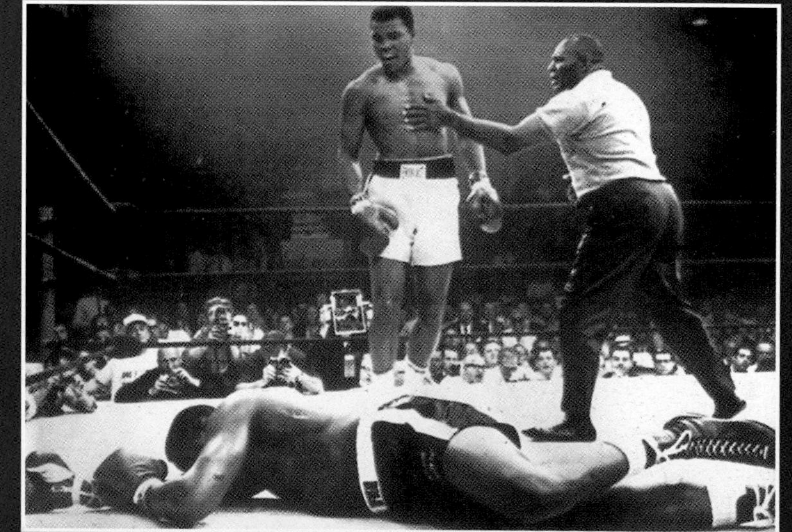

MAKING OF A LEGEND: CLAY WINS THE WORLD HEAVYWEIGHT TITLE FOR THE FIRST TIME, LEAVING THE GIANT SONNY LISTON POLEAXED ON THE CANVAS. THE FORMIDABLE LISTON HAD BEEN THOUGHT UNBEATABLE; NOW THAT MANTLE WOULD FALL TO ALI

1065
WESTMINSTER ABBEY
Building of the original abbey was completed in 1065. All but two of Britain's kings and queens have been crowned there.

1066
THE BATTLE OF HASTINGS
Probably the most famous date in English history. King Harold II died during the battle and William, Duke of Normandy (William the Conqueror), succeeded to the throne. The legend has grown that Harold was killed after being struck in the eye by an arrow. But scholars say the only evidence for this is the 224ft (68m) Bayeux Tapestry, made about 1067-70, which appears to show Harold being killed in that way.

1067
BATTLE ABBEY
A significant year for important buildings. Battle Abbey was founded in Sussex to commemorate William's victory the year before. At the same time, the cathedral at Canterbury, built by the Saxons, was burned down. And work started on the White Tower at the Tower of London.

'Only two things are infinite: the Universe and human stupidity – and I'm not sure about the former'

ALBERT EINSTEIN, INITIATOR OF THE AMERICAN ATOM BOMB

THE ATOMIC BOMB

THE UNITED STATES DROPPED THE ONLY TWO ATOM BOMBS USED IN WAR – ON HIROSHIMA AND NAGASAKI, JAPAN, IN 1945. THE TWO MASSIVE EXPLOSIONS LEFT OVER 200,000 DEAD OR SERIOUSLY INJURED. TODAY, THE USA IS ONE OF ONLY FIVE NATIONS – WITH RUSSIA, CHINA, BRITAIN AND FRANCE – PERMITTED TO HOLD NUCLEAR WEAPONS UNDER THE UNITED NATIONS NON-PROLIFERATION TREATY. HOWEVER, IT IS SAID THAT INDIA, PAKISTAN, ISRAEL, NORTH KOREA, IRAN AND IRAQ HAVE UNDISCLOSED ARSENALS. THERE'S A SCARY THOUGHT...

ASSASSINATIONS

TEN LEADERS WHO SURVIVED ASSASSINATION ATTEMPTS

(AND PROBABLY THOUGHT THEY WERE IMMORTAL ANYWAY)

CHARLES DE GAULLE *1961* A sacked general tries to blow up the French President's car. "A joke in very bad taste," he says.

ADOLF HITLER *1944* German officers blow up the Führer's HQ. Three die. He calls his attackers "criminally stupid".

RONALD REAGAN *1981* John Hinckley, a disc jockey, shoots the US President in the chest. "I forgot to duck," he says.

POPE JOHN PAUL II *1981* A Turk shoots the Pope to protest against US imperialism. Bystanders said he looked crazy.

MARGARET THATCHER *1984* Three die when an IRA bomb shatters the Brighton Grand Hotel, where the PM is staying for the Tory Conference.

FIDEL CASTRO *1956* Cuba's President Batista thinks rebel Castro is dead after his planes bomb Fidel's jungle hideout.

GEORGE WALLACE *1972* A white man shoots the segregationist Governor of Alabama and cripples him.

GERALD FORD *1975* Two women try to shoot the President in 17 days – one a member of Charles Manson's 'Family'.

SHAH OF IRAN *1965* Three die in a machine gun attack.

YASSER ARAFAT *1985* Fifty die as Israel bombs the Palestine Liberation Organisation HQ in Beirut, Lebanon.

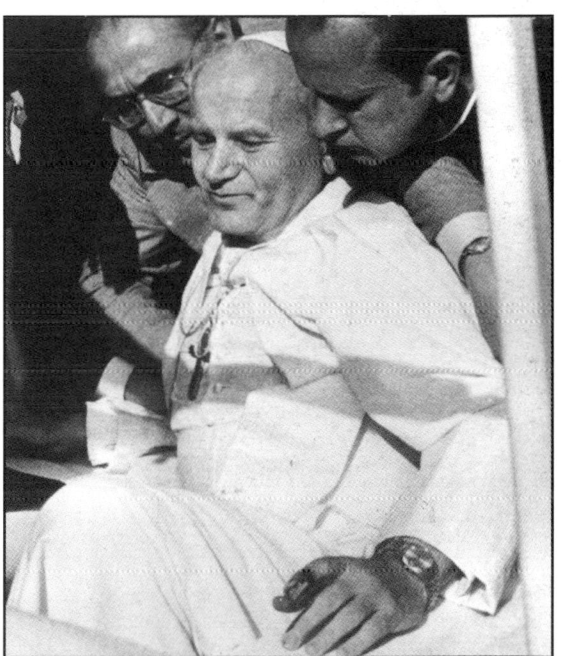

After the Pope was shot, he met his would-be assassin in prison, forgave him, and even let him kiss his hand

1076
'I'M SORRY' SAYS KING IN RAGS
Henry I was excommunicated by Pope Gregory VII after the king convoked a German council at Worms to depose the Pope. Henry's nobles demanded his climbdown. As a result the King had to spend three days standing barefoot in the snow, dressed in penitent's rags and begging forgiveness outside a castle at Canossa, Italy, where the Pope was staying.

1086
DOMESDAY BOOK
William the Conqueror ordered a survey of all the property in England and details of every manor were recorded in the famous Domesday Book. It included how many people lived there and so what taxes needed to be paid. It was called Domesday (day of doom) because there was no way anybody could escape its judgment.

1088
THE FIRST UNIVERSITY
The University of Bologna in Italy, which still exists, is generally regarded as the prototype of universities today. Established in the 11th century, it focused on law studies and attracted scholars from all over Europe.

ALICE IN WONDERLAND

FOR ALICE, THE MAD HATTER'S TEA PARTY WAS – LIKE MANY OF HER ENCOUNTERS – A TRIAL BY LOGIC: *'Take some more tea,' the March Hare said to Alice, very earnestly. 'I've had nothing yet,' Alice replied in an offended tone, 'so I can't take more.' 'You mean you can't take less,' said the Hatter: 'It's very easy to take more than nothing.'*

Alice's Adventures in Wonderland began as a story told to a real little girl called Alice Liddell, daughter of a family befriended by its author, Charles Lutwidge Dodgson – better known as Lewis Carroll.

Dodgson was a shy, stuttering Oxford don, a studious bachelor and brilliant mathematician. Born in 1832, the third of 11 children (with seven sisters), he was said only to be comfortable in the company of little girls, whom he amused with stories and liked to photograph naked. In our day it is hard to view such a situation entirely innocently, and indeed relations between Dodgson and Alice's family were later suddenly severed in mysterious circumstances.

Nevertheless, Alice's story

'Curiouser and curiouser!'

THE DUCHESS – A PEPPERY TYRANT WITH A VICTORIAN LINE IN CHILDCARE: *'Speak roughly to your little boy, And beat him when he sneezes; He only does it to annoy, Because he knows it teases'*

JANE AUSTEN

Jane Austen's witty English romances are as popular now as when she died in 1817. The BBC's *Pride and Prejudice* sparked Austen-mania in 1995, followed by Emma Thompson's *Sense and Sensibility* (left, with Kate Winslet) and Gwyneth Paltrow as *Emma*. There was even a US teen movie – *Clueless* – based on *Emma*.

For years Austen was derided as glib and 'female', but today the whole world loves her heroines' heaving bosoms.

As Austen (right) wrote in *Mansfield Park*: "Let other pens dwell on guilt and misery. I quit such odious subjects as soon as I can."

1095
POPE LAUNCHES THE FIRST CRUSADE
Pope Urban II launched the Crusades by calling on Christian Europe to recapture the Holy Land. In his historic Clermont Address he said that "a race from the kingdom of the Persians, an accursed race, wholly alienated from God, has violently invaded the lands of the Christians and has depopulated them by pillage and fire, killing captives by cruel tortures". There were eight Crusades over the next 200 years. All but the first were failures.

1102
EDWARD THE CONFESSOR'S STAYING POWER
Rumours that the body of Edward the Confessor, who had died 36 years earlier in 1066, had not decayed were found to be true after Henry I allowed his tomb to be opened. One bishop was stopped from snipping a piece off the dead King's white beard for a souvenir. In 1163, the body, astonishingly still undecayed, was transferred to a new shrine on the orders of Henry II.

– published in 1865 – would become an enduring classic of children's literature. Brilliantly illustrated by Sir John Tenniel, the cartoonish dream-fantasy of white rabbits running late, bloodthirsty card-queens and hookah-smoking caterpillars has become a staple of our cultural background. We all grew up with the Mad Hatter, the March Hare, the Cheshire Cat and *Through the Looking-Glass*'s Tweedledum and Tweedledee.

Alice made Dodgson famous. Since his death in 1898, her adventures have spawned hundreds of films, plays, pantomimes, books and pieces of music, and the characters have appeared on adverts, posters and stamps. There is even a psychological condition known as Mad Hatter's disease!

Perhaps part of the appeal is that the whimsy is rooted in logic – Dodgson liked to compose mathematical puzzles, and several appear in the story. But what charms us most is that, for all its silliness, this topsy-turvy world somehow makes sense – as the child in each of us instinctively understands.

ADVERTISING

The first ten commercials broadcast on British TV, 1955

1. *Gibbs SR toothpaste*
2. *Cadbury's drinking chocolate*
3. *Kraft cheese*
4. *Dunlop tyres*
5. *Woman magazine*
6. *Surf washing powder*
7. *National Benzole petrol*
8. *Lux soap*
9. *Ford cars*
10. *Guinness*

AIRCRAFT

1903 *Eight days before Christmas, engineers Wilbur and Orville Wright unveil their gift to package tourists of the future as the first airplane leaves the ground in their home town of Kittyhawk, North Carolina, piloted by Orville himself. In the same year, Henry Ford set up his car-making company. The future starts here...*

1969 *Concorde was supposed to usher in a new era of aviation. But although it still breaks the sound barrier flying from London to New York at 1336 mph, the 13 Concorde planes may not be replaced when they wear out in 2010. Supersonic travel is too expensive, so our grandchildren may never see one of the marvels of our time*

1130
Early Gothic Architecture
Originating in the early 12th century, Gothic architecture is epitomised by its pointed arches and large stained-glass windows. Around 1130, architects discovered new techniques which enabled them to build bigger and higher buildings. Critics who found the style ugly named it Gothic after the barbarian Goths.

1137
Eleanor of Aquitaine
In 1137, Eleanor of Aquitaine inherited so much land that she became one of the most powerful women in Europe. Her second husband became King Henry II of England.

1139
Crossbow Outlawed
The crossbow had become such a deadly and feared weapon that Catholics meeting in 1139 decided to ban it. Opponents of the weapon were horrified that it could hurl a missile 300 metres (328 yards) and was capable of piercing chain mail. But the ban applied only to using it against Christians and was widely flouted. The crossbow remained popular until it was succeeded in the 15th century by an even more devilish weapon – the firearm.

AMERICAN WAR OF INDEPENDENCE

The American Revolution was a potent symbol of a people's fight for freedom. From 1763, Britain imposed a series of unpopular taxes on its 13 North American colonies.

War began on April 9, 1775, when British soldiers and American revolutionaries clashed at the Massachusetts towns of Lexington and Concord. The Americans sought reconciliation but King George III refused, so the union declared independence on July 4, 1776. After France allied itself with America, the British caved in at Yorktown, Virginia.

After eight years' conflict, the Treaty of Paris gave independence to the United States on September 3, 1783. George Washington, who had led the US army, became the first President of a nation that would grow to be the most powerful on earth.

The Boston Tea Party was no party. Britain's 1773 Tea Act exempted its East India Company from taxes, so American protesters dumped 342 chests of tea in Boston harbour, sparking the Revolution

THE ALAMO

Originally built in the city of San Antonio as a colonial Spanish mission, the Alamo was the scene of a famous battle during the war for Texan independence. Dissatisfied with the Mexican government, Texas had decided to sever relations in the winter of 1835-6. In response the Mexican general, Santa Anna, marched 4,000 men on San Antonio.

The city's 189 Texans retreated to the Alamo – Jim Bowie and Davy Crockett among them. Short on ammunition and cut off from reinforcements, they held out for 12 days, even using their rifles as clubs, but were eventually massacred.

However, their defiance bought valuable time, and Texas later won its independence from Mexico.

"Remember the Alamo!" became a famous battle cry. John Wayne certainly did – he directed and starred in the classic 1960 movie which made the Alamo a legend.

AMERICAN CIVIL WAR

This bloody dispute was really a clash between two ways of life: the breakaway Confederacy of Southern states, with their agricultural economy and black slave labour, against the city-based Northern Yankees, opposed to slavery and keen to keep the Union intact. War began in 1861 when Southern troops fired at a Union military outpost, and ended four years later when Confederate General Robert E Lee surrendered in Virginia.

The first modern war, it involved trench warfare, ironclad ships, mines and submarines. The death toll was just as modern: 620,000 – almost as many Americans as in all other conflicts put together, including two World Wars and Vietnam.

Robert E Lee: a brilliant general, but his Civil War ended in defeat

Wild frontiersman

HOLLYWOOD HERO JOHN WAYNE PLAYED DAVY CROCKETT IN HIS OWN FILM OF THE ALAMO – "THE MISSION THAT BECAME A FORTRESS... THE FORTRESS THAT BECAME A SHRINE". AS EVER, HE DIED WITH ALL GUNS BLAZING

1140
ANTI-SEMITISM SWEEPS EUROPE
After a 12-year-old boy was found murdered in Norwich, rumours spread that he had been sacrificed by Jews. The story caused a wave of anti-Semitism to sweep across England and spread to France. The boy, a skinner's apprentice, became St William of Norwich.

1150
THE TEMPLE OF ANGKOR WAT
This magnificent Buddhist temple in Kampuchea (formerly Cambodia) is one of the most impressive buildings in the world. It was built during the reign of King Suryavarman II at Angkor, capital of the Khmer Empire from the 9th to the 15th century.

1154
CHARTRES CATHEDRAL
Work began on Chartres Cathedral, near Paris in 1154. No sooner had it been built, however, than it was destroyed by fire, apart from a few carved portals. It was rebuilt in the High Gothic style and remains one of the world's finest examples of such architecture.

ACTORS

LIFELINES

Hollywood standard-setters who have brought laughter, tears and a sexual frisson to the century's cinema-goers

Tom Hanks
The genial boy-next-door who can do no wrong, Hanks won back-to-back Best Actor Oscars in 1993 and 1994 for *Philadelphia* and *Forrest Gump*.

Leonardo DiCaprio
The latest in a long line of handsome Hollywood rebels, DiCaprio's lead role in *Titanic* – the top-grossing movie up to 1999 – made him today's hottest property.

Marlon Brando
The original Method actor, Brando's Oscar-winning performance as *The Godfather* has a strong claim to being the greatest ever.

Marilyn Monroe
The original 'candle in the wind' and Hollywood's best-loved sex symbol, Monroe took on mythic proportions after her troubled death at just 35.

Charlie Chaplin
Undisputed king of the silent screen comedies, Chaplin's 'little tramp' remains cinema's most recognisable character.

Fred Astaire and Ginger Rogers
He was Hollywood's greatest dancer, she was his perfect foil. They teamed in ten films including *Top Hat*, packed with set-piece classics such as 'Isn't It A Lovely Day?'.

Gwyneth Paltrow
Paltrow's performance in *Shakespeare in Love* won her the last Best Actress Oscar of the Millennium. Cue floods of tears and instant world fame…

Robert De Niro
The greatest living film actor? De Niro put on 60lb to play boxer Jake La Motta – and win a second Oscar – in *Raging Bull*.

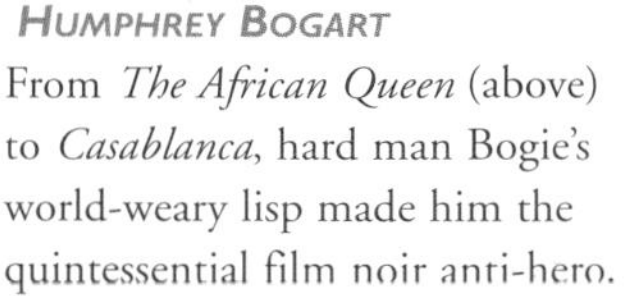

Katharine Hepburn
Her record of 12 Oscar nominations and four wins – three after the age of 60 – remains unbeaten to this day.

Humphrey Bogart
From *The African Queen* (above) to *Casablanca*, hard man Bogie's world-weary lisp made him the quintessential film noir anti-hero.

***Hans Christian Andersen**, 1805-1875, wrote fairy stories such as The Ugly Duckling and The Little Mermaid. A Dane, his life story became a Hollywood musical in 1952, starring Danny Kaye.*

***Julie Andrews**, born in 1935, is the typically English star of such films as Mary Poppins and The Sound Of Music – though the singer-actress has constantly tried to shrug off the image. In 1998, throat surgery threatened to end her career.*

***Louis 'Satchmo' Armstrong** was the world's favourite jazz man. Born in New Orleans in 1901, he shaped the course of jazz as a trumpeter, and went to No 1 as a singer in 1968 on 'Wonderful World'. His voice still graces TV ads long after his death in 1971*

A

1170
The Murder of Thomas Becket
Despite being made Archbishop of Canterbury by Henry II, Thomas Becket fell out with the King, particularly over his attempts to control the affairs of the Catholic Church. In 1170, after the King's despairing utterance, "Who will rid me of this troublesome priest?", four of Henry's knights murdered Becket. Rome later declared him a saint and in 1174, as well as being forced to do penance at Becket's tomb at Canterbury, Henry was flogged by monks.

1171
Miracle Cures
A cult of worship surrounding Thomas Becket began when the custodian of his shrine in the crypt of Canterbury Cathedral revealed that there had been 14 miraculous cures among pilgrims who had come to pray before Becket.

1178
Lunar Explosion
Fear and panic ensued after an explosion on the Moon was widely visible across Britain. Modern scientists have theorised that it was caused by the impact of a meteor causing the crater now known as Giordano Bruno.

BJORN BORG

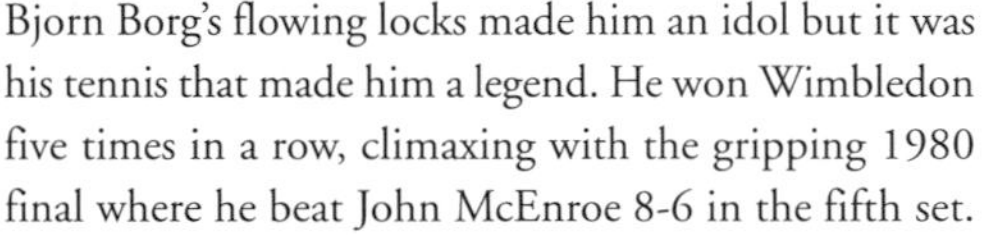

Bjorn Borg's flowing locks made him an idol but it was his tennis that made him a legend. He won Wimbledon five times in a row, climaxing with the gripping 1980 final where he beat John McEnroe 8-6 in the fifth set.

BORIS BECKER

In 1985 Boris Becker became Wimbledon's youngest men's champion and the first unseeded winner. He was also Germany's first champion and, as the Berlin Wall came down, Becker proved himself unusually passionate and outspoken for a sportsman. He made his Wimbledon bow in 1999, having won it three times.

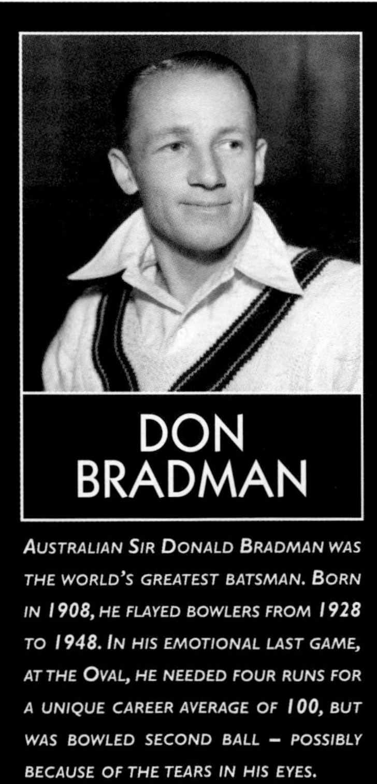

DON BRADMAN

AUSTRALIAN SIR DONALD BRADMAN WAS THE WORLD'S GREATEST BATSMAN. BORN IN **1908**, HE FLAYED BOWLERS FROM **1928** TO **1948**. IN HIS EMOTIONAL LAST GAME, AT THE OVAL, HE NEEDED FOUR RUNS FOR A UNIQUE CAREER AVERAGE OF **100**, BUT WAS BOWLED SECOND BALL – POSSIBLY BECAUSE OF THE TEARS IN HIS EYES.

GEORGE BEST

It's 1977. George Best, 31, looks a happy man. Yet in the eyes of the world he was a tragedy. For five years he had swanned around with various Miss Worlds, falling out of night-clubs, playing the odd low-key football game. Yet in the Sixties, the Northern Irish genius was Europe's best footballer, winning the 1968 European Cup Final for Manchester United almost solo. Did the 'fifth Beatle' waste his talent? Best's message was always: "Je ne regrette rien."

IAN BOTHAM

'BEEFY' BOTHAM'S IMMORTALITY WAS ASSURED IN **1981** WHEN, WITH ENGLAND FOLLOWING ON, SEVEN WICKETS DOWN, STILL **92** BEHIND AUSTRALIA'S FIRST INNINGS, HE THRASHED **149** NOT OUT TO SET UP A MIRACULOUS WIN. HE TOOK A RECORD **383** TEST WICKETS AND SCORED **5200** RUNS, BUT HIS CAVALIER ATTITUDE MADE HIM A VILLAIN TO THE CRICKET ESTABLISHMENT – AND A HERO TO MILLIONS.

1189
RICHARD THE LIONHEART
King Richard I, dubbed the Lionheart, reigned for 10 years (1189-99) and started as he meant to go on – fighting wars. He began by setting off on the Third Crusade and continued campaigns for another five years before, almost inevitably, being killed by an arrow during a skirmish in 1199. He remains a legendary and heroic figure.

1192
SAMURAI AND SHOGUNS
Shoguns, who were military dictators, were the rulers of Japan from the late 12th century to the late 19th century. The first of the shogunates was the Kamakura, which lasted from 1185 until 1333.

1196
GENGHIS KHAN
His real name was Temujin, but the world knows him as Genghis Khan – supreme ruler. He came to power among the Mongols in 1196. His people were illiterate, poor and nomadic. But from them he formed well-disciplined armies that would conquer much of the world from China to Europe.

THE BEANO

This comic cost tuppence (1p) when it appeared on July 30, 1938. Today it would cost £6800. That's the record sum paid at auction for a first edition. The *Beano* was launched soon after its stablemate *The Dandy* by DC Thomson, the Scottish publisher of *Wizard* and the *Rover* since the 1920s.

The first *Beano* had an ostrich called Big Eggo on the front, where Dennis the Menace now takes pride of place. Lord Snooty was also in the first *Beano*, and lasted into the Nineties. But the comic really took off when the rebels took over: Dennis arrived in 1951, followed by Roger the Dodger, Minnie the Minx and the Bash Street Kids. Their exploits propelled *The Beano* to a Fifties peak of two million copies a week. The look of *The Beano* was largely down to its long-serving editor George Moonie and a galaxy of comic illustrators such as David Law, Dudley D Watkins, Ken Reid, Mal Judge and Leo Baxendale.

To celebrate its 60th birthday in 1998, *The Beano* launched an Internet website. It's a long way from Big Eggo.

1951 ***Dennis the Menace arrives in The Beano, followed by Minnie the Minx. Comics will never be the same again***

BLACK ADDER AND MR BEAN

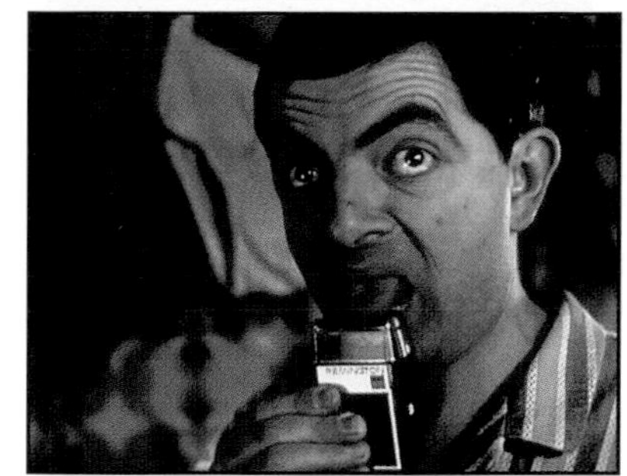

Rowan Atkinson's gurning power knows no limits. First there was Black Adder (1983) – a truly Millennial series, created by Richard Curtis and Ben Elton, with the same characters reappearing in different centuries. Atkinson and Curtis then created Mr Bean, the accident-prone twit who brought slapstick back to TV. Bean: The Ultimate Disaster Movie (1997) is the most successful British film ever, because you can understand slapstick in any language

THE BBC

The BBC remains a cherished institution – witness the furore in 1999 over its new director-general, Greg Dyke. Dyke was seen by some as unsuitable because he had given money to the Labour Party. Others welcomed him as the man to reform the culture of "excessive paper-pushing" associated with his predecessor Sir John Birt.

> **'Nation shall speak unto Nation'**
> **BBC MOTTO, ADAPTED FROM THE OLD TESTAMENT**

Britain's publicly-funded broadcasting service went on air in 1922. The BBC received its royal charter in 1927 under John Reith, who outlined a blueprint to entertain and inform. When the TV service began in 1936, 7000 people queued to watch three sets at Olympia.

The BBC still enjoys a reputation for independence and quality. Its World Service was vital in occupied countries during the Second World War, and still is in many parts of the world with no other reliable source of news.

ENID BLYTON

From the Secret Seven and the Famous Five to Noddy and Big-Ears, the prolific output of Enid Blyton (1897-1968) has cornered a huge share of the 20th-century bedtime-story market. The one-time governess was an astute businesswoman, who made £100,000 a year in the 1950s with her recipe of "giving children what they want" – a mirror image of the den-building, gang-forming world of childhood. But she was not without her critics. Her sexism and racism may perhaps be put down to her (unhappy) Edwardian upbringing, but educationists also charged her with an impoverished vocabulary. Most tellingly, her daughter Imogen Smallwood remembered her as "a distant authority, a clever person, an imaginative actress, but never or almost never, a mother".

LIFELINES

***Ludwig van Beethoven** took music to places it had never been before – or since. Born in Bonn, Germany, in 1770, he studied under Haydn in Vienna, where he wrote his nine symphonies. An obsessive worker, he did his best work after he went deaf. His Fifth Symphony, with its doom-laden four-note motif, may be the ultimate musical masterpiece. When he died in 1827, thousands lined the streets. Including, maybe, his 'Immortal Beloved' – the unknown woman to whom he penned a famous, unposted letter, the subject of a 1994 Gary Oldman film.*

***Johann Sebastian Bach** (1685-1750) is pop's favourite composer. The German organist's masterpieces such as the Brandenburg Concertos inspired the 'Air On A G String' Hamlet cigar ads and Procol Harum's 'A Whiter Shade Of Pale'. In the year 2000 it is 250 years since his death, so prepare for Bach mania.*

B

1200 FOOT FASHION Small female feet went down big with men in China at the start of the 13th century. So mothers would bind their daughters' feet tightly with silk, hoping to have warped them into the desired lotus petal shape by the time they were of marriageable age. The painful custom spread to other parts of the world.

1215 MAGNA CARTA On June 15, 1215, at Runnymede, King John was forced by rebellious barons to sign the Great Charter of Liberties, or Magna Carta. It established the basis of constitutional government and legal rights of citizens which exist to this day.

1220 TRANSLATION OF ST THOMAS King Henry III and a host of bishops and lords were present as the bones of Thomas Becket were carried from the crypt of Canterbury Cathedral to a splendid new shrine in Trinity Chapel which had just been built.

THE BEATLES

Rock is a battlefield, with each generation gunning for the one before. Sometimes it's deliberate – the first thing the punks of 1976 did was to declare war on the hippies of '67. But The Beatles did it inadvertently, creating a musical revolution that destroyed the careers of the American artists who had been their heroes.

Until John Lennon, Paul McCartney, Ringo Starr and George Harrison emerged from Liverpool's Cavern Club in 1963 playing their hyped-up Merseybeat, pop music was strictly made in the USA. The Beatles' drive and flair changed all that. Four cocky young men with four distinct personalities, they broke new ground by playing their own instruments and writing their own songs – and within weeks, the packaged British solo singers and instrumental groups of the Fifties were as old hat as their quiffs.

Of the 21 singles The Beatles released in seven years, 18 went to No 1, the others to No 2. At least 16 have achieved classic status, while a song that wasn't a single – Paul McCartney's 'Yesterday' – is now the most-recorded of all time, with well over 2,500 versions.

As architects of cultural change, The Beatles were as influential as Leonardo da Vinci. Their *Sergeant Pepper's Lonely Hearts Club Band* is as untouchable as the Mona Lisa, Beethoven's Fifth and *Romeo and Juliet.* Lennon provoked outrage when he said: "We're as popular as Jesus now" – but in 1966 he was right. Millennium men indeed.

Watch out, world! The Beatles in 1963, from left: Paul McCartney, Ringo Starr, John Lennon and George Harrison

Fab Four who took America by storm

THE BEATLES TOUCHED DOWN IN NEW YORK ON FEBRUARY 7 1964 (RIGHT), TO BE GREETED BY SCREAMING CROWDS. ON APRIL 4, THEY MADE HISTORY BY OCCUPYING ALL OF THE TOP FIVE PLACES IN THE AMERICAN SINGLES CHART. NO WONDER THEY CALLED IT THE BRITISH INVASION...

1	Can't Buy Me Love	The Beatles
2	Twist And Shout	The Beatles
3	She Loves You	The Beatles
4	I Want To Hold Your Hand	The Beatles
5	Please Please Me	The Beatles

TEN BEATLES SONGS AND WHO OR WHAT INSPIRED THEM

A HARD DAY'S NIGHT The title was inspired by a comment from Ringo (as was 'Eight Days A Week'), but John wrote the song for Julian, his baby son (*"But when I get home to you, I find the things that you do, will make me feel all right"*).

SOMETHING Written by George for his wife Patti. *"Something in the way she moves, attracts me like no other lover."*

ELEANOR RIGBY Paul claimed he made it up, but there is a gravestone for Eleanor Rigby ('Died 10th Oct 1939 Aged 44 Years. Asleep') in St Peter's, Woolton – where Paul first met John at a church fête.

LUCY IN THE SKY WITH DIAMONDS Long after it wouldn't have mattered, John insisted this song had nothing to do with the drug LSD but was inspired by a picture painted by four-year-old Lucy O'Donnell – a friend of his son Julian, who described it as "Lucy in the sky with diamonds".

A DAY IN THE LIFE This song was about lots of things but the line *"He blew his mind out in a car"* was inspired by the death in a car of Tara Browne, an Irish heir who was related to the Guinness family. He was friendly with Paul.

THINGS WE SAID TODAY Written by Paul for Jane Asher. *"We'll go on and on."* Alas not.

WE CAN WORK IT OUT Once again for Jane Asher. *"Try to see it my way,"* begged Paul, but she would have none of it.

JANE ASHER AND PAUL

YOU'VE GOT TO HIDE YOUR LOVE AWAY Supposedly written by John for manager Brian Epstein. The love he had to "hide" was his homosexuality, which was still illegal.

SHE'S LEAVING HOME Paul read a newspaper story about teenage runaway Melanie Coe. Her father said: "She has everything here", echoed in *"We gave her everything money could buy"*. Unknown to Paul, he had actually met the girl when he had presented her with a prize on *Ready Steady Go!* four years earlier.

I SAW HER STANDING THERE Iris Caldwell was indeed just 17 when Paul saw her dancing in a nightclub. Iris, the sister of Liverpool rocker Rory Storm, went out with Paul for two years.

1224
ST THOMAS AQUINAS
Born around 1224, philosopher and theologian St Thomas Aquinas spent six years writing his *Summa Theologica*, or *Summary of Theology*, which he left unfinished in 1273. It formed a coherent set of beliefs which are still the basis of Roman Catholic teachings.

1231
THE INQUISITION
All Christians in Europe during the Middle Ages were considered members of one Church, with the Pope as its head. In 1231 Pope Gregory IX set up the Inquisition to seek out and either pardon, or kill, dissenters from the faith. It lasted until 1908, when it was renamed the Holy Office.

1240
BIRTH OF PARLIAMENT
The Great Council which offered advice to the Monarch began, about this time, to be called 'Parliament'. Knights of the Shire began helping its deliberations, thus widening its role and influence. Edward I (1239-1307) was the first King to call regular Parliaments.

BRIT POP

Mean, moody, sullen, streetwise – the style was set in the Sixties and recycled ever since. For most of the Millennium, music evolved slowly. So if time has stood still for British guitar groups since 1964, don't call the Fashion Police

1964 The Yardbirds

1965 The Who

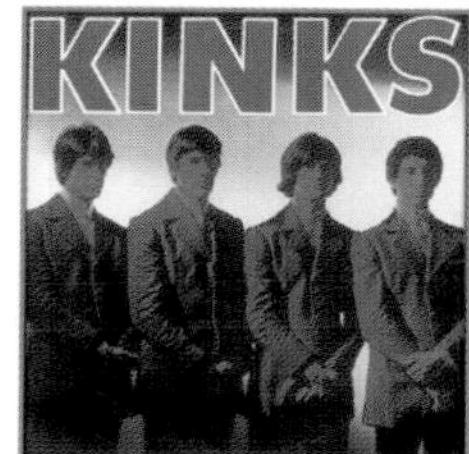

1965 The Kinks

1977 The Clash

1977 The Jam

1979 The Pretenders

1994 Pulp

1995 The Verve

1996 The Charlatans

It's not just the surly look that remains the same. British guitar pop is one musical fashion that never goes away. Oasis draw from The Beatles, Blur from The Kinks, Suede from David Bowie. Pretender Chrissie Hynde so wanted to be Ray Davies of The Kinks that she married him. In time, each band loses its fizz, but there'll always be another Britpop group along soon.

THE BEACH BOYS

California's Beach Boys invented surf music by adding close harmonies to Chuck Berry guitar riffs. Then came The Beatles. Brian Wilson's desperation to outdo them led to gorgeous classics such as 'Good Vibrations' (a No 1 in 1966) and 'God Only Knows' – but led him to a drug-induced nervous breakdown.

BRIT ART

In the Sixties, The Who wore Pop Art and John Lennon fell for an artist called Yoko Ono. Now Art is the new rock and roll: Damien Hirst is as big a star as Blur, for whom he directed a video. Hirst won the Turner Prize in 1995 with *Mother and Child Divided* – a bisected cow and calf in a glass cage – and led the way for Rachel Whiteread, Jake & Dinos Chapman and the Brit Art pack, whose crowning came at the Royal Academy's 1998 Sensation show. Their most famous patron is David Bowie, who writes for *Modern Painters* magazine.

DAVID BOWIE

David Bowie, born in 1947, found fame with 'Space Oddity' (1969) and invented glam rock in 1972 with *Ziggy Stardust and the Spiders From Mars* (below). The first pop star to employ the tactic of changing persona with every record – now in drag, now in a suit – his influence far outweighs his record sales.

THE BEE GEES

Maurice, Robin and Barry Gibb are the only group with No 1 hits in three decades: 1960s: 'Massachusetts' and 'I've Gotta Get A Message To You'. 1970s: 'Night Fever' and 'Tragedy'. 1980s: 'You Win Again'. And in the 1990s, Take That had a No 1 with a cover of 'How Deep Is Your Love'.

LIFELINES

Chuck Berry *virtually invented rock and roll guitar. Born in 1926, he was also rock's first poet, in songs such as 'Sweet Little Sixteen' (1958) and "You Never Can Tell' (1964) – but his only No 1 was the smutty 'My Ding-A-Ling' (1972).*

Geoffrey Boycott, *a brilliant but often controversial cricketer, opened the batting for England throughout his career. Born in Yorkshire in 1940, he scored his 100th first-class century in 1977 and is now a tough-talking commentator.*

James Brown *is the 'godfather' of US funk and R&B. Born in 1928, his career has spanned five decades. Hits like 'Say It Loud, I'm Black And Proud' made him an icon who could (and did) stop a race riot.*

1281
First Kamikaze
About 140,000 Mongols, the biggest naval force ever seen, attacked Japan in 1281. Fighting went on for two months before a typhoon destroyed the Mongol fleet and their dispirited army ashore was defeated. The Japanese thought a kamikaze – 'divine wind' – was sent to help them. In the Second World War, Japan tried to create another divine wind by sending suicide pilots – kamikazes – against the enemy.

1284
Wales Conquered
Edward I finally conquered Wales after eight years of war and rebellion. The Statute of Wales was enacted, annexing Wales to England and making it subject to the same laws. Seven hundred and fifteen years later, Tony Blair began to reverse the process.

1290
Child Bride
In an attempt to unite the crowns of England and Scotland, arrangements were made for the marriage of Margaret, Queen of Scotland, to Edward of Caernarvon. He was aged six, and Margaret, the 'Maid of Norway', was seven. The marriage never took place because she fell ill and died on the way to the ceremony.

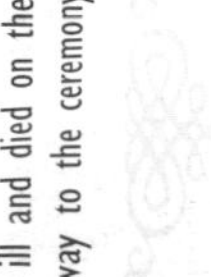

LIFELINES

Christiaan Barnard, *born in 1922, performed the first human heart transplant in Cape Town in 1967. The patient, 54-year-old Louis Washkansky, lived for just 18 days, but it remains the greatest achievement in surgery.*

Mrs Beeton *would be a TV personality if she was around today. Born Isabella Mayson in 1836, she died in childbirth aged 29, having spent four years writing her great cookery book, Beeton's Household Management.*

Irving Berlin *couldn't read or write music, but he composed 1500 songs including White Christmas. Born in Russia, he was a penniless US immigrant who became a millionaire through his music and died in 1989 aged 101.*

THE BLITZ

Adolf Hitler first deployed a new form of warfare called the Blitzkrieg – or 'lightning war' – when Germany invaded Poland in September 1939. Fast-moving tanks destroyed defences while bombers disrupted supplies and communications.

He began blitzing England's cities – London, Coventry, Liverpool – from the air in August 1940, destroying a million homes and killing 40,000 civilians. Evacuations helped to minimise losses, and Londoners took to sleeping in the tube stations (above) and endured the blanket bombing until June 1941, when the Luftwaffe was diverted to Russia.

'If the British Empire lasts a thousand years, men will still say: This was their finest hour'

Winston Churchill, June 18, 1940

THE BRITISH EMPIRE

Before the First World War, the British Empire covered a fifth of the planet and included a quarter of the world's population. It began in the 16th century under Elizabeth I and ended under Elizabeth II, having become a Commonwealth of Nations in 1931. All the countries are now independent, apart from these:

The ten (populated) British dependent territories

Bermuda (population 60,000); Cayman Islands (33,600); Gibraltar (30,000); Turks & Caicos Islands (19,000); British Virgin Islands (16,108); Montserrat (9,000 before the 1996 earthquake but now hardly any); Anguilla (8,960); St Helena (5644); Falkland Islands (2121); Pitcairn Island (54).

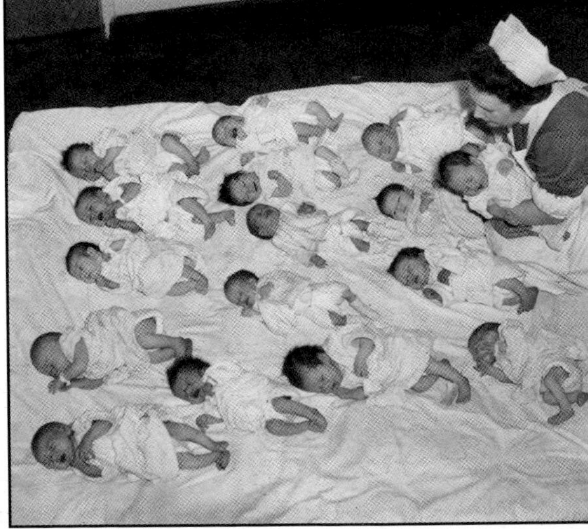

BABY BOOM

As the troops returned from the Second World War, so began the baby boom. Between 1941 and 1945 just under four million babies were born in Britain. Post-war, between 1946 and 1950, this shot up to over 4,500,000. The sheer number of baby boomers has made them a major force through each subsequent decade (think of them as the Sixties generation), but the crisis will come around 2010 – when they all start claiming their old age pension.

1296
Stone of Destiny
Edward I announced that he had decided to take control of the Scottish government. To enforce the point he ordered the symbolic transfer of the Stone of Destiny from the Abbey at Scone to Westminster Abbey. It would not be returned until 700 years later.

1300
Dante's 'Divine Comedy'
The *Divine Comedy* by Dante Alighieri, completed shortly before his death in 1321, was the first literary masterpiece written in Italian, not Latin. A journey through Hell, Purgatory and Paradise, it paved the way for the Italian Renaissance.

1305
Wallace Executed
Scottish national hero William Wallace was betrayed and captured by English soldiers. Wallace almost destroyed the English army at Stirling in 1297 and went on to devastate northern England. In London, his execution took the form of being hanged, drawn and quartered.

St Paul's Cathedral stood out against the German Blittzkreig, symbolising London's resistance

BATTLE OF BRITAIN

As the countries of Europe fell one by one to the Nazis, Britain – fortuitously separated from the continent by a sleeve of water – stood as the last bastion against Hitler's aggressive expansion.

Hitler planned a coastal invasion, Operation Sea Lion, for September 15, 1940, but knew that he would have to destroy the RAF first. The Luftwaffe began bombing Britain, but young British pilots (average age 23) boldly defended the skies in their nippy Spitfires (above) and Hurricanes. The Luftwaffe outnumbered the British, but was outfought: 900 RAF planes were lost, but 1700 German planes were downed. The invasion was shelved.

'Never in the field of human conflict was so much owed by so many to so few'
WINSTON CHURCHILL, AUGUST 20, 1940

BRIEF ENCOUNTER

David Lean's classic weepie *Brief Encounter* – written and produced by Noël Coward – made stars of Trevor Howard and Celia Johnson. One of the first great post-war British movies, it won cinema-goers' hearts in 1945 with its love-torn protagonists stealing a moment of passion in a world of splintered relationships as the Second World War ended.

THE BRIDGE ON THE RIVER KWAI

Brief Encounter director David Lean returned to a wartime theme in 1957 – of a very different kind. *The Bridge on the River Kwai* won Oscars for Lean and Alec Guinness (above right) as the British officer whose men are forced by their Japanese captors to build a bridge. It was a true story.

The bridge, in Thailand, was a testament to British engineering and endurance in conditions of extreme heat and cruelty (37 per cent of Japanese POWs died as against two per cent in Germany). Yet the bridge they built is still there today.

BUTLIN'S

Before the package holiday in the 1970s gave Britons easy access to the Med, holidays meant only one thing: Butlin's. Billy Butlin opened his first holiday camp in Skegness in 1936, and by the Sixties they were so popular that Mr Butlin was knighted for bringing the nation knobbly knees competitions.

Butlin's has just spent £139 million to "take the British weather out of the British holiday", and is recruiting 200 new redcoats. They will no doubt hope to emulate ex-redcoats Sir Cliff Richard, Michael Barrymore and Des O'Connor.

BINGO

ORIGINALLY CALLED HOUSEY-HOUSEY, BINGO TOOK OFF IN THE TWENTIES WHEN NEWSPAPERS USED IT AS A SALES GIMMICK. RECENTLY BINGO HAS HAD A MILLENNIAL FACELIFT. NO LONGER THE SOLE DOMAIN OF RETIRED LADIES, BINGO HALLS NOW BOAST BARS, RESTAURANTS AND OTHER ENTERTAINMENTS. IT SEEMS TO BE WORKING, AS THE BIG COMPANIES CLAIM THREE MILLION MEMBERS. NOW THAT'S A LOT OF PENSIONS – AND A LOT OF ART DECO CINEMA BUILDINGS SAVED FROM DEMOLITION.

1322
EARL OF TREASON
The Earl of Lancaster became the first peer of the realm to be sentenced to death for high treason (against Edward II).

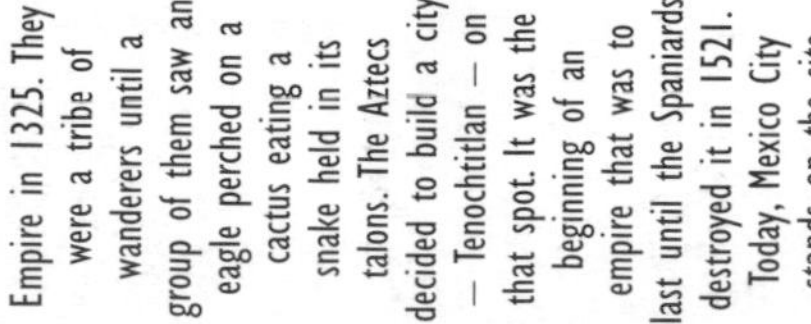

1325
AZTEC EMPIRE
It was a vision, so legend has it, that started the Aztec Empire in 1325. They were a tribe of wanderers until a group of them saw an eagle perched on a cactus eating a snake held in its talons. The Aztecs decided to build a city – Tenochtitlan – on that spot. It was the beginning of an empire that was to last until the Spaniards destroyed it in 1521. Today, Mexico City stands on the site of the vision.

1332
THE NEW PARLIAMENT
The division of Parliament into two houses – the Lords and the Commoners – was recorded for the first time in 1332.

1337
THE HUNDRED YEARS' WAR
England and France were at loggerheads, and when French king Philip VI halted the wool trade, war broke out. It lasted on and off for over a century, including Agincourt and Joan of Arc's campaign. France finally won.

LIFELINES

Robert Burns *(1759-96) was as Scottish as haggis. 'Rabbie' Burns broke with custom by writing poetry in Scots dialect. Now, every New Year's Eve, even the Sassenachs attempt at least one stanza of his 'Auld Lang Syne'.*

Roger Bannister *ran the first four-minute mile. Born in Middlesex in 1929, his time of 3min 59.4sec at Oxford in 1954 earned him immortality. Bannister, who has had a distinguished medical career, was knighted in 1975.*

Lord Byron *(1788-1824) was a great romantic writer, the creator, in his epic poem Childe Harold, of the moody, angst-ridden hero – not unlike Byron himself. He toured all over Europe, finally dying as a freedom fighter in Greece.*

'The only thing worse than people talking about the Sixties is people talking about football'

David Bailey

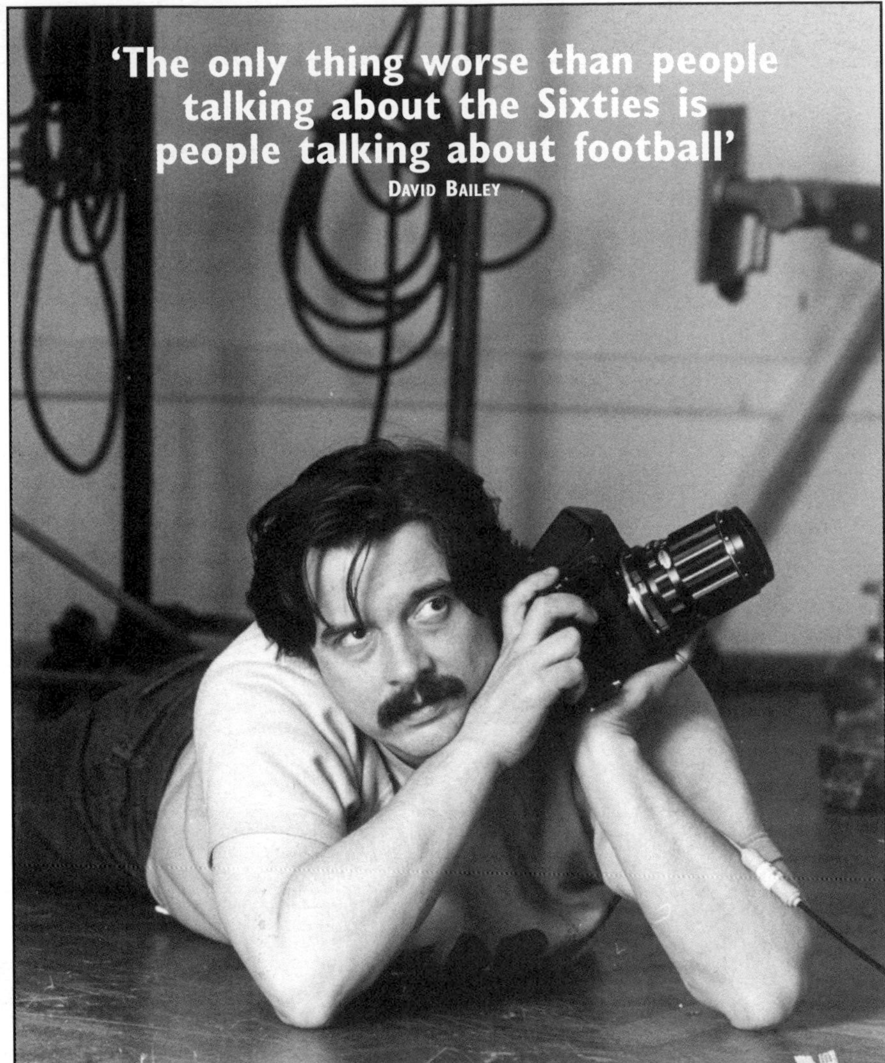

SIR CECIL BEATON AND DAVID BAILEY

David Bailey and Sir Cecil Beaton are probably the best-known British photographers of the century. Fashion photographers both, they gave us the images we love of the great celebrities of their day. Beaton's portraits of Greta Garbo, the aristocracy and the royals, and Bailey's pictures of Mick Jagger, Sixties icon Jean Shrimpton and his wives Catherine Deneuve and Marie Helvin, had a huge influence on the world's glossy magazines. Beaton (1904-80) also designed stage sets such as the 1971 *My Fair Lady* (left) while Bailey (born in 1938) famously lived the life of the stars he pictured.

EMILY BRONTE

Emily Brontë's only novel, Wuthering Heights, was published in 1847 with little success – the same year as her sister Charlotte's Jane Eyre. One year later Emily's life was cut short at the age of 30, leaving us to speculate what other heights she might have reached. Wuthering Heights has become a literary classic, with the brooding Heathcliff played in films by Laurence Olivier (1939), Timothy Dalton (1971) and Ralph Fiennes (1992, above), as well as a Nineties stage show starring Cliff Richard. But the most remarkable reworking of Wuthering Heights was by Kate Bush. Born on Emily Brontë's 140th birthday, Bush made it a No 1 record in 1978 – and launched her own startlingly original career.

KATE BUSH

1346
Debut of the Longbow
The English longbow was used for the first time in continental warfare in 1346 – and with devastating effect. A French army of mounted men-at-arms was destroyed by King Edward III's dismounted army of soldiers and archers at the Battle of Crécy. The English had been outnumbered four to one. The longbow, particularly in skilled English hands, was to be a formidable weapon of war for 200 years.

1347
The Black Death
Kipchak nomads from Euro-Asia laid siege to a Genoese trading post in the Crimea in 1347. Using catapults, they hurled plague-infected corpses over the town's walls. Scholars now believe this could have been the source of the plague, which originated from rats' fleas, in the European community. It was to kill 25 million people – a quarter of the continent's population – and first swept across Britain in 1349.

BEQUESTS

A Scotsman bequeathed each of his two daughters her weight in £1 notes. The elder, slimmer daughter received £51,200 while her sister got £57,433.

In 1856, Heinrich Heine, the German poet, left everything to his wife only on the condition that she remarried "so that there will be at least one man to regret my death".

Toby, a poodle living in New York, was bequeathed £15 million by his owner, Ella Wendel, when she died in 1931.

A wealthy American banker left a codicil in his will cutting out two members of his family: "To my wife and her lover, I leave the knowledge I wasn't the fool she thought I was. To my son, I leave the pleasure of earning a living: for 25 years he thought the pleasure was mine."

In 1955, Juan Potomachi, an Argentinian, left more than £25,000 to the local theatre on condition that they used his skull when performing *Hamlet.*

An Irishman left £1500 to the Department of Health & Social Security (as it then was) to repay the money he had received while on the dole.

In 1765, John Hart left his brother a gun and a bullet "in the hope that he will put the same through his head when the money is spent".

In 1960, Samuel Bratt left $330,000 to his wife – who never let him smoke – on condition that she smoked five cigars a day.

CELEBRITY BEQUESTS

G B SHAW

MARILYN MONROE

F SCOTT FITZGERALD

BOB FOSSE, the choreographer who won an Oscar for *Cabaret*, left $378.79 each to 66 people to "have dinner on me" in 1987. These included Liza Minnelli, Dustin Hoffman and Melanie Griffith.

MARILYN MONROE left all her "personal effects and clothing" in 1962 to Lee Strasberg, her acting coach, to "distribute among my friends, colleagues and those to whom I am devoted".

F SCOTT FITZGERALD, author of *The Great Gatsby*, drew up a will in 1937 specifying "a funeral in keeping with my station in life". Three years later, a much poorer Fitzgerald amended this to "cheapest funeral". His funeral cost just $613.25.

GEORGE BERNARD SHAW, the author of *Pygmalion*, left much of his estate in 1950 for the purpose of replacing the alphabet with a more efficient alphabet of over 40 letters. It was never achieved.

WILLIAM SHAKESPEARE bequeathed his wife, Anne, "my second best bed". This has been interpreted as a snub. In fact, his "second best bed" was probably the one most used by the two of them and was therefore a sentimental gesture.

RICHARD SHERIDAN, British dramatist, told his son he was cutting him out of his will with just a shilling. His son replied: "I'm sorry to hear that, sir. You don't happen to have the shilling on you now, do you?"

HIERONYMUS BOSCH

HIERONYMUS BOSCH INVENTED SURREALISM 400 YEARS BEFORE DALI. THE DUTCHMAN'S MASTERPIECE IS THE GARDEN OF EARTHLY DELIGHTS – THREE PANELS DEPICTING FIRST THE GARDEN OF EDEN, THEN HUMAN SINS, AND FINALLY A NIGHTMARISH HELL (LEFT). BOSCH, BORN IN ABOUT 1450, LIVED IN THE MEDIEVAL WALLED CITY OF S'HERTOGENBOSCH, A LONG WAY FROM RENAISSANCE ITALY, BUT HIS INFLUENCE HAS REACHED ALMOST AS FAR. HE DIED IN 1516.

BALLET

DARCEY BUSSELL'S BEST OF THE MILLENNIUM

BALLET

ROMEO AND JULIET

"*Romeo and Juliet* is my favourite ballet of the Millennium, and probably will be forever. It's really challenging to dance, as you have to be an actress as well as a dancer onstage. Prokofiev's music makes me cry every time, whether I'm performing to it or watching someone else. *Romeo and Juliet* is a classic that will run and run."

DARCEY BUSSELL (LEFT) IS THE PRINCIPAL DANCER WITH THE ROYAL BALLET. SHE HAS APPEARED IN SWAN LAKE, THE SLEEPING BEAUTY, THE NUTCRACKER – AND AS JULIET.

1348 ORDER OF THE GARTER FOUNDED The Order of the Garter was founded to encourage chivalry and military adventures. It began as a fraternity consisting of King Edward III and 25 knights. Recipients in modern times include Sir Winston Churchill, Lord (Harold) Wilson and Baroness (Margaret) Thatcher.

1349 BOCCACCIO'S 'DECAMERON' Italian poet and scholar Giovanni Boccaccio was a father of the Italian Renaissance. In his celebrated Decameron, ten people hide in the countryside for ten days to escape the plague, and each tells ten stories. Chaucer drew upon the work for *The Canterbury Tales*.

1362 ENGLISH SPOKEN HERE English became the official language in Parliament and the law courts, instead of French.

1370 LIMOGES MASSACRE Edward, the Black Prince, King Edward III's warrior son, ordered 3,000 French people in Limoges to be put to death for opposing the English.

THE BICYCLE

One of the greatest gaffes of the Millennium was when Scotsman Kirkpatrick Macmillan failed to patent his invention of the bicycle in 1840. Since then, from the penny farthing (above) to the mountain bike, the bicycle has never looked back, with 800 million now used worldwide. An energy-efficient, non-polluting mode of transport, this most simple of machines will still hold an important role in the new millennium.

ISAMBARD KINGDOM BRUNEL

PROBABLY THE GREATEST BRITISH ENGINEER OF THE MILLENNIUM, BRUNEL WAS BORN IN 1806. HE HELPED HIS FATHER, MARC, TO PLAN THE ROTHERHITHE TUNNEL UNDER THE THAMES BEFORE DESIGNING THE CLIFTON SUSPENSION BRIDGE – STILL ONE OF THE FINEST BRIDGES IN THE WORLD. HE ALSO BUILT 1,600 MILES OF RAILWAY AND DESIGNED THE LARGEST SHIP OF THE 19TH CENTURY, THE GREAT EASTERN, BEFORE HIS DEATH IN 1859.

BALLOONING

In 1999 Brian Jones and Bertrand Piccard – a Briton and a Swiss – pipped Richard Branson to 'the last aviation feat' of ballooning round the world. Yet the balloon was the first flying machine – invented by France's Montgolfier brothers, Joseph and Jacques, in 1783 (left). Their problem was navigation; they even tried oars. Maybe that's where Branson went wrong?

JAMES BOND

It began as a series of sexy spy novels by a former British intelligence agent – and became the most successful film series ever. Here's one 007 fan fact for every James Bond film to date…

DR NO 1962 (RIGHT)
Sean Connery was the 'original' Bond, of course – but he wasn't actually the first. That was Barry Nelson, who played Bond in a 1954 American TV version of *Casino Royale.* In the Ian Fleming novel *Dr No,* Honey Ryder came out of the ocean wearing only a belt. Ursula Andress (pictured with Connery) wore a white bikini.

FROM RUSSIA WITH LOVE 1963
The film used 200 live rats, some of which escaped and ran amok on the streets of Madrid.

GOLDFINGER 1964
Enter Bond's most famous car – the Aston Martin DB5 with revolving number plates, pop-up bullet-proof shield and ejector seat.

THUNDERBALL 1965
To meet demand, New York's Paramount Theatre had to show the film 24 hours a day.

YOU ONLY LIVE TWICE 1967
Aki's Toyota was Japan's first convertible.

ON HER MAJESTY'S SECRET SERVICE 1969
Diana Rigg disliked George Lazenby, who played Bond, so she ate garlic before their love scenes.

DIAMONDS ARE FOREVER 1971
Bond's most memorable car stunt: he drives his Ford Mustang down a narrow alleyway on two wheels, then sets it back on four wheels.

LIVE AND LET DIE 1973
Roger's Moore's first Bond movie. Whenever filming went wrong, crew members would shout: "Send for Sean!"

THE MAN WITH THE GOLDEN GUN 1974
Villain Christopher Lee, the famous horror movie actor, was author Ian Fleming's cousin.

MOONRAKER 1979
The one where 007 goes into space. The opening parachute shots took five weeks to film.

FOR YOUR EYES ONLY 1981
Carole Bouquet (Melina) was originally asked to play Holly Goodhead in *Moonraker.*

OCTOPUSSY 1983
The title airplane sequence was set to be shot at Angel Falls, Venezuela, but the river dried up.

A VIEW TO A KILL 1985
Patrick Macnee (Bond's accomplice) starred in the Bond-style Sixties TV series *The Avengers.*

THE LIVING DAYLIGHTS 1987
Pierce Brosnan plays Bond for the first time on the 25th anniversary of *Dr No.*

LICENCE TO KILL 1989
When Bond is being shot at by machine guns, the bullets' ricochets play out the Bond theme.

GOLDENEYE 1995
Eunice Grayson appeared in the first two Bond films. Her daughter Karen, 24, is in *Goldeneye.*

TOMORROW NEVER DIES 1997 (LEFT)
Bond's best joke was cut. At the end, after his car crashes through the roof of the Avis hire car office, he quips to the Avis employee: "I left the keys in the car." The line was edited out.

1377 THE FIRST POLL TAX
Parliament introduced a poll tax of 4d (about 1.5p) on everyone aged 12 to 60. In 1380, there was a further tax of one shilling (5p) a head. The measures led to widespread revolt. A little over 600 years later, Margaret Thatcher was to find history repeating itself.

1381 THE PEASANTS' REVOLT
Peasants led by Wat Tyler demanded the abolition of serfdom, fair rents and the execution of leading figures including the Lord Chancellor and the Lord Treasurer. They sacked towns in Kent and Essex before entering London. While Tyler was talking with the King at Smithfield, the Mayor stabbed and killed him.

1381 THE BIBLE IN ENGLISH
Theologian John Wycliffe believed people should read the Bible themselves and not rely on priests to interpret it. Translation took a year but the Church was not happy and Wycliffe was denounced by Pope Gregory XI.

LIFELINES

William Blake, *born in London's Soho in 1757, was a poet and painter of mind-blowing vision. His hymn Jerusalem remains England's great anthem, while his Book of Job illustrations retain a mystic power. He died in 1827.*

Sandro Botticelli *(1444-1510) painted in an inventive style that epitomised the Italian Renaissance. He was patronised by Florence's Medici family, and his famous Birth of Venus is the star attraction in that city's Uffizi gallery.*

Tony Blair, *born in 1953, became the youngest British Prime Minister of the century when his centrist 'New Labour' ended 18 years of Tory rule in 1997. His wife, Cherie Booth, is a leading lawyer.*

BRIGITTE BARDOT

Brigitte Bardot was the original 'sex kitten' of the late-Fifties and Sixties. Born in 1934, the Parisienne actress found fame in 1956 with her sexually unihibited performance in And God Created Woman, directed by her then husband Roger Vadim. Married four times, she made her last movie in 1973. After that, France's favourite pin-up became a recluse, devoted to animal welfare.

BEAU BRUMMELL

Beau Brummell was the 18th century's most dedicated follower of fashion. Born in 1778, he was a renowned dandy who introduced long trousers as everyday wear for men. An in-demand socialite and friend of the Prince of Wales, he ran up heavy gambling debts which forced him to flee to France – where he died, in 1840, in an asylum.

LUCILLE BALL

CILLA BLACK

The public's love affair with Lucille Ball and Cilla Black proves the power of the girl next door. Lucy, star of 'I Love Lucy', was the face of US TV from 1951 to the Seventies. Singer-turned-gameshow host Cilla stole British hearts with 'Anyone Who Had A Heart' in 1964 and has kept them ever since. That's a lorra, lorra years...

1390
Canterbury Tales
The first great masterpiece of English literature was *The Canterbury Tales*, written by Geoffrey Chaucer around 1390. It tells the stories of a group of pilgrims heading for the shrine of Thomas Becket in Canterbury. They entertained themselves along the way with a number of comic and tragic tales.

1399
Farewell King
Henry Bolingbroke, Duke of Lancaster, who had been banished from the realm by Richard II, returned and forced the King to abdicate. Bolingbroke took the Crown to become Henry IV.

1400
Rebellion Suppressed
The Earls of Rutland, Kent, Salisbury and Huntingdon led a rebellion in an attempt to restore Richard II to the throne (see *1399*). It was crushed and all but Rutland were executed.

1400
King Murdered
Richard II, who had been held prisoner in Pontefract Castle in Yorkshire, disappeared and is believed to have been murdered. Later, to prove that he was dead, his corpse was put on public display in London.

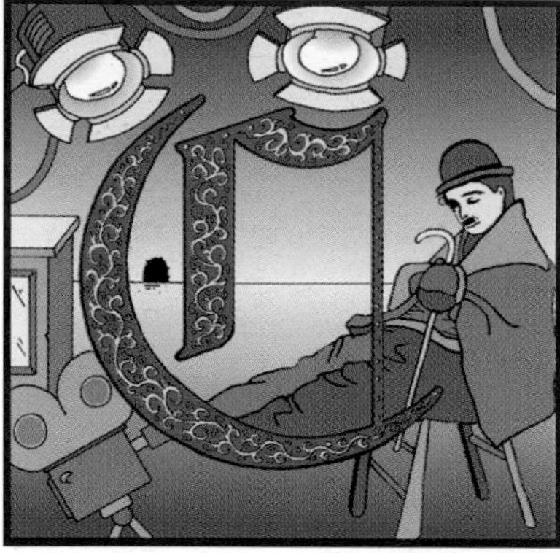

CENTENARIANS

Famous people who made it to 100 years old

George Burns (comedian) • Hal Roach (film producer)
Irving Berlin (songwriter) • Eubie Blake (pianist)
Rose Kennedy (mother of the Kennedy clan)
Sir Thomas Sopwith (aviation pioneer) • Manny Shinwell (politician)
Dame Freya Stark (explorer) • Lord Tom Denning (judge)

CASABLANCA

Hollywood's most emotive movie came out just after the USA entered the Second World War in 1942. Tough but tender Humphrey Bogart runs a bar in Casablanca – a haven for doomed souls fleeing the war. Enter his ex-lover Ingrid Bergman, now with her husband. Bogart struggles to do the right thing, as Sam the pianist "plays it again".

CENSORSHIP

Ten books which have been banned

The Adventures of Tom Sawyer (Mark Twain)
Banned by some London libraries (in politically-correct Labour boroughs) in the 1980s because of the book's 'racism' and 'sexism'.

Black Beauty (Anna Sewell)
Banned by the African country Namibia in the 1970s because the Government took offence at the 'racist' title.

The Scarlet Pimpernel (Baroness Orczy)
Banned by the Nazis because Baroness Orczy was Jewish.

Catcher In The Rye (J D Salinger)
Banned in Boron, California, in 1989 because of the word "goddamn".

Noddy (Enid Blyton)
Banned by several British libraries in the 1960s because Enid Blyton books weren't thought to be 'good' for children.

The Grapes of Wrath (John Steinbeck)
Banned from schools in Iowa, USA in 1980, after a parent complained that it was "vulgar and obscene".

The Joy of Sex (Alex Comfort)
Banned in Ireland from its publication in the 1960s until 1989 due to the book's uninhibited approach to sex and relationships.

Billy Bunter books (Frank Richards)
Banned from British libraries in the 1970s in case it led children to tease overweight schoolmates.

On The Origin of Species (Charles Darwin)
Banned in some US states because Darwin didn't accept the Bible's account of Creation.

My Friend Flicka (Mary O'Hara)
Banned from school reading lists in Clay County, Florida in 1990 because it uses the word "bitch" to describe a female dog.

1401
The Burning of Heretics
A new law allowed for heretics to be burned. William Sawtre, an East Anglian rector who preached unauthorised doctrines, was the first victim.

1407
The Great Explorer
Cheng Ho, the son of a noble Mongol family, was one of the world's great explorers. After being captured and castrated by the Chinese he gained favour with the Ming dynasty and became an influential court eunuch. In 1407, he commanded a fleet of 60 ships in the first of seven Indian Ocean expeditions. He visited the coast of East Africa a century before any European explorer.

1415
The Triumphs of Henry V
King Henry V invaded France, took Harfleur after a five-week siege – "For God, Harry and St George" – and then triumphed at the Battle of Agincourt, despite being outnumbered three to one by the French. It all inspired Shakespeare to write one of his great plays.

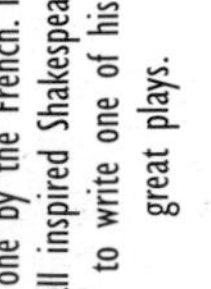

Cartoons have come a long way from Mickey Mouse. Matt Groening's The Simpsons created a complete small town, centred on the Simpson family. From left: Santa's Little Helper, Bart, Lisa, Maggie, Marge and Homer PICTURE COURTESY OF BSKYB

CARTOONS

When Chef from *South Park* reached No 1 with his 'Chocolate Salty Balls' early in 1999, it was the culmination of 200 years of cartoon capers. The first examples of cartoon animation were toys such as W G Horner's Zoetrope (1834), a revolving cylinder with slots through which viewers watched a series of drawings that appear to move.

The movie camera made possible the first cartoons as we know them, often using characters from newspaper strips such as Felix the Cat, created by Pat Sullivan in 1917. Then in 1928 a young man in Los Angeles – one Walt Disney – made the first cartoon with a soundtrack, *Steamboat Willie*, starring Mickey Mouse. Disney went on to make the first successful animated feature, *Snow White and the Seven Dwarfs* (1939).

Today's cartoons are increasingly sophisticated, blending film and computer techniques as in *Who Framed Roger Rabbit?*, in which real actors play against 'toons'. And in the likes of Matt Groening's *The Simpsons*, an everyday story of a blue-collar, smalltown family whose lives revolve around junk food and TV, they have achieved a new level of darkly satirical realism.

'As a nation we should be like The Waltons, not The Simpsons'

PRESIDENT GEORGE BUSH IN HIS 1991 STATE OF THE UNION ADDRESS

'Hey, we're like The Waltons. We're praying for the Depression to end too'

BART SIMPSON (IN THE CARTOON SERIES, BUSH LATER MOVED IN OPPOSITE THE SIMPSON FAMILY AND WAS LATER SPOTTED IN THE UNEMPLOYMENT QUEUE)

LIFELINES

Nat 'King' Cole *died in 1965, aged just 45. But he had achieved so much, winning polls as a jazz pianist, having hit records as a velvet-voiced pop singer, starring in the movie St Louis Blues, and heading his own TV series. Hated by some as a successful black performer, he was attacked onstage by white hoodlums in Alabama in 1956, though it was cancer that finally caught up with the mild-mannered non-militant.*

Bobby Charlton *survived the 1958 Munich air crash which killed eight of his Manchester United team-mates. He went on to play for his country 106 times, scoring 49 goals. Charlton, born in 1937, was a member of England's 1966 World Cup-winning team. A fine ambassador for the game, he was knighted in 1994 and has been guiding England's bid to stage the 2006 World Cup.*

1421
A QUEEN IS CROWNED
Henry V, having completed his conquest of Normandy, arrived at Dover with his French bride, Catherine, to an enthusiastic welcome. Many nobles waded into the sea to carry the pair in on their shoulders. Catherine's coronation was followed by a royal tour of the kingdom.

1421
FORBIDDEN CITY
Yung-lo, emperor of the Ming dynasty (1368-1644) decided in 1421 to move his capital from Nanjing to Beijing. There he built a vast imperial palace, known today as the Forbidden City.

1429
JOAN OF ARC
After claiming to have been directed by holy visions, the 17-year-old French farmer's daughter led the French armies into battle against the English in 1429. In 1431 she was denounced by the church as a heretic and burned at the stake, though later the same church declared her a saint.

C

CARS

If you think cars are increasing faster than people, you are not far wrong. Each year, 42 million cars, buses and trucks are made worldwide. Yet it is only a century since the first recognisable petrol engine motor car was built, shortly after Daimler-Benz's three-wheeled prototype (above), which looked more like a lawnmower.

The growth of the car began in the US. Henry Ford's moving assembly lines, installed in 1909, brought the car within everyone's reach. Industries like steel and rubber soared, and nothing was ever the same again.

Now comes the backlash. Every year 300,000 people die in accidents worldwide. Car pollution – carbon monoxide, hydrocarbons, nitrogen oxides – cloaks our cities in smog. Governments have now set emission standards, but it may be too late.

'The automobile changed our dress, manners, social customs, vacation habits, the shape of our cities, consumer purchasing patterns, common tastes and positions of intercourse'

WRITER JOHN KETAS

'A pedestrian is a man who has two cars – one being driven by his wife, the other by one of his children'

WRITER ROBERT BRADBURY

'I just solved the parking problem. I bought a parked car'

COMIC HENNY YOUNGMAN

THE CHANNEL TUNNEL

A TUNNEL LINKING BRITAIN TO FRANCE WAS FIRST PLANNED IN 1802, AND DIGGING ACTUALLY BEGAN IN 1878. THE 31-MILE (50KM) RAIL TUNNEL WAS NOT COMPLETED UNTIL 1994, AT A COST OF £8 BILLION. TYPICAL ANGLO-FRENCH 'CO-OPERATION', MAYBE – BUT IT REMAINS ONE OF THE ACHIEVEMENTS OF THE MILLENNIUM, THOUGH JAPAN'S SEIKAN RAIL TUNNEL (1988) IS ACTUALLY 4KM LONGER.

THE COUNTRY

COUNTRYFIED QUOTATIONS

'THE COUNTRY HAS CHARMS ONLY FOR THOSE NOT OBLIGED TO STAY THERE'
Artist Edouard Manet

'IT IS PURE UNADULTERATED COUNTRY LIFE. THEY GET UP EARLY BECAUSE THEY HAVE SO MUCH TO DO AND GO TO BED EARLY BECAUSE THEY HAVE SO LITTLE TO THINK ABOUT'
Playwright Oscar Wilde

'I AM AT TWO WITH NATURE'
Film director Woody Allen

1441 DUCHESS OF SORCERY After admitting at a trial that she dabbled in sorcery, the Duchess of Gloucester was sentenced to public penance and life imprisonment.

1455 WARS OF THE ROSES A series of civil wars between the House of Lancaster, represented by a red rose, and the white rose House of York. The two were finally drawn together 31 years later by the marriage of Lancastrian Henry Tudor (Henry VII) and Elizabeth of York.

1474 CAXTON'S FIRST BOOK William Caxton, inventor of the printing press, printed the first book in English – *The Recuyell of the Historyes of Troye*. Six years later (1480) he printed *The Chronicles of England*.

1478 SPANISH INQUISITION The start of the most brutal of the European inquisitions in which so-called heretics were tortured and burnt at the stake.

HRISTIANITY

A quarter of the planet are Christians – its biggest religious grouping – and since 1400 most of us have reckoned time from the supposed year of Christ's birth.

In the Middle Ages, monasteries became the repository of knowledge, and Christianity was the main inspiration for art. But it was a source of division too.

In 1054 disagreements over the Pope's authority produced a schism between Eastern Orthodox and Roman Catholic churches which has never been resolved. In the 16th century Martin Luther's Reformation movement divided Catholics from Protestants, and Henry VIII established the Church of England.

The Queen remains 'Defender of the Faith' to this day, though her son would prefer to reign as 'defender of faiths' in a multi-ethnic Britain where the most practised religion is actually Islam.

THE COLD

The coldest temperature ever recorded on Earth was -85 degrees Fahrenheit (-64.8 Celsius) at Eismitte, Greenland in 1987. The lowest ever in the UK was 0°F (-17.8C).

SIR MALCOLM CAMPBELL AND DONALD CAMPBELL

The second most famous boat crash in history – Donald's Bluebird flips over and disintegrates

Like father like son. England's Campbell clan were the fastest men on Earth – along with *Bluebird*, as they named all their record-breaking cars and boats. Sir Malcolm (1885-1949) set the pace, holding land and water speed records from 1927, and breaking the 300mph land-speed barrier at Bonneville Salt Flats, Utah, in 1935. Donald *(right)*, born in 1921, took up the baton, hitting a land speed of 403mph and a water speed of 276mph. But tragedy struck in 1967 on Lake Coniston when his *Bluebird* turbo-jet hydroplane hit a log and crashed at an unofficial speed of 328 mph.

Sir Malcolm's Bluebird in 1934

THE CITY

CITYFIED SAYINGS

'THERE IS NO SOLITUDE IN THE WORLD LIKE THAT OF THE BIG CITY'
Novelist Kathleen Norris

'CITIES, LIKE CATS, WILL REVEAL THEMSELVES AT NIGHT'
Poet Rupert Brooke

'FARMERS WORRY DURING THE GROWING SEASON, BUT TOWN PEOPLE WORRY ALL THE TIME'
Writer Edgar Watson Howe

THEN The Romans built sophisticated walled cities all over Europe, but when the Roman Empire crumbled, the continent's tribes went back to farming and the cities waned. By the ninth century, however, London – won back from the Danes by Alfred of Wessex in 886 – was a prosperous Saxon trading centre with a merchant navy and new wharves. In the 1200s its population was 40,000.

NOW The 18th-century Industrial Revolution turned Britain's cities into manufacturing centres as out-of-work farm workers flocked to the new factory jobs. Manchester, for instance, grew from 6000 people in 1685 to 303,000 in 1851. Today, two-fifths of the world live in urban areas, and there are about 225 cities of over a million people. New York had 33,000 people in 1790; today the figure is 7.5 million. London is now home to 6.5 million.

TEN CITIES WHICH HAVE HAD THEIR NAMES CHANGED

CONSTANTINOPLE (to Istanbul)
SAIGON (to Ho Chi Minh City)
TENOCHTITLÁN (to Mexico City)
PEKING (to Beijing)
DANZIG (to Gdansk)
EDO (to Tokyo)
SALISBURY (to Harare)
LENINGRAD (to St Petersburg)
NEW AMSTERDAM (to New York)
CHRISTIANA (to Oslo)

1481
FOUNDING OF INDEPENDENT RUSSIA
The grand prince of Moscow, Ivan Vasilyevich – also known as Ivan III or Ivan the Great – finally defeated the Tatars' Golden Hordes, going on to create a unified Russian nation.

1483
MURDER IN THE TOWER
Twelve-year-old Prince Edward and his brother the Duke of York were held in the Tower of London, after being labelled 'technically' as bastards by the Church. That meant Edward's claim to the throne was invalid. The Duke of Gloucester was then crowned King Richard III and the princes in the Tower were murdered, almost certainly on the orders of the newly crowned King.

1491
ENTER KING HENRY VIII
Henry VIII was born. He married six times, beheaded two wives, broke away from the Catholic church to form the Church of England, put to death Catholics who failed to recognise his church – and more or less anybody else who stood in his way. Yet he was popular. He also fathered Elizabeth I, one of the greatest monarchs.

CHILDHOOD

THEN Children in the Middle Ages had a rough time. Babies were hung up on hooks on the wall out of the way, and children were put to work early. Girls learned to cook, sew and weave; boys learned farming or a trade. Only the upper classes were educated. Youths were married off as soon as they could have sex.

NOW It was the Victorians who first popularised the idea of childhood as a period of innocence and wonder requiring protection. The first statutory age of consent came into English law in 1885, after a journalist purchased a young girl to prove that sexual slavery really existed. Books like Charles Kingsley's *The Water Babies* drew attention to the plight of working children; the 1833 Factory Act was the first enforceable child labour law.

Tubbies take over

CHILDREN'S FIRST SIGHT OF TV USED TO BE WATCH WITH MOTHER. NOW IT'S THE TELETUBBIES, NOT JUST IN THE UK BUT ALL ROUND THE WORLD

THE HOUSE OF COMMONS

Quaint practices of our elected rulers

- Yeomen dressed in Tudor uniform (right) still ritually search the cellars of the House of Commons for Gunpowder.
- The Speaker of the House of Commons is obliged to show extreme reluctance on taking office.
- Until a recent reform, an MP wishing to raise a point during a vote had to wear a collapsible black top hat and remain "seated and covered".
- When Black Rod comes to the House of Commons for the State Opening of Parliament, he is traditionally refused admission.
- If an MP wants to disrupt business and empty the chamber, he can merely say 'I spy strangers'.
- MPs can wave their order papers and shout "Hear hear" to signal approval of a speech but they're not allowed to clap.

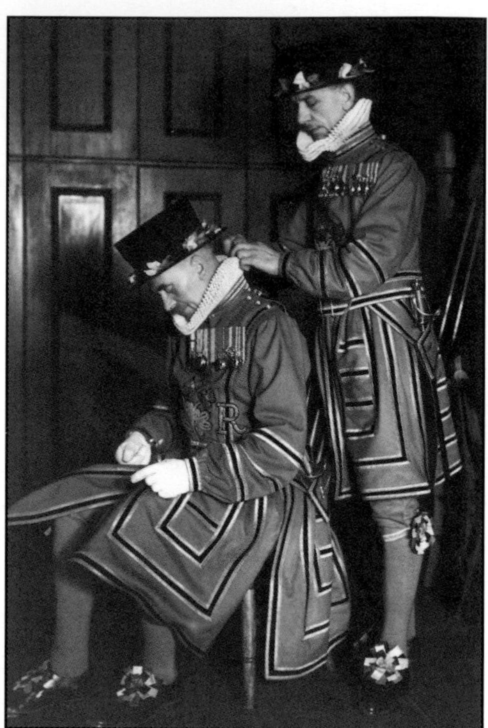

THE CIVIL WAR

The causes of the Civil War were religious, economic and constitutional, all rooted in a power struggle between King Charles I and Parliament. Thwarted in his attempts to raise taxes, and with Parliament trying to increase its powers, Charles sought to arrest five MPs in the Commons in March 1642. He failed, and left a hostile capital to seek support in the provinces.

War between the Cavaliers (Royalists) and Roundheads (Parliamentarians) broke out in July. In three major battles Charles won control of north and west England, and Wales. But by 1645 Oliver Cromwell's full-time professional New Model Army, and the Scots, controlled most of England. Charles was executed in 1649 and his son, Charles II, defeated and exiled in 1651. For a decade, England became a republic.

KING CHARLES I

Born in 1600, Charles I cuts an almost tragic figure on the stage of British history. A devoted husband and art-lover, with a slight stammer, he proved fatally rigid in his beliefs. He ruthlessly persecuted the Puritans, and his inflexibility made civil war inevitable. He was executed for treason in 1649.

OLIVER CROMWELL

Puritan MP Oliver Cromwell, born in 1599, masterminded the Civil War victory. He oversaw Charles' execution, and became head of an English Commonwealth. In 1653 a military coup made him Lord Protector. He declined to be king but was just as powerful; on his death in 1658, his son Richard succeeded him.

1492 COLUMBUS DISCOVERS THE NEW WORLD Spain supported Christopher Columbus as he sailed west seeking a new route to the riches of Asia. He knew the world was round, but not how big it was, and when he reached the Bahamas he thought he had found Asia.

1497 THE CORNISH REBELLION Fifteen thousand Cornishmen, objecting to paying taxes for a war against Scotland, marched on London. When they got there they soon realised what they were up against and many fled back home. The rest were crushed by the King's soldiers and their leaders put to death.

1497 CABOT EXPLORES CANADA Italian sea captain John Cabot was hired by Henry VII to find a northern route to Asia. His explorations of Newfoundland and the Atlantic coast gave England claim to territory in North America. Fifty years later his son Sebastian opened up a new route to Russia.

JOHN CONSTABLE

John Constable is probably Britain's favourite painter. His 19th-century landscapes may have acquired a cosiness with familiarity, but their realism was radical at the time and much admired by the French Impressionists. Constable (1776-1837) lived on the Essex-Suffolk border in East Bergholt, a stone's throw from the site of The Haywain on the River Stour. The area is now known as Constable country, and hundreds wander the fields each weekend, seeking the timeless idyll of Constable's art.

CAPITAL PUNISHMENT

Some of Britain's more bizarre executions from the era of the noose

In 1679, Messrs Green, Berry and Hill were hanged at Tyburn for a murder they committed on … Greenberry Hill

In 1885, John Lee was to be hanged at Exeter Gaol for murdering his employer. But when the hangman put the noose round his neck, the scaffold wouldn't work. Three times the scaffold was tested. Three times it refused to drop with Lee standing there. He was later reprieved and became famous as 'The Man They Couldn't Hang'.

In 1264, Inetta De Balsham was hanged at 9am. The King's messenger arrived a few seconds later with a reprieve. The hangman ran to cut the rope with a sword. The victim's face had already turned blue, but she survived.

In the 18th and 19th centuries, people – including children – were hanged for incredibly trivial offences. In 1819, Thomas Wildish was hanged for letter-stealing; in 1750, Benjamin Beckonfield was hanged for stealing a hat; in 1833, a nine-year-old boy was hanged for stealing a pennyworth of paint; in 1782, a 14 year-old girl was hanged for being in the company of gypsies.

Being a hangman was no insurance against being hanged. Four English hangmen were hanged: Cratwell in 1538 for robbing a booth at St Bartholomew's Fair; Stump-leg in 1558 for thieving; Pascha Rose in 1686 for housebreaking; and John Price in 1718 for murdering an old woman. He who lives by the rope…

PRINCE CHARLES

A brush with the heir to the throne

Prince Charles is the first heir to the throne to have gone to school, taken a university degree, made a parachute jump (though on his first jump his legs got caught up and there was nearly a disaster) and been divorced (although Kings – as opposed to heirs – have beaten him to this dubious achievement).

At Cambridge he wanted to join the university Labour Club but the Master of his College, Lord (Rab) Butler said no.

He owns 100 loo seats and takes his own wooden seat with him on trips overseas.

He bought two miniature chastity belts in 1974 to use as loo paper holders.

Things he owns include: Dartmoor Prison; any whale or porpoise washed up on a Cornish beach; the village of Daglingworth, Gloucs; and the right to 300 puffins, as an annual tithe, from the inhabitants of the Scilly Isles.

He had to shave off his beard when he left the Navy – but collected his shavings, put them in matchboxes and sent them to members of his family who had disliked his beard.

Among the awards he has won are 'Hooligan of The Year' from the RSPCA in 1978 after he went boar-hunting in Liechtenstein and 'Best Dressed Man of The Year' by the *Tailor And Cutter* in 1954 (when he was five years old).

He first allowed himself to be photographed with Camilla Parker Bowles in January 1999 at her sister's 50th birthday party

1500 Hello Fleet Street
Dutchman Wynkyn de Worde, William Caxton's principal assistant, set up his press in Fleet Street, London, and began printing pamphlets and books. It was the start of Fleet Street's historic connection with printing, which would continue until computers displaced typographers in the 1980s.

1500 African Slave Trade
Europeans began capturing Africans and transporting them by sea to the Caribbean islands and Brazil, where they were sold into slavery. England took control of the slave trade in 1713.

1502 Rio is Born
On January 1, 1502, Portuguese explorers landed at Guanabara Bay on the coast of South America. Not very imaginatively, they named the place Rio de Janeiro (River of January).

1504 First Watch
Although the sundial existed around 2400BC, and the first clock was invented in 1360AD, it wasn't until 1504 that a pocket-sized timepiece was created by German locksmith Peter Henlein. Later, it was called a watch.

CATS

Cats have been pets for 5000 years, since the Egyptians tamed African wild cats to protect farms from mice and snakes. Cats became sacred and were mummified.

In Europe in the Middle Ages, however, cats were linked to witchcraft and thousands were killed. The resulting increase in rats brought the bubonic plague.

Later, cats regained popularity as rodent-exterminators. The first cat show was held in London in 1871, and they recently overtook dogs as pets for the first time.

'If a dog jumps on to your lap it is because he is fond of you. If a cat does the same thing it is because your lap is warmer'

A N Whitehead, English philosopher

Animals are magic in adverts, as Freddie (above) will attest. Freddie, the Go Cat cat, earns about £350 a day. Most actors might object to being forced to spend a day eating cat food for the cameras, but Freddie loves it. In the cat pack, Freddie ranks second only to Arthur

CHIPS

- The 'British' chip was actually first made in France – French fries indeed.
- The first mention of chips in Britain came in an 1854 recipe book, *Shilling Cookery.* Chef Alexis Soyer described "thin cut potatoes cooked in oil".
- Britons eat two million tonnes of chips every year – that's 37 kg each.
- In the 1950s there were 30,000 fish and chip shops in the UK. Now there are 8500. Nevertheless, fish and chips are still our most popular takeaway.
- Fish and chip shops are most popular in Scotland and the north of England. One in three people in chip-loving Yorkshire goes to a chippy every week.
- Sixty-nine per cent of us put salt on our chips; 57 per cent vinegar; 24 per cent tomato ketchup; eight per cent brown sauce; five per cent mayonnaise and two per cent gravy (yuk!)
- As for what we eat with our chips, the winner is fish (27 per cent) followed by baked beans, chicken, packet meals, sausages, hot meat pies, burgers (surprisingly only six per cent), pizza and steak.
- British chip consumption has risen by 800 per cent in the past 15 years. We spend £83 million a year on oven chips.

CHOCOLATE

The Ten Oldest Chocolate Bars in the UK

Fry's Chocolate Cream (1875)
Cadbury's Dairy Milk (1905)
Cadbury's Bournville (1908)
Cadbury's Flake (1911)
Fry's Turkish Delight (1914)
Cadbury's Fruit & Nut (1921)
Terry's 1767 Bitter Bar (1922)
Cadbury's Crunchie (1929)
Cadbury's Whole Nut (1930)
Terry's Waifa Bar (1934)

1509 Henry VIII's First Bride
Accomplished scholar, sportsman and musician, 17-year-old Prince Hal became King Henry VIII. Within two months he married Catherine of Aragon. But she was unable to give him the son that he desperately wanted – and that's how all the trouble began.

1517 Luther Hammers Home His Points
German priest Martin Luther nailed his 95 theses to the door of Wittenberg's Palace church, marking the beginning of the Reformation. He denounced the selling of papal indulgences and criticised a number of ecclesiastical practices.

1521 Thanks, Henry
King Henry VIII, still at this stage in the Vatican's good books, was endowed with the title Defender of the Faith by Pope Leo X. It was a reward for his stand against papal critic Martin Luther (see 1517). On Henry's orders a number of Lutheran books were ceremoniously burned.

COOKERY

Cookery used to be a classroom chore. Now we learn from TV stars such as the Naked Chef (Jamie Oliver, right) and zany Ainsley Harriott (below)

THEN Cooking over small, open fires began over 1.5 million years ago, and the Egyptians baked bread in clay ovens. A thousand years ago, most Europeans cooked on a fireplace, roasting meat on a spit and heating other food in a kettle. A typical British diet would have included poultry, grains, grapes, beans, cabbage and turnips. The Crusaders would soon enliven this, bringing home a taste for spices, a passion which helped open up international trade and stimulate the exploration of new lands.

NOW Immigration and tourism have led to much more diverse diets – Chinese, Mexican and Indian food are now part of the British staple diet – while technological innovations like the microwave oven have slashed cooking times. In the West, increasing obesity and animal rights issues have prompted a preoccupation with healthy eating. More people than ever eat out, and we expect our take-aways to be delivered. Another growing trend, conversely, is the rise of cooking as a hobby, abetted by the rise and rise of the TV chef.

COMPUTERS

The computer must be the major invention of the Millennium. From your wrist watch to your microwave, we depend on the microchip for almost everything. The computer has made many industries redundant and created many others, changed our language and accelerated the very pace of life.

The first commercial computers were made in the 1950s. In 1961 some 10,000 were in use; in 1970, 100,000; by 1990, 100 million.

The silicon-chip microprocessor, born in the 1960s, was the real breakthrough. It allowed computer circuits to be compressed, and paved the way for the personal computer – which not only created a new kind of game for kids of all ages, but also made computers affordable for any business.

Only agriculture today brings in more money worldwide than the computer industry. And the Internet, a global network of computers linked by phone lines, is creating another revolution.

But what about the Millennium bug? All those computers set to mistake the year 2000 for 1900...

If computers operate everything from salary payments to fighter jets, what would happen if they all broke down?

Girl power comes to the PC screen with Lara Croft, heroine of Tomb Raider, the most successful computer game ever

LIFELINES

Bing Crosby, *the all-time great crooner, was born in 1903. He started his career with the Paul Whiteman Orchestra in the Twenties and soon became a pioneer of US radio. His many films include the 'Road' series with Bob Hope and Dorothy Lamour, and he won an Oscar for his performance in Going My Way. He died in 1977 but his 1942 recording of 'White Christmas' will outlast us all.*

Geoffrey Chaucer, *born in 1340, was the father of English poetry. His Canterbury Tales, told by a group of pilgrims, was the first great book in English. A stage musical of the book ran for five years, 1968-73, and an animated film was released in 1998. Chaucer died in 1400 and was the first person buried in what has become known as Poets Corner in Westminster Abbey.*

1530 Astronomical Revelations In 1530 Polish astronomer Nicolas Copernicus said that Earth span on its axis (though he also thought the planets revolved around Earth). The Roman Catholic Church disagreed and Copernicus's work was not published until shortly before his death in 1543.

1534 The Reformation After the Pope refused to allow Henry VIII to divorce Catherine of Aragon, the King installed himself as head of the Church of England. His removal of papal authority was a milestone in the worldwide Reformation – the movement against the corruption and worldliness of the Roman Catholic Church in the 16th century.

1540 Horse Racing Begins The first recorded horse-race meeting in Britain was held at Roodeye Field – now the Roodeye – at Chester.

1543 True Religion An Act for the Advancement of True Religion became law. It said that the labouring classes were forbidden to read the scriptures.

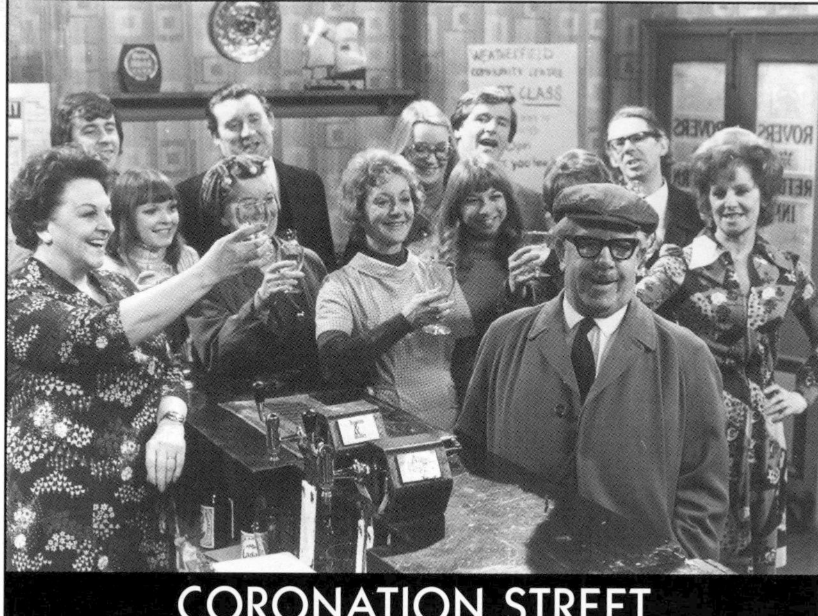

CORONATION STREET

***Coronation Street* is Britain's most successful TV programme, having been at or near the top of the ratings ever since its launch in December 1960. Time has stood still in Salford's cobbled streets and folk like grumpy Albert Tatlock (above) are now part of our heritage**

COMMERCE

THE TEN OLDEST SURVIVING BUSINESSES IN THE UK

ABERDEEN HARBOUR BOARD (FOUNDED 1136) ● CAMBRIDGE UNIVERSITY PRESS (1534)
OXFORD UNIVERSITY PRESS (1586) ● DURTNELL LTD (BUILDERS 1591)
OLD BUSHMILLS DISTILLERY COMPANY LTD (WHISKEY DISTILLERS 1608) ● THE POST OFFICE (1635)
ALLDAYS, PEACOCK & COMPANY LTD (MAKERS OF FANS 1650) ● HAYS LTD (OFFICE SERVICES 1651)
VANDOME & HART LTD (WEIGHING MACHINE MAKERS 1660) ● JAMES GIBBONS LTD (LOCKSMITHS 1670)

CHRISTMAS

❄ The first Royal Christmas broadcast was made by King George V on radio. Nowadays the Queen's Christmas broadcast is always recorded.

❄ Since 1900, there have only been eight white Christmasses in London. The most recent was in 1976.

❄ William The Conqueror was crowned King of England on Christmas Day, 1066.

❄ Christmas was officially abolished for ten years from 1642 because the Puritans hated people having fun.

❄ Armenians celebrate Christmas on January 19. How nice to be able to buy all your presents in the sales!

❄ Indiana, USA has a town called Santa Claus which runs courses for department store Santas. 'Graduates' get a BSc (Bachelor of Santa Clausing).

JOHN CLEESE

***Fawlty Towers* was written by John Cleese and his then wife Connie Booth – who played the irascible Basil Fawlty and pert Polly Sherman respectively. Their co-stars were Prunella Scales as Sybil (the 'dragon') and Andrew Sachs as the waiter, Manuel**

John Cleese created not one but three of Britain's greatest comedy triumphs. The anarchic *Monty Python's Flying Circus*, with Eric Idle, Michael Palin, Terry Jones, Terry Gilliam and Graham Chapman, was the template for post-Sixties comedy. Almost incredibly, Cleese topped that in the Seventies with *Fawlty Towers*, taking the sitcom to new heights: only 13 episodes, but every moment a gem. Then in 1988 he paved the way for the new wave of British comedy films with the worldwide blockbuster *A Fish Called Wanda*. A comic genius indeed.

Sadly, Tommy Cooper died "just like that"

TOMMY COOPER

NO ONE MADE SO MANY LAUGH BY DOING SO LITTLE. TOMMY COOPER ONLY HAD TO STAND ON STAGE AND GRIN NERVOUSLY TO HAVE HIS AUDIENCE IN STITCHES. COOPER'S ACT REVOLVED AROUND HIS CONJURING TRICKS, WHICH WOULD GO HILARIOUSLY WRONG UNTIL THE MOMENT WHEN HE SUDDENLY GOT IT TRIUMPHANTLY RIGHT.

COOPER, BORN IN CAERPHILLY IN 1922, WAS A MUSIC HALL MAN WHO BECAME A TELLY SUPERSTAR – HIS TOMMY COOPER HOUR WAS A CHART-TOPPER IN 1974 AND '75. WHEN HE DIED OF A HEART ATTACK DURING A LIVE TV SHOW IN 1984, THE NATIONAL SENSE OF LOSS WAS MADE EVEN GREATER BY THE REALISATION THAT WE HAD SOMEHOW TAKEN THIS TRAGI-COMIC GIANT FOR GRANTED.

1545 MARY ROSE SINKS
Henry VIII's warship *Mary Rose* was leaving the Solent when it heeled over and sank at a cost of 700 lives. The dismayed King watched the disaster from Southsea Castle. In 1982, 437 years later, the Prince of Wales watched as the wreck of the ship was brought to the surface to be preserved.

1547 IVAN THE TERRIBLE
Having ruled Russia for 14 years, Ivan the Terrible decided in 1547 he would be crowned as the first Russian Czar. He died in 1584 having introduced welcome reforms, but his reign was marred by a campaign of terror against the nobility. More than 3,000 were put to death. Aptly-named Ivan also killed his son in a fit of rage.

1547 VAGRANTS FOR SLAVES
The Vagrant Act was passed. It meant that on the approval of two magistrates, anyone wanting an able-bodied vagrant as a slave could brand him with a 'V' and keep him in slavery for two years.

CHARLIE CHAPLIN

Remembered mainly for his bowler-hatted little tramp character, British-born actor, director, writer and composer Charlie Chaplin (1889-1977) achieved great success in Hollywood with silent movies such as *The Kid* (1921) and *The Gold Rush* (1925). His later films included *The Great Dictator* (1940), in which he lampooned Adolf Hitler. Chaplin, who quit the US in 1953 after being accused of being a Communist, won two Oscars in 1929 and 1973, and was knighted in 1975.

Times have changed in the West – in Hollywood's version anyway. Once, cowboys were box-office certs. Now their stetsons are old hat, and you're more likely to see women in a western, such as Bad Girls with Madeleine Stowe, Andie MacDowell, Mary Stuart Masterson and Drew Barrymore

COWBOYS

The laconic, toughly independent figure of the cowboy – the performer of daring feats who worked hard, played hard, and slept under the stars on the wide-open prairies – is a major part of western folklore. His heyday was from the 1860s to the 1880s, as cattle-raising became big business in Texas following the American Civil War.

At that time 100,000 men on horseback were employed to tend great herds of cattle on vast stretches of unfenced land known as the open range. They took cattle on demanding trail drives, moving herds up to 1600 km to the nearest railroad station for transporting to east coast dinner plates. Trails could last three months and the hazards were many, including cattle rustlers, snake bites and stampedes.

The cowboys helped to cement the economy of the emerging American West, but by 1890 the spread of farming and railroads made many of them redundant.

Yet the cowboy spirit lives on in thousands of films, books and cartoons. The screen cowboy's heyday was the 1950s, when TV abounded with weekly series such as *Wagon Train*, *The Lone Ranger* and *Rawhide*, starring Clint Eastwood. And as recently as 1992, Eastwood won Oscars for his bruisingly realistic western *Unforgiven*.

1548
HENRY'S SIXTH WIFE DIES
Catherine Parr, the sixth wife of Henry VIII – who, like her predecessors, had been unable to give him the robust male heir that he desperately craved, – died, ironically while in childbirth for her second husband, Lord Seymour. Henry had died 18 months earlier.

1556
ARCHBISHOP BURNED TO DEATH
As the persecution of Protestants got well under way in Britain under the rule of Catholic Queen Mary I, Thomas Cranmer was burned at the stake in Oxford, condemned as a traitor and heretic. The unfortunate Cranmer had been appointed the first Protestant Archbishop of Canterbury by Henry VIII in 1533.

1558
ELIZABETH I CROWNED
Elizabeth I became Queen at the age of 25 and remained on the throne for 45 years. Under Elizabeth – "the Virgin Queen" who never married – the nation flourished politically, militarily and culturally. Her nickname reflected her popularity – Good Queen Bess.

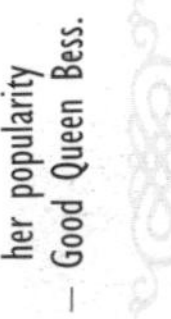

Churchill – the bow tie and victory sign were the trademarks; unflinching determination was the hallmark

SIR WINSTON CHURCHILL

Winston Churchill was perceived as half man, half bulldog by the British public during the Second World War – an icon representing the nation's ability to hang on against an overwhelming foe.

Born in 1874, he became a legend during the Boer War when he made a dramatic escape from internment in Pretoria. Becoming a member of Parliament, he switched sides when it suited him. He held various Government posts, but fell from favour with his then fellow Conservatives – until war broke out in 1939 and the country knew it needed the great warrior at the helm.

After becoming Premier in May 1940, Churchill forever seemed on hand in a crisis, clad in a siren suit, chomping on a trademark cigar and making a V-sign indicating British invincibility. In our darkest hour, Churchill was Britain's light. He worked non-stop on relationships with America and Russia and was generally regarded as the architect of the Allies' victory.

Yet, with the war won, he was promptly ditched by the British public, who voted in Clement Attlee's Labour administration. Even then Churchill refused to give up, and won an amazing election victory in 1951 at the age of 77. He finally resigned four years later after suffering a stroke.

A prolific but self-deprecating historian, he won the Nobel Prize for literature in 1953.

After his death in 1965 he lay in state for three days in Westminster Abbey before a funeral at St Paul's Cathedral. The greatest Briton of the century – and arguably of the Millennium – is buried near his ancestral home at Blenheim Palace, Oxfordshire.

Queen Coco

THE EPITOME OF FRENCH CHIC, COCO CHANEL RULED PARISIAN HAUTE COUTURE FOR 50 YEARS. HER ELEGANTLY CASUAL INVENTIONS ARE NOW CLASSICS – JERSEY SUITS, COSTUME JEWELS AND THE 'LITTLE BLACK DRESS'. BUT COCO, WHO DIED IN 1971, WILL BE BEST REMEMBERED FOR A FRAGRANCE AND A NUMBER – CHANEL NO 5, INTRODUCED IN 1922 AND STILL HUGELY POPULAR.

THE CALENDAR

THEN Calendars have always struggled to reconcile solar time with lunar time. In 1000, Britain was still using Julius Caesar's calendar. The Roman calendar had been drifting – by Caesar's era, autumn was arriving in July – so he divided the year into 12 months of 31, 30 or 29 days and moved the year start from March 1 to January 1. To put the calendar back on track, he instituted a year of 445 days – the so-called 'year of confusion'. Even so, his year was still 11 minutes out.

NOW In 1752 we adopted the Gregorian calendar, devised in the 1580s by Pope Gregory XIII. The year 2000 in the Hebrew calendar is 5761, while in the Chinese calendar it is 'the 17th year in the 78th cycle' – and the year of the dragon.

Calendars with stars such as Caprice are more popular now than ever

1562 BRITAIN'S SLAVE TRADE Britain became seriously involved in the slave trade when Sir John Hawkins took on board 300 African slaves from a Portuguese slave ship. Two years later, Queen Elizabeth loaned Hawkins a ship provided she received a share of the slave trade profits.

1562 BRITAIN'S FIRST CONSERVATORY Sir William Cecil, one of Elizabeth I's right-hand men, had a conservatory built to protect his sub-tropical plants – brought to him during this age of exploration – from the English climate. It is believed to have been the first conservatory built in Britain.

1564 THE BARD IS BORN Born on St George's Day, William Shakespeare is acknowledged as the greatest-ever writer in the English language. As one 20th century biographer put it: "No writer of any land or any age has ever had popularity and renown on such a colossal and astounding scale."

COSMETICS

Catherine Deneuve for Chanel

CHANEL

French screen goddess Catherine Deneuve was for many years the elegant face of Chanel fragrances

THEN The prudish Victorians frowned upon make-up, despite its venerable past: the Romans, for instance, used kohl to darken brows. By 1900, respectable women in Britain still made only modest use of rouge and powder, and it was left to the French to pioneer many of today's formulas. After the First World War the Brits and Americans finally discarded their prejudices, persuaded by advertising and the cinema, whose female idols were perfectly made-up.

NOW Over 5000 ingredients are used in cosmetics, which are required by law to be safe. There is also pressure to make them 'cruelty-free'. Anita Roddick's ethical beauty company The Body Shop has led this movement, with plant-based products and campaigns against animal testing. She also declines to claim miraculous results for her products. Men are now under the sort of pressure to look good that women have long known, and male grooming products are booming.

In 1999 Max Factor moved the cosmetics advertising war to a new level by signing pop superstar Madonna

COINCIDENCES

TEN BIZARRE HAPPENINGS

BABY LUCK: In 1975, in Detroit, a baby fell out of a building 14 storeys up. Luckily, it landed on a man named Joseph Figlock and so survived. A year later, another baby fell from the same building and survived by falling on … Joseph Figlock.

LIVE MUSHROOMS: A nun in Clwyd tried but failed to grow mushrooms in the convent grounds. Since her death in 1986, mushrooms have grown on her grave every autumn.

SPONTANEOUS COMBUSTION: In 1938, 22-year-old Phyllis Newcombe combusted spontaneously at a dance hall during a waltz. Many people witnessed it. In a similar event, British pensioner Euphemia Johnson died when she suddenly burst into flames while enjoying her afternoon tea.

A GOLDEN SHEEP: In 1984, a Greek priest was cooking a sheep's head when he discovered that it had a jaw made of 14-carat gold (worth £4,000). The sheep had been owned by his brother-in-law, who couldn't explain it – nor could the Greek Ministry of Agriculture.

ABRAHAM LINCOLN'S GHOST: The ghost of the assassinated US President is said to haunt the White House. Among those who have 'seen' it are a maid who was in the room with First Lady Eleanor Roosevelt and Queen Wilhelmina of the Netherlands. Similarly, Anne Boleyn's ghost is said to revisit her childhood haunt, Blickling Hall in Norfolk, on May 19, the date she was executed in 1536.

DOUBLE PROOF: A pair of identical American twin boys were separated at birth in 1940 and adopted by different people who didn't know each other. Each boy was named James, each boy married a woman named Linda, had a son named James Alan, and was then divorced. When they eventually met up at the age of 39, they found they shared the same hobbies, experiences and tastes.

LET IT RAIN: In 1986, Judge Samuel King was annoyed that some jurors were absent from his Californian court because of heavy rain. So he issued a decree: "I hereby order that it cease raining by Tuesday." California suffered a five-year drought. So in 1991, the judge decreed: "Rain shall fall in California beginning February 27." Later that day, California had its heaviest rainfall in a decade.

DEAD AGAIN: In Bermuda, two brothers were killed precisely one year apart at the age of 17 by the same taxi driver carrying the same passenger on the same street.The two boys had each been riding the same moped.

FISHY FACT: In 1969, a Finnish farmer was cutting wood when, in the middle of an aspen log, he found a dried fish.There was no way the fish could have got there, yet there it was.

A TIME TO DIE: Charles Davies died at 3.00 in the morning at his sister's house in Leicester. When she phoned his home in Leeds to tell his wife, she found that Charles's wife had also just died … at 3.00 in the morning.

LIFELINES

AGATHA CHRISTIE, *born in 1890, was the archetypal English mystery writer, the creator of Hercule Poirot and Miss Marples. Her play The Mousetrap has been running in London since 1952. She died in 1976, five years after she was made a Dame.*

RAYMOND CHANDLER, *born in 1888, was the archetypal American mystery writer, the creator of tough private eye Philip Marlowe. Raised in Europe, Chandler's novels include The Big Sleep and The Long Goodbye. He died in 1959.*

DENIS COMPTON *(1918-1997) was England's most dashing sportsman. The Brylcreem boy's 1947 record of most runs (3816) and centuries (18) in a cricket season still stands, and he also played football for Arsenal and England. Howzat!*

1572 ENTER BEN JONSON English poet and dramatist Ben Jonson was born in Westminster in 1572. His first play, *Every Man in His Humour*, was performed in 1598. The plot is thin but will always be remembered mainly because of the name of one of the actors who performed in it – William Shakespeare.

1581 THE FIRST ARK ROYAL Sir Walter Raleigh had a magnificent new ship built, called the *Ark Raleigh*, which he sold to Queen Elizabeth I for her flagship. It became the first *Ark Royal*.

1582 THE FIRST WATERWORKS Britain's first waterworks were built in London and for the first time water was pumped to private houses.

1582 THE GREGORIAN CALENDAR The year in which Pope Gregory XIII formulated the calendar in use today. Previously, most countries had deemed Christmas or Easter the start of a new year, but under Gregory's plan New Year's Day would be January 1.

DICTIONARY

The first English dictionary, Robert Cawdrey's The Table Alphabeticall of Hard Words (1604), defined about 3000 words. The ultimate dictionary in any language remains the Oxford English Dictionary (OED), with 291,500 entries describing 615,100 words in 22 volumes. Our favourite new words are:

- *MOUSE POTATO – an Internet couch potato.*
- *IRRITAINMENT – an infuriating media spectacle that you can't help watching (such as the O J Simpson trial).*

THE DERBY

Ten firsts for the world's greatest flat race

1780 The first Derby is won by Diomed.
1787 The first Earl of Derby to win the race is Edward Stanley with his horse Sir Peter Teazle.
1801 Eleanor becomes the first filly to win both The Derby and, the following day, The Oaks.
1828 The first dead heat.
1894 Earl Rosebery is the first Prime Minister to own a Derby winner.
1895 The Derby is the first horse race to be filmed.
1909 The first winning horse to be owned by a reigning monarch is King Edward VII's Minoru.
1932 The Derby is the first horse race to be televised.
1949 The first photo finish in a Derby.
1967 Starting stalls are used for the first time.

CHARLES DICKENS

Ethan Hawke and Gwyneth Paltrow as Pip and Estella in the 1998 Great Expectations

The tale of a great novelist in ten chapters

1. Dickens was born in 1812. His father, a navy pay clerk, lost his job and wound up in a debtors' prison. Young Charles had to work in a blacking factory to help the family.

2. Dickens' father was the model for the ever-optimistic Mr Micawber in David Copperfield.

3. W C Fields played Micawber in the 1935 film with typical gusto. When told that Dickens hadn't written about Micawber juggling, he replied: "He probably forgot."

4. Later, Dickens was a journalist – starting as a court reporter and graduating to editor.

5. Dickens gave dramatic readings of his books and sometimes got so excited that he fainted.

6. Dickens' novels have often been chosen on Desert Island Discs – including Eric Clapton (Barnaby Rudge), Ernie Wise (Edwin Drood) and Frankie Howerd (David Copperfield).

7. Dickens called his wife, Kate, his "dearest mouse" and his "darling pig".

8. An insomniac, his bed had to point north and he lay in the centre.

9. Dickens fell "deeply and intimately" in love with his wife's sister Mary when she lived with them. Mary died aged 17 and he wore her ring for the rest of his life.

10. He then fell for his wife's sister Georgina. When Dickens and his wife separated after 22 years and ten children, Georgina stayed with him. He asked to be buried next to Mary but was buried, in 1870, in Westminster Abbey.

1588
THE SPANISH ARMADA
Philip II of Spain sent an armada of 130 ships bearing 30,000 men to attack England. It was partly a Papal-backed holy war against Protestant Elizabeth and partly retaliation over what Spain saw as English piracy. The armada was defeated, leaving England free to develop trade and colonisation across the world.

1589
THE WORLD'S FIRST LOO
Inventor John Harrington installed the world's first flushing wc at his home in Kelston, near Bath. In 1592, Queen Elizabeth visited his home, tried it out and ordered one for herself.

1599
ENTER OLIVER CROMWELL
In the year that Oliver Cromwell was born there were, perhaps portentously, simmering disagreements between monarchy and Parliament. It all led to a declaration of rights by the House of Commons known as The Great Protestation.

LIFELINES

Fyodor Dostoyevsky, *born in 1821, had a deep insight into the criminal mind. Hardly surprising, as he spent four years in a Siberian prison. Sentenced to death for his ideas, Dostoyevsky survived to become one of the great writers of his age. He displayed great psychological insight, influencing other novelists and Sigmund Freud, through such books as Crime And Punishment. He died in 1881.*

Alexandre Dumas *was France's answer to Dickens – a huge 19th-century talent who lived life with the swash-buckling vim of his classic novels The Three Musketeers, The Man in the Iron Mask and The Count of Monte Cristo. A brazen literary thief, he transformed his sources with immense verve. By the time he died in 1870, aged 68, he had amassed and squandered several fortunes.*

Above: Lady Diana Spencer wrestles with her train on the steps of St Paul's. Below: Princess Diana campaigning against land mines in Bosnia, and visiting Pakistan

DIANA

People related to the late Diana, Princess of Wales

Prime Minister **Sir Winston Churchill** *(4th cousin, twice removed)*
Hollywood great **Humphrey Bogart** *(7th cousin, twice removed)*
Author **Louisa May Alcott** *(7th cousin, four times removed)*
Adventurer **T E Lawrence** of Arabia *(4th cousin, three times removed)*
German statesman **Otto Von Bismarck** *(8th cousin, five times removed)*
Soldier statesman **Oliver Cromwell** *(1st cousin, 11 times removed)*
Novelist **Jane Austen** *(7th cousin, six times removed)*
President **Franklin D Roosevelt** *(7th cousin, three times removed)*
Vanished earl **Lord Lucan** *(2nd cousin, once removed)*
Film director **Orson Welles** *(8th cousin, twice removed)*

1603
Death of Elizabeth I
After a triumphant reign of 45 years, Elizabeth died, aged 69. The subsequent accession of James VI of Scotland as James I of England united the two nations. Elizabeth's funeral was held at Westminster Abbey on April 28, 1603.

1603
Raleigh Arrested
After the death of Elizabeth, Sir Walter Raleigh was arrested and accused of plotting to overthrow James I. He was tried for treason and sent to the Tower. In 1618 he was executed.

1605
Gunpowder Plot
Frustrated at their failure to gain religious toleration, a group of Catholics decided to blow up the King and Parliament. The Gunpowder Plot was thwarted when 36 barrels of powder were discovered in the cellars of the Houses of Parliament. Some of the plotters were killed; others, including Guy Fawkes, were tortured and executed.

DOMESDAY BOOK

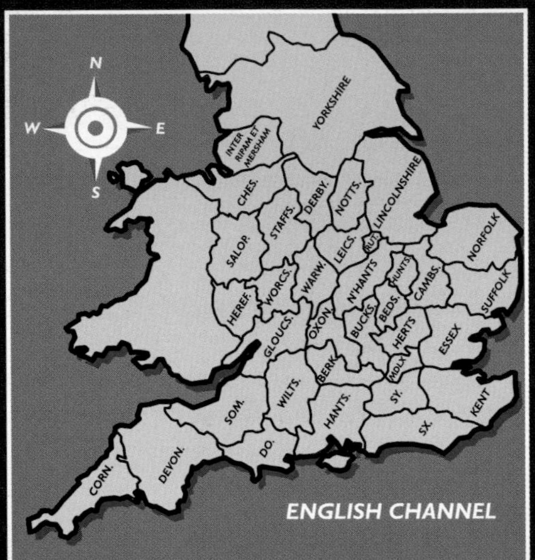

1086 ***The counties in the Domesday Book (above) have changed little in a millennium***

No one knows exactly why William the Conqueror commissioned the *Domesday Book*, but anyone who values their roots owes the Norman king a debt. The Book is an extraordinarily thorough listing of who lived where in England in 1086 and how many pigs, sheep, goats and slaves they owned.

Nine hundred years on, most of the towns and villages mentioned still exist. The counties have hardly changed: Yorkshire was huge; Middlesex and Huntingdonshire have only recently disappeared; Salopshire is now Shropshire. The book (below) reposes at the Public Record Office in London.

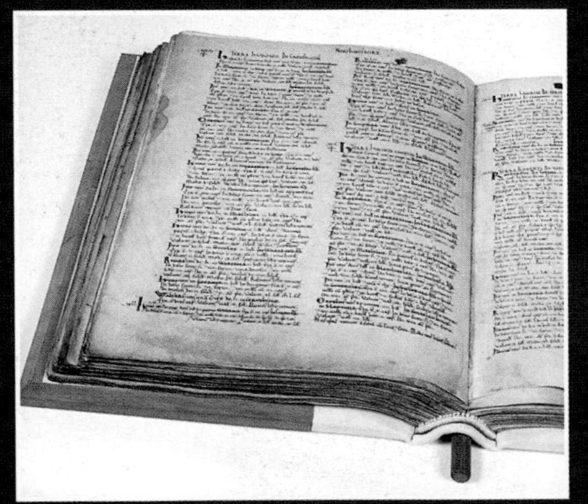

SALVADOR DALI

Genius or charlatan – the debate goes on a decade after Spanish artist Salvador Dali's death. But no one disputes that he had a great gift of showmanship which made him the century's most famous artist. Born in 1904, Dali led the Surrealist movement with beguiling dreamscapes such as 1931's The Persistence of Memory, where he first unveiled the evocative limp watches (below).

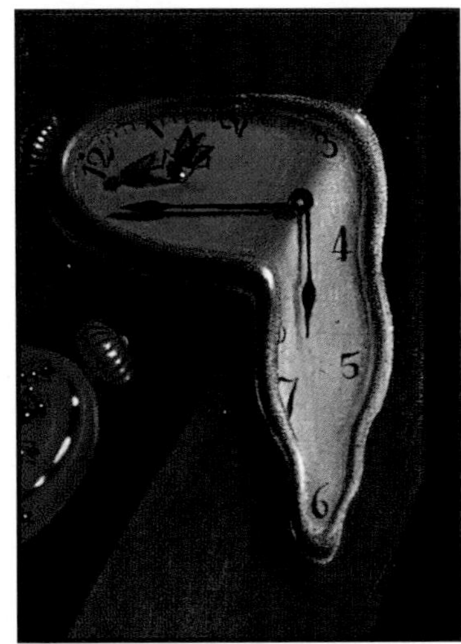

DOCTOR WHO

Secrets of the Tardis revealed

- *Doctor Who* holds the record as the world's longest-running science fiction TV series, running from 1963 till 1989.
- The first episode was broadcast on November 23 1963 – the day after President John F Kennedy was assassinated.
- The Daleks were so popular in Britain in the 1960s, they were even turned into a stage play. *The Curse of The Daleks* opened in London's West End on December 21, 1965.
- In 1983, there was a one-off 20th anniversary special entitled 'The Five Doctors' with Richard Hurndall standing in for William Hartnell, who had died in 1975. Patrick Troughton and Jon Pertwee both appeared. It also used footage from the unshown 'Shada' by Douglas Adams, starring Tom Baker. Patrick Troughton went on to appear in 'The Two Doctors', a three-episode story in 1985.
- Countries which have shown the series include Brunei, Cyprus, Australia, Ghana, Mexico, Sierra Leone, Holland, Tunisia and even Lebanon.
- The only Doctor who married an assistant – in real life – was Tom Baker, who married Lella Ward (who played his assistant Romana).

1611 FOUNDER OF HUDSON BAY
English navigator Henry Hudson, his son and seven sailors were cast adrift in a small boat after a mutiny. They were never seen again but the spot where he disappeared was later named after him – Hudson Bay.

1613 THE GLOBE BURNS DOWN
The Globe Theatre, on London's Bankside, where William Shakespeare acted and where his plays were performed, burned down in 1613 after a cannon fired during a performance of *Henry VIII* set the thatched roof on fire. It was rebuilt the following year, only to be pulled down in 1644 by Puritans objecting to "dens of thieves and a theatre of all lewdness." The new Globe was opened in 1996.

1625 ACCESSION OF CHARLES I
Twenty six years after Cromwell's birth, Charles I succeeded to the throne after the death of his father, James I.

1967 *Martin Sharp's famous psychedelic poster sums up the awe in which Dylan was held. Thirty years on, Sharp posters are collected as artworks in their own right*

BOB DYLAN

As a force of change, Bob Dylan ranks with The Beatles and Elvis. In the Sixties he influenced everyone from Jimi Hendrix to the Fabs themselves.

Blending the old with the unheard-of, the Bible with social protest, folk music with electric rock, he became a legend in his own lifetime – and all with a voice that David Bowie compared to 'sand and glue'.

The folk anthem 'Blowin' in the Wind' (1963) crystallised that era's youth politics, while 'Like A Rolling Stone' (1965) unveiled a psychedelic style that some fans saw as treachery.

A bad motorbike accident in 1966 kept Dylan from touring for seven years, but his music went on its bewildering way. The 1975 album *Blood on the Tracks*, with its bittersweet love songs, marked a new high.

When, in 1982, he was elected to the Songwriters' Hall of Fame, he said: "This is pretty amazing because I can't read or write a note of music."

What's Bob done lately?

- **1985: He is the last act at Live Aid**
- **1988: He hooks up with George Harrison and Roy Orbison in The Traveling Wilburys**
- **1997: His album Time Out of Mind is hailed as his best for years**

LIFELINES

Dante Alighieri, *born in 1265, was Italy's greatest poet. His masterpiece The Divine Comedy is an epic account of a journey through Hell, Purgatory and Paradise. Politically active, Dante was forced to flee from Florence and died in exile in 1321.*

Charles Darwin, *born in 1809, was England's greatest naturalist. He aroused worldwide controversy when he published his On The Origin Of Species, with its theory of evolution that questioned biblical teachings. He died in 1882.*

Bette Davis *was Hollywood's drama queen. Born in 1908, she won Oscars for Dangerous (1935) and Jezebel (1938). She became a horror star in Whatever Happened to Baby Jane? (1962), and died in 1989.*

DEATH

Jeremy Bentham

People whose parts were preserved after their death

Physicist **Albert Einstein's brain**
Poet **Percy Bysshe Shelley's heart**
Astronomer **Galileo's finger**
Russian leader **Lenin's brain**
Composer **Joseph Haydn's head**
Philosopher **Jeremy Bentham's head**
Missionary **Dr David Livingstone's heart**
President **George Washington's tooth**
King Richard II's jawbone
Novelist **Thomas Hardy's heart**
French Emperor **Napoleon's penis**

Dr David Livingstone

1642
Civil War
The English Civil War broke out between the Roundheads, those supporting Parliament, and the Cavaliers, those supporting the King. The Roundheads found a leader in Oliver Cromwell, a soldier and statesman. The war would lead to the execution of Charles I and the temporary abolition of the monarchy in England.

1649
King Charles Executed
Executioner Richard Brandon took the life of Charles I on a scaffold outside Whitehall. The King had been found guilty of treason by waging "unnatural, cruel and bloody wars". He was buried in St George's Chapel, Windsor. Charles II, crowned King of Scotland in 1651, then marched into England to claim his throne. Cromwell resisted and Charles was not crowned until 1660, the official restoration of the monarchy.

1650
Birth of the Quakers
George Fox, charged with illegal preaching, urged the judge at his trial to "tremble at the word of the Lord". The judge replied that Fox was the only quaker in the court. The name stuck.

DECLARATION OF INDEPENDENCE

A KEY WORK OF THE MILLENNIUM, THE AMERICAN DECLARATION OF INDEPENDENCE WAS DRAFTED BY A TEAM INCLUDING BEN FRANKLIN (STANDING), AND FUTURE US PRESIDENTS THOMAS JEFFERSON AND JOHN ADAMS

'We hold these truths to be self-evident, that all men are created equal, that they are endowed by their Creator with certain unalienable rights, that among these are life, liberty and the pursuit of happiness'

THE AMERICAN DECLARATION OF INDEPENDENCE, JULY 4, 1776

DECLARATION OF HUMAN RIGHTS

THE DECLARATION OF HUMAN RIGHTS WAS ONE OF THE FIRST DOCUMENTS ISSUED BY THE UNITED NATIONS. UNFORTUNATELY IT HAS NO LEGAL STANDING, AND HAS BEEN ABUSED EVER SINCE. BUT AT LEAST IT EXISTS...

'All human beings are born free and equal in dignity and rights'

THE UNIVERSAL DECLARATION OF HUMAN RIGHTS, 1948

The film Saving Private Ryan showed that the heroism of D-Day remains undimmed by the passage of time

D-DAY

Steven Spielberg's movie *Saving Private Ryan* has brought home the bloody reality of D-Day to a generation whose fathers and grandfathers had actually fought to secure their freedom.

The turning point of the Second World War in Europe, the D-Day landings on the Normandy coast on June 6, 1944 marked the largest seaborne invasion in history, and put paid to Hitler's boast that his defences were unbreachable.

Led by General Eisenhower, Operation Overlord brought Allied forces ashore along a 100-kilometre stretch of five beaches code-named Utah, Omaha, Gold, Juno and Sword. Overnight, 2700 ships carrying 176,000 soldiers followed a fleet of minesweepers across the English Channel, while paratroopers dropped behind Nazi lines to capture bridges and railway tracks. At 6.30am, the troops stormed ashore to surprise the Germans, who had expected an invasion attempt near Calais.

"We will fight them on the beaches," Prime Minister Churchill had pledged, and so the Allies did, surviving heavy shelling and machine-gun fire to secure all five beaches. An artificial harbour was built, a pipeline brought fuel across the Channel, and by the end of June, a million soldiers had landed. The Allied advance could begin.

1652
ANYONE FOR TEA?
While England was at war with the Netherlands a small quantity of tea was discovered on a captured Dutch ship. It was brought back, introducing tea to the country for the first time. Ten years later, tea-drinking began at the royal Court.

1658
CROMWELL DIES
On September 3, 1658, Oliver Cromwell died from pneumonia and was buried in Westminster Abbey. His famous effigy is seen holding an orb and sceptre and wearing a crown. He was succeeded by his son, Richard, as Lord Protector of the Commonwealth of England, Scotland and Ireland. Cromwell had held the post from December 1653.

1660
AN ACTRESS ON STAGE!
The theatres were reopened after being shut down by the Puritans. The first woman to appear as an actress on stage did so as Desdemona in Shakespeare's *Othello*.

DISEASES

THEN Disease was rife in the Middle Ages. Epidemics such as leprosy swept Europe, while in the 14th century the Black Death (bubonic plague) accounted for a third of the continent's population. Hundreds of thousands lost their lives to smallpox, meningitis and tetanus. Poor sanitation and ignorance compounded the problem. But the new Millennium saw the first charitable hospitals and medical schools.

NOW In 1900, the average life expectancy in Europe was only about 50 years. Now it's closer to 75, thanks to a huge leap in medical knowledge, along with better nutrition and hygiene. Research into vitamins helped eradicate beriberi, rickets and scurvy. Penicillin and hundreds of other drugs now contain diseases such as tuberculosis and smallpox. But medicine is faced with new challenges in the form of auto-immune conditions such as AIDS. And we have yet to fully understand heart disease and cancer – the chief causes of death in the West.

DNA

DNA is the very blueprint of who you are. It is the chemical which carries the genetic code of every living thing, determining its individual characteristics; it's what makes us all different. It was Englishman Francis Crick and American James Watson who first built a model of the DNA molecule in 1953, showing it as a twisting ladder. Their work may one day eradicate inherited diseases, but it has also led us into the moral minefield of genetic engineering. Dolly the sheep (above) was cloned from another sheep's DNA; human clones can't be far behind.

ISADORA DUNCAN

'What one has not experienced, one will never understand in print'
Isadora Duncan

Isadora Duncan's life was like the plot for a Ken Russell movie – which indeed it became (played by fellow free spirit Vanessa Redgrave).

The creator of modern dance, born in San Francisco in 1878, she graced the world's stages dressed in the skimpiest of Greek tunics or less.

Her life off stage was equally wild. Her two children – one by a stage designer, the other by the heir to a sewing machine fortune – died in a car that sank in the Seine. Her marriage to a young Russian in 1922 ended in his suicide.

Isadora died in 1927, as dramatically as she lived, when her scarf caught in the spokes of a car wheel and strangled her.

DESERT ISLAND DISCS

THE TOP TEN BOOKS CHOSEN SINCE THE PROGRAMME STARTED

1. **Encyclopaedia Britannica**
2. **An encyclopaedia**
3. **War and Peace** *(Leo Tolstoy)*
4. **Remembrance of Things Past** *(Marcel Proust)*
5. **The Oxford Book of English Verse**
6. **The Decline and Fall of the Roman Empire** *(Edward Gibbon)*
7. **The Oxford English Dictionary**
8. **The Lord of The Rings** *(J R R Tolkien)*
9. **Alice in Wonderland** *(Lewis Carroll)*
10. **The combined novels of Charles Dickens**

LIFELINES

Richard Dimbleby *(1913-65) was Britain's favourite broadcaster. A radio war correspondent, he later became a TV commentator, the voice of all great state occasions. His sons David and Jonathan have followed in his footsteps.*

Benjamin Disraeli *was the leading Conservative of the 19th century. Born in 1804, he was a novelist who became Prime Minister in 1868 and 1874-80, his perennial rival being the Liberals' William Gladstone. He died a year after losing office.*

Sir Francis Drake *made history by sailing round the world. Devon born, in 1545, he delayed a Spanish invasion of England by burning ships in Cadiz harbour, and in 1588 destroyed the Spanish Armada. He died in 1596.*

1660 Pepys Begins His Diary
Samuel Pepys started writing his celebrated diary. As well as detailing London society of the time, he wrote graphically about the Plague of 1664-65 and the Great Fire of 1666.

1665 The Great Plague
An outbreak of the Bubonic Plague swept through London in 1664 to 1665, claiming about 70,000 lives. There had been several outbreaks of the plague, known as the Black Death since the 14th century *(see 1347)* but this terrible outbreak was the last in Britain. The nursery song, *Ring a Ring o' Roses* is believed to have originated at this time referring to a red rash that appeared on victims before their almost certain death.

1665 Newton's Discoveries
Sir Isaac Newton saw that apple fall, or so the story goes. True or not, his theories, including the one on gravity, proved to be some of the most influential of the Millennium. Equally important were his laws of motion which established the science of mechanics. He went on to discover calculus and invented the first reflecting telescope.

Forget Southend-on-Sea: *these days a child's idea of a day out is a trip to Paris to meet Mickey Mouse, explore Sleeping Beauty's castle in Fantasyland, and visit the future on the virtual reality rides of Discoveryland. It's a small world, they sing – and an expensive one*

DISNEY

"I've seen a house fly!" For most of this century, the kaleidoscopic sights and sounds of Disney's feature-length animated films have excited children's imaginations everywhere.

Disney's characters – Mickey Mouse, Donald Duck, Bambi, Mary Poppins and the rest – must rank among the best-known on the planet.

Goofy, Pluto and Donald first appeared in *Silly Symphonies* in 1929. Disney's 1932 cartoon *Flowers and Trees* was the first ever in Technicolor, and over the years his studio would win more than 50 Oscars for technical innovation.

Though he drew little himself, Disney oversaw the heyday of the full-length films, beginning with *Snow White and the Seven Dwarfs* (1937) and including *Fantasia* (1940), *Dumbo* (1941), *Lady and the Tramp* (1955) and *The Jungle Book* (1967). The studio adapted easily to TV, producing a weekly show and branching out into non-animated films.

Disney laid the foundations of a global industry of theme parks and merchandising when he opened Disneyland in Anaheim, California in 1955. Today there is Disney World in Florida (incorporating the futuristic Epcot Center) and theme parks in Tokyo and Paris, the latter now attracting more visitors than Notre Dame.

TEN NAMES WALT DISNEY REJECTED FOR SNOW WHITE'S SEVEN DWARFS

GLOOMY	WHEEZY
SHIRTY	SNIFFY
WOEFUL	WEEPY
LAZY	SNOOPY
PUFFY	SHORTY

(The names chosen were Doc, Grumpy, Dopey, Sleepy, Happy, Sneezy and Bashful)

The Walt Disney story in ten episodes

1. Born on December 5 1901, Walt(er) Elias Disney started drawing cartoons in exchange for free haircuts.

2. *During the First World War, Disney tried to join both the US and Canadian armies but was refused because he was only 16.*

3. He finally went to France as a Red Cross ambulance driver. On return he worked as a postal clerk in Kansas City.

4. *He started the Laugh-O-Gram Corporation, a vehicle for his animated fairy tales, in Kansas City in 1921 – but went bankrupt.*

5. In 1923 he went to Hollywood, taking all his worldly goods: a jacket, a pair of trousers, a shirt, two sets of underwear and a few drawing materials.

6. *For four years, Disney and wife Lillian Bounds lived in poverty.*

7. In 1927 Disney was inspired by the mice in his studio to create a cartoon mouse. He called him Mortimer but his wife said Mickey sounded better.

8. *Disney himself supplied the voice for Mickey in the 1928 hit talkie Steamboat Willie. He once said: "I love Mickey more than any woman I've ever known."*

9. When he set out to make a film of *Peter Pan*, he couldn't think of how to depict Tinker Bell. In the end, he decided to model her on the ideal American woman: Marilyn Monroe.

10. *By the time of his death on December 15, 1966 at the age of 65, Disney had won 32 Oscars – more than anyone else in history.*

1666 GREAT FIRE OF LONDON
A year after the Great Plague, London was devastated by a fire which lasted four days, affecting 80 per cent of the city. St Paul's Cathedral was among the buildings destoyed. The fire began in a bakehouse in Pudding Lane. Incredibly, only a recorded nine people were killed.

1666 TAJ MAHAL MAN DIES
Shah Jahan, a Mogul emperor of India who was a descendant of Genghis Khan, died aged 74. He is the man who built the Taj Mahal as a mausoleum for his beloved wife Mumtaz-i-Mahal. Shah Jaha was in a jail overlooking the Taj Mahal at the time of his death, having been overthrown by his own son. He was entombed beside his wife.

1669 BIG YEAR FOR 'BEEFEATERS'
The Warders of the Tower of London earned their now famous nickname, supposedly because of their reputation for eating large daily rations of beef.

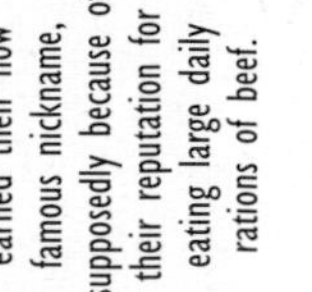

DEBENHAM & FREEBODY'S

COMMENCES MONDAY Next, July 5th

SALE

And Continues FOR TWELVE DAYS ONLY

EXCEPTIONAL BARGAINS IN ALL DEPARTMENTS

TAILORED SHIRT JUMPER SALE PRICE 21/9

PRACTICAL KNICKERS SALE PRICE 16/9

BECOMING HAT SALE PRICE 25/9

EVENING GOWN SALE PRICE 15½ Gns.

USEFUL STOCKINETTE JUMPER SUIT SALE PRICE 35/6

ATTRACTIVE HAT SALE PRICE 27/6

SERVICEABLE WALKING SHOE SALE PRICE 25/9

METAL BROCADE EVENING SHOE SALE PRICE 29/6

REMNANT DAYS FRIDAYS AND SATURDAYS

WIGMORE ST. and WELBECK ST., LONDON, W.1

QUICK SERVICE BUFFET Iced Drinks. Tea. Coffee. Sandwiches. Pastries.

DEPARTMENT STORES

Department stores have dominated town centres since Victorian times, when shopkeepers realised the appeal of 'one-stop shopping' – particularly to finely dressed ladies climbing in and out of carriages. Most department stores started as single shops whose proprietors had expanded by buying up adjacent properties. Although the early stores sold mainly fabric and made-to-measure clothing, the range of goods steadily expanded, and the prices and stock were adapted to the spending power of the increasing lower middle class.

In their heyday, they used gimmicks which make today's window displays and in-store promotions pale in comparison. Pauldens – the first shop in Manchester with electric lights after the store's founder bought all the lighting equipment used for the Manchester Jubilee Exhibition in 1887 – had live lions and tigers in one of its windows, and many Mancunians saw their first 'moving pictures' in another of its displays.

Other innovations included Kennards of Croydon commandeering two elephants to walk along Croydon high street advertising the store's 'jumbo' birthday sale (Kennards' managing director was arrested for bringing the town centre to a standstill). In-store pet shows, donkey rides, snake charmers, orchestras and cabaret acts were commonplace.

Celebrity appearances – including British aviator Amy Johnson and Betty Driver, who plays Betty Williams, née Turpin, in *Coronation Street* – were another potent promotional ploy.

Self-service was introduced after the Second World War when British department stores, albeit rather grudgingly, followed the lead of similar stores in America. Considering themselves bespoke establishments with the focus very much on polite, attentive shop assistants who ran around catering to every whim of their clientele, the British stores found it hard to take a more *laissez-faire* approach whereby the customer simply helped themselves to goods and carried them singlehandedly to the till.

Nevertheless, it proved a wise move. Department stores continued to flourish, and today there are around 800 in Britain, where shoppers can still buy everything from pins to pets under one roof.

Debenhams is one of the pioneers of department stores. In 1778 – the same year that Captain Cook discovered Hawaii – William Franks opened a small, upmarket haberdashery store in Wigmore Street, London, which became Debenham and Clark in 1813. The company really took off in the late 19th century when Frank Debenham linked the family name to that of his mother, Caroline Freebody (top left), and began taking over other stores such as Kennards (bottom left and right)

LIFELINES

MILES DAVIS was one of the most important figures in modern jazz. A trumpeter, born in 1926, classics such as Sketches of Spain relied on understatement instead of the frantic approach of musicians such as Dizzy Gillespie. He died in 1991.

DANIEL DEFOE is mainly remembered for writing Robinson Crusoe, though his bawdy classic Moll Flanders has also appeared as a film and TV series. A prolific author, born in London in 1660, he was also a secret agent. Defoe died in 1731.

RENÉ DESCARTES (1596-1650) has been called the Father of Modern Philosophy, his theories stemming from his belief that "I think, therefore I am". His own existence, he argued, proved the existence of God.

D

1671
THE DAY THEY STOLE THE CROWN JEWELS
Colonel Thomas Blood was an adventurous Irishman who went to see the royal regalia at the Tower of London disguised as a priest. He and his gang then managed to steal the Crown Jewels and make their way out of the Tower with them. But they were caught in the street. Blood was pardoned after persuading King Charles II that his execution would almost certainly trigger a revolution.

1682
HALLEY'S COMET
Edmund Halley, the Astronomer Royal, noticed a bright comet in the sky. His research showed that it had returned every 76 years and was seen just before the Battle of Hastings.

1685
DEATH OF CHARLES II
Charles II, the man who had restored the Monarchy to Britain, suffered an apoplectic fit and died four days later. Charles liked to have a good time and was known as the Merry Monarch. One of his mistresses was Nell Gwyn and he was said to have fathered at least 14 illegitimate children.

ELIZABETH I

The Virgin Queen came to the throne in a position of great weakness – heir-less, husband-less; a Protestant in a still Catholic country bitterly divided by religion.

Yet by the end of her 45-year reign – which began in 1558 – Elizabeth I had sent explorers to open up the New World, encouraged a new era of prosperity based on trade, taken control of the seas by defeating the invincible Spanish Armada, and witnessed an extraordinary flourishing of English literature. Not for nothing did hers become 'The Golden Age'.

Elizabeth (1533-1603) returned the country to the Church of England, which her father Henry VIII had founded and her sister, 'Bloody' Mary I, had tried to abolish. Shrewdly she used her single status as a bargaining tool, welcoming both Catholic and Protestant suitors but committing to no one.

And her patronage encouraged many great writers: Ben Jonson, Christopher Marlowe, Edmund Spenser … and, oh yes, William Shakespeare.

Australian actress Cate Blanchett played Elizabeth in the 1998 British film Elizabeth

EDWARD VIII & MRS SIMPSON

Crises in the Royal Family are not new. Edward VIII will forever be known as the man who refused to lay down his wife for his crown. Edward, born in 1894, became king in 1936, but refused to relinquish his American fiancée Wallis Simpson – a divorcee. Ten months into his reign Edward abdicated to marry Wallis, throwing the monarchy into turmoil. His brother, George VI, restored the crown's credibility with his diligence during the war, while Edward went into self-imposed exile. He died in 1972 and many – including the Queen – never forgave him.

1953 ***Long to reign over us indeed. In the 46 years since Princess Elizabeth became Queen in the first televised coronation, she has been a rock in a sea of change***

ELIZABETH II

In 1953, with Hillary scaling Everest and Britain shaking off wartime austerity, the new Queen must have looked forward with hope. Yet in the last decade she has seen three children's marriages end in divorce, bowed to pressure to pay tax, and taken the brunt of public distress after the death of Diana, Princess of Wales. And most of that came after her 1992 'annus horribilis'.

The goings-on of the next generation – from Diana's *Panorama* confessions to Charles' taped chats with his mistress – have led to growing public scepticism about the monarchy. The weakening of the Commonwealth, together with the new Scottish and Welsh assemblies and the proposed end of hereditary peers in the Lords, will only add to this.

Yet the Queen stays resolutely above the fray, ever distant and dutiful – qualities for which, as poet Philip Larkin saw, she may yet be recognised: "In times when nothing stood but worsened or grew strange, there was one constant good: she did not change."

1685
PROTESTANT CRACKDOWN
King Louis XIV of France revoked the Edict of Nantes, stripping French Protestant Huguenots of the religious and civil liberties granted to them by Henry IV of France.

1687
PARTHENON BLOWN UP
The Parthenon in Athens, one of the greatest classical monuments, was reduced to the ruin that it is today during a battle in 1687. Gunpowder supplies accidentally exploded when Venetians attacked the Turks who were holding the Acropolis. The explosion blew off the roof and extensively damaged the walls.

1687
ISAAC NEWTON'S 'PRINCIPIA'
Sir Isaac Newton's *Mathematical Principles of Natural Philosophy*, or the *Principia*, served as the basis of modern physics until the early 20th century when Einstein changed things. Newton's book covered the three laws of motion and his theory of universal gravitation.

'I know I have the body of a weak and feeble woman, but I have the heart and stomach of a king – and a king of England too'

EDUCATION

THEN At the turn of the Millennium, only children destined for a religious vocation received schooling. They would be taught along classical lines – grammar, logic, rhetoric, arithmetic, geometry, astronomy – in monastery and cathedral schools. All parents were expected to understand the laws of Christianity, and to pass them on to their children. Many children were apprenticed to skilled masters, for on-the-job training. The 12th century saw the first universities, with students as young as ten. By 1500, there were about 80 universities in Europe. The invention of printing in the 14th century sent literacy levels soaring.

NOW The world today has 900 million students and 40 million teachers. Britain took longer than many other European countries to form a state-controlled educational system, which did not emerge until this century. The morning assembly remains compulsory, however. As in most Western countries, full-time education is compulsory between the ages of five and 16. More than nine children in ten go to state schools rather than private. The split exam system of O-levels and CSEs was replaced in 1988 by the all-comers' General Certificate of Secondary Education. The 1980s also saw the start of a National Curriculum of basic school subjects. Literacy remains a concern, however, and the present Labour administration has pledged new targets for the 'three Rs'.

ETON

PRINCE HARRY ON HIS FIRST DAY AT ETON IN SEPTEMBER 1998, LOOKING FOR ALL THE WORLD LIKE AN URCHIN WHO STOLE THE CLOTHES OF AN ETON TOFF – LIKE THE CHAP ON THE LEFT, PICTURED IN 1937. WILLS AND HARRY BOTH GO TO THE WORLD'S MOST FAMOUS PUBLIC SCHOOL, A POTENT SYMBOL OF THE UNCHANGING HIERARCHY OF BRITISH SOCIETY

LIFELINES

***EDWARD THE CONFESSOR**, born around 1003, was an ultra-religious English king who rebuilt Westminster Abbey. His lack of an heir led to a dispute over the throne, resulting in the Norman invasion following his death in 1066.*

***T S ELIOT** is the British poet whose writings inspired Cats, the world's longest-running musical. Born in America in 1888, his masterpiece was The Waste Land, which has long been regarded as the definitive 20th-century poem. He died in 1965.*

***CHRIS EVERT** was the first female million-dollar tennis player. Born in 1954, Evert was a teenage prodigy and is renowned for her two-handed backhand. A three-times Wimbledon winner, she won 21 Grand Slam titles.*

1688
WILLIAM OF ORANGE
It began when a son was born to King James II and with him came the prospect of a succession of Catholic kings. It was not a prospect everyone relished and the King's son-in-law, William of Orange, was invited by Parliament to save Britain from Catholicism. He accepted. James II's reign was soon legally over and the Crown was given jointly to William III and Mary II in 1689.

1697
ST PAUL'S CATHEDRAL REOPENED
The official reopening and consecration of the rebuilt cathedral took place on December 2, 1697, although work on it would continue until 1710. One of London's most beautiful and famous landmarks, it was rebuilt by Sir Christopher Wren after being destroyed in the Great Fire of London (see 1666). The building is seen as Wren's crowning achievement.

ENGLAND

THEN Albion, Blighty, 'this sceptr'd isle'... Though no longer at the peak of its powers, England has had a good Millennium. Its traders, explorers and colonists opened up the New World and founded the largest empire in history. English democracy is emulated all over the world. England produced Newton, Shakespeare, and the inventors of the Industrial Revolution. England became part of Great Britain with the 1707 Act of Union, and has since seen the sun set on its dominions.

'A nation of shopkeepers'
NAPOLEON BONAPARTE, 1815

'England expects that every man will do his duty'
LORD NELSON AT THE BATTLE OF TRAFALGAR, 1805 (THE SHOPKEEPERS WON)

NOW As the Welsh, Scottish and Irish assert their identities, the English character is more confusing. The English love eccentricity but are fiercely anti-intellectual. England's hooligans demolish foreign towns, its politicians stand cautiously at the edge of Europe, yet the world speaks its language. The English are famously inhibited, but they wept in the streets for Diana and brought you The Beatles and Damien Hirst. England is a paradox – and the English would have it no other way.

'If I should die, think only this of me: that there's some corner of a foreign field that is for ever England'
RUPERT BROOKE, 'THE SOLDIER', 1914

EARTH

THEN In the year 1000, people thought the heavens revolved around the Earth. The idea that the Earth was round, however, is as old as Pythagoras. In 1543, Polish astronomer Copernicus sparked a revolution by proposing that the stars and planets actually go round the Sun, a theory confirmed by the telescopic observations of the Italian Galileo. The year after Galileo's death, 1642, saw the birth of Isaac Newton, an English scientist destined to make a still more radical discovery: gravity, which he used to explain the movements of the planets and the behaviour of objects on this one.

NOW The advent of space travel and advances in astronomy have placed our planet in a new perspective. It is a spinning ball of rock and water (70 per cent water to 30 per cent land at the surface) that is one of nine planets in orbit around the Sun – one of billions of stars that make up the Milky Way galaxy, which is one of billions of galaxies that make up our infinite and (according to Einstein) expanding Universe. Over 4.5 billion years old, Earth remains – to our knowledge – the only inhabited mass in the cosmos.

The Earth seen from Apollo 16 in 1972. A thousand years ago, people thought the Earth might be round, but they didn't know how pretty it looks

1707
FORMATION OF GREAT BRITAIN
England, Wales and Scotland became Great Britain under the Act of Union. A second Act in 1801 brought in Ireland to form the United Kingdom.

1709
THE REAL CRUSOE
Castaway sailor Alexander Selkirk was rescued after spending five years alone on the uninhabited Juan Fernandez islands off the coast of Chile. Writer Daniel Defoe based his novel Robinson Crusoe on the true-life story.

1711
THE FIRST ASCOT
The first Ascot horse race meeting was held on August 7, 1711. It was attended by Queen Anne who began the 'high society' traditions associated with the event.

1712
THE SPELL IS BROKEN
The last execution for witchcraft took place in Britain. Over the centuries, thousands of people were put to death for indulging in witchcraft.

THE EIFFEL TOWER

1889 ***At 984ft, Alexandre Eiffel's tower in Paris was the world's tallest until the Chrysler Building, New York, went up in 1930***

THE TEN TALLEST BUILDINGS IN THE WORLD

1. **Petronas Tower I**	*Kuala Lumpur, Malaysia*	*1483ft*	*1997*
2. **Petronas Tower II**	*Kuala Lumpur, Malaysia*	*1483ft*	*1997*
3. **Sears Tower**	*Chicago, USA*	*1450ft*	*1974*
4. **Jin Mao Building**	*Shanghai, China*	*1380ft*	*1998*
5. **One World Trade Center**	*New York, USA*	*1368ft*	*1972*
6. **Two World Trade Center**	*New York, USA*	*1362ft*	*1973*
7. **Empire State Building**	*New York, USA*	*1250ft*	*1931*
8. **Central Plaza**	*Hong Kong, China*	*1227ft*	*1992*
9. **Bank of China**	*Hong Kong, China*	*1209ft*	*1989*
10. **Emirates Towers One**	*Dubai, UAE*	*1161ft*	*2000*

● *Britain's tallest building is Canary Wharf, London (800ft). Our tallest planned building is the Green Bird Project, London (1450ft, date unknown)*

THE EMPIRE STATE BUILDING

1931 ***Manhattan's monolith cost $41 million to build but a lack of renters in the Depression forced it to rely on sightseers. Today it's still high in the charts***

LIFELINES

Albert Einstein, *who died in 1955, is the Millennium's best-known scientist. The fact that he published a theory of relativity is known to almost everyone. German-born in 1879, he fled to America when Hitler came to power. In 1939 he warned President Roosevelt of probable atomic warfare. Though the A-bomb was developed as a result of his theories, he took no part in its manufacture.*

Dwight D Eisenhower *encouraged most of America to wear I Like Ike badges when he successfully ran for President in 1952, and again in 1956. Born in 1890, he was Supreme Commander of the Allied Forces during the Second World War before taking up a political career with the Republican party, almost assured of the presidency in an age dominated by the Cold War. He died in 1969.*

1714
Calling Germany
Queen Anne died on August 1, the last of the Stuart monarchs. She had failed to produce an heir, although not through want of trying – she became pregnant 18 times. Under the 1701 Act of Settlement Prince George Louis of Hanover was called in, a German who spoke no English. He became King George I.

1714
First Typewriter
English inventor Henry Mill took out a patent for the first typewriter. The record shows it was designed 'for the impressing or transcribing of letters singly or progressively one after another, as in writing'.

1721
The First PM
Sir Robert Walpole was Britain's first Prime Minister. With an eye on the purse-strings, he was also First Lord of the Treasury and Chancellor of the Exchequer.

1722
Death of a Warrior
Britain's most successful military commander, the Duke of Marlborough, died on June 16, 1722. His line was to produce another great Briton – Winston Churchill.

EXPLORERS

Who was the greatest explorer? Many of the candidates are British, such as **SIR ERNEST SHACKLETON**, who in 1909 got within 97 miles of the South Pole, or **ROBERT FALCON SCOTT**, who reached the Pole in January 1912, only to find that Norwegian Roald Amundsen got there a month earlier. All five of Scott's party died in the Antarctic blizzards.

Perhaps one might nominate **DAVID LIVINGSTON**, the Scottish missionary who discovered Africa's Victoria Falls, or **HENRY MORTON STANLEY**, the Welshman who tracked him down. Or **LEIF ERIKSSON**, the Viking who reached Newfoundland 1000 years ago; **UMBERTO NOBILE**, the Italian who crossed the North Pole in an airship in 1926; or the Anglo-Swiss team of **BRIAN JONES** and **BERTRAND PICCARD**, who only this year made the first nonstop round-the-world balloon flight.

But why ponder when we can ask a true great? **SIR RANULPH FIENNES** has led over 20 expeditions, reaching both Poles and finding the 'Atlantis of the Sands' in the Oman desert. In 1992 he and Dr Mike Stroud made the longest unsupported Polar journey – 97 days dragging 500lb sledges about 1400 miles – to achieve the first unassisted crossing of the Antarctic continent. Who better to nominate his explorer of the Millennium?

SIR RANULPH FIENNES'
BEST OF THE MILLENNIUM
EXPLORERS

CAPTAIN COOK

"The results of James Cook's explorations were more far-reaching in terms of follow-up, trade and civilisation than the other close contenders such as Christopher Columbus. Cook not only explored the Pacific Ocean, Australasia and Antarctica, but also travelled as far north as Vancouver and the Bering Strait in 1778. I wish I could claim him as my inspiration, but I'm afraid I get seasick in a boat!"

MOUNT EVEREST

1953 ***The greatest challenge on earth was to climb Mount Everest, the world's highest mountain. On May 29, 1953, Nepalese Sherpa Tenzing Norgay (centre) and New Zealander Edmund Hillary (right) reached the 29,022ft Himalayan peak, where they spent just 15 minutes, leaving behind a Union Jack, a Nepal national flag and a United Nations flag. The expedition was led by Britain's Colonel John Hunt (left)***

THE ENVIRONMENT

The environment only became something to worry about once we realised what we had done to it. The trouble began in the industrial 19th century, with factory smoke smothering cities in soot. The London 'pea-souper' was as fatal as it was famous.

Today, industry has switched to cleaner fuels, but the vociferous Green movements of the West still have any number of targets: how to dispose of nuclear waste; the extinction of plants and animals; the contamination of the food chain by man-made chemicals; global warming and flooding as the ozone layer disappears.

The first Green MPs were elected in West Germany in 1983, while the flamboyant direct action group Greenpeace has grown from humble Canadian roots in 1971 to employ 1330 people in 30 countries, with five million supporters.

In Britain, anti-road protests have turned eco-warriors such as Swampy (left) into stars for 15 minutes. But where once they might have been seen as a nuisance, now they find unlikely support. Because when it comes to the environment, we are realising that we all have a vested interest.

1725
PETER THE GREAT DIES
Peter, who had taken the title of Emperor of Russia, was intent on transforming his country into a modern, cultural nation by adopting Western styles and customs. It was epitomised by the building from scratch of St Petersburg, as close to the West as possible. The beautiful city, crammed with art treasures, was meant to rival anything in Europe.

1729
AN ORIGINAL VIEW OF THINGS
The apparent shift in the position of stars as a result of the Earth's movement was discovered by astronomer James Bradley. It was the first confirmation of Copernicus' theory of the Earth moving around the Sun.

1731
WOUND THAT LED TO WAR
Captain Jenkins of the English ship Rebecca lost an ear during a skirmish with Spanish coastguards. It was an excuse eight years later for a war against the Spanish – the War of Jenkins' Ear.

EVA PERON

'Her life was insane. The best way to tell her story is through a musical because she was larger than life'
TIM RICE

EVITA

ONE OF THE MANY MYSTERIES ABOUT EVA PERÓN IS WHAT INSPIRED TIM RICE AND ANDREW LLOYD WEBBER TO WRITE A MUSICAL ABOUT HER. BUT THEY DID, AND THE RAGS-TO-RICHES STORY OF THE WIFE OF ARGENTINA'S FASCIST PRESIDENT HAS PROVED AN ENDURING SHOWBIZ HIT.

THE 1978 STAGE SHOW RAN FOR EIGHT YEARS IN LONDON. ITS SUCCESS IN NEW YORK PAVED THE WAY FOR OTHER BRITISH MUSICALS SUCH AS CATS.

THE 1996 MOVIE GAVE MADONNA (LEFT) A HIT WITH 'DON'T CRY FOR ME ARGENTINA' 20 YEARS AFTER JULIE COVINGTON'S NO 1.

AS FOR EVA, REVERED BY HER PEOPLE, SHE DIED OF CANCER IN 1952 AGED 33. JUST THINK OF ALL THE ROYALTIES SHE MISSED...

LIFELINES

CLINT EASTWOOD's bid for star status began when he was cast as Rowdy Yates in the TV series Rawhide. From there it was a short hop to spaghetti westerns and hard cop Dirty Harry. Born in 1930, Eastwood is also a successful film director.

GARETH EDWARDS MBE, born 1947, was appointed captain of the Welsh rugby team when he was 20 years old. One of the all-time greats, his international career included a run of 53 games in a row, 13 of them as captain.

GEORGE ELIOT, born Mary Ann Evans in 1819, was a free-thinker who wrote several major novels, including Middlemarch. It was published serially in 1871-2 and became a hit TV series in 1994. She died in 1880.

EPONYMS

PEOPLE WHO GAVE THEIR NAMES TO THINGS

1. SAMUEL PLIMSOLL was a coal merchant and MP who cared about safety at sea. He invented the Plimsoll Line, to limit the cargo a ship could carry. He also gave his name to the canvas shoes worn by sailors: plimsolls.

2. SIR GEORGE EVEREST was surveyor-general of India from 1830-43 and gave his name to its highest mountain. For an eminent Victorian, he was modestly named. Mount Ponsonby-Smythe would have been a challenge only to social climbers.

3. THE 7TH EARL OF CARDIGAN led the Charge of the Light Brigade at the Battle of Balaclava in 1854. He called the long-sleeved woollen waistcoat he wore under his coat a Cardigan. The name stuck.

4. THE 5TH EARL OF LONSDALE was a huge boxing fan. The belt given to any British boxer who wins the same title three times is named after him.

5. PETER NISSEN, a Canadian who fought for the British in the First World War, invented the corrugated iron Nissen hut as a shelter for men and equipment on the Western Front.

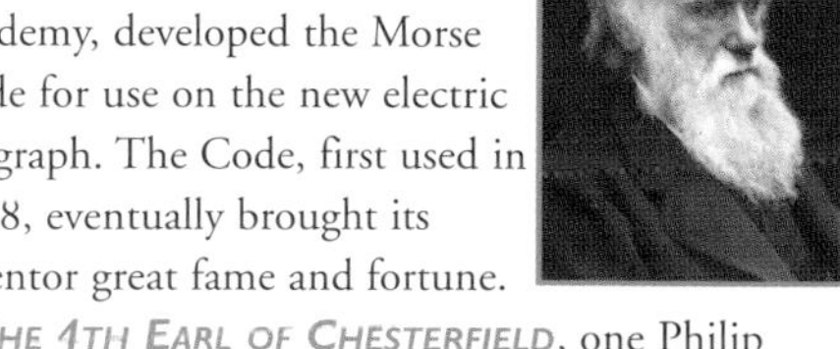

6. SAMUEL MORSE, an American artist who exhibited at the Royal Academy, developed the Morse Code for use on the new electric telegraph. The Code, first used in 1838, eventually brought its inventor great fame and fortune.

7. THE 4TH EARL OF CHESTERFIELD, one Philip Dormer Stanhope, was an 18th-century politician. No doubt he was a well-padded gent, because he gave his name to a sofa.

8. CHARLES MACINTOSH (no 'k') was a Scottish industrial chemist who patented his Mackintosh waterproof coat in 1823. He made his discovery by accident while trying to find something to do with a manufacturing by-product.

9. JEAN NICOT found a rather unfortunate way to achieve immortality. Nicot was the French ambassador to Portugal from 1559-1561. There he tried tobacco, and took some back with him to France – where the tobacco plant Nicotiana was named after him. From Nicotiana, of course, we get the word nicotine.

10. LOUIS BRAILLE was a Frenchman who went blind as a child. He invented his system of raised type when he was a teacher of the blind. In 1829, at just 20, he published his first book in braille. Sadly, he died in his early forties.

1739 DICK TURPIN HANGED The notorious highwayman Dick Turpin was hanged in York on April 7, 1739. He had been accused of murder, smuggling, cattle-stealing and holding up stagecoaches.

1740 RATIONS OF GROG Admiral Edward Vernon was known in his day as 'Old Grog' because he always wore a grogram coat – one made of a coarse wool and silk fabric. But around 1740 he was responsible for the naval rum ration being weakened with water. After that the drink was always referred to as 'grog'.

1743 LAST KING IN BATTLE George II was the last British King to lead troops into battle. He commanded the Pragmatic Army – made up of British, Hanoverian and Hessian soldiers – at the Battle of Dettingen, where the French lost.

1745 THE NATIONAL ANTHEM The first known performance of the National Anthem, 'God Save the King' was at the Drury Lane Theatre on September 28, 1745.

FILMS

This century has belonged to the cinema, and the cinema has belonged to Hollywood. Ever since the first studios began sprouting up in southern California in the 1910s, its films have entertained the world.

DW Griffith's *The Birth of a Nation* (1915), an epic American history, won praise for its artistry despite its racist slant. The silent comedians – Buster Keaton, Charlie Chaplin, Harold Lloyd – shaped a golden age under the influence of director Mack Sennett. Al Jolson's spoken words in *The Jazz Singer* (1927) heralded the talkie. Gangster flicks like *Scarface* (1933) reflected the realities of the Depression; Busby Berkeley's elaborate musicals offered escape. New genres flourished such as horror and the screwball comedy, including *It Happened One Night* (1931) and *Bringing up Baby* (1938). The hugely popular *Gone with the Wind* (1939) and Orson Welles' innovative *Citizen Kane* (1941) ended the period on a high.

Cinema went to war. Chaplin's *The Great Dictator* (1940) lampooned Hitler, while the tear-jerking *Casablanca* (1943) sacrificed romance on the altar of the greater good. Later, films such as Stanley Kubrick's nuclear comedy *Dr Strangelove* (1964) and Michael Cimino's *The Deer Hunter* (1978) would show film's powerful capacity for anti-war dissent.

Meanwhile, Alfred Hitchcock's *Psycho* (1960) made its London-born director a byword for suspense. Francis Ford Coppola dissected the Mafia with *The Godfather* (1972); and Martin Scorsese's bruising portrayals of the US male began with *Mean Streets* (1973).

'Photography is truth. The cinema is truth 24 times a second'

Jean-Luc Godard

Britain's heyday came with Ealing comedies such as *The Lavender Hill Mob* (1951), and tough Sixties capers such as *Get Carter*. After decades in the doldrums, the Nineties saw a surge in British regional creativity with *Trainspotting* and *The Full Monty*.

Top of the Hollywood heap today are two old-fashioned entertainers. Steven Spielberg made *Jaws* (1975) and *ET* (1982), but has since turned to weightier themes such as the Holocaust (*Schindler's List*). However, George Lucas's *Star Wars* 'prequel' shows he has no intention of growing up.

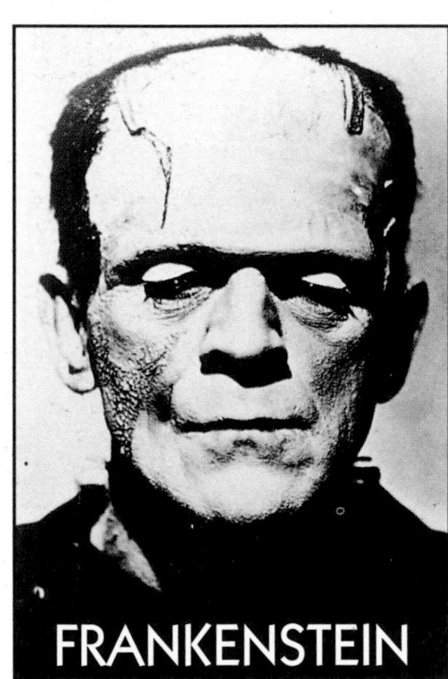

FRANKENSTEIN

Mary Shelley's creation is the greatest in the annals of horror because we fear the Monster yet sympathise with his plight at the hands of Dr Frankenstein. Since Boris Karloff first wore the neck bolts in 1931 (above), there have been at least 40 films – including Frankenstein General Hospital! With cloning set to make the myth a reality, Kenneth Branagh remade the story in 1994 with Robert de Niro as the Monster

The Full Monty (1997) struck a chord beyond its makers' wildest dreams. A bigger hit in Britain than even Four Weddings and a Funeral, it made Robert Carlyle (left) a star, and gave Hot Chocolate a huge hit with the 24-year-old You Sexy Thing

Ten wonderful film gaffes

In ***The Maltese Falcon (1941)***, as Humphrey Bogart slaps Peter Lorre, his bow-tie changes from dots to stripes.

In ***Speed (1994)***, Jeff Daniels is shot in the left leg but limps on the right.

In ***The Last Temptation of Christ (1988)***, you can see the label in Christ's robe.

In ***The Doors (1991)***, Meg Ryan calls Val Kilmer 'Val' instead of 'Jim' (see also *The War of The Roses*, in which Michael Douglas calls Danny De Vito's character 'De Vito').

In ***Rear Window (1954)***, the cast on James Stewart's leg switches legs.

In ***Robin Hood: Prince of Thieves (1991)***, the Sheriff uses the expression '10.30'. Unfortunately, clocks didn't exist in the 12th century.

In ***Spartacus (1960)***, you can clearly see a vaccination scar on Kirk Douglas's arm.

In ***48 Hrs (1982)***, Eddie Murphy is handcuffed when he leaves jail. The handcuffs then disappear but later reappear.

In ***Born On The Fourth of July (1989)***, you can hear 'American Pie' – three years before it was released.

In ***The Bible (1966)***, Adam has a belly button (think about it!).

1750
Industrial Revolution
The industrialisation of Britain began about this time, which would eventually lead to the country becoming the highly prosperous "workshop of the world". The revolution was fuelled by inventions such as James Watt's steam engine and Hargreaves' 'Spinning Jenny'.

1750
First Umbrella
A man called Jonas Hanway is recorded as being the first male seen walking in London sheltering from the rain with an umbrella. He received continuous jeers and cat-calls.

1752
The New New Year
In Britain, New Year's Day was celebrated on January 1, 1752 for the first time following adoption of the Gregorian calendar (see 1582). Before that the New Year officially began on March 25. The change caused a loss of the days from September 3 to September 13 and there was outcry from some people who believed their lives had been shortened by eleven days.

FOUR WEDDINGS AND A FUNERAL

FOUR WEDDINGS AND A FUNERAL STARTS WITH THE LONGEST STRING OF SWEAR WORDS IN ANY MAINSTREAM MOVIE. YET THIS BAWDY ROMANCE WAS A HUGE HIT IN PRIM AMERICA AND MADE STARS OF HUGH GRANT AND ANDIE MACDOWELL AS A BLUSHING ENGLISHMAN AND SEXY AMERICAN WHO MEET AT A WEDDING. RELEASED IN 1994, IT POPULARISED W H AUDEN'S POEM STOP ALL THE CLOCKS, GAVE WET WET WET A HUGE NO I WITH 'LOVE IS ALL AROUND' AND PAVED THE WAY FOR WRITER RICHARD CURTIS'S 1999 COLLABORATION WITH GRANT IN NOTTING HILL.

THE TEN GREATEST FILMS OF ALL TIME
(AS VOTED BY THE MEMBERS OF THE BRITISH FILM INSTITUTE)

1. *Casablanca (1942)*
2. *Les Enfants Du Paradis (1945)*
3. *Citizen Kane (1941)*
4. *Singin' in the Rain (1952)*
5. *2001: A Space Odyssey (1968)*
6. *Some Like It Hot (1959)*
7. *Seven Samurai (1954)*
8. *Gone With The Wind (1939)*
9. *The Third Man (1949)*
10. *One Flew Over the Cuckoo's Nest (1975)*

TEN CLASSIC MOVIES WHICH DIDN'T WIN A SINGLE OSCAR

The Lady Vanishes (1938)
The Maltese Falcon (1941)
The Big Sleep (1946)
Oliver Twist (1948)
Kind Hearts And Coronets (1949)
Singin' In The Rain (1952)
The Caine Mutiny (1954)
Cat On A Hot Tin Roof (1958)
North By Northwest (1959)
Lenny (1974)

LIFELINES

SIGMUND FREUD'S *theories regarding the unconscious mind and sexual repression in childhood were some of the most controversial this century. An Austrian psychiatrist born in 1856, he fled the Nazis to live in London, where he died in 1939.*

ST FRANCIS OF ASSISI, *who loved animals, was made the patron saint of ecologists in 1980. A friar born in 1181, he is said to have received the stigmata – the wounds of Jesus – on his hands two years before he died in 1226.*

JANE FONDA, *born in 1937, is part of a Hollywood dynasty, has been an Oscar-winner twice, achieved fame as a political activist nicknamed Hanoi Jane and, more recently, become the star of fitness videos.*

F

1757
EMPIRE IN INDIA
English soldier and statesman Robert Clive defeated the Indian rulers of Bengal, paving the way for a British Empire in India. In 1774, depressed by allegations of corruption, he committed suicide.

1758
BIRTH OF LORD NELSON
Born in Norfolk, Horatio Nelson was one of Britain's great naval commanders. He destroyed the French fleet at the Battle of the Nile in 1798 and wiped out the Danish fleet at the Battle of Copenhagen in 1801. When ordered to retreat at this battle, Nelson, blind in his right eye, lifted his telescope to his eye patch and said that he did not see any signal.

1759
BRITISH MUSEUM OPENS
Lottery money of £300,000 was used to create the British Museum in London. It was advertised as "a general repository for all arts and sciences".

FARMING

THEN Nearly everyone farmed 1000 years ago, on estates owned by rich lords and worked by peasants. With no labour-saving tools, farming was hard – though a harness had been developed to hitch a horse (instead of the slower ox) to a plough. Selective breeding produced the Guernsey dairy cow by 1100.

NOW Agriculture is still the world's most important industry, employing half of the world's workers on a third of the planet's land. But recently in the West, farming has suffered from a spate of food scares (salmonella, BSE, red meat) and pro-animal campaigns. The big trend now is for organic food – fresh produce, fish and meat that has been reared or grown according to strict guidelines.

FOOD

THEN The Western diet was enlivened by the culinary discoveries of its explorers and seamen. The Crusaders developed a taste for spices and Middle Eastern foods, while Columbus' voyage of 1492 opened up a new world of food, bringing Europeans chocolate, peanuts, peppers, pineapples and tomatoes.

NOW We are more diet-conscious than ever. While developing countries are malnourished, the West has seen the rise of eating disorders (in men as well as women) and obesity. The popularity of 'health foods' reflects consumer concern about environmental issues such as pollution and genetically modified food. Vitamin supplements are used by many as 'insurance' to make up for missing nutrients.

Ten people who had food named after them

Giuseppe Garibaldi (Garibaldi biscuits)
Viscount François de Chateaubriand (Chateaubriand steak)
James Logan (The loganberry)
John Montague, 4th Earl of Sandwich (The sandwich)
Forrest Mars (The Mars Bar)
Sir William Gage (The greengage)
Sally Lunn (Sally Lunn cakes)
Dame Nellie Melba (Peach Melba and Melba toast)
Jean & Theodor Tobler (Toblerone)
Lord Woolton (Woolton pie)

Ten people who had drinks named after them

Queen Mary I (Bloody Mary)
Tom Harvey (Harvey Wallbanger)
Dr Louis Perrier (Perrier)
Jacob Schweppe (Schweppes Indian tonic)
Alexander The Great (Brandy Alexander)
St Benedictine of Nursia (Benedictine)
Mickey Finn (Mickey Finn)
Tom Collins (Tom Collins)
James & William Horlick (Horlicks)
Dom Perignon (Dom Perignon Champagne)

FAMINE

A 1984 BBC report on famine in Ethiopia galvanised rock star Bob Geldof. The result: Band Aid's 'Do They Know It's Christmas' single, the 1985 Live Aid concerts, and over £40 million raised in relief

THEN Famine is not always caused by drought. In the 14th century, famine hit western Europe when several years of rains rotted crops. In 1841-51, Ireland's potato crop was devastated by disease; 2.5 million died or emigrated. In the 1870s, dry weather caused a famine that killed five million in India and nine million in China.

NOW Famine, sadly, is still with us. Half a billion people are malnourished. Food shortages in developing countries are made worse by instability. A million Biafrans starved when food supplies were blockaded in the Nigerian civil war (1967-70). In the 1980s, famine hit Africa's dry Sahel region. Worst hit was Ethiopia, where again civil war hampered relief efforts.

The first FA Cup Final at Wembley in 1923 was almost a disaster as 200,000 people managed to get into a stadium designed for 100,000. PC George Storey and his white horse helped clear the pitch peacefully before Bolton beat West Ham 2-0

1765 Stamp Act A tax on American colonists. Official documents and newspapers had to bear a stamp to prove that duty had been paid. This tax was among the grievances that led to the War of Independence.

1769 Steam Power James Watt patented his steam engine invention. Then he and John Roebuck, founder of the Carron iron works, built a full-sized engine for a trial run. It did not work.

1770 Cook Reaches Australia Sailing across the Pacific Ocean, British explorer James Cook landed at Botany Bay on the east coast of Australia and declared it British territory.

1775 American War of Independence The American colonies declared independence on July 4, 1776, but war against Britain raged on for a further five years. In 1787 the colonies – now states – joined forces to become a nation.

THE FRENCH REVOLUTION

The French Revolution of 1789-99 introduced ideas of democracy and justice to Europe which could never again be ignored.

France was a divided country, with a complacent monarchy, a resentful peasant class, and severe war debts. To raise money, Louis XVI was forced to call the Estates General, the nearest thing to a parliament. Unsuspectingly he gave the people a forum to air their many grievances; when demands went unmet, they took to the streets.

The fearsome Bastille prison was stormed, a revolutionary government was set up, and peasants rose up against nobles. France was turned on its head as elected assemblies took control. Supreme monarchy gave way to a republic, under the slogan 'Liberty, Equality, Fraternity'.

King and queen were beheaded, the Church's assets were plundered, and the Revolution became more radical. In the infamous Reign of Terror, thousands suspected of anti-revolutionary leanings were sent to the guillotine. Eventually many of the democratic reforms were undone, and Napoleon Bonaparte came to power. Nevertheless, the Revolution's impact was enormous, thanks to its insistence that individuals have rights simply because they are human.

1789 ***The storming of the Bastille on July 14, 1789 was crucial to the French Revolution. The Bastille, a medieval fortress prison in Paris, was the symbol of the king's power. When it fell to the common people, Louis XVI's days were numbered***

LIFELINES

***Aretha Franklin**, the Queen of Soul, was born in Memphis in 1942. The daughter of a preacher, she sang pop with a gospel fervour. Unlike many Sixties soul singers, Aretha has endured on record and in films such as The Blues Brothers.*

***Henry Ford**, born in 1863, created the Model T – the first mass-produced car. He resolved assembly line monotony and a high labour turnover by doubling the standard wage, and when he died in 1947 was worth an estimated £700 million.*

***Anne Frank** is one of the best-known victims of the Nazis, thanks to the diary she kept as a child in the Second World War. A Jew born in 1929, she hid in an Amsterdam factory before being taken to Belsen and killed in 1945.*

FOOTBALL

Where once the people might have united for a religious festival or the visit of a monarch, now perhaps only football has the power to enthral an entire nation, an entire world. Pele's 'beautiful game' is an obsession, boosted by giant screens in pubs and novels like Nick Hornby's *Fever Pitch*. In the new all-seater stadia, hooligans have given way to families, and female followers are rising.

'Some people think football is a matter of life and death. I can assure them it is much more serious than that'

LIVERPOOL MANAGER BILL SHANKLY, 1981

The last World Cup, France 1998, pitted Iran against the US in a match described as the 'ultimate political football'. Iran scored a 2-1 victory over the 'Great Satan'. That football can now embrace such political combinations shows it has gained the sort of benevolent internationalism which, in the wake of revelations of Olympic corruption, the IOC would kill for.

Football has always dealt in extreme emotion. It has had its fair share of tragedies, not least the 1989 Hillsborough disaster, Britain's worst sport-related accident. Poorly-policed Liverpool fans were directed into the wrong part of the stadium, crushing people at the front against fences designed, ironically, for crowd control; 95 died. In the same era, a riot by Liverpool fans in Brussels led to the deaths of 39 Juventus supporters, and a fire at Bradford killed 56.

But football scales the heights, too. In Paris, in 1998, victory for the French saw more people on the streets of the capital than at any time since the end of the last World War.

Football today: French star Zinedine Zidane and the World Cup are engulfed by photographers

1775 U.S. Navy Launched In America, the Second Continental Congress authorised the acquisition of a fleet of ships. It was the birth of the United States' Navy.

1778 Cook Discovers Hawaii Explorer James Cook discovered a group of islands in the Pacific that the local inhabitants told him were called Hawaii. He didn't like the name and after claiming the territory on behalf of the Crown, he named them the Sandwich Islands.

1781 The Celestial Bed An eccentric doctor from Edinburgh, Dr James Graham, began a trend in fashionable London for bizarre treatments. He offered childless couples a night on his 'Celestial Bed' for £50, claiming it would solve all their problems.

1783 The Youngest Prime Minister William Pitt became Britain's youngest-ever Prime Minister at the age of 24. He brought in income tax (see 1799), and passed the Act of Union (1800) setting up links between England and Ireland.

FIREWORKS

● We have the Victorians to thank for the link between November 5 and fireworks. For some 200 years after the Gunpowder Plot, it was celebrated as a victory over Catholicism. It was a day of great rowdiness – but the British got bored with it until, in the last century, some bright spark decided to let off some fireworks…

● ***In 1990, a family in Basingstoke, Hampshire, went to a public fireworks display because they thought doing it at home was dangerous. They came back to find that their house had been set on fire by a neighbour's rocket.***

● In Lewes, East Sussex, they take their Guy Fawkes Night very seriously indeed. After a torch-lit parade with 10,000 people, they burn not only Guy Fawkes, but also the Pope – in remembrance of the 17 Protestant martyrs executed at the stake by Bloody Mary.

GUY FAWKES

On November 5, we celebrate the capture of Guy Fawkes, who tried to blow up the Houses of Parliament along with Protestant King James I in 1605. He was tortured, hanged and then (while still alive) cut down. His genitals were cut off – while he was forced to watch – and he was disembowelled. He was then decapitated and his body was cut in quarters. Just to make sure…

● ***In 1988, six people were taken to hospital after a rocket fired from the Orpington Liberal Club's bonfire landed on the Conservatives' bonfire party. It was, of course, an accident…***

● On November 5 1988, the smoke from millions of fireworks and Guy Fawkes bonfires created so much smog in the damp autumnal air that Heathrow, Gatwick and other airports were closed.

THE FAMILY

THEN Until the 18th century, most families lived and worked in the kind of proximity that many today would consider claustrophobic, often sharing space with servants and orphaned, sick or elderly relatives. Everyone made a contribution according to their age and expertise, with the father the undisputed head. Families also provided their own social life, playing games and music together in the evenings.

NOW The modern family has changed beyond recognition. The family as a unit has increasingly fragmented, as divorce rates soar and family members move away in search of work. Fertility rates are now so low in most European countries that in the next century these societies will 'depopulate' themselves. Marriages, like births, are in decline, and around one in every three British and American children are now born out of wedlock.

FASHION

THE EVER-CHANGING LOOKS THAT DEFINED A MILLENNIUM

1780s
BUSTLES AND BONNET HATS

1870s
BEADS AND LATTICE SLEEVES

1920s
CLOCHE HATS AND FUR

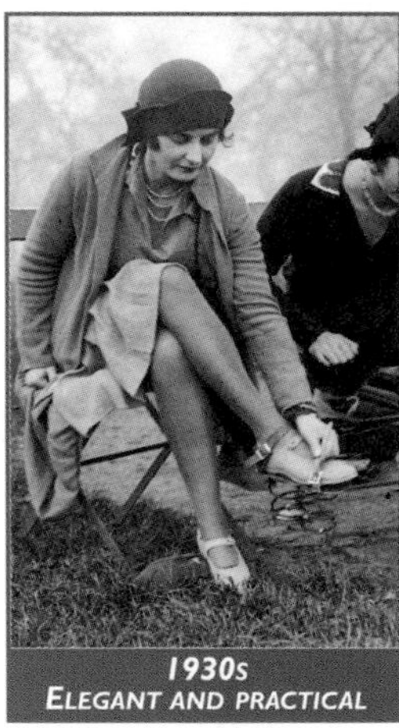

1930s
ELEGANT AND PRACTICAL

1950s
FITTED WAISTS, FULL SKIRTS

1960s
SHORT AND SIMPLE

1970s
BRIGHT AND BRASH

1980s
RIPPED JEANS, HARD TIMES

1990s
SHORT SKIRTS, CROPPED TOPS

1788
FIRST PENAL COLONY
Because of overcrowded prisons, a penal colony was set up in Australia. The first eleven ships carrying 778 convicts arrived at Sydney Harbour in 1788.

1788
STRANGE, BUT TRUE
Murderer William Brodie was hanged in Edinburgh. His story prompted Robert Louis Stevenson to write *The Strange Case of Dr Jekyll and Mr Hyde.*

1789
MUTINY ON THE BOUNTY
In the South Seas, Captain William Bligh and 18 officers and men of *HMS Bounty* were set adrift in an open boat by mutineers led by First Officer Fletcher Christian. The mutiny arose from harsh conditions imposed by Bligh and the warm reception the crew had received from women in Tahiti when they collected consignments of breadfruit. Against all odds, Bligh survived after drifting for 3,500 miles, landing at Timor. Descendants of the mutineers still live in the Pitcairn Islands.

FASHION SUPERMODELS

Leggy Texan Jerry Hall, right, and the exotic-looking Marie Helvin, left, were queens of the catwalk and the gossip columns in the late Seventies and through into the Eighties. But it wasn't until the Nineties that the term 'supermodel' was first coined. Kate Moss, centre, born in unromantic Croydon in 1974, was not only the face of the 1990s but also the first supermodel 'waif'. Signed up in 1988, her Calvin Klein advertisements made her the world's best-known model

In the last 1000 years, clothing styles have moved from drab uniformity to explosive diversity. Until recently, the clothes a person wore denoted their place in society. In the 14th century, as the nobility began to lose political power, they dressed more elaborately to distinguish themselves from the middle class. Later, a 17th-century law required lower-class men to wear woollen caps, while their superiors wore imported velvet.

Fashions filtered down from court: wigs arrived in the mid-17th century after France's Louis XIII wore one to hide his baldness, while 19th-century English women emulated Queen Victoria's stout figure with puffy, padded dresses. Haute couture developed from court, too, as the wealthy hired dress-makers to help them keep up with the trends. In the 19th century, mass manufacture made fashions cheaper and less indicative of status.

This century, fashion has exploded, with teenagers setting the pace by aiming to wear anything their parents didn't.

Today, fashion continues to oscillate wildly between enduring classics and individualism, with designers such as Ozwald Boateng, 32, successfully combining the two. His trademark traditional suits with a sharp Sixties edge have attracted customers as diverse as Tony Blair and George Michael, and Boateng (right) is quick to acknowledge the influence of masters such as Hardy Amies, who brought classic couture to the high street.

OZWALD BOATENG'S BEST OF THE MILLENNIUM

FASHION DESIGNERS

HARDY AMIES

"I love Amies' quintessential British style, which has spanned so many decades. His designs are very traditional (right), and I admire his unerring attention to detail and ability to achieve the right look for the occasion. If I too reach 90, I hope I'll be as involved in my label as he is with his today."

LIFELINES

***BENJAMIN FRANKLIN** proved that lightning was electricity by flying a kite in a storm. Born in 1706, he also helped draft the US Declaration of Independence and negotiate a peace settlement with Britain in 1783, seven years before his death.*

***MARGOT FONTEYN**, born in 1919, was the supreme British ballerina from the Forties through to the Seventies. She formed a legendary partnership with Rudolph Nureyev as part of the Royal Ballet, and died in 1991.*

***BOB FITZSIMMONS** was the first British world heavyweight champion. Cornish-born in 1862, he won both the world middleweight and heavyweight titles. He fought past the age of 50, retiring three years before his death in 1917.*

1789
THE FRENCH REVOLUTION
A ten-year revolution which began when parliament refused to grant taxes to Louis XVI and his extravagant queen, Marie Antoinette. Soon a republic was declared, the king and queen were executed on the guillotine, as were thousands of aristocrats during the Reign of Terror from 1793-94. The revolution ended when army general Napoleon Bonaparte seized power in 1799.

1791
MOZART THE PAUPER
Composer Wolfgang Amadeus Mozart died of kidney failure, aged 35. The musical genius, who composed his first symphony at the age of nine, died penniless and was given a pauper's funeral in Vienna.

1791
ABOLITION OF SLAVERY
A motion for the abolition of slavery, proposed by William Wilberforce, was passed by Parliament.

1792
THE WHITE HOUSE
George Washington laid the cornerstone of the White House in Washington DC. John Adams was the first President to occupy it in 1800.

GLOBE THEATRE

1599 ***Shakespeare's favourite stage is built, burnt down, rebuilt and demolished all in the space of 45 years***

1997 ***An exact replica of the Globe reopens on the same site by the Thames. Ticket prices have gone up, though***

THE GREAT FIRE OF LONDON

It was a costly accident – but without it we might never have had St Paul's Cathedral. The Great Fire broke out in the royal bakery in Pudding Lane, near Tower Bridge, on September 2, 1666.

London's crowded wooden houses provided the perfect conditions – it was also an unusually dry summer – and the flames, fanned by a strong east wind, raged for five days. In the process, most of the City of London as far west as the Temple was destroyed, together with 13,000 houses, 89 parish churches and the old St Paul's. With no fire-fighting service, an operation was mounted to make an open strip the flames couldn't cross; Charles II personally oversaw the demolitions.

The fire was a blessing in disguise: the area that was gone had been a breeding-ground for disease, and new brick and stone buildings replaced the old wooden ones.

The new St Paul's, designed by Sir Christopher Wren, became a symbol of defiance in another great London fire, when in 1940 German bombers sought to torch the city from the air.

GREENWICH MEAN TIME

Greenwich must rival Jerusalem as the ultimate Millennial location. Time and space are very different, of course, but if time has a home, then this venerable south London borough is it.

Charles II founded a Royal Observatory at Greenwich in 1675; its job was to study celestial bodies and determine time more accurately. The meridian of longitude passing through Greenwich was adopted by an international conference in 1884 as the 'prime meridian', the starting point of the world's time zones. The conference fixed 12 time zones west of Greenwich and 12 to the east; these meet on the other side of the globe – exactly halfway round from Greenwich – on the International Date Line.

As the point on the Earth from which time is traditionally measured, Greenwich was thought to be the obvious site for the Millennium Dome, the focus for Britain's Millennium celebrations. The hope is that it will attract millions of visitors, in the spirit of the Great Exhibition of 1851 and the Festival of Britain of 1951. Will it work? Only time will tell.

The Observatory keeps an eye on the time

1796
SHAKESPEARE'S 'LOST PLAY'
On April 2, 1796, crowds flocked to Drury Lane theatre to see a performance of *Vortigern and Rowena* – "a long-lost play by Shakespeare". Only later was it exposed as a fake, written by a 17-year-old Londoner. At least he didn't call it *Ethel and The Pirates!*

1797
WHERE DID YOU GET THAT HAT?
The first top hat was worn on the streets of London, causing much excitement among the crowds. The wearer, a Mr James Hetherington, was arrested for breaching the peace. The charges against him were that he had "appeared on the highway wearing a tall structure of shining lustre calculated to disturb timid people."

1797
THE FIRST PARACHUTE
In 1797, French balloonist André Garnerin made the first parachute out of canvas and used it when he jumped out of a balloon. The first parachute jump from a plane didn't happen until 1912.

FLORENCE GRIFFITH JOYNER

'Flo-Jo' was the most glamorous athlete ever – but also, perhaps, the most tragically flawed. Even before she flew home to the USA from the 1988 Seoul Olympics carrying three gold medals, one silver medal and two world records, other athletes were insisting that she was a drugs cheat.

Flo-Jo retired after the Games, aged 29, had a baby and started training for the marathon. If she really was taking steroids, she had avoided getting caught like fellow sprinter Ben Johnson.

But a worse fate awaited her. In 1998 she died of a brain tumour – and this time, sadly, she was not there with her beautiful smile to rebut the rumours herself.

THOMAS GAINSBOROUGH

Thomas Gainsborough left us a great record of both the people and the scenery of the 18th century. Even at the age of eight, his teacher declared: "That boy will be a genius!" – and he was right.

Works such as Robert Andrews and his Wife (right), painted in about 1748 when Gainsborough was in his twenties, would have been commissioned by the sitters, and the artist would have been required to portray not only the elegant lord of the manor and his pretty wife – which he did with great accuracy – but also their grand estate.

John Constable, who inherited Gainsborough's mantle of England's greatest creator of country scenes, said: "On looking at these paintings, we find tears in our eyes, and know not what brought them."

LIFELINES

Yuri Gagarin *was the first man in space, aboard Vostok I in 1961. Born in 1934, he came to represent Soviet space-race supremacy over the USA – but having survived the ultimate mission, he died in a plane crash in 1968.*

Galileo Galilei *was the first astronomer to use a telescope. He also used a pendulum as a clock. Born in Italy in 1564, Galileo's theories made him an enemy of the church. He was finally pardoned in 1984, 342 years after his death.*

Greta Garbo *played her greatest movie role of Anna Karenina twice – before and after the invention of sound. Born in Sweden in 1905, she retired in 1941 saying "I want to be alone", and remained a recluse until her death in 1990.*

1799
Income Tax Introduced
Prime Minister William Pitt introduced income tax at two shillings in the pound (ten per cent). Highly unpopular, the measure was brought in to help pay for the (also unpopular) war against Napoleon's France.

1801
Steam Power's Sad Debut
The first steam-powered vehicle to run on British roads was wheeled out by inventor Richard Trevithick, despite warnings from James Watt that high pressure would cause the engine to explode. Trevithick and friends went to an inn, leaving the boiler fire burning while inside. They came out to find a pile of burned-out wreckage.

1802
Channel Tunnel Plan Launched
The first plans to build a tunnel linking France and Britain were proposed by French engineer Albert Mathieu. He envisaged horse-drawn carriages travelling through a candle-lit tunnel.

TRULY GREAT BRITAIN

Ways in which Britain is top of the world

In Queen Victoria, we boast the longest-reigning queen the world has ever known

Highest (joint) percentage of the population which is literate

Britain has more duty-free sales than any other country in the world

We have the busiest international airport in the world in London Heathrow

More public lending libraries than any other country in the world

The three most-published authors of all time are all British: William Shakespeare, Charles Dickens and Sir Walter Scott

London has the longest underground railway network in the world

We publish more books than any other country in the world

Highest (joint) percentage of the population which has access to sanitation services

The longest running show in the world – The Mousetrap, which opened in 1952

Highest proportionate number of botanical gardens and zoos in the world

The top air ace of the First World War (Edward Mannock – 73 kills)

More makes of car (52) than any other country in the 200-strong shortlist for Car of the Century

ICI is the world's largest paint manufacturer

Ways in which Britain makes the world's top ten

Only five countries (Sri Lanka, India, Israel, Argentina and the Central African Republic) had a female Prime Minister or President before we did (Margaret Thatcher)

Only one country (Japan) has had more monarchs

Only two countries (Thailand and Monaco) boast a longer-reigning living monarch than our Queen

Only one country (the USA) has won more Nobel Prizes

Only four countries (France, USA, Spain and Italy) attract more tourists a year than we do

Only three countries (USA, France, Italy) have more turkeys

Only three countries (Japan, Denmark and China) have a longer suspension bridge than the Humber Bridge, which is 1,410 metres long

Only one country in the world (the USA) has a larger reference library than our British Library

Only one language (Mandarin Chinese) is spoken by more people in the world than English

Only one country (Russia with Lenin) boasts a more translated author than our own Agatha Christie

Only eight countries (Saudi Arabia, USA, Russia, Iran, Mexico, China, Venezuela and Norway) produce more oil than we do

Only three countries (USA, France and Japan) have more nuclear reactors than we do

Only seven countries (USA, France, Germany, Italy, Switzerland, Holland and Japan) have greater gold reserves than we do

Only seven countries in the world (USA, Japan, Germany, France, South Korea, Canada and Spain) produce more vehicles than we do

Only four countries (USA, Japan, Germany and Brazil) have more VCRs than we do

Only four countries (USA, Japan, Germany and France) have a higher Gross National Product than we have

Only two countries (Libya and Algeria) have a longer name than the United Kingdom of Great Britain and Northern Ireland

Other areas in which Britain is top of the world

Underwear (more sold here proportionately than anywhere else)

Pain control and care of the terminally ill

Speakers and sound systems

Regulating in-vitro fertilisation treatment and research

Manufacture of fruit machines

Making explosives

Training of designers and provision of design services

Aviation technology

Financial services

The provision of computers in schools

Electronics

Surveillance equipment

Children's book publishing

Car design

Drug testing in athletics

Virtual reality technology

Genetic research

Keyhole surgery to correct antenatal deformities in babies

Theatre in education

Ballroom dancing

Satellite decoders

Biotechnology

Child immunisation

Safety standards on household goods

Giving up smoking

Mechanical diggers

1805 Battle of Trafalgar
Nelson raised his famous signal, "England expects that every man will do his duty" at the Battle of Trafalgar. He emerged victorious against a joint Spanish-French fleet off the coast of Portugal. But the great naval commander lost his life in the encounter.

1809 The Birth of Braille
Louis Braille was born in France in 1809. He was blinded in an accident when he was a boy and later invented his reading system for the blind, using punch marks in paper. The system was developed and used across the world. Braille died in 1852.

1811 First Siamese Twins
Chang and Eng, the original Siamese twins, were born in Siam, joined from breastbone to navel. The twins spent much of their lives in the US, where they formed an exhibit in a travelling show. They both married and had several normal children.

Things Britain gave to the world

Television	Traffic lights	Garden cities
Postage stamps	Soap flakes	The hearse
Football	The disposable nappy	Christmas cards
The railway	Airline meals	The mini skirt
Tennis	The Underground	Punk rock
Sell-by dates on food	Package tours	Cricket
	The BBC World Service	

GOVERNMENT

The United Kingdom has no written constitution, yet its system of government – the 'mother of parliaments' – is one of the oldest and most respected in the world, and a model for many others.

The origins of Parliament go back over a millennium, to early councils of nobles and high-ranking clergy who advised the king on policy and law. After the Norman Conquest in 1066, the assembly became known as the Great Council and met three times a year.

In the early 13th century, King John would summon knights to a 'parliament' to approve new taxes; a few decades later Simon de Montfort, during his brief rule, brought in town representatives. Thus the Lords and Commons developed, and by the mid-14th century, the first MPs were meeting separately from the nobles – though they could not yet make laws.

Parliament gained its real powers during the English Civil War, when MPs defied the wishes of the king, and effectively put an end to the idea that the monarch was answerable only to God. Parliament ordered the beheading of Charles I, and in 1689 passed the Bill of Rights to ensure free and frequent debate. In 1707 Great Britain was unified under a single Parliament.

Today, the House of Lords seems to be slowly fading away. In 1911 it lost its right to veto laws in the making, and under Tony Blair's Government it will lose its hereditary peers. Exactly who will replace them, however, has yet to be decided.

The Queen opens Parliament in full pomp

LIFELINES

***Bob Geldof** is Britain's scruffiest knight. Born in 1954, he led Dublin band The Boomtown Rats but is best-known as organiser of 1985's Live Aid – raising £48 million for famine relief – and for his ill-starred marriage to Paula Yates.*

***William Ewart Gladstone**, born in 1809, was one of Britain's most reformist prime ministers. A Liberal, heartily disliked by Queen Victoria, he won four elections but failed to bring Home Rule to Ireland and resigned in 1894, four years before his death.*

***Lady Godiva** rode naked through Coventry to induce her husband Leofric, Earl of Mercia, to reduce the town's taxes. The tabloid press wasn't around in the 11th century – but Peeping Tom was, and he couldn't help looking.*

G

1812
The First Waltz
A new dance-craze reached Britain – the waltz. It had already swept across Europe.

1812
It's War against U.S.
As a result of its war with Napoleon, during which England stopped American ships from trading with France, England went to war with the United States in 1812. The whole thing petered out a couple of years later when England lifted its embargo.

1814
Frozen Thames
The freezing of British rivers became a regular feature from the 15th to the 19th century during what scientists call the 'little ice age'. Londoners would hold fairs, known as frost fairs, on the frozen Thames. The last was in 1814.

1815
Britain Defeats Napoleon
Following his disastrous Russian defeat in 1812 and the subsequent invasion of France by the Allied armies, Napoleon Bonaparte was forced to abdicate and live in exile on the Italian island of Elba. He escaped, regained power, but was defeated by Wellington at Waterloo. Bonaparte's final exile was to St Helena, off the coast of Africa.

GOYA

Francisco de Goya was already Spain's leading Court artist, renowned for his ravishing yet honest portraits, when, at 62, he turned to a new style for his Disasters of War etchings. Inspired by the slaughter when Napoleon invaded Spain in 1808, these graphic pictures showed war as it had never been seen before. Goya's execution scenes were remodelled in 1994 by Brit Art brats Jake and Dinos Chapman, using amputated shop dummies

GENOCIDE

On the scale of evil, genocide – the deliberate attempt to wipe out a race or a religious group – is as low as you can go. Yet, despite its recurrence throughout humanity's bloody history, only recently were such atrocities formally condemned by international law – by the newly-formed United Nations in 1949.

This was a reaction to the Holocaust, the Nazis' systematic extermination of the Jews, but other episodes this century might also be taken into consideration. The First World War saw 1.5 million Armenians killed by Turkey, which may be considered the first modern attempt to eliminate a population. One might also cite the mass killings of Cambodia's Khmer Rouge regime in the Seventies, and China's ongoing annexing of Tibet.

Cambodian skulls bear testimony to the Khmer Rouge's slaughter in 1975-79

GREETINGS CARDS

On April 23, 1995, a new greetings card was introduced: the St George's Day card. Within two years, it was selling 50,000 a year. It is the latest example of how commercial ingenuity has helped to create a tradition that goes back two centuries.

The first 'greeting cards' appeared in the 18th century – decorated visiting cards, often picturing an ancient ruin. New Year's cards spread from Germany, and led to the first Valentine's cards, which were handmade and delicately coloured. Mass production began in the US in the 1840s, and alongside sentimental Valentines there were cruel and rude 'anti-Valentines'. Britain's penny post (1840) added to the craze, and the first Christmas card, showing a Victorian family at dinner, was sent in 1843.

The industry has never looked back, forever finding new occasions we never knew we had to mark, like Father's Day, but also offering messages that would once have been made by letter – "With deepest sympathy", "Welcome to your new home", and so on. By the time you read this, you will no doubt have received your first "Happy New Millennium" card…

CARY GRANT

CARY GRANT HAD GREAT CHARM AND COMIC TIMING – ASSETS THAT MADE HIM A HOLLYWOOD ICON FOR 30 YEARS. BORN ARCHIBALD LEACH IN 1904, THE ELOQUENT BRIT WAS A FAVOURITE WITH ALFRED HITCHCOCK, WHO CAST HIM IN THE CLASSIC NORTH BY NORTHWEST AND WITH INGRID BERGMAN IN NOTORIOUS (LEFT). BUT ONLY AN HONORARY OSCAR CAME GRANT'S WAY

1817
JANE AUSTEN DIES
Renowned novelist Jane Austen died at a lodging house in Winchester on July 18. She had lived to see Pride and Prejudice become an established classic.

1818
HERE STANDS CANADA
Britain and the United States formally agreed that the Canadian border would be set at the 49th parallel.

1818
FRANKENSTEIN REARS HIS HEAD
The classic horror story of Dr Frankenstein and the monster he created was completed and published. The gripping tale, later to be immortalised by Hollywood, was written by Mary Shelley.

1819
BEGINNING OF AN ERA
Victoria, the future long-reigning Queen, was born on May 24, 1819 at Kensington Palace. She was to spend much of her later life devastated by the loss of her beloved Albert and was to give her name to an era of prim morality and expanding Empire.

CLARK GABLE AND GONE WITH THE WIND

When Hollywood mogul David Selznick paid $50,000 for a novel by first-time writer Margaret Mitchell, people said he was mad. But by the time Gone With The Wind premiered in Atlanta, Georgia on December 15, 1939, the book was already a best-seller and the film was the most keenly awaited in history. The following month, the epic love story set against the American Civil War won nine Oscars, including Best Film. One of the few involved who didn't win a statuette was Clark Gable – Rhett Butler to Vivien Leigh's Scarlett O'Hara – but frankly, my dear, he couldn't give a damn. In 1998 a new restored, digitally enhanced version gave a new generation of film-goers a taste of what the fuss was all about.

GULLIVER'S TRAVELS

Many people who think they know *Gulliver's Travels* are actually familiar only with the children's version. A pity, because the real thing is a disturbing masterpiece.

In Jonathan Swift's satire – published in 1726 ship's surgeon Lemuel Gulliver relates his fantastic adventures in distant lands. Gulliver is shipwrecked in Lilliput, where the people are only 15cm high and he is able to put out a fire in their city by passing a well-aimed jet of water. In Brobdingnag, the people are giants and he is befriended by a nine-year-old girl "not above 40 foot high, being little for her age". Here women amuse themselves by placing him down their cleavage. Finally Gulliver meets the Houyhnhnms – a race of wise talking horses who tame herds of human-like Yahoos.

By this time Gulliver is so disgusted by his own race that he opts to live in a stable. Swift's tale was sadly reflected in his own life. Born in Ireland in 1667, he suffered a mental breakdown before his death in 1745.

Gulliver's Travels was recently made into a lavish TV mini-series featuring former *Cheers* star Ted Danson.

LIFELINES

Sir Alec Guinness *is an actor of whom it has been said: "He's an all-star cast in his own person." Born in 1914, he arrived on screen in 1946 and soon became Britain's most versatile film star, playing eight characters in Kind Hearts And Coronets alone. A 1958 Oscar-winner for The Bridge on the River Kwai, he starred on TV in the Seventies as spy-master George Smiley, and lent weight to Star Wars.*

Mahatma Gandhi *proved non-violence could win out by leading India to independence in 1947. A frail, gentle man, born in 1869, he first fought against racial discrimination in South Africa, then returned home to lead the nationalist movement to ultimate triumph. However, he died violently at the hands of a religious fanatic in 1948. His story became an Oscar-winning film in 1982.*

1820 Discovery of Antarctica Rumours of an icy land mass at the bottom of the world had existed for centuries. In 1820 it was confirmed. Three men – Edward Bransfield from England, Fabian Gottlieb von Bellingshausen from Russia and Nathaniel Palmer from the United States – all independently claimed to have seen it.

1821 The Electric Motor Michael Faraday, an English chemist and scientist, invented the electric motor from which the electric generator was later developed.

1825 Enter the Steam Train *The Active*, the first steam locomotive to carry goods and passengers, travelled for 27 miles along the Stockton to Darlington railway line.

1827 Invention of Photography The first camera – the camera obscura – could offer only non-permanent images. In 1827 Frenchman Joseph-Nicéphore Niepce found a way to preserve the image chemically and produced the first photograph.

THE GRAND NATIONAL

The Grand National is Britain's toughest test of horse and rider. It was first run in 1839, and soon the 30 jumps of the four-and-a-half mile Aintree course – the notorious Becher's Brook water hazard, the Canal Turn, Valentine's – had entered popular mythology.

Several horses have won the National twice, but only the legendary Red Rum has managed a trio of victories, in 1973, 1974, and in 1977.

The most moving moment, however, was the 1981 victory by Aldaniti, ridden by Bob Champion, who fought cancer to gallop home to victory.

No one who witnessed it will forget the farcical 'Grand National that never was' of 1993, when a mix-up with the starting tape led to the race being abandoned. Several runners were unaware, and proceeded to finish the course anyway.

JOHN FRANCOME'S BEST OF THE MILLENNIUM

NATIONAL WINNERS

John Francome is one of Britain's most successful jockeys. In 1970-85 he rode a record 1138 winners over fences and was seven times National Hunt champion jockey.

RED RUM *(RIGHT)*

"Red Rum has to be the greatest Grand National winner ever. He won the race at his first attempt in 1973, in nine minutes 1.9 seconds, breaking the course record by 19 seconds. He then competed at Aintree for the next four seasons, winning again in 1974 and 1977 and finishing in second place in 1975 and 1976. Red Rum never made a mistake and was a genuine character. He cost 6000 guineas, won over £114,000 and went on to make even more money from personal appearances."

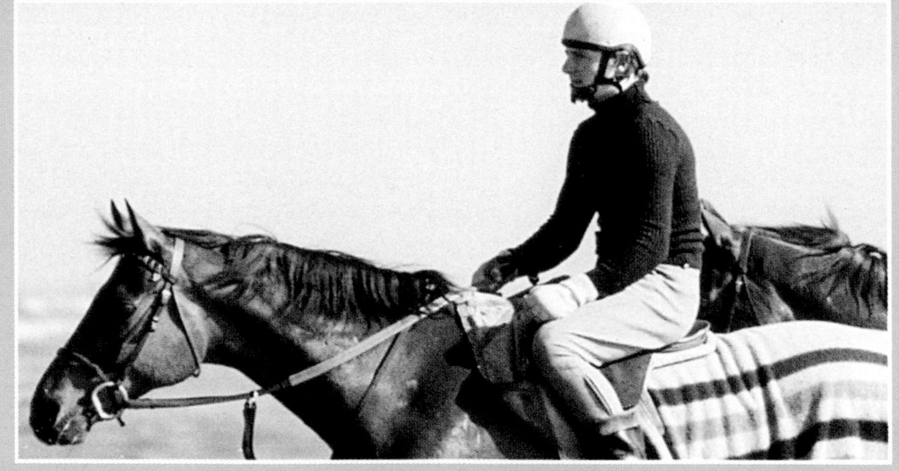

1828 INDEPENDENCE FOR GREECE Greece had been battling for independence from Turkey for seven years when Russia, France and Great Britain stepped in and forced the Turks to comply.

1829 THE FIRST BOAT RACE The first Oxford v Cambridge boat race was held over a two-and-a-quarter mile course from Hambledon Lock to Henley Bridge. Oxford won.

1829 THE BRITISH BOBBY The Metropolitan Police Act gave London its first modern police force. It was pushed through by Prime Minister Robert Peel, whose Christian name resulted in policemen being nicknamed 'Bobbies'. Peel is regarded as the founder of the modern Conservative Party.

1830 BELGIUM FREED Belgium was given independence, after being part of the Netherlands for 30 years.

GAMBLING

Trying to win money by guessing the outcome of an event has a long and chequered history. Casinos have existed since the 17th century, but rumour has constantly linked them with organised crime – as in the 1995 film *Casino*, starring Sharon Stone (above).

In Las Vegas, extra oxygen is pumped into the rooms and clocks are hidden to keep punters awake and spending money. Gamblers also have to buy enough petrol to leave the city before entering; they may not have enough left on the way out…

Betting on the horses is doubtless as old as horse racing itself. In the 14th century, the royal court was entertained by placing bets on 'running horse matches', where a knight-at-arms would challenge a rival in a gruelling cross-country course.

Ladbroke's, the world's largest bookmaker, began a century ago; to qualify for an account, you needed to be in the society who's who, *Debrett's*. The biggest ever horse racing payout was $1,627,084 (£988,211), won by Britons Anthony Speelman and Nicholas Cowan on a nine-horse accumulator bet at Santa Anita racecourse, California, in 1987.

A growing trend is spread-betting, which allows you to bet on variables such as the number of throw-ins in a football match. Fiendishly, the more right you are, the more you win. And the more wrong, the more you lose…

STEFFI GRAF

Steffi Graf is the only person ever to have achieved tennis's Golden Slam, by winning the first Olympic tennis title in 1988 – the same year she became the fifth player to do the Grand Slam of the US, French, Australian and Wimbledon titles. Graf, born in 1969, possesses a ferocious forehand that enabled her to achieve her Grand Slam on four surfaces – the only person to do so. In a monumental career, she has won Wimbledon seven times, the US Open five times, the French Championship six times, and the Australian Championship four times. Perhaps her most remarkable feat came in 1999 when, after a two-year hiatus from her trophy-winning exploits due to injury, she stormed back to win in Paris (above) and reach the Wimbledon final.

GAMES

THEN The oldest book of games, *Libro de Juegos* (1282), mentions chess, dice, backgammon and board games. The book was written for "all those looking for a pleasant pastime which will bring them comfort and dispel their boredom". This age-old ideal led to many ingenious games, often of Asian origin such as chess and go, which can earn players big money today. Card games were a dominant form of entertainment for centuries and, as in the novels of Jane Austen, often formed the centrepiece of social gatherings.

NOW Board games underwent a revolution in the 1960s, when strategic war games such as Risk came into vogue, followed by fantasy role-play games like Dungeons and Dragons. The expertise passed from players to games-makers, who produced electronic-sensor tests such as Operation! and 3-D teasers such as Mousetrap. Trivial Pursuit mined the apparently endless demand for general knowledge quizzes, which continues on TV and in pubs. And with Playstation and Gameboy, the playground has turned completely virtual.

LIFELINES

***Graham Greene** (1904-91) is probably Britain's novelist of the century. Many of his books – filled with corruption and Catholic angst – made great films, including Brighton Rock, The Heart Of The Matter and The Third Man.*

***George Gershwin** (1898-1937) was one of the finest American popular composers. As well as Broadway musicals – some composed with his brother Ira – he wrote semi-classical pieces and the black opera Porgy And Bess.*

***Alberto Giacometti**, born in 1901, made skinny an in-thing in surreal sculpture. The Swiss sculptor's almost primitive wire-framed works had a similar appeal to Lowry's matchstick people. He died in 1966.*

G

1833 Birth of the Tabloids Benjamin Day, a 23-year-old printer, launched the *New York Sun*, the first tabloid newspaper. Its four pages were filled with articles meant to entertain its readers, rather than inform them about the news of the day. Day also hit on the novel idea of hiring boys to sell it on the streets.

1834 Martyrs Sentenced Six farm labourers from Tolpuddle, Dorset, were sentenced to be transported to a penal colony in Australia for forming a trade union. They became known as the Tolpuddle Martyrs.

1835 Houses of Parliament Sir Charles Barry and Augustus Pugin started building the Houses of Parliament. They were completed in 1867.

1836 The Great Trek Unhappy with British rule in South Africa's Cape region, the white Afrikaners, known as Boers, started trekking north into non-colonised areas. They finally settled in the Natal, Transvaal, and Orange Free State regions of southern Africa.

HENRY VIII

Cruel and domineering yet charismatic and gifted, Henry VIII made England a great naval power, spent his father's fortune on wars, and united the rivals who had fought the War of the Roses simply by being born to a Lancastrian father and Yorkist mother in 1491. But he will always be remembered as the monarch with six wives who effectively started a new religion to get his own way.

Desperate for a male heir, Henry defied the Pope and had his marriage to his brother's widow Catherine of Aragon annulled in 1533 so he could marry Anne Boleyn. With two Parliamentary Acts he separated the Roman Catholic church from the Church of England, of which he now became supreme head.

Henry and Catherine had a daughter who later became Mary I. Meanwhile Anne Boleyn had a daughter, after which Henry had her beheaded for infidelity. Jane Seymour had a son, then died; Anne of Cleves was divorced; Catherine Howard executed. Only Catherine Parr – wife No 6 – survived him.

At the end of his life in 1547, Henry was bloated and syphilitic, with a running ulcer on his leg and a tyrannical temper. But he had kept the nation behind him through sheer force of personality. "When at last death claimed him," it was said, "few felt relief and most were in despair."

Henry VIII by portrait maestro Hans Holbein

SHERLOCK HOLMES

Mrs Hudson. 221b Baker Street. The violin and tobacco pouch… Sherlock Holmes – creation of doctor, adventure writer and spiritualist Sir Arthur Conan Doyle – is the detective's detective. Eagle-nosed, gaunt and clinically clever, Holmes's powers of observation effortlessly outdo the attempts of Scotland Yard as he unravels complex criminal narratives from the scantiest clues. He first appeared in A Study in Scarlet (1887), and the many stories which followed have inspired hundreds of film and TV adaptations, notably Basil Rathbone's Hollywood version and Jeremy Brett's inch-perfect portrayal for Granada. As always events are recounted by trusty Dr Watson, Holmes's room-mate and friend. Their partnership is simply elementary.

HAMPTON COURT

Can red brick be beautiful? Visit Hampton Court Palace and the answer is yes. Built on the River Thames by Cardinal Wolsey in 1515-25 for King Henry VIII, Hampton Court is Britain's largest royal palace, and the first open to the public. Its gardens are the most visited in Britain – 1.2 million of us went there in 1998

1839
THE FIRST BICYCLE
Invented by Scottish blacksmith Kirkpatrick Macmillan, the first bicycle had two pedals attached to rods that moved backwards and forwards alternately, propelling the back wheel. The first chain-driven cycle, similar to today's machines, was John Starley's Rover safety cycle of 1885.

1840
THE PENNY BLACK
The first adhesive postage stamp, the Penny Black, was issued with the introduction of a prepaid postal system. The first Penny Black was stuck on a letter to George Waterman, of Thame, Oxfordshire. Now rare, Penny Blacks could be worth thousands of pounds.

1841
LIVINGSTONE'S MISSION
Scottish missionary and explorer David Livingstone went to Africa in 1841, mapped the Zambezi River and discovered the Victoria Falls. He spent the rest of his life exploring the interior, introducing Christianity and trying to end slavery. He died in 1873 in Zambia.

THE BATTLE OF HASTINGS

THE BATTLE OF HASTINGS ACTUALLY TOOK PLACE SIX MILES INLAND. IN 1066, KING HAROLD II'S ANGLO-SAXONS HAD SEEN OFF THE VIKINGS IN YORK, THEN HAD TO MARCH SOUTH TO FACE THE INVADING DUKE WILLIAM OF NORMANDY. THE EXHAUSTED TROOPS HELD OUT ALL DAY, BUT WERE LURED INTO A TRAP WHEN THE NORMANS PRETENDED TO FLEE. HAROLD DIED WITH AN ARROW THROUGH HIS EYE AND WILLIAM BECAME THE CONQUEROR. THE 70-METRE BAYEUX TAPESTRY – MADE IN ENGLAND IN CELEBRATON – HANGS IN NORMANDY, AND IS ONE OF THE GREAT ARTWORKS OF THE MILLENNIUM.

HORSE RACING

THEN People have raced horses for as long as they have ridden them. In the 12th century, Archbishop of Canterbury Thomas Becket spoke of how "the jockies, inspired with thoughts of applause, clap spurs to the willing horses, brandish their whips and cheer them with their cries". 'Steeplechases' were just that: a race cross-country to an agreed landmark such as a steeple. The first established racecourse was at Chester (1540); the Newmarket Gold Cup began in 1634. Charles II made Newmarket the headquarters of the Turf, and himself rode to victory in 1671.

NOW The shape of horse racing today originated in the 18th century. The Jockey Club was founded in 1727, the first *Racing Calendar* was published in 1773, the Derby began in 1780, and the first *General Stud Book* appeared in 1791. In Victoria's time, racing was much as it is today, except that riders sat upright in the saddle. Women were allowed to race on the flat from 1975. Racing enjoyed its biggest sensation for many a year at Royal Ascot in 1996, when Frankie Dettori (left) became the first jockey ever to race all seven winners on a card. At odds of 25,091-1, some smaller bookies were completely wiped out, and the big boys lost nearly £30 million.

HOUSES

THEN In 1000, many Europeans lived in the shadow of a large castle. In times of conflict, villagers would shelter in the Great Hall. In the Middle Ages, new towns arose. Houses were built in narrow streets, with walls of wattle and daub – a mix of sticks, clay, water and even dung. By the 15th century, houses were in the Renaissance style, copying classical designs with wide staircases and spacious rooms.

NOW Demand for houses soared as the population grew in the 19th century. The first housing estates were built round factories, like Lever's Port Sunlight, Liverpool. A 1960s attempt to solve housing needs with high-rise tower blocks proved ill-judged, leading to social isolation and crime; many have been demolished. Nor have we managed to house everyone: 600 people a night sleep rough in London.

VACLAV HAVEL

Vaclav Havel, born in 1936, is the playwright who became President. Jailed for four years in 1979 for dissent against the Czech Communists, he was elected leader of the free Czech Republic in 1993.

STEPHEN HAWKING

Physicist Stephen Hawking's courage has amazed millions. Born in 1942, wheelchair-bound, talking by voice synthesizer, he inspired the black holes theory and wrote A Brief History of Time (1988).

1845 IRISH POTATO FAMINE The cold, wet summer of 1845 wiped out virtually all of Ireland's potato crop, and almost a million people – a quarter of the population – died from starvation and disease. Over the next few years hundreds of thousands emigrated to America.

1846 FIRST GAME OF BASEBALL The first official game of baseball was a clash between the New York Nine and Knickerbocker Club, held at the Elysian Fields, Hoboken, New Jersey.

1848 THE COMMUNIST MANIFESTO German political and economic theorist Karl Marx, helped by political thinker Friedrich Engels, wrote the *Communist Manifesto*, introducing the philosophy behind communism to the world. The aim was to create a classless society. Instead, a succession of repressive regimes emerged.

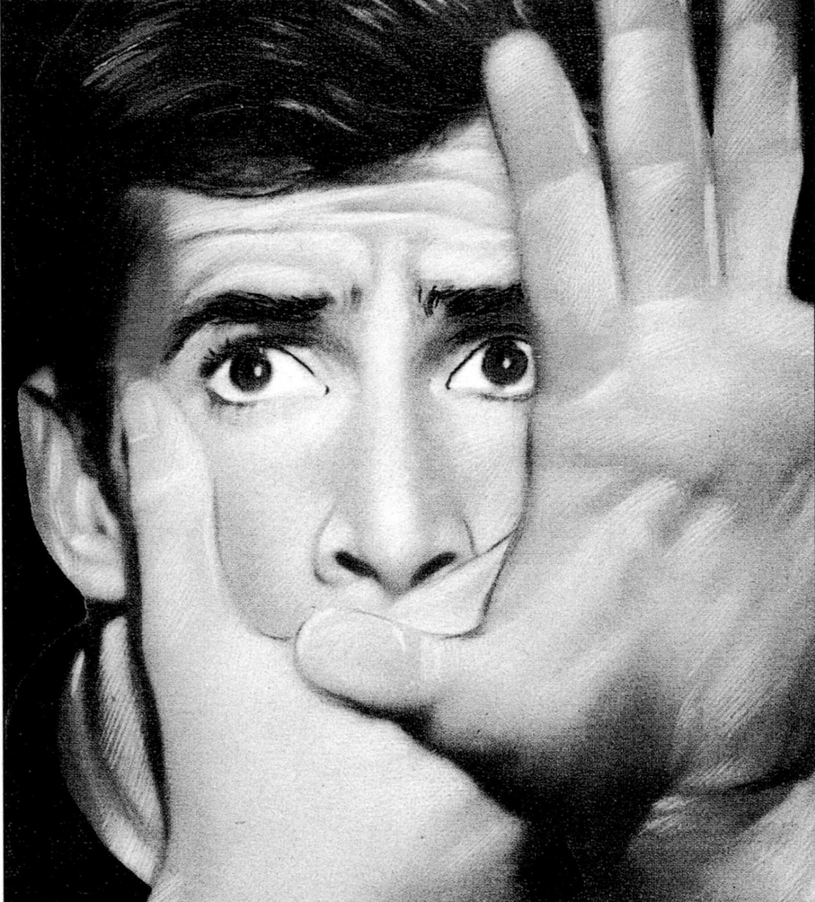

Psycho, starring Anthony Perkins, broke all the rules. In the ad for the film, Alfred Hitchcock blatantly gave away most of the plot. The heroine, Janet Leigh, dies just a third of the way in, which was unheard-of. A man wrote to Hitchcock complaining that his daughter refused to take a shower after seeing *Psycho*. Hitch wrote back: "Send her to the dry cleaners."

ALFRED HITCHCOCK

In life, as in his films, Sir Alfred Hitchcock loved to shock. Once, in a packed lift, he turned to a friend and said loudly: "I didn't think the old man would bleed so much."

British-born in 1899, the 'Master of Suspense' worked in Hollywood for four decades up to his death in 1980, making films that showed a mastery of the cinema. He loved a moral dilemma: in *I Confess* (1953), a priest accused of murder can't prove his innocence without breaking the sacred seal of the confessional.

Above all, he knew how to terrify his audience, as anyone who has seen *Psycho* (1960) and *The Birds* (1963) will testify.

'Hitch' also liked to make signature cameo appearances in his own films, and fans take delight in spotting the moment when his unmistakable portly profile heaves into view.

And though he understood well the cinemagoer's perspective ("The length of the film should be directly related to the endurance of the human bladder"), he was notoriously callous about actors.

"I didn't say actors are cattle," he once defended himself. "What I said was, actors should be *treated* like cattle."

'Psycho has a very interesting construction. I was playing the audience, like an organ'

ALFRED HITCHCOCK 1962

HORROR

Frankenstein, the first modern horror icon, owes his existence to Mary Shelley who in 1818 wrote a supernatural tale to titillate her husband Percy Shelley and his fellow Romantic poet Lord Byron. Frankenstein is a student from Geneva who breathes life into a hideous creature he has built from dead body-parts. This creature, unlike later incarnations, was sensitive and intelligent, capable of reading Goethe and deeply hurt by people's reaction to his appearance.

The first Hollywood versions of this and another classic horror tale, *Dracula*, starring Bela Lugosi, appeared in 1931. The genre has never looked back since, moving through Thirties Wolf Men and Houses of Wax to the interplanetary nasties of the sci-fi Fifties (*Invasion of the Body Snatchers*, *I Married a Monster from Outer Space*) to the post-war output of Hammer Films, an independent British outfit which made stars of Christopher Lee and Peter Cushing in countless low-budget Dracula and Frankenstein movies.

Alfred Hitchcock's *Psycho* (1960) now seems positively restrained compared to *The Exorcist* (1973), which itself opened the door for a new generation of video nasties (and their many sequels), usually based on the teen massacre formula: *Friday the 13th* (1980), *The Evil Dead* (1983) and *A Nightmare on Elm Street* (1984), which brought us child-murdering, razor-fingered monster Freddy Krueger.

Today's biggest-selling horror writer is Stephen King, who has the sort of power that allowed him to get made a second film version of his book *The Shining* because he didn't like the original – even though it had been directed by the great Stanley Kubrick.

Meanwhile, on-screen horror has moved on to become interactive, with video games such as *Mortal Kombat* in which players can bask in gore to their hearts' content.

Christopher Lee really got his teeth into *Dracula* – he played him in eight films

1848
CALIFORNIA GOLD RUSH
In 1848, gold was accidentally discovered on a site where a sawmill was being built. When President Polk made a statement about it later in the year, the California Gold Rush was on, bringing with it an unending stream of 'Forty-niners' anxious to make their fortune.

1849
FIRST WOMAN DOCTOR
Elizabeth Blackwell was awarded her MD in New York to become the first woman doctor in the United States.

1850
SINKING OUR DIFFERENCES
The first communication cable was laid under the English Channel from Dover to Calais. It enabled telegraphs to be sent between Britain and France.

1852
FAREWELL TO A HERO
Death of the Duke of Wellington, the naval hero who defeated Napoleon and served as Prime Minister. He died at Walmer Castle, Kent, and was buried at St Paul's Cathedral.

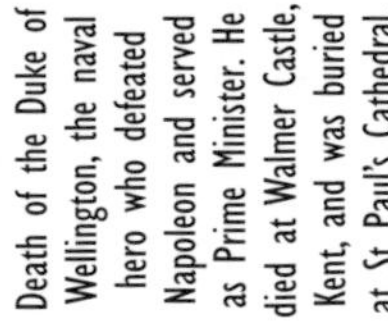

RITA HAYWORTH

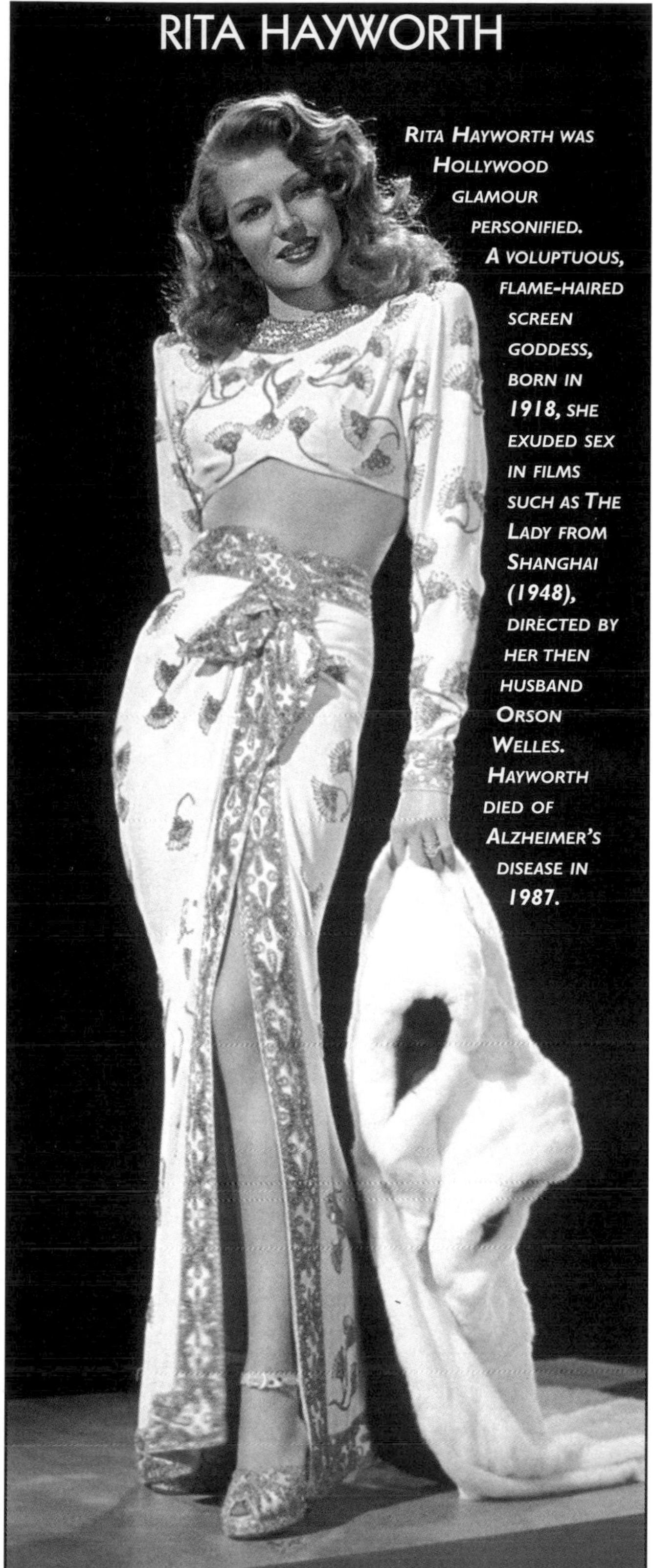

Rita Hayworth was Hollywood glamour personified. A voluptuous, flame-haired screen goddess, born in 1918, she exuded sex in films such as The Lady from Shanghai (1948), directed by her then husband Orson Welles. Hayworth died of Alzheimer's disease in 1987.

HONOURS

Winston Churchill turned down the Order of the Garter after losing the 1945 General Election, saying: "I could not accept the Order of the Garter from my Sovereign when I have received the order of the boot from the people." He did accept it eventually.

Men stripped of honours for committing crimes include: Sir Roger Casement (hanged for treason, 1916), Lester Piggott (lost his OBE after being jailed for tax evasion, 1988) and Lord Michael Spens (lost his MBE when jailed for theft, 1975).

Others stripped of their honours include Italian dictator Mussolini (Order of the Bath, 1940) and spies Kim Philby (OBE, 1965) and Anthony Blunt (Knight Commander of the Royal Victorian Order, 1979).

John Lennon (above, second left) returned his MBE in 1969 citing three reasons: the UK's involvement in Vietnam, the war in Biafra and because 'Cold Turkey' (his latest record) was slipping down the charts.

MEN WHO WERE AWARDED HONORARY KNIGHTHOODS

J Edgar Hoover *(1947)*
Douglas Fairbanks Jr *(1949)*
Kurt Waldheim *(1969)*
Chaim Herzog *(1971)*
Alistair Cooke *(1973)*
Sidney Poitier *(1974)*
Dean Rusk *(1976)*
Bernard Haitink *(1977)*
François Mitterrand *(1984)*
Bob Geldof *(1986)*
Caspar Weinberger *(1988)*
Magnus Magnusson *(1989)*
Richard Giordano *(1989)*
Ronald Reagan *(1989)*
Alfred Brendel *(1989)*
Norman Schwarzkopf *(1991)*
Lech Walesa *(1991)*
Perez de Cuellar *(1991)*
George Bush *(1993)*
Colin Powell *(1993)*
Cyrus Vance *(1994)*
Henry Kissinger *(1995)*
André Previn *(1996)*
Pele *(1997)*

MEN WHO TURNED DOWN KNIGHTHOODS

Graham Greene
Alastair Sim (right)
J B Priestley
Augustus John
Henry Moore
Francis Bacon
T S Eliot
Michael Faraday
E M Forster
Joe Gormley
(though he accepted a peerage)

THE HUMAN BODY

THEN Until the 16th century, it was thought that blood vessels carried both blood and air, and that only the arteries contained blood alone. Blood apparently formed in the liver and was carried via the lungs into the heart, where it was mixed with air and distributed. English physician William Harvey changed all that in 1628, by showing that the blood vessels carry no air, and uncovering the whole pattern and direction of blood circulation in the human body.

NOW Nowadays, when a bit of body wears out, science can often come up with a new part to compensate. They've even started growing them. But today's achievements are just the tip of the biotechnological iceberg: scientists say they will soon be able to reactivate paralysed muscles with electrodes, insert pelvic hips designed with 3-D imaging (to get the fit just right) and prescribe light-sensitive 'silicon implant' glasses, directly attached to the nerves behind the wearer's eyes.

1852 GREAT ORMOND STREET FIRST
Eliza Armstrong, aged three-and-a-half, was the first young patient at London's famous Great Ormond Street children's hospital.

1852 FOR YOUR CONVENIENCE
Britain's first 'Gents' public toilet opened in Fleet Street, London. The first 'Ladies' opened at nearby Bedford Street, off the Strand, soon after.

1853 THE FIRST LIFE POLICY
According to records in London, the first life insurance policy was sold in 1853. When a claim was made, the insurance company refused to pay, but was forced to do so after the dispute was taken to court.

1854 THE CRIMEAN WAR
Britain, France and Turkey declared war on Russia because of Russian expansion into the Ottoman Empire. The fighting, which included the Charge of the Light Brigade, took place on the Crimean Peninsula. Nurse Florence Nightingale tended the wounded and became an almost saintly figure. Russia lost.

ADOLF HITLER

This small-time Austrian painter rose to power in a Germany devastated by the defeat of the First World War. Hitler had had a good war – he was twice decorated for bravery – but it left his country crippled by reparation payments. In Vienna in 1919, Hitler joined the little-known German Workers' Party, forerunner of the Nazi movement, building up membership with stirring speeches promising to return Germany to its past glories and putting together a private army of storm troopers.

He was imprisoned after leading an attempt to overthrow the Bavarian state government in 1923 and while inside he wrote *Mein Kampf* (My Struggle), which argued that a dictatorship was the only way to save Germany from Communism and the Jews, whom he blamed for corrupting German life.

On his release Hitler rebuilt his party, gaining support from trade unions, farmers and industrialists. He offered a plan to ease the depression of 1930, and in elections two years later his party won most seats.

By 1933 Hitler had made himself dictator and set about eliminating the opposition: trade unions, a free press and political parties were outlawed. Jews were ostracised, and German children were indoctrinated early in the Nazi way.

Hitler provoked war in 1939 by invading Poland. He went on to bring death to about 11 million people because he believed they were inferior, such as Jews, gypsies, homosexuals and mental patients, or politically dangerous – such as Communists and priests. The war killed 55 million in all. Three million Soviet prisoners of war alone were starved and worked to death.

With the Allies marching on Berlin, Hitler and his mistress Eva Braun committed suicide in their bunker on April 30, 1945.

THE HOLOCAUST

The Holocaust was uniquely evil – the first time in history that a government had tried to murder an entire people. Hitler's hatred of the Jews was prefigured in his book, *Mein Kampf.* Once in power he began excluding Jews from jobs and citizenship, and forbidding them to marry Aryans. On 'Crystal Night' in 1938, synagogues were burnt down and Jews were forced to emigrate.

The 'final solution' for the Jewish problem turned from exodus to extermination some time early in the war. By the end of 1941, SS squads had killed half a million Jews. By 1942 all Jews were deported to extermination camps. By the end of the war, six million people had been murdered, mainly in six death camps in Poland, the largest of which was Auschwitz (right).

LIFELINES

***HOWARD HUGHES** designed both the biggest aircraft in the world and a bra for his protégé, voluptuous movie star Jane Russell. Born 1905, the aircraft maker became one of the world's richest men, but he died a recluse in 1976.*

***BOB HOPE** is the greatest stand-up comedian of the century. British born, in 1903, he starred in scores of films – notably the 'Road' series with Bing Crosby – and, says Milton Berle, "owns so much property in America that he must be Japanese".*

***JOHN LEE HOOKER** is, with BB King, the last giant of the blues. Born in 1917, his raw style on songs like 'Dimples' inspired the likes of Van Morrison, who queue to guest on his award-winning albums.*

1854 FIRST GIRLS' SCHOOL
Britain's first public school for girls, the Cheltenham Ladies College, was opened.

1856 THE MILK MAN
Scientist Louis Pasteur discovered that milk could be purified by heating it at a low temperature.

1856 THE FIRST VC
Queen Victoria instituted the Victoria Cross, the highest military decoration, awarded for conspicuous gallantry. Until the supply ran out in 1942, all the medals were made from cannon captured from the Russians at the siege of Sebastopol in the Crimean War.

1859 KAISER BILL IS BORN
Queen Victoria's grandson, Germany's Kaiser Wilhelm II, was born in 1859. He was known disparagingly by First World War British troops as 'Kaiser Bill'. After Germany's defeat in 1918 he abdicated and fled to Holland. In 1941, Hitler gave him a military funeral.

HELICOPTERS

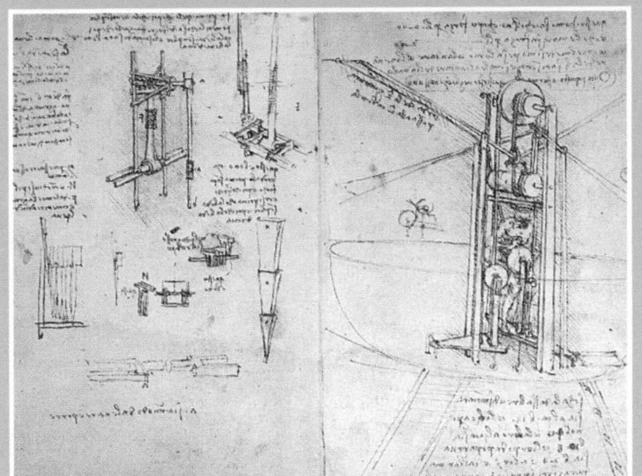

1495 ***Leonardo da Vinci draws a flying machine, writing backwards to keep his invention secret***

1967 ***Leonardo's code is cracked – and American helicopters rule the skies in the Vietnam War***

HOVERCRAFT

Is it a boat? Is it a plane? The first hovercraft, designed by Britain's Christopher Cockerell, has lift-off in 1959. These craft are now a familiar sight, crossing the Channel in just 35 minutes

HOSPITALS

THEN The oldest hospital in existence – the Hotel Dieu in Paris – goes back to the 7th century. Hospitals were founded in the affluent city-states of Italy – Genoa, Florence, Venice, Milan – in the 14th century. They had trained nurses, junior doctors to help administer treatments prescribed by experts, and even female doctors for women. They were only for the rich, however; the poor relied on apothecaries, herbalists and 'wise women'.

NOW In the 19th century, ether and chloroform were used as anaesthetics. Hygiene became more important: in 1865 Lister began using a carbolic acid spray to kill germs in the air. Schools for nursing were founded, and hospitals offered rooms to private patients. After the Second World War, the Labour government created the National Health Service, but its funding and organisation remain hot topics of debate today.

THE HINDENBURG DISASTER

The famous Hindenburg crash of 1937 was not actually the worst airship disaster. That occurred four years earlier, when a US Navy airship crashed, killing 73. Britain's worst airship crash came in 1930 when the R101 hit a hill in France and exploded, killing 44 people, on a journey to India. Yes, India! The Hindenburg, as big as the Titanic, had flown from Germany to America when it exploded, killing 33. Hitler decided hydrogen-filled airships were too dangerous, and for once the rest of the world agreed with him.

1859 Darwin's Theory of Evolution The publication of Charles Darwin's *On the Origin of Species by Means of Natural Selection* caused a rift between science and religion which still exists. Scientists accept Darwin's theory that life forms, including man, altered their appearance as they adapted to changing environments. Some theologians still believe that all species were created by God in their present form.

1860 The First Antiseptic The first operation using antiseptic was carried out by Joseph Lister at Glasgow infirmary – on his own sister.

1863 Gettysburg Address This famous speech was delivered by Abraham Lincoln while dedicating a Civil War cemetery at Gettysburg, Pennsylvania. He spoke of "government of the people, by the people, and for the people".

1863 First Tube Service London's first Tube service opened, the Metropolitan line between Paddington and Farringdon.

HALLEY'S COMET

English astronomer Edmond Halley (1656-1742) made several important advances, including a way to measure the distance between Sun and Earth. But we remember him best for his comet.

Comets were previously thought to appear at random, until Halley proved that comets seen in 1531 and 1607 followed an identical path to a 1682 comet, and so were one and the same. Comets therefore formed part of the solar system, orbiting the Sun – once every 77 years, in the case of Halley's Comet, which can only be seen from Earth as its orbit nears the Sun.

It was first photographed in 1909-11. In 1986, several unmanned spacecraft observed it at close range.

Earth passes through the orbit of Halley's Comet every May and October, when pieces of the dust left behind by the comet burn up on entering our atmosphere and make meteor showers.

BILL HALEY & HIS COMETS

Bill Haley, born in 1925, already seemed middle-aged in the 1950s. Yet when 'Rock Around The Clock' – recorded on April 12, 1954 – was featured in the film Blackboard Jungle, it sold over 25 million copies and became the signature tune of the rock 'n' roll era. An unlikely icon, Haley died in 1981.

HOLIDAYS

THEN The first holidays were, as the name suggests, 'holy' days, marking out events of special religious significance. As Christianity swept through Europe, it incorporated many pagan special days and gave them its own spin: Easter and Christmas are both based on earlier feasts. Holy days did not always have the associations of leisure that we give them today; church attendance and sometimes fasting (on Good Friday for example) were expected.

NOW In Latin countries, people celebrate their 'name day' – the feast day in the Roman Catholic calendar of the saint after whom they are named. In Britain, bank holidays were established by Act of Parliament, signalling days on which banks and other institutions were to shut. They change with increasing frequency; in 1999 the Queen approved a New Year's Eve bank holiday to mark the Millennium.

HEINZ BAKED BEANS

BEANZ HAVE MEANT HEINZ EVER SINCE HJ HEINZ PRODUCED ITS FIRST BATCH OF 'OVEN-BAKED BEANS WITH PORK & TOMATO SAUCE' IN PITTSBURGH, USA, IN 1895.

IN BRITAIN THEY WERE FIRST SOLD BY FORTNUM & MASON AND WERE INITIALLY A LUXURY ITEM COSTING 9D (4P).

BY THE SECOND WORLD WAR, BEANS WERE ONE OF THE ESSENTIAL FOODS ON THE 'POINTS' RATIONING SCHEME.

AROUND 1.5 MILLION CANS ARE NOW SOLD DAILY WORLDWIDE.

1865
SECRET PAST
After retired army surgeon James Barry died in London, aged 73, a post-mortem revealed that "he" was a woman and had given birth to a child.

1865
LINCOLN SHOT
While watching a play in a theatre, United States President Abraham Lincoln was shot in the head by actor John Wilkes Booth. Conspiracy theories still abound.

1866
DISCOVERY OF GENES
Gregor Mendel, an Austrian monk, discovered that when different strains of peas were crossed, certain traits were passed from one generation to another via what he called "discrete hereditary elements". These are now known as genes.

1867
AMERICA BUYS ALASKA
The United States bought Alaska from Russia for $7,200,000 (£4,360,000 at today's rates). Neither knew that Alaska was to become a major oil source of the world.

THE HIT PARADE

The first record charts appeared in 1896-1899 when *The Phonoscope* magazine printed monthly lists, but the term Hit Parade didn't become fashionable until the 1930s, when a radio show called *Your Hit Parade*, ranking America's most popular songs, became required listening.

The first accurate sales chart appeared in America's *Billboard* magazine in July 1940. Glenn Miller's 'Chattanooga Choo Choo' was the first Gold Record, for selling a million copies in 1941 – though many earlier records had sold a million, the first being Enrico Caruso's 1903 waxing 'Vesti La Giubba'.

1952 VERA LYNN

In Britain, music charts were based on sheet music until 1952, when Maurice Kinn, the new owner of the *New Musical Express*, launched a record sales chart, believing it to have reader appeal. He was proved correct when the paper, which had been selling poorly, gained sales of 100,000.

Here are some of the landmark charts from the past five decades.

1998 THE SPICE GIRLS

NOVEMBER 15, 1952
THE FIRST EVER BRITISH TOP TEN

1	*Here In My Heart*	Al Martino
2	*You Belong To Me*	Jo Stafford
3	*Somewhere Along The Way*	Nat King Cole
4	*Isle Of Innisfree*	Bing Crosby
5	*Feet Up*	Guy Mitchell
6	*Half As Much*	Rosemary Clooney
7	*Forget Me Not*	Vera Lynn
7	*Sugarbush*	Doris Day & Frankie Laine
8	*Blue Tango*	Ray Martin
9	*Homing Waltz*	Vera Lynn
10	*Auf Wiedersehen (Sweetheart)*	Vera Lynn

The first Top 10 was actually a Top 11, as two records tied for No 7

AUGUST 6, 1964
THEY DON'T MAKE 'EM LIKE THAT ANY MORE

1	*A Hard Day's Night*	The Beatles
2	*Do Wah Diddy Diddy*	Manfred Mann
3	*Call Up The Groups*	Barron Knights
4	*It's All Over Now*	The Rolling Stones
5	*I Just Don't Know What To Do With Myself*	Dusty Springfield
6	*Tobacco Road*	The Nashville Teens
7	*On The Beach*	Cliff Richard
8	*House Of The Rising Sun*	The Animals
9	*I Won't Forget You*	Jim Reeves
10	*I Get Around*	The Beach Boys

The Beatles rubbing shoulders with the Stones, Beach Boys, Dusty, The Animals ... and in 1964-66 the chart was like that every week!

1985 MADONNA

AUGUST 24, 1985
THE RISE OF GIRL POWER

1	*Into The Groove*	Madonna
2	*Holiday*	Madonna
3	*I Got You Babe*	UB40 with Chrissie Hynde
4	*Running Up That Hill*	Kate Bush
5	*Money For Nothing*	Dire Straits
6	*We Don't Need Another Hero*	Tina Turner
7	*Drive*	The Cars
8	*White Wedding*	Billy Idol
9	*There Must Be An Angel*	Eurythmics
10	*Say I'm Your Number One*	Princess

Madonna's double leads the way as women stage a chart take-over which looks set to continue into the next Millennium

CHRISTMAS 1998
THE SPICE GIRLS' HAT-TRICK

1	*Goodbye*	The Spice Girls
2	*Chocolate Salty Balls*	Chef
3	*Especially For You*	Denise and Johnny
4	*Believe*	Cher
5	*To You I Belong*	B*Witched
6	*Heartbeat/Tragedy*	Steps
7	*End Of The Line*	Honeyz
8	*When You're Gone*	Bryan Adams featuring Melanie C
9	*She Wants You*	Billie
10	*Cruise Into Christmas Medley*	Jane McDonald

The Spice Girls matched The Beatles' feat in 1963-65 by having the Christmas No 1 in 1996 ('2 Become 1'), 1997 ('Too Much') and 1998

H

1868 THE LAST PUBLIC EXECUTION
The last public execution in England took place on May 26 outside London's Newgate prison. Michael Barret was hanged for setting off a bomb which killed 12 people.

1869 SUEZ CANAL OPENED
The ten-year construction of the 114 mile-long shipping canal running between the Mediterranean and the Red Sea was completed in 1869.

1870 CHARLES DICKENS DIES
One of Britain's greatest novelists, Charles Dickens died on June 9. He painted a vivid picture of life in Victorian England, creating memorable characters. His work could be warm and humorous, but he also wrote of suffering and cruelty which he worked to expose.

1871 GREAT FIRE OF CHICAGO
The great fire of Chicago spread for four square miles, gutted 17,500 buildings, left 300 dead and 90,000 homeless. The damage was put at $200 million. Legend says it started when a cow kicked over a lantern in a barn.

LIFELINES

THOMAS HARDY'S *romantic novels so shocked the Victorians that he confined himself to poetry in later life to avoid controversy. Born in 1840, his Wessex tales such as Tess of the d'Urbervilles (1891) have become lavish films and TV series. He died in 1928.*

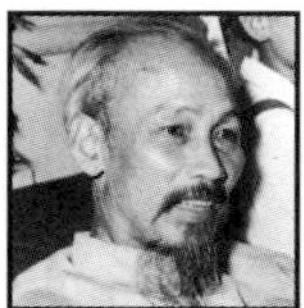

HO CHI-MINH *was Asia's David to America's Goliath. As the Communist president of North Vietnam, he masterminded the fight against the US-assisted South Vietnam. He died in 1969, aged 79, three years before the US left Vietnam.*

ERNEST HEMINGWAY, *born in 1899, was America's most famous novelist of the century – a tough guy who wrote tough-guy yarns such as A Farewell To Arms and For Whom The Bell Tolls. He shot himself in 1961.*

TONY HANCOCK

Tony Hancock is remembered as the very epitome of the tortured clown, the man who could make everyone laugh but himself. Born in 1924, from the start of his career he battled with nerves to emulate his father, an amateur entertainer, as a stand-up comic in RAF concert parties.

He progressed through cabaret and pantomime to star in *Hancock's Half Hour*, a radio series written for him by Ray Galton and Alan Simpson. In it he perfected the lugubrious comic persona for which he will be remembered, a self-important nonentity whose social and intellectual aspirations were constantly thwarted by the mediocrity of his abilities and circumstances.

The comedy, of course, lay in Hancock's total inability to spot this disparity, in his chronic lack of self-knowledge. Transferred to telly, the series won record rating figures, and the videos of the shows – most featuring Sid James – are now hugely successful.

Hancock, in a case of life imitating art, decided he could do without his regular writers and co-stars, and moved unsuccessfully into various solo or 'artistic' projects such as the film *The Rebel* (1960). After a dismal round of failed projects and lapses into alcoholism, he committed suicide in Australia in 1968, whilst attempting another comeback.

The note simply said: "Things seemed to go wrong too many times."

'A pint? That's nearly an armful!'

TONY HANCOCK'S MOST FAMOUS LINE, IN THE BLOOD DONOR, 1961

Anthony Aloysius St John Hancock, of 23 Railway Cuttings, East Cheam, was one of TV's best-loved characters. Writers Galton and Simpson went on to create Steptoe and Son

JIMI HENDRIX

Jimi Hendrix was rock's guitar genius. An American who found fame in London, he invented heavy metal in 'Purple Haze' and wrote his own myth in the blues-rooted 'Voodoo Chile'. Playing up to his outrageous image, he was never destined for longevity. Hendrix, born in 1942, was dead by 1970.

HOROSCOPES

THEN After centuries of decline at the expense of Christianity, astrology began to be popular again in Britain in the 12th century. By the 16th its influence was particularly strong and backed by royal approval: Queen Elizabeth I chose an auspicious date on which to be crowned after consultations with her astrologer, and herbalists like Culpeper would prescribe remedies according to your birth chart as well as your illness. Astrology was a topic of great public debate, and hundreds of books arguing for or against it were published.

NOW Scientists reject the claims of astrology on the grounds that the position of Earth in space has changed since the ancient times when horoscopes were devised, so the zodiac signs no longer match the constellations for which they were named. For most of us, astrology is a bit of harmless fun, and checking the 'stars' for any coincidence with reality is as far as it goes. Yet one prediction is a cert: any tabloid which left out the horoscopes would quickly go out of business.

1871
DR LIVINGSTONE, I PRESUME?
Welshman Henry Stanley became a correspondent for the *New York Herald* and was told by his editor to find missionary-explorer David Livingstone who was missing in Africa. The almost impossible and exhausting search ended near Lake Tanganyika in 1871 when Stanley finally tracked down his quarry and asked: "Dr Livingstone, I presume?"

1872
LEARNING THE OCEAN'S SECRETS
The invention of a primitive sonar device by Lord Kelvin led to the discovery of the Mid-Atlantic Ridge. It was an important milestone in mankind's understanding of plate tectonics.

1876
CUSTER'S LAST STAND
Up to 4,000 Sioux Indians attacked US General Custer and 250 of his men near the Little Bighorn river in Montana. Only one scout survived 'Custer's Last Stand'. White America was outraged, swore revenge, and within a year the Sioux tribe was broken and defeated.

DAVID HOCKNEY

David Hockney is Britain's most famous living artist. Relentlessly innovative, Hockney has created paintings, photoportraits, theatre designs, fax art and lithographs.

His best-known style is the bright poster colours and broad strokes of his swimming pool pictures, with that blend of modernism and accessibility that makes him so popular.

Born in Bradford in 1937, Hockney declared himself a conscientious objector when he came of age and did his National Service as a hospital orderly.

After finding fame as an early Sixties Pop artist, he moved away from abstract art and has focused his painting on his personal interests and background, including his homosexuality and his family – as in the sparsely honest portrait of *My Parents* (1977). In the Sixties he earned enough from his *A Rake's Progress* etchings to move to Los Angeles, where he still lives. An etching series from 1970 illustrates six fairy tales by the Brothers Grimm.

More recently, he has taken yet another new direction, painting warmly nostalgic landscapes of his native Yorkshire.

1970 ***The painting Mr and Mrs Clark and Percy – a portrait of swinging London fashion designers Ossie Clark and Celia Birtwell – showed David Hockney turning from Pop to representative art***

HARRY HOUDINI

Harry Houdini, born in Budapest in 1874, was the greatest escape artist ever. He even got out when chained underwater.

Yet he never tried to make people believe in magic, and often exposed those who did, such as fake mediums.

He died in 1926, after a punch received during a stunt burst his appendix – but he left a challenge for spiritualists to contact him via a coded message.

No one ever did.

HOMOSEXUALITY

For most of the Millennium, gay sex has been outlawed. Playwright Oscar Wilde was jailed in 1895 for supporting 'the love that dare not speak its name'. Later, Hitler simply practised sexual cleansing on his gay population.

The UK decriminalised consenting homosexual acts in 1967. Another turning point came in 1969, when New York police raided a gay bar in Greenwich Village called the Stonewall. Drinkers refused to come quietly, and suddenly 'gay revolution' was on the map. In 1973, the American Psychiatric Association removed homosexuality from its manual of mental illnesses.

But a new illness, AIDS, would provoke an epidemic of deaths among gays and intravenous drug users, providing more ammunition for the prejudiced.

Now we have openly gay MPs and celebrities (though notably few in Hollywood), and the age of consent has been lowered to 18. But the bombing in early 1999 of a gay pub in London shows that, for some, blind hatred remains the only response to homosexuality.

1876
Invention of the Telephone
Edinburgh-born inventor Alexander Graham Bell received a patent for his invention of the telephone in March 1876. His first 'phone call' had actually taken place on June 5, 1875, when he managed to transmit a message to his assistant. The Bell Telephone Company was set up in 1877 and lasted for more than a century – until 1984. Bell also founded the journal Science.

1877
Dead Heat in Boat Race
For the only time since the world-famous rowing event was first staged in 1829, the Oxford-Cambridge boat race ended in a dead heat.

1879
Bright Idea
Let there be electric light! The world was about to be lit up thanks to American inventor Thomas Edison. After experimenting in his workshop with an electric incandescent lamp fitted with a carbonized filament, Edison managed to keep it lit for more than 13 hours.

IRELAND

The central theme of Ireland's Millennium has been its relations with England. Since the 12th century, when King Henry II and his Normans invaded Ireland (having just done the same to England), the Irish have resisted attempts to conquer them, enduring war, poverty, famine, and political and religious persecution along the way.

In 1607, the English government planted the six counties of Ulster with English and Scottish settlers, and in 1650 Oliver Cromwell crushed an Irish Catholic rebellion during the English Civil War. The Irish Free State – southern Ireland – finally secured independence in 1921, and Eire became a republic in 1949.

In Ulster the Catholics complained of official prejudice, while Protestants feared being absorbed into the Republic. In the 1960s, violence broke out and the British army came in. The IRA and Protestant armed groups have since killed hundreds.

The 1985 Anglo-Irish agreement and 1993's Downing Street Declaration paved the way for the 1998 Good Friday Agreement, which finally brought a ceasefire and elections to a Northern Irish assembly. But issues such as the decommissioning of paramilitary arms remain unresolved.

1903 The Telephone Booth

1589 The Flush Toilet

1855 The Refrigerator

INVENTIONS MADE IN BRITAIN

The Slide Rule 1621
The Pressure Cooker 1679
The Match 1680
The Machine-Gun 1718
The Chronometer 1735
The Flush Toilet 1589
The Power Loom 1785
Gas Lighting 1792
The Locomotive 1804
The Photographic Lens 1812
The Electromagnet 1824
Modern Rainwear 1830
The Lawn Mower 1830
The Computer 1835
The Bicycle 1840
The Travel Agency 1841
The Glider 1853
Steel (production) 1854
The Refrigerator 1855
Linoleum 1860
Colour Photography 1861
The Stapler 1868
The Vending Machine 1883
The Thermos 1892
The Loudspeaker 1900
The Electric Vacuum Cleaner 1901
Car Disc Brakes 1902
The Telephone Booth 1903
The Geiger Counter 1908
Stainless Steel 1913
The Turbojet 1928
The Decompression Chamber 1929
The Food Processor 1947
The Integrated Circuit 1952
The Hovercraft 1955
Acrylic Paint 1964
The CAT Scanner 1972
Test-Tube Babies 1978
Genetic Fingerprinting 1987

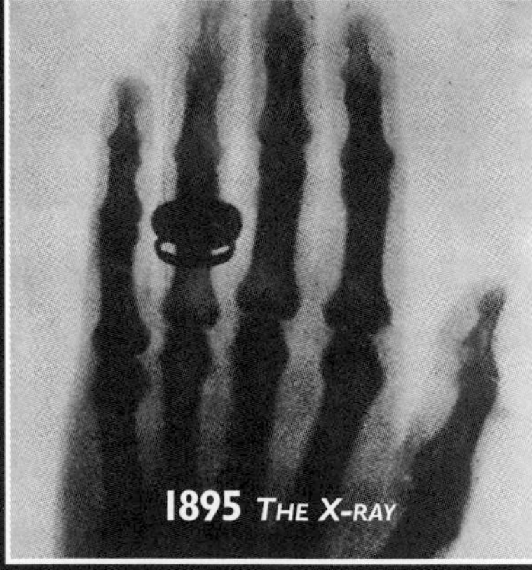

1895 The X-ray

Ten indispensable inventions of the 19th century

Elastic (1820)
The fax machine (1843)
The can opener (1860)
The cylinder lock (1860)
The telephone (1876)
The record player (1877)
The car (1884)
Aspirin (1889)
The vacuum flask (1892)
The X-ray (1895)

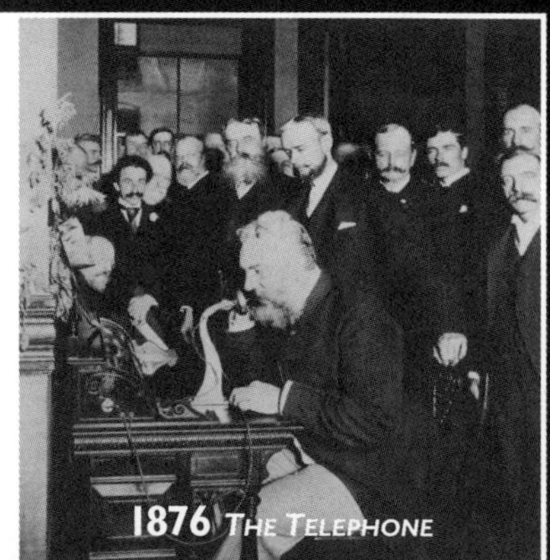

1876 The Telephone

1879 The First Woolworth's
Frank W. Woolworth opened his first F.W. Woolworth Co 5 and 10 Cent Store in Lancaster, Pennsylvania. As the name suggests, everything inside cost either five or ten cents. The store's success led to the eventual growth of a worldwide Woolworth chain. Frank's earlier five cent store in New York was a flop.

1879 Start of the Zulu War
The Zulu War began between Britain and the natives of Zululand in Southern Africa. It included the celebrated Battle of Rorke's Drift (filmed as Zulu, starring Michael Caine) where a handful of British soldiers successfully resisted a Zulu army.

1880 First Telephone Directory
The London Telephone Company published the first telephone directory in London. It contained only 255 entries.

LIFELINES

HENRIK IBSEN *was Norway's greatest playwright. Darkly realistic plays such as A Doll's House revolutionised European drama. Born in 1828, he spent his most creative years abroad, returning to Norway before his death in 1906.*

CHRISTOPHER ISHERWOOD *(1904-86) invented Sally Bowles, heroine of the film Cabaret. English novelist Isherwood lived the decadent pre-war Berlin life with his friend WH Auden. Defiantly gay, he quit Germany in 1939 to become a US citizen.*

POPE INNOCENT III *(1160-1216) was the most powerful Pope. Founder of the Papal Empire, he wielded authority over secular rulers and even the succession of the Roman Emperor, influencing every part of society.*

Thomas Telford's Caledonian Canal was one of the great waterways of the Industrial Revolution. Linking the North Sea to the Irish Sea across the Scottish Highlands, it took 44 years to build and was completed in 1847

THE INDUSTRIAL REVOLUTION

In the 18th century, Britain was the world's leading colonial power. It had vast deposits of coal and iron, and large colonial markets for finished iron and textile goods. The pressure was on to keep up with demand.

Inventions such as flying shuttles for weaving, and new iron-making processes, found a cheap source of power in the steam engine.

Factories and mills sprang up everywhere, bringing together the machines and the workers needed to operate them. Housing estates were built around the factories, helping create whole new cities. Canals were built and roads resurfaced to carry raw materials and goods. Banks emerged to underwrite the expansion.

Working conditions were harsh – even children worked 12-14 hours a day – and the division of labour made work increasingly monotonous.

The sudden influx from rural areas often led to overcrowding and disease. Trade unions were initially banned and workers had no vote. But the growing middle classes benefited as universities sprang up to educate a new class of engineers and professionals.

Mass production made new comforts and labour-saving devices available to those who could afford them. Britain was no longer a rural society, but an urban, industrial one.

Without the Industrial Revolution we would never have had the telephone or the computer – or the traffic jam and the hole in the ozone layer.

INFLATION

Millennia come, millennia go, but one truth is constant: prices always go up. Sometimes they rise quickly. In the 1970s, when the oil-producing countries hiked their prices by 400 per cent, the annual rate of inflation hit 26 per cent in the UK and 172 per cent in Argentina.

And sometimes (but not often) prices almost stand still. At the end of the Millennium, the annual inflation rate in Britain is 1.3 per cent. So in a year's time, today's £1 will be worth 99p.

What £1 bought you 100 years ago would cost an amazing £69.33 today. And in 1959, £1 would have bought the equivalent of £19.74 today. Here are some typical price changes in the past 40 years:

HOW PRICES HAVE CHANGED

	1959		1999
Loaf of bread	*11d*	*(5p)*	*61p*
1 lb butter	*4s 4d*	*(22p)*	*£1.56p*
Pint of milk	*8d*	*(3p)*	*35p*
1 lb oranges	*1s*	*(5p)*	*72p*
1 lb sugar	*1s 4d*	*(7p)*	*28p*
1 lb bacon	*3s*	*(15p)*	*£1.65p*

EDDIE IZZARD

Eddie Izzard, born in 1962, is "the funniest man in Britain", says John Cleese. Izzard's surreal raps about being an "action transvestite" have made him a world star, and he now looks set for a major acting career

1883 KRAKATOA ERUPTS
A series of eruptions from Krakatoa, a volcano in the East Indies, could be heard 2,200 miles away. Ash was propelled nearly 50 miles into the air and fell over 500,000 square miles of the surrounding area. Dust from the explosion affected climates around the world.

1884 GREENWICH SETS THE STANDARD
Greenwich Mean Time was accepted as the universal time from which standard times around the world were calculated.

1886 STATUE OF LIBERTY
The Statue of Liberty was inaugurated on Liberty Island in New York Harbor by President Grover Cleveland. Standing 151 ft (49m) without its pedestal, the statue, officially called Liberty Enlightening the World, was a gift to the United States from France to commemorate the friendship between the two nations.

INDIAN RESTAURANTS

Many Indian restaurants are not Indian at all – four out of five in Britain are Bangladeshi. The confusion goes back to Bangladesh's independence from India in 1971. As this was the start of the UK curry boom, the 'Indian' tag stuck. The first 'Indians' appeared in the 1960s, and the British, normally wary eaters, soon took them to their hearts, though not without turning the delicately spiced cuisine into a macho test of endurance. There are 10,600 Indian restaurants in Britain. In 1999, for the first time, Michelin's British guide listed more 'Indians' (64) than French or English *cordon bleu* restaurants.

ISLAM

THEN After Mohammed's death in 632AD, Islam quickly took over the Middle East and gradually built up an empire that engulfed the Persian and Christian Byzantine empires and spread a sophisticated civilisation into Iraq, Palestine, Syria, North Africa, India and Spain, and later Asia and Indonesia. Learning was part of religious duty, and classical knowledge was translated into Arabic. Muslim scholars developed astronomy, medicine, philosophy, mathematics and chemistry. Muslim art and architecture gave the world many magnificent structures, such as the Taj Mahal in India and the Mosque in Cordoba.

NOW Islam presents the last challenge to the Western way of life – capitalist, industrialised, increasingly non-religious – that is rapidly taking over the world. The expulsion of the modernising Shah of Iran (1979), for instance, was followed by the installation of a traditional Islamic state, as has happened more recently in Afghanistan and Algeria. Fundamentalists murdered President Sadat of Eygpt in 1981, two years after he made peace with Israel. The Middle East remains the focal point of world stability, something Saddam Hussein tried to exploit when he sought the support of Muslims after invading Kuwait in the 1990 Gulf conflict. Worldwide, there are 1.3 billion Muslims today.

The Card Players (1890) by Paul Cézanne – the 'father of modern art' – eschewed fine painting in favour of emotion. Claude Monet's Houses of Parliament at Sunset (1904) owed a lot to Turner – though there was probably less smog in Turner's day

IMPRESSIONISM AND POST-IMPRESSIONISM

'The Christopher Columbus of a new continent of form'

CLIVE BELL, ART CRITIC, ON CÉZANNE

The Impressionists – Degas, Manet, Monet, Pissarro, Renoir – had a huge influence on art. Meeting in Parisian cafés in the 1860s, they shared a distrust of imaginative, academic art, and of the Romantic idea that art should communicate intense emotion. Instead, influenced by photography, they wanted to record the fleeting moment.

They used bright colours and sketchy brushwork to convey light, and loved to paint in the open air. Degas painted horse races and dances, Renoir pretty women and children, and many others chose landscapes. Monet, whose picture *Impression: Sunrise* gave the group its name, took to painting series of pictures with the same subject – haystacks, Rouen Cathedral – at different times of day.

The reaction of the Post-Impressionists – Cézanne, Gauguin, Van Gogh – was to return emotion to painting. Cézanne tried to capture the underlying structure of nature; Gauguin painted more symbolically; Van Gogh used colour and texture unrealistically, to show powerful inner feeling. Their work prefigured other developments, notably Cubism.

1886
THE FIRST SOCCER CAPS
The Football Association Council approved the idea of caps being given to international players.

1886
FIRST TASTE OF COCA-COLA
Originally marketed as a syrup, the drink was formulated by chemist John S. Pemberton to cure headaches. A year later he sold the formula to another chemist, Asa Briggs Candler, who used it to flavour soda water and called it Coca-Cola.

1888
JACK THE RIPPER
1888 was the year of Jack the Ripper, the notorious murderer who killed and mutilated six London prostitutes. On December 3, the body of Montague Druitt, a prominent suspect, was found floating in the Thames. The identity of the Ripper was never discovered.

1891
THE LONG, LONG RAILROAD
Russia started building its transcontinental railroad, the Trans-Siberian line. The 5,900-mile link was finished in 1905.

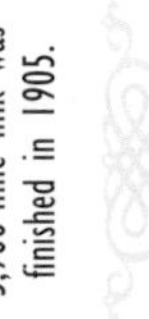

Christ has inspired artists all through the Millennium. Two painters whose work ranged from the sublime to the grotesque were Hieronymus Bosch and his spiritual heir, Salvador Dali, and these pictures visit those extremes. In Christ Crowned With Thorns (1480), Bosch depicts Jesus lost in a crowd of ugly characters while, below, in Christ of St John of the Cross (1951), Dali transforms Christ's agony into beauty

JESUS CHRIST

THEN A thousand years ago, in these solidly Christian isles, Christ was indisputably the Son of God. Christianity provided the principles by which people lived; its calendar was the fabric of everyday life; the church was the village focal point. Christ's teaching helped to unify an ethnically diverse population of Vikings, Saxons and Celts. The Pope was the most powerful figure in Europe, and the Anglo-Saxon and Scottish kings – Macbeth among them – all made the arduous pilgrimage to Rome to receive his blessing.

NOW Britain is often referred to as a post-Christian society. Few question Christ's historical existence, however, and admire him as an ethical leader. But his divinity, virginal conception and bodily resurrection are often disputed – even from within the Church. In the 1980s the Bishop of Durham caused a storm by denying the Resurrection, which he called 'a conjuring trick', and claiming that Mary was a 'symbolic Virgin'. Church attendance has fallen from 9.1 million adults in 1970 to 6.4 million in 1995.

THE KING JAMES BIBLE

The King James Bible, the 'Authorised Version', was put together by a group of about 50 scholars under James I and published in 1611. They worked together to agree a version that would be acceptable to all Christian groups, and to make the best of earlier English translations. The text is largely based on a vigorous 16th-century translation from the Greek by William Tyndale. Unusually for a piece of committee work, the elegance and expressiveness of the language soon turned it into a literary and spiritual classic, and made it the standard Bible for English-speaking Protestants well into the 20th century. Many hanker for its return still.

JODRELL BANK

Jodrell Bank, near Manchester, was the world's largest telescope when it was rushed into operation in 1957 to track the orbit of Sputnik-I, the first Soviet satellite. The giant radio telescope has since made pioneering radar studies of meteors, the moon and the astronomical bodies known as pulsars, and mapped 'cosmic radio sources'.

LIFELINES

GLENDA JACKSON, born in 1936, had few challenges left as an actress after winning two Oscars and appearing with Morecambe and Wise. So she turned to politics, becoming Labour's Minister for Transport, then running for Mayor of London.

JAMES JOYCE's ideas streamed on to paper in a manner that revolutionised the novel. Born in Dublin in 1882, he experimented with language, though classics such as Ulysses were once seen as pornography. He died in 1941.

JOAN OF ARC said her mission from God was to reclaim France from the English. Born in 1412, she led armies to victory but failed to take Paris. She was found guilty of witchcraft by her own countrymen and burnt at the stake in 1431.

1893 VOTING RIGHTS FOR WOMEN New Zealand was the first country to grant women the right to vote. In Britain they had to wait until 1918, and then only those aged 30 or above qualified. In 1928, the right to vote was given to all British women aged 21 and over.

1894 THE FIRST STRIP-TEASE It happened at the Divan Fayonau Music Hall, Paris. The act was billed as 'Le Coucher d'Yvette' and depicted a girl taking off her clothes to go to bed. It was the first known public strip-tease.

1894 THE FIRST CAR RACE Held in France, from Paris to Rouen, the first car race was over a distance of 50 miles. The winner's average speed was just over six miles an hour.

LIFELINES

Jesse James, *born in 1847, has been shot in the back countless times. The most notorious gang leader in the Wild West was a cold-blooded killer. But the way he died in 1882, shot by a reward-seeker, made him the hero of 100 films.*

Dr Samuel Johnson *(1709-84) ruled London's 18th-century literary scene. A prolific writer of essays and poetry, as well as his famous dictionary, his life was documented by his friend James Boswell. He was buried in Westminster Abbey.*

Ben Johnson *is the Millennium's best-known cheat. Born in Canada in 1961, he 'won' the 1988 Olympic 100 metres. But a drugs test showed he owed it to anabolic steroids and he was disqualified with appropriate speed.*

MICHAEL JACKSON

'I am the one who will dance on the floor in the round'
'Billie Jean', 1982

1996
Brit Awards

Michael Jackson has been in the public spotlight most of his extraordinary life, during which he has become *the* celebrity of the 20th century. In recent years, however, a lot of the attention can't have been much fun.

Born in 1958, he had his first hit at 11, when the Jackson 5's exhilarating Motown confection 'I Want You Back' ushered in the 1970s, hitting No 1 in both Britain and America.

Soon Michael's distinctive treble vocals were appearing on records both with his brothers and in his own right. But by 1979 the group's fortunes had begun to falter, and Michael struck out

1972
Jackson Five at the London Palladium

ELTON JOHN

In 1997 Elton John sang a poignant version of 'Candle in the Wind' – originally written about Marilyn Monroe – at the funeral of his friend Princess Diana. By the end of the Millennium it had made £33 million for her memorial fund. The flamboyant singer, pianist and football club owner – born Reg Dwight in 1947 – shot to fame in the Seventies with hits including 'Your Song', 'Rocket Man' and 'Crocodile Rock'.

JANIS JOPLIN

With her wild, drug-fuelled lifestyle and brash but charismatic onstage presence, blues singer Janis Joplin quickly established herself as a Sixties rock icon – and just as quickly burnt herself out. In October 1970, a month after the death of Jimi Hendrix and nine months before that of The Doors' Jim Morrison, she died of a heroin overdose at the age of 27.

MILLENNIUM TIME LINE

1895
FA Cup Stolen
Football's FA Cup was stolen from a sports shop in Birmingham and never seen again. In 1963 – 68 years later – a man claimed that he had melted it down for counterfeit half-crown coins.

1896
The First Car Show
The first Horseless Carriage Show opened to the motor trade at the Imperial Institute in London. There were ten models on show.

1896
First Car Victim
Mrs Bridget Driscoll, of Croydon, Surrey, apparently froze in panic when she saw a motor vehicle hurtling towards her at 4mph. She was the first person in Britain to be knocked down and killed by a car.

1896
Nobel's Legacy
Dynamite inventor Alfred Nobel died, leaving a fund to provide Nobel Prizes for those making the greatest contribution in the fields of physics, chemistry, physiology or medicine, literature and peace.

alone with his classic *Off the Wall* album, which sold 10 million. Then came *Thriller* (1982), the best-selling album of all time: 40 million sales, No 1 in every Western country. The singles ruled the charts, boosted by extravagant videos featuring Jackson's divine dancing that would culminate in a horror-movie epic with a voiceover by Vincent Price to accompany the title track.

After that, the only way was down. Though Jackson remains a huge-selling artist, the music has been swamped by gossip about his private life: his retreat into a lonely Peter Pan world complete with fairground rides, pet chimpanzee and visits from other ex-child stars (Brooke Shields, Liz Taylor); the plastic surgery and changing skin colour; the ill-starred marriage to Lisa Presley, the allegations of child abuse (settled out of court); and the strange circumstances of the birth of his child.

At the 1996 Brit Awards, Pulp's Jarvis Cocker caught the turning mood when he disrupted Jackson's Messianic rendition of 'Earth Song'. Cocker called it "a protest at the way Michael Jackson sees himself as some Christ-like figure with the power of healing". Michael's reply could be a comment on his life in the spotlight: "I am immensely proud that the show went on."

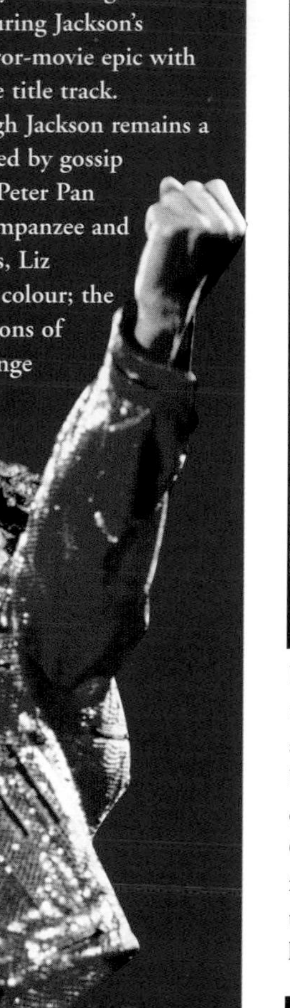

1982
THRILLER TOUR

AL JOLSON

Calling himself the World's Greatest Entertainer, singer and comedian Al Jolson (1886-1950) started in vaudeville. A white man, he would imitate black minstrels on songs such as 'Mammy', 'Sonny Boy' and 'Swanee', going down on one knee with arms outstretched. He later starred in numerous films, including *The Jazz Singer* (1927) – the first motion picture with sound.

JACK THE RIPPER

No one knows who Jack the Ripper actually was, though people just won't give up guessing. What is known is that between August 31 and November 9, 1888, the bodies of six prostitutes were found in London's East End, all with throats cut and flesh slashed. A huge investigation followed, involving police searches, citizen patrols, bloodhounds and fortune-tellers. Three prime suspects – all thought to be insane – were identified and released owing to insufficient evidence. Complaints of police incompetence led to the resignation of Sir Charles Warren, Commissioner of Scotland Yard – on the day before the sixth murder. The police received hundreds of letters from people claiming to be Jack. One contained part of a victim's kidney, and was addressed 'from Hell'; it was thought to be authentic. Still, the English love a criminal who gets away with it, and to this day there is a busy little industry in Jack the Ripper walks and paperbacks claiming to have solved the murders at last.

JEKYLL AND HYDE

The Strange Case of Dr Jekyll and Mr Hyde is one of those stories that most of us are vaguely familiar with, but few have actually read.

Robert Louis Stevenson's tale, written in 1886, tells of a physician who becomes fascinated with the mix of good and bad in his own nature. He discovers a drug that enables him to create a separate personality which will take on all his evil instincts. His alter ego, the repulsive-looking Hyde, begins to take control and Jekyll fights a losing battle.

The novel's title has slipped into the language and is nowadays used to describe virtually anyone with variable moods.

It has been filmed several times; the best, made in 1931, starred Fredric March (left).

1896 OLYMPIC GAMES
Established in 776BC at Olympia, Greece, the Olympic Games were abolished in 394AD. They were revived in 1896 and Athens was chosen to hold the first Olympics of modern times.

1896 KLONDIKE GOLD RUSH
Thousands rushed to northern Canada's Klondike River region where gold was discovered in 1896. By 1900, the area had been all but stripped of the precious metal.

1897 BRITAIN'S FIRST DRUNK DRIVER
The first conviction for drunken driving came on September 10, 1897. The shamed offender was one George Smith – a London taxi driver.

1899 THE BOER WAR
Dutch settlers – Boers – who were seeking independence in South Africa, went to war with Britain. They lost and in 1902, under the Treaty of Pretoria, the disputed Transvaal and Orange Free State became British colonies. Lord Kitchener, made famous by his "Your Country Needs You" First World War poster, led the British forces.

KELLOGG'S CORNFLAKES

A packet of Kellogg's Cornflakes is to be found in one in two of the nation's households at any one time. W K Kellogg invented the flake in Michigan in 1898, when he left a sheet of wheat to soak overnight. When rolled, the sheet broke into flakes, which out of curiosity he baked. Kellogg's hit the UK in 1924, though the cockerel mascot – Cornelius – did not appear until 1964. Cornflakes aren't just for breakfast: in a Kellogg's survey, 26 per cent of people were found to like eating a bowl last thing at night.

JOHN F KENNEDY

JFK seemed to have it all. A dashing war hero from a prominent Boston family, he became America's youngest President in 1960 at the age of 43, defusing his Republican opponent Richard Nixon's claim that he was too young by beating him in head-to-head TV debates.

His Presidency nearly foundered just a year later in the Bay of Pigs – a disastrous attempted invasion of Cuba – and he then risked nuclear war in facing down the USSR's Nikita Khrushchev in the Cuban missile crisis. But the US prospered under its vigorous President and his high-profile clan – an American royal family.

And then 'the shot that was heard around the world' tore the fabric of Camelot to shreds. Kennedy was assassinated on November 22, 1963 when shots were fired at his motorcade in Dallas, Texas. Lee Harvey Oswald was arrested, but was shot dead in police custody by one Jack Ruby, who also died in custody.

Kennedy's death traumatised America, but his afterlife has been a mire of sexual revelations and conspiracy theories, allegedly involving everyone from the CIA to Marilyn Monroe.

'Ask not what your country can do for you. Ask what you can do for your country'

John F Kennedy, Presidential Inauguration speech

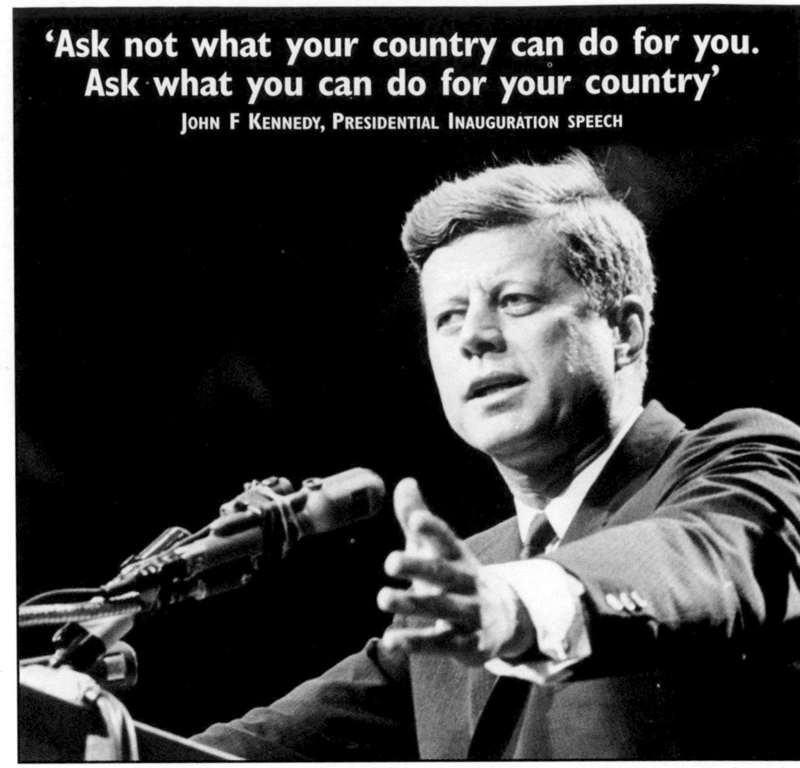

"Where were you when Kennedy was shot?" JFK's assassination was the most dramatic incident of the early TV age, and for a moment time stood still

MARTIN LUTHER KING JR

'I have a dream that my four little children will one day live in a nation where they will not be judged by the colour of their skin but by the content of their character'

Martin Luther King Jr, Washington civil rights march, 1963

Martin Luther King's 'I have a dream' speech, delivered at a peaceful 1963 march in Washington before a diverse crowd of 300,000 people, is perhaps the most powerful piece of oratory since the Second World War. The speech, with its Biblical rhythms, set the burgeoning civil rights movement in its proper context. This was no petty protest, but a righteous call for an end to racism and discrimination.

King demanded equal rights in work and education for black people, not to mention the freedom to sit where they liked on a bus. (Rosa Parks had been arrested in 1955 for refusing to move to the back seats.)

Eventually, in 1964, the wide-ranging Civil Rights Act was passed. But racist violence continued. King, whose non-violent stance had won him a Nobel Prize, was shot in Memphis in 1968. A white ex-convict, James Earl Ray, later pleaded guilty, but never declared any motive. Black people rioted in 100 cities.

Martin Luther King Jr making the speech for which he will always be remembered, on August 28, 1963

1900 Birth of Sinn Fein
Sinn Fein, meaning 'Ourselves Alone', was established to promote the cause of home rule for Ireland. It was founded by Irish Republican Arthur Griffith.

1900 Oscar Wilde Dies
Irish poet and dramatist Oscar Wilde died, aged 46, in an obscure Paris hotel on November 30. The literary genius was penniless and a broken man after serving two years' hard labour, convicted of homosexual offences.

1901 Australian Commonwealth
At the beginning of the 20th century Australia was still made up of a number of British colonies. To help establish an Australian national identity, the British Parliament passed the Constitution Act on July 9, 1901, creating an Australian federation.

STANLEY KUBRICK

STANLEY KUBRICK (RIGHT) WAS THE MILLENNIUM'S MOST IMAGINATIVE FILM-MAKER. BORN IN NEW YORK IN 1928, HIS MOVIES SPANNED A HUGE RANGE, BUT EACH WAS A LANDMARK. IN LOLITA (1962), A MIDDLE-AGED MAN FALLS FOR A 15-YEAR-OLD GIRL. IN DR STRANGELOVE (1963), PETER SELLERS TURNS ATOMIC WAR INTO A JOKE. 2001: A SPACE ODYSSEY (1968) MADE SPACE TRAVEL A PSYCHEDELIC TRIP. A CLOCKWORK ORANGE (1971) WAS WITHDRAWN BY KUBRICK AFTER ITS RELEASE BECAUSE ITS GRAPHIC VIOLENCE PROVOKED OUTRAGE – IT HAS NOT BEEN SCREENED IN BRITAIN SINCE. THE SHINING (1980) WAS ONE OF THE SCARIEST FILMS EVER. KUBRICK DIED IN 1999 LEAVING ONE LAST FILM – EYES WIDE SHUT, STARRING NICOLE KIDMAN AND TOM CRUISE.

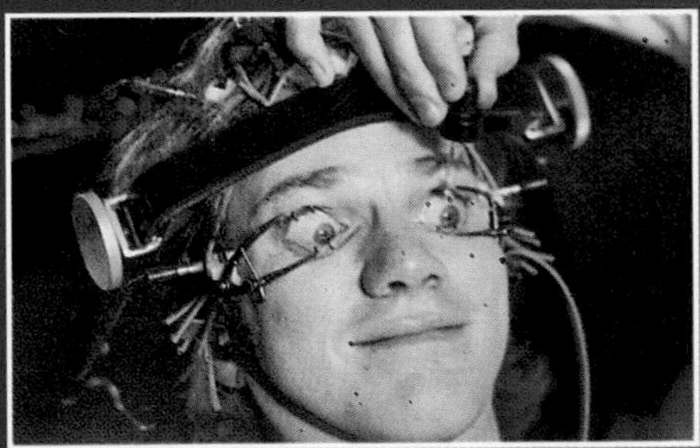

ABOVE: Scenes from A Clockwork Orange
LEFT: Jack Nicholson in The Shining
BELOW: Peter Sellers as Dr Strangelove

STEPHEN KING

STEPHEN KING (LEFT) IS THE MODERN MASTER OF SUSPENSE. HIS NOVELS HAVE BEEN MADE INTO INNUMERABLE HORROR MOVIES – MOST NOTABLY THE SHINING, STARRING JACK NICHOLSON, AND BRIAN DE PALMA'S CARRIE. BORN IN 1947, THE AMERICAN AUTHOR HAS WRITTEN OVER 20 BEST-SELLERS INCLUDING MISERY, THE STAND AND SALEM'S LOT. HE NEARLY DIED IN A CAR ACCIDENT IN 1999.

KIDNAPPINGS

FAMOUS ABDUCTIONS

CHARLES LINDBERGH JR, the baby of aviator Charles Lindbergh, was kidnapped in New Jersey in 1932 and murdered. German immigrant Bruno Hauptmann went to the electric chair but there is now doubt about his guilt.

ALDO MORO, ex-Prime Minister of Italy, was kidnapped and killed by the Red Brigade in 1978.

JOHN PAUL GETTY III was kidnapped by Italian gangsters in Rome in 1973 and held for six months. They cut off his ear and sent it to his family, who paid $2.5 million ransom for his release. The gang was caught and sent to jail.

GEOFFREY JACKSON, the British Ambassador to Uruguay, was held by left-wing guerrillas for eight months in 1971. He was released unharmed.

JOHN MCCARTHY, TERRY WAITE and **BRIAN KEENAN** – two British, one Irish – were abducted separately in Beirut in 1986 and 1987 by Shi'ite Moslems and held for over $4^1/_2$ years.

BARBARA MACKLE, the daughter of a wealthy Florida builder, was buried alive for 83 hours while her kidnappers (who were later caught and jailed) fled. Her first words to her rescuers were: "You're the handsomest men I've ever seen."

PATTY HEARST, a 19-year-old heiress, was kidnapped by the Symbionese Liberation Army in California in 1974 – and joined them. She took part in a bank robbery and ended up in jail.

THE KRAY TWINS

Sixties gangsters Reggie and Ronnie Kray loved to mingle with film stars and boxers in their West End nightclub. But finally the law caught up with them after Reggie butchered small-time hoodlum Jack 'The Hat' McVitie, and they were sentenced to life. When Ronnie died in 1995 in Broadmoor Hospital for the Criminally Insane, Reggie made a brief public appearance at his funeral, a showy affair attended by hosts of celebs.

LIFELINES

FRANZ KAFKA *(1883-1924) was a huge influence on both writers and film-makers. A Czech, he wrote his dark, tortured novels such as The Trial in German. He was played by Jeremy Irons in the 1991 film Kafka.*

BILLIE JEAN KING *was one of the most competitive tennis players ever. Born in 1943, she is equally fierce about women's rights in sport, and beat 1939 Wimbledon champion Bobby Riggs after he challenged her to a battle of the sexes.*

RUDYARD KIPLING'S *Jungle Books added to most people's childhood entertainment long before Disney released their film potential. Born in Bombay in 1865, Kipling was a fine short story writer and the first Englishman to win a Nobel Prize for literature. He died in 1936.*

1901
TEXAS OIL BOOM
A vast oil well was discovered at Spindletop Hill, near Beaumont, East Texas. From there, a number of global oil companies developed, including Texaco and Gulf.

1902
THE FIRST FINGERPRINT CONVICTION
The first conviction made on the basis of fingerprint evidence came after a house in Denmark Hill, London, was broken into and some billiard balls stolen. Known villain Harry Jackson left a clear thumb-print on a newly painted window-sill. He was jailed for seven years after admitting other burglaries.

1903
FIRST TOUR DE FRANCE
The first Tour de France, the world's best known cycling race, was held with about 60 competitors facing a gruelling route from Paris to Marseilles and back over three weeks.

LANGUAGES

THEN In the Middle Ages the world's lingua franca was Latin. How many languages were spoken worldwide 1000 years ago can only be a matter of speculation, but it was surely more than now. The last speaker of Manx died this century, a minor celeb pictured on postcards. But dying languages *can* survive: Hebrew was resuscitated in the new state of Israel, while Catalan, suppressed under Franco, is now thriving.

NOW There are still several thousand languages spoken in the world: about 1000 Native American languages, 1000 African, and 700 on New Guinea alone. India has over 150, Russia 100, and China several dozen. But fewer than 100 of these are spoken by 95 per cent of the world's population. Chinese accounts for 20 per cent alone, followed by English, Spanish, Russian and Hindi. It is American English, however, which has asserted itself as the international language. The only remaining indigenous languages in Britain are English, Welsh, Irish and Gaelic, while the most commonly spoken foreign language is the Indian dialect Urdu. Here's the same greeting in each of them:

IRISH: *Fáilte chuig an Méle bliain nua*
GAELIC: *Fàilte gu an ath mhìle bliadhna*
URDU: *Khush Amded Sadi-e-nau*
WELSH: *Croeso I'r Mileniwm Newydd*
ENGLISH: *Welcome to the new Millennium!*

THE TOP TEN BOOKS OF ALL TIME
(ACCORDING TO THE MEMBERS OF THE FOLIO SOCIETY)

1. ***LORD OF THE RINGS*** (J R R Tolkien)
2. ***PRIDE AND PREJUDICE*** (Jane Austen)
3. ***DAVID COPPERFIELD*** (Charles Dickens)
4. ***THE COMPLETE PLAYS OF WILLIAM SHAKESPEARE***
5. ***WAR AND PEACE*** (Leo Tolstoy)
6. ***THE WIND IN THE WILLOWS*** (Kenneth Grahame)
7. ***MIDDLEMARCH*** (George Eliot)
8. ***ANIMAL FARM*** (George Orwell)
9. ***TESS OF THE D'URBEVILLES*** (Thomas Hardy)
10. ***THE JUNGLE BOOK*** (Rudyard Kipling)

BURT LANCASTER

The most famous kiss in movie history. Burt Lancaster smooches in the surf with Deborah Kerr in the 1953 classic From Here To Eternity – an embrace made all the more shocking because it was uptight Burt breaking his code of honour. Like his buddy Kirk Douglas, Lancaster played every part as if struggling to contain the volcanic emotions within – an approach that would seem out of place in today's dressed-down cinema (and indeed, in his last two great films, Atlantic City and Local Hero, Lancaster is an ageing man out of his time). He died in 1994, aged 80 – a true Hollywood giant.

D H LAWRENCE

DAVID HERBERT LAWRENCE (1885-1930) WAS THE MARTIN AMIS OF HIS DAY, A WRITER YOU COULD LOVE OR HATE BUT NEVER IGNORE. SONS AND LOVERS (1913) IS A PARTLY AUTOBIOGRAPHICAL ACCOUNT OF THE SON OF A REFINED MOTHER AND VIOLENT FATHER. WOMEN IN LOVE (1920) AND LADY CHATTERLEY'S LOVER (1928) EXPRESSED HIS VIEW THAT WESTERN CULTURE HAD BEEN ALIENATED BY INDUSTRIALISATION, AND NEEDED TO REDISCOVER ITS PRIMITIVE INSTINCTS. BUT IT WAS THE DELIBERATELY PROVOCATIVE SEX SCENES THAT GOT HIS BOOKS BANNED.

1903
INVENTION OF THE AIRPLANE
The first airplane was devised and built by Orville and Wilbur Wright in Dayton, Ohio. It made its first successful flight, lasting 12 seconds, on December 17, 1903.

1904
PANAMA CANAL
Construction of this impressive shipping canal, running between southern and central America and linking the Atlantic and Pacific oceans, was begun in 1904 and completed ten years later.

1905
SPARKLING NEWS
The largest ever diamond, the 3,106-carat Cullinan, was found in Pretoria, South Africa. It was acquired by Edward VII.

1905
RUSSIAN REVOLUTION
The first Russian Revolution began in 1905 when 500 protesting workers were killed by Czar Nicholas II's troops in St Petersburg – Russia's 'Bloody Sunday'. The second revolutionary movement in 1917 ended the Czar's rule – and his life.

LITERATURE

Books and their original titles

Lady Chatterley's Lover *(D H Lawrence)* Tenderness
Treasure Island *(Robert Louis Stevenson)* The Sea-Cook
Jaws *(Peter Benchley)* The Summer of The Shark
War And Peace *(Leo Tolstoy)* All's Well That Ends Well
Moby Dick *(Herman Melville)* The Whale
Of Mice And Men *(John Steinbeck)* Something That Happened
The Great Gatsby *(F Scott Fitzgerald)* The High-Bouncing Lover
Gone With The Wind *(Margaret Mitchell)* Bå! Ba! Black Sheep
Frankenstein *(Mary Shelley)* Prometheus Unchained
Roots *(Alex Haley)* Before This Anger
The Postman Always Rings Twice *(James M Cain)* Bar-B-Q
The Mill On The Floss *(George Eliot)* Sister Maggie
Portnoy's Complaint *(Philip Roth)* A Jewish Patient Begins His Analysis
A Portrait Of The Artist As A Young Man *(James Joyce)* Stephen Hero
East of Eden *(John Steinbeck)* The Salinas Valley
The Time Machine *(H G Wells)* The Chronic Argonauts
The Man With The Golden Arm *(Nelson Algren)* Night Without Mercy
Catch 22 *(Joseph Heller)* Catch 18

The first lines of ten of the Millennium's greatest novels

... BUT CAN YOU MATCH THE OPENING LINE TO THE NOVEL IT COMES FROM? *(The answers are overleaf)*

Read the ten famous opening lines below, then try to decide...

1 "It was a cold bright day in April, and the clocks were striking 13."

2 "Hale knew, before he had been in Brighton three hours, that they meant to murder him."

3 "As Gregor Samsa woke one morning from uneasy dreams he found himself transformed in his bed into a gigantic insect."

4 "Dr Iannis had enjoyed a satisfactory day in which none of his patients had died or got any worse."

5 "Happy families are all alike, but an unhappy family is unhappy in its own way."

6 "There were 117 psychoanalysts on the Pan Am flight to Vienna and I'd been treated by at least six of them."

7 "On top of everything, the cancer wing was number 13."

8 "The sweat wis lashing oafay Sick Boy; he wis trembling."

9 "It is a truth universally acknowledged, that a single man in possession of a good fortune must be in want of a wife."

10 "The Mole had been working very hard all morning, spring-cleaning his little home."

... which novel does each come from?

- **A** ***The Wind in the Willows*** by Kenneth Grahame
- **B** ***Cancer Ward*** by Aleksandr Solzhenitsyn
- **C** ***Brighton Rock*** by Graham Greene
- **D** ***Pride and Prejudice*** by Jane Austen
- **E** ***Anna Karenina*** by Leo Tolstoy
- **F** ***Fear of Flying*** by Erica Jong
- **G** ***Trainspotting*** by Irvine Welsh
- **H** ***1984*** by George Orwell
- **I** ***Metamorphosis*** by Franz Kafka
- **J** ***Captain Corelli's Mandolin*** by Louis de Bernières

LADY CHATTERLEY'S LOVER

Lady Chatterley is Connie, the unhappy wife of English aristocrat Sir Clifford, whose impotence (due to a war wound) is echoed by his emotional frigidity.

She runs away with her gamekeeper, Mellors, a strong, forthright individualist whose work with nature means that he has not been contaminated by industry.

This being D H Lawrence, there is plenty of frank language and graphic love-making, though hardly anything that would now be considered shocking. Nevertheless, it was seized upon by the British authorities and banned as an immoral work after its publication in 1928.

Only in 1960 was 'the English language's best-known dirty book' made available to the British public again, with the novelty of being able to read this 'smut' on the tube (right). Penguin won a famous case, with the likes of E M Forster and John Mortimer testifying that the book had 'redeeming value'. The decision opened a new era of freedom in publishing.

LIFELINES

***Joe Louis**, born in 1914, was a great boxer and folk hero. The Brown Bomber, who died in 1981, made a record 25 defences of his world heavyweight title, each causing joy in Harlem, where he headed a revue at the Apollo.*

***Arthur Lowe** was probably Britain's best-loved character actor. Born in 1914, he found fame as Leonard Swindley in Coronation Street, but was even more pompous (and funnier) as Captain Mainwaring in Dad's Army. He died in 1982.*

***Laurel & Hardy** were the original odd couple, making the world laugh in both silent films and talkies. The thin, watery-eyed Englishman Stan Laurel (1890-1965) and fat, self-important American Oliver Hardy (1892-1957) made over 200 movies.*

1906
San Francisco Earthquake
One of the worst earthquakes of the second millennium occurred on April 18, 1906, in San Francisco. The resulting fires destroyed large areas of the city and about 700 people died.

1906
The First Corn Flakes
Corn 'flakes' produced by the Battle Creek Toasted Cornflake Company of Michigan went on sale for the first time. Will K Kellogg, founder of the company, said that customers just needed to add milk and sugar and they would immediately have a healthy breakfast ready to eat.

1907
The First Mothers' Day
Anna Jarvis, an early American feminist who ran a women's suffrage and temperance movement in Philadelphia, pioneered the idea of a Mothers' Day. It caught on around the world.

LIFELINES

***V I Lenin** led the Russian revolution of 1917, forming the first Communist state. Born in 1870, he lived in exile until his war-torn country sought new leadership. He died in 1924 and was embalmed in a Red Square mausoleum.*

***David Lloyd George** was a fiery Welsh orator who became Prime Minister during the First World War. A Liberal, born in 1863, he introduced the old age pension and unemployment insurance during his 55 years as an MP. He died in 1945.*

***Abraham Lincoln**, born in 1809, was elected President of the Union in 1860 but he failed to stop the secession of the South, and brother killed brother in the Civil War that ensued. Five days after the South surrendered in 1865, the man they called Honest Abe was assassinated.*

LEONARDO DA VINCI

Leonardo da Vinci was *the* Renaissance man. Not just one of the world's great painters, his genius extended to anatomy, astronomy, botany, geometry and geology.

Born in Vinci, Italy, in 1452, Leonardo became court artist to the Duke of Milan, where he painted his magnificent *The Last Supper* (above) in 1498 on a wall in the monastery of Santa Maria delle Grazie.

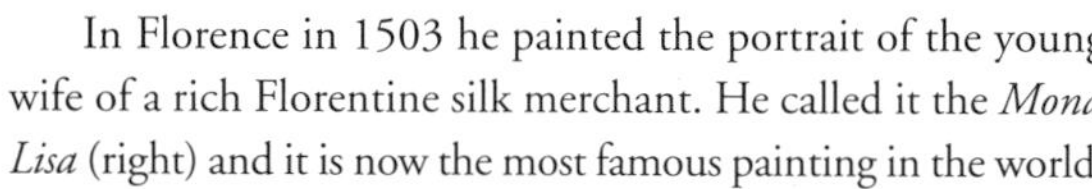

In Florence in 1503 he painted the portrait of the young wife of a rich Florentine silk merchant. He called it the *Mona Lisa* (right) and it is now the most famous painting in the world.

From 1515 until his death in 1519, he served as 'first painter and engineer and architect' to Francis I of France, and his notebooks show a torrent of prophetic ideas. Studying the flight of birds, he drew up hundreds of inventions, including the parachute and the helicopter. (Modern inventors who have built some of his designs are amazed at their accuracy.)

He transformed the art of drawing, making anatomical sketches which didn't just show the parts of the body with unprecedented precision, but explained their interaction too. Few of his paintings have survived the Millennium, but those we do have are almost literally priceless.

The Last Supper (above) has caused a fuss for 500 years. Leonardo painted it on a refectory wall, to give the impression that Christ and the disciples were actually in the dining room, and the painted plaster soon began to flake. It has been restored eight times, but never to critics' satisfaction. The latest remake, unveiled in 1999, has been called a pastiche of a Leonardo. If so, it's a fate that has befallen him often before. The Mona Lisa is the world's most parodied picture, having been 'redone' Dada-style by Marcel Duchamp in 1919, Pop-style by Andy Warhol in 1980, smoking a joint and even as a cat. Ask her what she thinks of it herself and she'll just smile enigmatically…

THE LOTTERY

'It could be you' was the infuriatingly tempting slogan which in 1994 launched Britain's first national lottery since 1826. To the original Saturday night draw were added Scratchcards (1995), a Wednesday draw (1997) and the Easy Play game (1998). The biggest lottery spend came in 1996, when Britons shelled out £128 million in hope of a £42 million rollover. The lottery's popularity has declined, but 61 per cent of households still took part in 1998. By 1999 the lottery had raised £6.6 billion for the arts, charities, heritage, sport and Millennium projects such as village halls and cycleways – with £44 million going on Year 2000 festivities, centring on the Millennium Dome.

'Best of luck for the future and please play the National Lottery again'

From a National Lottery letter to Paul Maddison in 1995 – accompanying a cheque for £22,590,830

FAMOUS LAST WORDS

"I'm still alive." – *Caligula*

"OK, I won't." – *Elvis Presley, after his girlfriend told him not to fall asleep in the bathroom*

"Sir, I beg your pardon." – *Marie Antoinette, to her executioner, after she accidentally trod on his foot*

"Dying is a very dull affair. My advice to you is to have nothing whatever to do with it." – *W Somerset Maugham*

"Never felt better." – *Douglas Fairbanks Sr*

The first lines of ten great novels (see previous page)
1-H, 2-C, 3-I, 4-J, 5-E, 6-F, 7-B, 8-G, 9-D, 10-A

Millennium Time Line

1907 First Boy Scouts
British army officer Lieutenant General Robert SS Baden-Powell held the first Boy Scouts' camp. His sister Agnes started the Girl Guides in 1910.

1908 Debut of the Model T
Henry Ford's Model T, a 'universal car' designed for the masses, went on sale. Ford famously offered customers "any colour they like, so long as it's black".

1908 First Beauty Contest
Britain's first international beauty contest was held at the Pier Hippodrome in Folkestone, Kent.

1909 The South Africa Act
A historic Act which brought together the British colonies of the Cape, Natal, Transvaal and Orange Free State established an all-white South African government, denied the black majority the right to vote and led, later, to the system of segregated society known as apartheid.

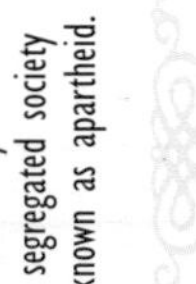

THE LOCH NESS MONSTER

There was a monster in Loch Ness a millennium ago, or so seventh-century Saint Adamnan believed. This famous 1934 photo is actually a fake, but that did not stop Cheers star Ted Danson and pals visiting the Scottish Highlands in 1996 to make Loch Ness – a film seen almost as rarely as Nessie herself.

CARL LEWIS

There was no finer sight in athletics throughout the Millennium than Carl Lewis bounding up the long-jump runway on the way to yet another gold medal. This extraordinary American athlete won the Olympic long jump title four times – culminating in an astonishing victory in 1996 at the age of 35 – and collected nine gold medals in all. In 1984 he equalled Jesse Owens' feat of winning the long jump, 100 metres, 100 metres relay and 200 metres, but his 100 metres triumph in 1988 was tarnished when it came by dint of Ben Johnson's drugs disqualification. No one ever accused Lewis of cheating…

LORD LUCAN

Richard 'Lucky' Lucan has been seen as often as Nessie since the 1974 night when he vanished after his estranged wife Veronica found their children's nanny Sandra Rivett beaten to death in their London home. The earl's car was found abandoned by the sea, and Lady Lucan accused him of murder and then suicide.

LIFE ON EARTH

"There is no mystery in the almost universal interest in television films about natural history. Unlike so much of what is on television, such films are about reality."

David Attenborough should know, having made innumerable wonderful nature series in his 47-year career – the greatest being the worldwide hit *Life on Earth* (1974), which made TV superstars of both Britain's favourite naturalist and the mountain gorillas of Rwanda. A Millennium masterpiece indeed.

1909 Marconi's Prize
Italian physicist Guglielmo Marconi received the Nobel Prize for physics in 1909 for establishing modern radio communications.

1910 King Deposed
King Manuel II became the last King of Portugal when he was deposed by a revolt and the country became a republic.

1910 Get a Job Here
The first 80 Labour Exchanges opened in Britain offering jobs to the unemployed. Later, they were to be renamed Job Centres.

1911 Amundsen Wins Race to The South Pole
Norwegian explorer Roald Amundsen won the race to be the first man at the South Pole. He made it on December 14, 1911. A British team, led by Captain Robert Scott (Scott of the Antarctic), would not arrive until the following month, only to find a Norwegian flag in place. Heartbroken Scott and his team all perished on the return journey, just 11 miles from a supply base.

MICHELANGELO

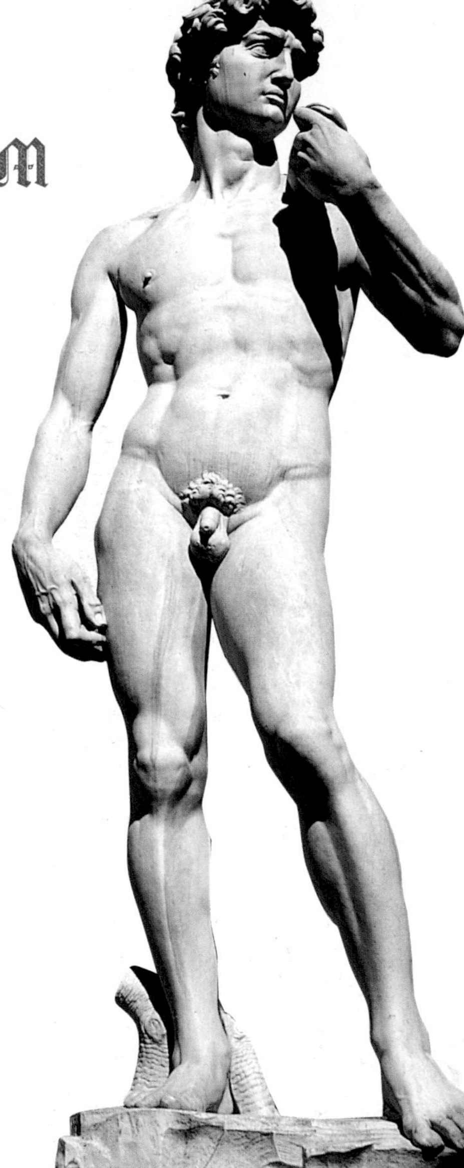

Five hundred years young, Michelangelo's Sistine Chapel ceiling still draws huge crowds, while the Creation of Adam (above) recently inspired the film E.T. and ads for BT. It could be the greatest painting of the Millennium – while his David (left) may be the greatest sculpture

Painter, sculptor, architect, poet and giant of the Renaissance, Michelangelo has been called the greatest artist who ever lived. His paintings and sculptures depict figures of great power and emotional intensity, whose energy seems to lift them beyond the merely human.

His marble statue of David (left) portrays the leader of the Israelites as a fierce warrior – part adolescent potential and part ideal manhood. It became the symbol of a new Florentine republic. Such was Michelangelo's enthusiasm that he would dissect corpses to understand their workings. The same enthusiasm also led him to take on vast projects that were almost beyond him.

Pope Julian II commissioned him to paint the vaulting ceiling of the Sistine Chapel in the Vatican, which took four years and culminated in nine scenes from the Book of Genesis, including the famous *Creation of Adam* (above). The technique is fresco, paint applied quickly to damp plaster. From 1536 to 1541 he worked on *The Last Judgment*, a fresco for the altar wall of the Sistine Chapel. A single scene covering the entire wall represents the resurrection and mankind's day of reckoning, with souls spilling from tombs towards Heaven or Hell.

The work was criticised for its nudity and several of the figures were later 'dressed' by a disciple – only to be undressed by restorers in the 1990s. It remains arguably the greatest artwork of the Millennium.

'I am dying just as I am beginning to learn the alphabet of my profession'

MICHELANGELO BUONAROTTI, 1564, ON HIS DEATHBED, AGED 89

1911
KILLER GUST
Freak weather conditions in Bradford, Yorkshire, in February, caused a gust of wind to pick up a schoolgirl and lift her 20 feet off the ground. The fall, as the wind dropped, killed the unfortunate child.

1912
TITANIC GOES DOWN
White Star Line's *Titanic*, the world's largest and most luxurious ocean liner, was believed to be unsinkable. But on April 14, 1912, four days into its maiden voyage from Southampton to New York, it hit an iceberg and sank. Of the 2,224 people on board, 1,515 perished.

1912
CHILD EMPEROR ABDICATES
China's five-year-old boy-emperor Pu Yi unknowingly abdicated following a nationalist rebellion which established a new republic. Pu Yi's weeping aunt stood beside him as she read out the deed of abdication ending the 267-year rule of the Qing dynasty and 3,000 years of monarchy.

MAGNA CARTA

The Magna Carta is the foundation stone of the English system of government which has been adopted as a democratic model worldwide.

The 'Great Charter' was triggered by the actions of King John, who came to the throne in 1199. There were no limits to John's powers and he abused them fully, increasing taxes willy-nilly, selling royal positions to the highest bidder and deciding court cases arbitrarily. In 1213 a group of barons and church leaders demanded an end to John's injustices, and raised an army to force the King's hand.

In June 1215 he signed their list of rights (left) at Runnymede, a meadow by the Thames near London.

Though the Magna Carta protected the rights of aristocrats, it did little for the people at large. But it placed a check on royal power. Its 63 articles granted church freedom from royal interference, forbade the raising of taxes without the barons' consent, and decreed that no man could be imprisoned without the lawful judgment of his peers.

These would later be the basis of English law and were used in the 17th century in establishing Parliament as a representative law-making body.

THE MONARCHY

1760-1820
KING GEORGE III

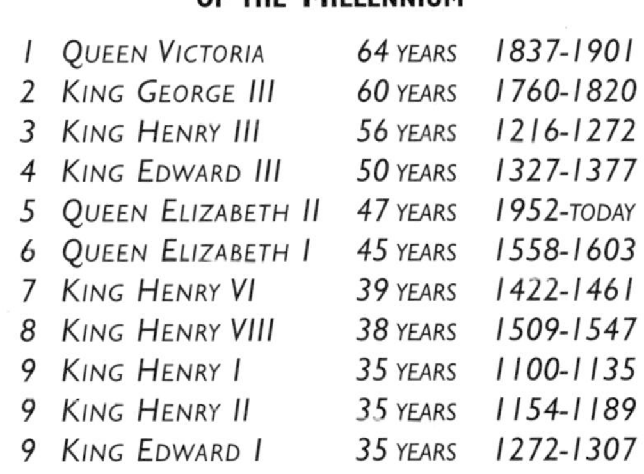

The longest-serving British monarchs of the Millennium

1	Queen Victoria	64 years	1837-1901
2	King George III	60 years	1760-1820
3	King Henry III	56 years	1216-1272
4	King Edward III	50 years	1327-1377
5	Queen Elizabeth II	47 years	1952-today
6	Queen Elizabeth I	45 years	1558-1603
7	King Henry VI	39 years	1422-1461
8	King Henry VIII	38 years	1509-1547
9	King Henry I	35 years	1100-1135
9	King Henry II	35 years	1154-1189
9	King Edward I	35 years	1272-1307

1100-1135
KING HENRY I

1558-1603
QUEEN ELIZABETH I

1837-1901
QUEEN VICTORIA

1272-1307
KING EDWARD I

LIFELINES

MARY, QUEEN OF SCOTS, led a life of drama. Born in 1542 while her father was dying, she was Queen of Scotland at a week old. At 16, marriage made her Queen of France. When her husband died, she returned to Scotland, but in 1568 the people turned against her and she fled to England. Her cousin Elizabeth I, seeing her as a threat, imprisoned her for 19 years and finally had her beheaded in 1587.

MARIE ANTOINETTE had a simple solution to the starving French people's plea that they had no bread: "Let them eat cake." Born in 1755, the daughter of the all-powerful Empress Maria Theresa of Austria, she married Louis XVI of France – and dominated him. Her blatant extravagance helped provoke the French Revolution, and both she and Louis were duly guillotined in 1793.

1912 THAMES TUNNEL The Woolwich Tunnel was opened under the River Thames in London.

1914 'THE WAR TO END WAR' Outbreak of the First World War. The four-year conflict cost nine million lives, with another 27 million injured. Survivors believed they had fought 'the war to end all wars'.

1915 TRAIN DISASTER More than 200 Scots Guards on their way to the war in France were killed when three trains collided near Gretna Green. Shocked survivors, staggering from the scene, were mistaken by local people for German prisoners of war and were stoned.

1915 THE FIRST ZEPPELINS Aerial bombardment of Britain began for the first time. German Zeppelin airships dropped bombs on King's Lynn and Great Yarmouth, killing more than 20 people.

MARILYN MONROE

Norma Jean Baker was born in poverty in 1926, an abused orphan who married a small-town policeman at 16. By the time of her death at the age of just 36, she was a screen goddess, the reputed lover of the President, and the greatest sex symbol of all time.

It was a heady journey, and an uneasy one. Norma shot to fame as Marilyn Monroe in a series of sexpot roles in which her powerful sensuality and hour-glass figure obscured her gift for comic acting.

By the time she was getting parts that allowed her to play it for laughs or show some range – *The Seven Year Itch* (1955), *Bus Stop* (1956), *The Prince and the Showgirl* (1957) – her personal life was disintegrating. She agonised over the imperfections of her image, despite – or perhaps because of – being a fantasy figure for millions of men. Her marriages to all-American heroes (baseball legend Joe DiMaggio, playwright Arthur Miller) did not provide the security she craved.

Desperate to be taken seriously as an actress, she went back to study at Lee Strasberg's Actors Studio – the cradle of Method – and her final films, among them *Some Like It Hot* (1959) and *The Misfits* (1961), were her best.

In hindsight she seems most at ease in her many musical numbers: 'I Want to be Loved by You', 'Diamonds Are a Girl's Best Friend', 'My Heart Belongs to Daddy'…

But the culture which had propelled her to unimaginable stardom did nothing to protect her from the personal consequences. On August 5, 1962, her housekeeper found her dead, an empty bottle of sedatives by her side. A sex object soon becomes a thing, Marilyn once observed. "I hate being a thing."

Marilyn Monroe surrounded by letters from admirers in 1952. One of the most adored women in the world, who could literally have drowned in her weekly fan mail, she was also one of the loneliest…

MADONNA

If a pop star aims to set the agenda, then Madonna – born Madonna Louise Ciccone in 1958 – is the ultimate star. Ever in the right place at the right time, her rise paralleled that of the music video.

'Like a Virgin' and 'Material Girl' – the anthem of the materialistic Eighties – set out her stall: raw sexuality, girl power, lapsed Catholicism, and an obsession with iconic women such as Marilyn Monroe. Teenage girls everywhere took to exposing their midriffs and wearing giant crucifixes.

Restlessly inventive, Madonna tried on a succession of images: haute couture, erotica, grunge, mysticism. She won the star role in *Evita*, and made it a success. After the failure of her marriage to Brat Pack actor Sean Penn, she had a daughter, Lourdes, with her personal trainer.

'A woman who pulled herself up by the bra straps'

Bette Midler on Madonna

Still a chart-topper, she is the most powerful woman in pop, with her own publishing, film and recording companies – no wonder *Forbes* magazine dubbed her America's Smartest Businesswoman. Even now she never fails to surprise, not least by signing up to advertise Max Factor make-up on TV. Surely she can't need the cash?

1916
Lawrence of Arabia
English army lieutenant Thomas Edward Lawrence became a guerrilla fighter helping the Arabs in their struggle against the Ottoman Empire. Portrayed as a hero and flamboyant character by the Press, he became known as Lawrence of Arabia. His story was told in the Oscar-winning David Lean film of 1962, starring Peter O'Toole.

1916
First Birth Clinic
Margaret Sanger, a nurse who worked among the poor in New York, opened a birth control clinc in Brooklyn. It was the first of its kind.

1917
Execution of Mata Hari
Her real name was Margarete Gertrude Zelle, a Dutch-born dancer working in Paris during the First World War. Using the stage name Mata Hari, she took a number of influential men as lovers and is thought to have spied for both France and Germany. The French executed her for espionage.

LIFELINES

LIZA MINNELLI *is truly her mother's daughter. Born in 1946, Liza took after Judy Garland as a child singer/dancer/actress, and became a star in 1972 when she won an Oscar for Cabaret. A 1994 hip replacement has slowed her career.*

GUSTAV MAHLER *(1860-1911) is the link from 19th to 20th century music. The Austrian's ten symphonies are so complex that No 8 is known as the Symphony of A Thousand because it requires so many musicians and singers.*

ED MOSES *ran the 400-metres hurdles 122 times between 1977 and 1987 without defeat. A double Olympic and World Champion, Moses, born in 1955, used his prominence to improve other athletes' lot.*

MARRIAGE

THEN Under ancient English law, a girl could marry at 12 and a boy at 14 – a tightening-up of the original church law which put the ages at 11 and 13. Children as young as seven could lawfully contract marriage – often to cement economic ties between two families – which would turn into marriage proper as soon as the young couple were capable of consummating their relationship. Marriages would be avoided during Lent and Advent, when the Church banned sexual relations. Most marriages took place between harvest and Christmas – when supplies for wedding feasts would be plentiful.

NOW Until the latter half of this century, and especially in Catholic countries, to 'live in sin' or to divorce your partner was to court scandal. Today, cohabitation and divorce are the norm. The number of non-married women cohabiting in Britain has doubled since 1981, to 25 per cent. Remarriages now account for two-fifths of all marriages. In 1996, there were 185,000 first marriages – half the 1970 total. The average age for first-time brides and grooms has risen to 27 and 29 years old respectively.

MARRIAGE ADDICTS

MARRIED NINE TIMES

Hollywood celeb Zsa Zsa Gabor, Beach Boy Mike Love

MARRIED EIGHT TIMES

Child stars Mickey Rooney, Elizabeth Taylor (twice to Richard Burton)

MARRIED SEVEN TIMES

Forties 'Sweater Girl' Lana Turner, comedian Richard Pryor, Stan Laurel (three times to the same woman; his partner Oliver Hardy married four times)

MARRIED SIX TIMES

Silent movie queen Gloria Swanson (who married for the sixth time at 79), Sir Rex Harrison, Johnny 'Tarzan' Weissmuller, King Henry VIII, TV presenter Larry King, novelists Harold Robbins and Norman Mailer, actress Hedy Lamarr, country stars Steve Earle, Jerry Lee Lewis and Tom Mix

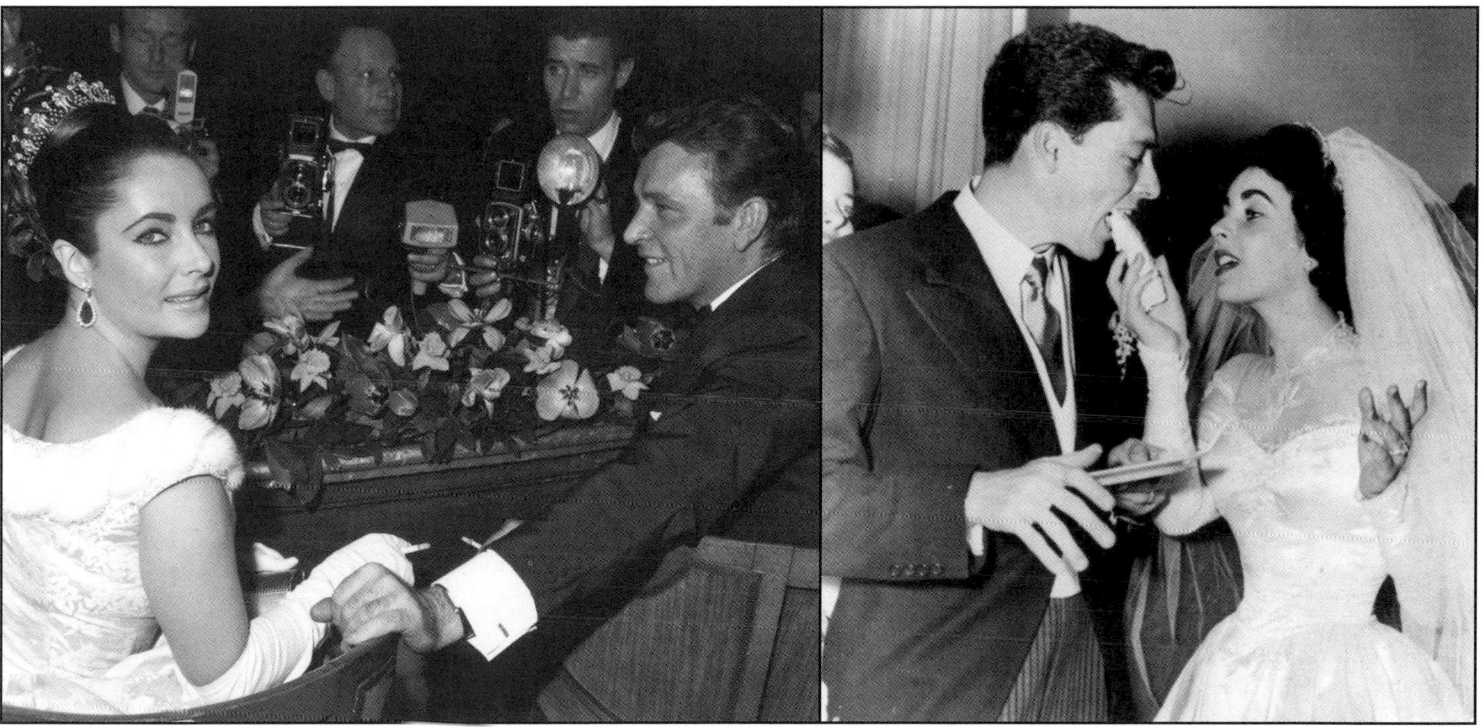

Elizabeth Taylor married her Cleopatra co-star Richard Burton in 1964 (above left) and again in 1975. The first of her weddings was in 1950 to Nick Hilton

McDONALD'S

McDonald's is the burger that ate the planet. If capitalism has conquered the world for good, then McDonald's must be its proudest cheerleader. By the end of 1999, the largest global 'food-service retailer' will have 25,000 restaurants in 115 countries. The McDonald's Golden Arches adorn premises from Tahiti to Belarus, from the Arctic Circle to New Zealand. Though the meals are famously the same wherever you go, there is the odd local variation: beef-free burgers in India, McChicken Korma Naans in Britain, pastries and espresso in Portugal. Net income for the year 1998 was £1 billion. So stable and all-pervasive is the Big Mac that *The Economist* has even adopted it as a yardstick for comparing currency values.

1917 RUSSIAN REVOLUTION Beginning with the forced abdication of Czar Nicholas II, and ending with the installation of a Communist regime led by Lenin, the Russian Revolution of 1917 was to bring about the birth of the Union of Soviet Socialist Republics. The Czar and his family were at first held prisoner, but were later taken to some woods outside St Petersburg and shot dead.

1917 BUFFALO BILL IS DEAD William 'Buffalo Bill' Cody died, aged 71. Originally a Pony Express rider, he fought in the Civil War, then went into business supplying meat to men building the Kansas Pacific railway, earning his nickname. He went on to scout for the Cavalry and fought in Indian wars. Finally, he set up a travelling Wild West show that toured Europe.

1918 MUTINY BY GERMAN FLEET Mutiny broke out in the German fleet at the port of Kiel. The revolt spread through Germany and led to a general strike in Berlin which paralysed the government.

LIFELINES

George Michael *is arguably Britain's only pop superstar whose career began after the Sixties. Born in 1963, he became a teen idol with Wham! then went solo in 1986, and has even managed to shrug off a high-profile sex conviction.*

Karl Marx's *theories about a classless society led to the rise of communism. A German, born in 1818, he settled in London to write books advocating the overthrow of capitalism, including Das Kapital. He died in 1883.*

W Somerset Maugham *(1874-1965) wrote spy stories based on his time as a secret agent in Russia. But he is best known for such novels as Of Human Bondage and The Moon and Sixpence (about Paul Gauguin).*

MOTOR SPORT

The first lap of the 1989 French Grand Prix came to a sudden end when Mauricio Gugelmin of Brazil had a spectacular crash. The car was destroyed but Gugelmin walked away – and continued the race in a spare car

Henry Ford liked to test new models by racing them on speedways. In 1903, Barney Olfield set a world record of 60mph in his Ford-Cooper 999. Car makers soon saw the benefits of racing as a way to showcase the company; buy a Ferrari or a Jag, and you could share in spirit the victories of the glorious machines at Le Mans (first raced in 1906), Monte Carlo (1911) or the Indianapolis 500 (1911).

The first racing drivers were dashing heroes who disregarded the dangers: Oldfield himself called his sport a 'Roman circus' and spent his last years preaching road safety. But from Britain's Peter Collins (killed in 1954) to Brazil's Ayrton Senna (1994), the lure of speed has always been bound up with the threat of death – which may be one reason why Formula 1 is the world's biggest spectator sport.

The last of the gentleman-swashbucklers was James Hunt, who won a famously tight Drivers' Championship in 1976. Despite increased safety regulations, crashes remain very much part of the attraction. And people will race anything with an engine – from lorries to cars driven backwards.

MOTORING

THEN Britain's first motorists had to put up with the Red Flag Law, which limited the speed of cars in town to just 2mph. In built-up areas, a man with a red flag literally walked in front of cars to enforce the limit. After the law's repeal in 1896, enthusiasts celebrated with an 'emancipation run' from London to Brighton, an event which still takes places every year in November, when vintage (ie pre-1905) crocks aim to reach the seaside town in under eight hours.

NOW Cars, initially used for touring by enthusiasts, were first bought in bulk by farmers and other country folk. Mass production brought demand for better roads. Britain's first stretch of motorway, the Preston bypass (now part of the M6) was completed in 1959. Today there are 2000 miles of motorway, yet traffic speeds are decreasing. The Department of Transport's 'stress maps', which monitor traffic flow, predict that the entire road network will be 'heavily congested' by 2020. The M25, for instance, will be at snail's pace all day, rather than just at peak hours.

STANLEY MATTHEWS

Stanley Matthews was England's greatest footballer. The 'Wizard of Dribble' made his debut for Stoke City at 17 in 1932, played for England for 22 years, and was voted Footballer of the Year at 48 – yes, 48 – after returning to Stoke to get them into the First Division. The first Footballer of the Year and the first European Footballer of the Year, his greatest match was the 1953 FA Cup Final when he mesmerised Bolton Wanderers to bring Blackpool back from 3-1 down to win 4-3.

MICK THE MILLER

The king of greyhounds, Mick the Miller was so famous that on his death in 1939 his body was embalmed and displayed at the Natural History Museum in London. Bred by a parish priest in Ireland, he set many world records, won the English Derby twice, and starred in the film of his life.

1918 The Fourteen Points
Creation of a League of Nations was among the Fourteen Points advocated by President Woodrow Wilson at the end of the First World War. Other points included arms reduction and self-determination for governments.

1919 The First Woman MP
Nancy, Lady Astor, the first female MP, took her seat in the House of Commons on December 1, representing Portsmouth.

1919 Nazi Party Founded
The Nazi Party was founded in Munich, Germany in 1919. Adolf Hitler was elected chairman in 1921.

1920 America Bans Alcohol
The manufacture, distribution and consumption of alcohol became illegal in the United States on January 16, 1920. But the highly unpopular law became impossible to enforce and was repealed in 1933.

MANCHESTER UNITED

Manchester United celebrate one of their greatest triumphs – winning the Premiership in 1999. The team went on to win the FA Cup and the European Cup, all in the space of ten days. Below: United's darkest hour, when their Elizabethan aircraft crashed while trying to take off in a snow storm in Munich. England prodigy Duncan Edwards was among eight players killed

In the folklore of football, no team in the world has experienced such extremes of tragedy and glory as Manchester United. Their place in the world's hearts was cemented by a terrible accident. In 1958, a plane carrying the Busby Babes – a young Manchester team of great promise managed by Sir Matt Busby – crashed during take-off on an icy runway at Munich, killing 23 people including eight players.

They were on their way back from playing Red Star Belgrade in the European Cup – a competition which they would become the first English team to win, a decade later, inspired by the supernaturally gifted George Best. By then, too, Bobby Charlton, a survivor of the Munich air disaster, had helped England to its moment of World Cup glory in 1966.

By the end of the 1999 season, the current United team had outdone even its own illustrious past with a unique treble of the League, FA Cup and European Cup. From Peter Schmeichel's 11th-hour penalty save against Arsenal in the FA Cup semi-final to their incredible comebacks against Juventus

and then Bayern Munich in the European Cup, there was an air of invincibility about this squad.

Awarded a corner as they trailed 1-0 against Bayern in the dying seconds of the European Cup Final, a TV commentator wailed, "They must score! They always score!" The excruciating pleasure of football derives from our very inability to influence events in this way. And yet score United did – twice. As a way to end the Millennium, it could not have seemed more right.

MARADONA

Diego Maradona was the only footballer to live up to the mantle of the 'new Pele'. With his stocky build, great skill and strength, he ran rings round defenders – as when he slalomed half the length of the pitch to score against England in the World Cup quarter-final in 1986, soon after his notorious 'Hand of God' goal. He led Argentina to victory in that World Cup (left) and to the Final in 1990, but was banned in 1991 for taking drugs. He started the 1994 World Cup, only to test positive again. On his comeback – after training with Ben Johnson! – he was done for drugs yet again and retired in 1997 on his 37th birthday. He plans to play himself in the film of his life.

1921
First Birth Control Clinic
Britain's first birth control clinic, run by Dr Marie Stopes, opened in London. Her frank and open speaking about sex shocked many and her advocation of contraception for all caused her to be ridiculed by the Press.

1921
Communism in China
The Chinese Communist Party was established in 1921, although it did not achieve power until after the Second World War.

1922
Fascists on the March
Fascist Blackshirts carried out their 'March on Rome' from Naples. It led to Benito Mussolini coming to power as a dictator.

1922
The Irish Free State
The Irish Parliament voted in favour of adopting a constitution for an Irish Free State. It was formally established before the end of the year. The name was used until 1937 while Ireland was a dominion within the British Commonwealth. The name was changed to Eire in 1932. In 1949, it was proclaimed a republic.

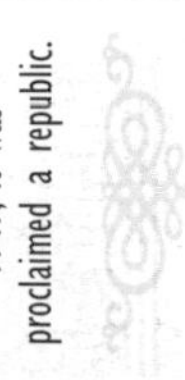

MODS AND ROCKERS

The rockers came first. They grew out of the Teddy boys of the Fifties, casting off the Edwardian drape coats and crepe-soled brothel creepers to put on leather jackets and winklepickers and go for burn-ups on their Norton motorbikes. The Mods arrived with the Swinging Sixties, in their neat little hipsters and button-down collars, riding their neat little Vespas and Lambrettas. And they hated the rockers on sight. So they liked nothing better than all riding down to Brighton on a bank holiday weekend and trying to beat each other to a pulp. By the mid-Sixties, every teenager in Britain wanted to be a Mod and the rockers spent most of their bank holiday time on the run. Later generations sanctified the Mods through the music of The Jam and the film Quadrophenia, but the rockers' legacy lives on in the form of the leather jacket. Unlike hipsters, it's one fashion that will never go away.

GLENN MILLER

Glenn Miller, born in 1904, was the American danceband leader whose music provided the great escape for ordinary people during the Second World War. Tunes like 'In The Mood' and 'Moonlight Serenade' hold bittersweet memories for millions. He died when his plane was lost over the English Channel in 1944.

BOB MARLEY

Bob Marley put reggae on the world map. With songs such as 'No Woman No Cry', 'Could You Be Loved' and 'I Shot the Sheriff', the dreadlocked Jamaican Rastafarian made reggae part of the rock vocabulary. He died from a brain tumour, aged 36, in May 1981.

MOZART

Wolfgang Amadeus Mozart was the Millennium's most brilliant child prodigy and probably its greatest musical genius. Born in Salzburg, Austria, in 1756, he soon mastered the clavier, violin and organ, and did a concert tour at the age of six with his sister that included a performance in the Viennese court of the Empress Maria Theresa. He wrote his first minuet at five, wrote a symphony at nine and his first opera at 14.

Able to write complex compositions in his head, Mozart wrote more than 50 symphonies and 27 piano concertos, as well as such great operas as *The Marriage Of Figaro*, *Don Giovanni*, *Cosi Fan Tutte* and *The Magic Flute.* Sadly, his financial acumen did not match his musical ability and he fell deeply in debt before his death in 1791. Composing frantically, he once wrote three symphonies in seven weeks.

Though the film *Amadeus* suggested that Mozart was murdered by jealous Italian composer Salieri, the theory seems unfounded. Even so, such is the fascination of Mozart and his music that Salzburg has become a place of pilgrimage.

1922
TUTANKHAMEN'S TOMB
Tutankhamen was king of Egypt from 1361-1352BC and died aged about 18. His virtually untouched tomb, filled with fabulous treasure, was discovered by English Egyptologist Howard Carter and Lord Carnarvon in 1922. It was one of the greatest archaeological discoveries. The death of Carnarvon during excavations and the fact that in England his dog died at the same time, confirmed the conviction of some people that the tomb was cursed.

1923
IT'S TIME FOR BIG BEN
The chimes of Big Ben were heard in London for the first time on December 31, 1923.

1924
DEATH OF LENIN
Vladimir Lenin, architect of the 1917 Russian Revolution, died of a brain haemorrhage in 1924. His preserved body was kept in a tomb in Moscow's Red Square and was a national shrine until the collapse of the Soviet Union in 1991.

MOTOWN

The Supremes

Motown, the music factory from the Motor City, provided the soundtrack for a generation. In 1959, Berry Gordy, a failed Detroit record store owner turned rhythm and blues songwriter who had formed his own production company, was persuaded by one of his artists – Smokey Robinson – to start a record label. He called it Tamla Motown…

The Supremes, Martha and the Vandellas, Little Stevie Wonder, The Four Tops, The Temptations, The Miracles, Marvin Gaye and later the Jackson 5 formed a stable that unleashed a torrent of polished love songs with catchy hooks, romantic strings, insistent bass lines and jangly tambourines. Behind the artists were a team of dazzling producer-writers led by Holland-Dozier-Holland ('Stop! In The Name of Love', 'Reach Out I'll Be There', 'You Can't Hurry Love') and Smokey Robinson ('My Guy', 'Tracks Of My Tears', 'My Girl'). No wonder Bob Dylan called Robinson "America's greatest living poet".

Gordy oversaw everything, from his artists' finances to their stage attire. In an era when racial tension in the US was rife, Motown's music effortlessly crossed the divide – The Supremes alone scored 12 No 1's in six years. The greatest record company of the Millennium? No contest.

Stevie Wonder

Smokey Robinson

Marvin Gaye

THE MINI

If any artefact proved that small is beautiful, it was the Mini – the most trendy British car of the Millennium.

Designed by Sir Alec Issigonis on the back of an envelope, the garish orange prototype Mini caught the mood of the Swinging Sixties even before its launch on August 26, 1959. Two million of them were sold in six years, the first Minis costing £459. Those eager to splash out included Lord Snowdon, Enzo Ferrari, Steve McQueen, the Aga Khan, Paul McCartney, Peter Sellers, Spike Milligan and George Harrison. More recent Mini fans have included David Bowie and Kate Moss.

Prince Charles bought one for Diana a year after they were married, while the Queen once took a famous ride around Windsor Park in a Mini, driven by Issigonis. The classic Mini escapade – the chase scene in the 1969 movie *The Italian Job* – was re-created 30 years later for a Martini advert, bringing the Mini back into style.

1924 Olympic Non-Runner
Deeply religious athlete Eric Liddell refused to run in the 100-metre heats at the Paris Olympics because they fell on a Sunday. But during the week he won the 400 metres in record-breaking time. His story was later told in the film *Chariots of Fire*.

1924 Beginning of Tyranny
Josef Stalin took control of the Communist Party, and the Soviet Union, following Lenin's death. Hailed as a great leader at the time, he became known as one of the world's cruellest dictators, responsible for millions of deaths.

1925 The Age of Television
John Logie Baird invented television in 1925. On January 27, 1926, members of the Royal Institute were given a demonstration at Baird's workshop in London's Soho.

1926 Emperor Enthroned
Michinomiya Hirohito was enthroned as Emperor of Japan on December 25, 1926 and was to become the nation's longest-reigning emperor. He died in 1989.

LIFELINES

Eddy Merckx *has been hailed as the greatest of all cyclists. Belgian-born in 1945, the man known as The Cannibal won the Tour de France a joint record five times in 1969-74, plus three world professional road-race championships.*

John Milton *wrote the epic poem Paradise Lost, a landmark in literature. Born in 1608, he went blind in 1652 but still completed his masterpiece in 1667. Paradise Regained followed in 1671, three years before his death.*

Montgomery of Alamein, *born in 1887, was Britain's top Second World War commander. After defeating Rommel in North Africa, he led armies through Italy and France, receiving the German surrender. Monty died in 1976.*

MURDOCH, MAXWELL AND THE MEDIA

At the end of the Millennium, every businessman in Britain wants to be a press baron. It's nothing new – in the 1920s, Max Beaverbrook made the *Daily Express* the cornerstone of a media empire and became a real Baron in the process. The difference in the satellite age is the world scale of the media moguls' ambition.

Beaverbrook was Canadian, and it is notable that his successors have tended to be foreigners. Rupert Murdoch – who owns *The Sun*, the *News of the World* and *The Times*, BSkyB TV and book publisher HarperCollins – was born in Australia in 1931. Already arguably the most powerful person in Britain, he tried in 1999 to buy the football giant Manchester United, but was blocked by the Government.

Murdoch's political influence is huge: when *The Sun* came out in favour of New Labour after decades of fervent Tory support, many wondered aloud what Tony Blair had had to offer Murdoch in exchange.

For an example of media abuse, one need look no further than Robert Maxwell, the Czech adventurer who became a Labour MP in the 1960s before taking over the *Daily Mirror*. Soon after his mysterious death over the side of his yacht in 1991, it emerged that Maxwell had plundered Mirror employees' pension funds to bolster his ailing business interests.

If Murdoch is the shadowy puppeteer, Maxwell's reasons for owning a newspaper were more transparent. He loved to see himself in the *Mirror* and it was said that he ran the newspaper "as a personal bulletin board to communicate with world leaders".

Rupert Murdoch made The Sun into Britain's best-selling daily newspaper. His great innovation was topless Page Three girls, so it caused shockwaves when he took over The Times in 1981. Robert Maxwell was a Labour MP in the 1960s but probably wielded greater power as the owner of The Sun's great rival, the Daily Mirror

MONEY

THEN On his travels to China in the 13th century, Marco Polo was amazed to find that the Chinese used paper money, not coins. "All receive it without hesitation," the Italian wrote, 'because they can dispose of it again in the purchase of merchandise they may require." The idea did not catch on in the West until the 17th century, when banks began issuing notes to depositors which could be exchanged for gold.

NOW In 1971, Britain left behind 'pounds shillings and pence' and switched to a new decimal coinage. Such delights as the threepenny bit and the tanner were henceforth available only in junk shops and coin collections. Later the decimal half-pence made its exit too. The pound note lost out to a chunky coin, which has this year gained a big £2 brother. But the most radical new item of legal tender is the euro, launched on January 4, 1999.

MONOPOLY

The world's favourite board game was launched in 1935. Since then, 160 million sets have been sold, and 500 million people have played it. It has been translated into 25 languages including Afrikaans, Croatian and Catalan, with the place names and currency changed accordingly.

Monopoly was popular among British prisoners of war in the Second World War. Hidden in secret compartments in their boards, which had been specially commissioned by the War Office and delivered by the Red Cross, they found silk maps showing escape routes, compasses and local currency. And they didn't even have to draw the Get Out Of Jail Free card!

Other variations include:

- A £15,000 set made for the underwater Monopoly marathon.
- A Braille edition produced in the 1970s.
- A chocolate Monopoly set, sold for £500.
- A $1 million set made of gold and precious stones by a San Francisco jeweller in 1988.
- A *Star Wars* set and a *Batman and Robin* set, created for Warner Bros stores in 1996.
- A World Cup edition, produced in 1998, with football stadiums in place of hotels and eight new playing pieces – a football, a boot, a whistle, a set of goals, a cap, a drink, a burger and the World Cup trophy.

1926
The General Strike
Britain's first General Strike was called by the TUC to support miners who were already on strike after being told their pay was to be cut. Ports, public transport, post and industry generally came to a halt for nine days. The Army and volunteers kept some essential services working.

1927
First Talking Film
The Jazz Singer, starring Al Jolson, is generally considered to be the first film to be released with integrated sound and vision. It was a huge success.

1927
First Atlantic Flight
American airmail pilot Charles A Lindbergh responded to a challenge from a group of businessmen and flew non-stop across the Atlantic from New York to Paris on May 20, 1927. His flight took over 33 hours, earning him $25,000 in prize money.

GROUCHO MARX

The Marx Brothers were the Millennium's funniest film-makers. The sons of New York German immigrants, they made a stream of madcap movies in the Thirties, including *Duck Soup*, *Horse Feathers*, *A Night at the Opera* and *Go West*. The world loved Harpo the dumb clown and piano-thumping Chico, but when wisecracking Groucho unzipped his lip, it was time to duck for cover...

Some gems of Marxist philosophy

"I don't want to belong to any club that would accept me as a member."

"I eat like a vulture: unfortunately, the resemblance doesn't end there."

"I've been around so long, I knew Doris Day before she was a virgin."

"I never forget a face but I'll make an exception in your case."

"They say a man is as old as the woman he feels."

"Go – and never darken my towels again."

"Only one man in a thousand is a leader of men: the other 999 follow men."

"Groucho isn't my real name, I'm breaking it in for a friend."

"We in this industry know that behind every successful screenwriter stands a woman. And behind her stands his wife."

"Time wounds all heels."

MORECAMBE AND WISE

"Bring me sunshine..." Morecambe and Wise enjoy a special place in the hearts of British performers today. Chris Evans used their signature song when signing off his quiz show *Don't Forget Your Toothbrush*, while Reeves and Mortimer set out to be a Morecambe and Wise for the Nineties.

Eric (1926-84) and Ernie (1925-99) made a successful transition from variety to TV, attracting huge audiences for their Christmas specials with their show-stopping setpieces in which a revered celebrity was expertly removed from his or her plinth. Shirley Bassey was made to sing wearing one stiletto and one hobnail boot, Angela Rippon emerged dancing from behind her newsdesk, and André Previn was ritually humiliated while trying to conduct his orchestra.

Somehow it made sense that they shared a bed. If it was good enough for Laurel and Hardy, it was good enough for them too.

SPIKE MILLIGAN

Spike Milligan is the Godfather of modern British comedy. His butterfly imagination provided most of the material for *The Goon Show*, a surrealistic radio series that ran for nine years from 1951. The Goons opened up a new direction in laughter-making, away from rote sketches and catch phrases to a fantasy world of silly voices and nonsensical plot lines.

Milligan, a sensitive man who has battled with depression all his life, has also written poetry, novels, autobiographies and children's books. Now in his eighties, he jokes: 'Every morning when I wake up I go to my wife and say: 'Who am I?' "

MONTY PYTHON'S FLYING CIRCUS

Between 1969 and 1974, *Monty Python's Flying Circus* was must-see TV. The natural heirs of *The Goons*, the Pythons combined extreme silliness with some savage attacks on the highbrow and the pompous in a free-associating format punctuated by Terry Gilliam's surreal cartoons.

Men in pinstripes – commuters, bank managers, men behind their desks – were their favourite target, and the repressed, over-polite Middle England they stood for.

The Ministry of Silly Walks, the transvestite lumberjack, the 'Summarise Proust' competition (first in bathing costumes, then in evening wear), the dead parrot sketch, the five Alan Whickers (right)... Throughout the English-speaking world the skits were memorised and repeated verbatim.

On the back of their popularity in America, the team went on to make three films: the medieval caper *Monty Python and the Holy Grail* (1975), the satire on Christianity *Monty Python's Life of Brian* (1979) and *Monty Python's Meaning of Life* (1983).

1927
Big Bang Theory
Belgian astronomer Georges Lemaître's theory, proposed in 1927, that the universe began with a huge explosion up to 20 billion years ago, is still accepted by many scientists. Some think the universe will eventually implode, others that it will simply continue expanding and cooling.

1927
First Meals in the Air
The first aircraft hot meals were served on an Imperial Airways flight from London to Paris. But the galley had facilities to provide food for only 18 passengers.

1928
Penicillin Discovered
Scottish bacteriologist Alexander Fleming discovered penicillin. It became – and remains – one of the most commonly used antibiotics.

1928
Oxford English Dictionary
Originally titled *A New English Dictionary on Historical Principles*, this comprehensive dictionary of the English language was first published on April 19, 1928. It had taken over 70 years to compile.

NELSON MANDELA

Nelson Mandela – the prisoner who became President – chivalrously called it "one of the greatest moments of my life" when he met the Spice Girls with Prince Charles in 1997

In 1999, at the age of 80, Nelson Mandela bowed out as President of South Africa. It marked the end of an extraordinary career, in which Mandela became one of the most respected world leaders of the century.

Mandela, who fought against apartheid as part of the African National Congress, was arrested in 1964 and imprisoned for life. The campaign for his release became an international cause, and eventually President F W De Klerk ordered Mandela's release in 1990. (The pair would be awarded the Nobel Peace Prize in 1993.)

After 26 years' captivity, at the age of 75, this dignified man moved rapidly from prisoner to President, without the slightest trace of triumphalism or vengeance.

For four days in April 1994, in the country's first free elections, Africans formed mile-long queues to vote for Mandela's vision of "a new South Africa where all South Africans are equal, where all South Africans work together to bring about security, peace and democracy in our country".

With Mandela now retired, many problems remain for South Africa – but they are the problems of a young democracy, not of a brutal and repressive police state.

'We have waited too long for our freedom. We can no longer wait'

NELSON MANDELA, FEBRUARY 11, 1990, ON THE DAY OF HIS RELEASE, AGED 71

1928
DEATH OF THOMAS HARDY
Novelist and poet Thomas Hardy died, aged 87. His body was interred in Westminster Abbey, close to Charles Dickens, but his heart was buried in the grave of his first wife, Emma, at the parish church of Stinsfield, Wessex. Hardy lived in his beloved Wessex for 40 years and all of his stories were based there.

1929
BIRTH OF YUGOSLAVIA
The Kingdom of Serbs, Croats and Slovenes adopted the name Yugoslavia.

1929
THE GREAT DEPRESSION
The collapse of the American stock market on October 24, 1929 was the start of the Great Depression, dragging Britain, Germany and Japan in its wake. From the streets of Wigan to the soup kitchens of New York, it brought mass unemployment and economic hardship to millions throughout the 1930s.

MURDERERS

Serial killers of the century

PEDRO ARMANDO LOPEZ **(Colombia, more than 300 victims)**
In the 1970s the 'Monster of The Andes' killed so many people (mostly women) in Peru, Colombia and Ecuador that police thought a large organisation was at work. He was caught in 1980 and sent down for life.

BRUNO LUDKE **(Germany, 85 victims)**
A mentally defective sex murderer of the 1930s, Ludke was caught and sent to a Nazi hospital to be experimented on. He died during an experiment.

DONALD HARVEY **(USA, more than 67 victims)**
Harvey – a Kentucky hospital orderly in the 1970s and 1980s – claimed his murders were mercy killings, but he also murdered his friends and homosexual lovers. He avoided the death sentence by a plea bargain.

WOU BOM-KON **(South Korea, 58 victims)**
Policeman Wou Bom-Kon, 27, was a 'spree' killer – someone who kills all his victims at once. He murdered his victims in eight hours after a row with his girlfriend, then blew himself up with a grenade.

ANDREI CHIKATILO **(Russia, more than 55 victims)**
Like the Yorkshire Ripper, the 'Rostov Ripper' was apprehended and released – because of a one-in-a-million fluke that his blood and semen samples didn't match. He was tried in an iron cage and executed in 1994.

JOHN WAYNE GACY **(USA, 33 victims)**
The 'Clown Killer' was a children's party entertainer who sexually abused, tortured and strangled 33 teenage boys in his Chicago home in 1972-78. He spent 14 years on Death Row and was executed in 1994.

SUZANNE FAZEKAS **(Hungary, more than 26 victims)**
Fazekas was a midwife who helped women murder their husbands. These women had had affairs with prisoners of war during the First World War and later found that their husbands couldn't satisfy them. Eight women were sentenced to death. Fazekas, fittingly, poisoned herself.

THEODORE 'TED' BUNDY **(USA, 23 victims)**
In 1974, while Bundy was working in the Washington crime commission, there was a spate of killings of young women. When he moved to Utah, the killings started there. He was captured in 1977 but escaped and killed more people before being arrested on a traffic violation. He was executed in 1989.

'The camera will never compete with the brush and canvas until such time as photographs can be taken in Heaven and Hell'
EDVARD MUNCH

EDVARD MUNCH

Edvard Munch put the pain into painting. The Norwegian's masterpiece, The Scream (1893), may strike a modern chord with its apocalyptic sky and androgynous figure, but its anguish is rooted in 19th-century hard times: illness and death had claimed most of his family. When Munch was 45 he received electric shock treatment for a nervous breakdown, and his later art was less angst-ridden. He died in 1944, aged 80.

LIFELINES

MAO TSE TUNG *plotted China's way ahead through Communism in his Little Red Book. Born in 1893, the son of a peasant, Mao led a civil war to set up the People's Republic, making China a superpower before his death in 1976.*

ROBERT MITCHUM, *sleepy-eyed and laconic, was one of Hollywood's most underrated actors. Born in 1917, he rose from B-movies to play great roles such as the psychopathic preacher in Night Of The Hunter. He died in 1997.*

GOLDA MEIR *(1898-1978) was the first female Prime Minister – she ruled Israel in 1969-74. A Russian-born, US-educated Zionist, she went to Palestine to work on a collective farm and formed the Labor Party in '67.*

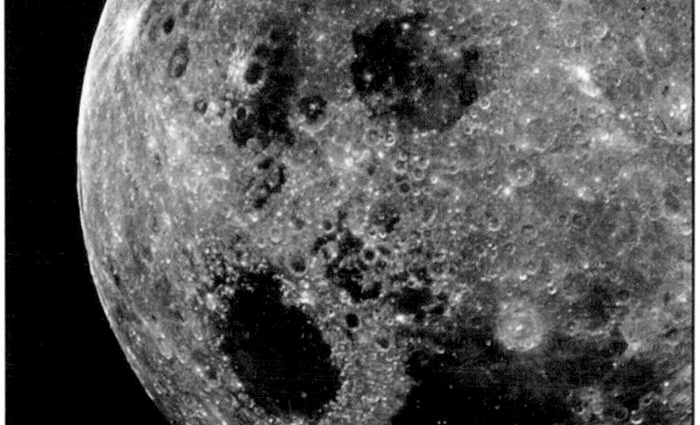

THE MOON

THEN By the beginning of the 17th century, early astronomers had already assembled many correct ideas about the Moon's size, shape, motion and distance from Earth. Galileo had made the first scientific observations with a crude telescope in 1609, and by 1645 the Polish astronomer Johann Hevelius had charted more than 250 formations on the Moon's surface. The most important breakthrough came from Sir Isaac Newton, who in 1687 was the first to explain the motion of the Moon and its tidal effect on Earth.

NOW The acceleration of astronomical studies and technology this century soon made space travel a real possibility. In 1959, the Soviet Union's *Luna 2* became the first spaceship to reach the Moon; that same year, *Luna 3* sent the first pictures back of the Moon's far side. In 1966-68, the United States launched five *Surveyor* spacecraft on the Moon, and photographed 98 per cent of the Moon's surface. The studies prepared the way for the first manned landing – *Apollo 11*, on July 20, 1969, the first of six *Apollo* landings. As Neil Armstrong put it: "That's one small step for man – one giant leap for mankind."

1930 PLUTO DISCOVERED Identified by American astronomer Clyde W Tombaugh as recently as 1930, Pluto is the most newly identified of the nine planets in our solar system. It is also the smallest and usually the farthest from the Sun. But because its 248-year orbit is highly elliptical, it is sometimes closer to the Sun than Neptune. It has been so since 1979, but that period will end with the start of the new Millennium.

1931 COMMONWEALTH FORMED The British Commonwealth of Nations was set up to draw together countries that were British colonies or dependencies. Many have since become independent, but remain members.

1932 IRAQ STANDS ALONE Iraq gained its independence from Britain and joined the League of Nations.

1933 NAZIS SHUN THE WORLD Ominously, Nazi Germany quit the League of Nations and announced it would withdraw from the Geneva Disarmament Conference.

THE NOVEL

With thousands of fiction books pouring out every year, we take it for granted that the novel has always been with us. Yet it has been the dominant literary form for only two centuries or so.

The first novels were Spanish tales like **Miguel de Cervantes**' *Don Quixote* (1605), about a middle-aged squire who fancies himself a heroic knight. **Aphra Behn**'s 1688 slave story *Oroonoko* is seen as the first English novel by a woman.

In the 18th century, the novel emerged as a distinct genre. **Jonathan Swift**, **Henry Fielding** and **Daniel Defoe** wrote about ordinary people rather than idealised types. **Laurence Sterne** showed how far the novel could go in *Tristram Shandy* (1760-67), with blank pages for the reader to fill in, and digressions on how the author is literally losing the plot.

Endlessly flexible, the novel proceeded through Gothic and historical romance to a peak in the 19th century with the society comedies of **Jane Austen** and the socially-conscious sagas of **Anthony Trollope** and **Charles Dickens**.

In France, **Gustave Flaubert** created an amoral heroine in *Madame Bovary* (1857), while Russia gave us such vast masterpieces as **Leo Tolstoy**'s *War and Peace* (1869) and **Fyodor Dostoyevsky**'s *The Brothers Karamazov* (1879-80).

This century, **James Joyce**, **Virginia Woolf** and **Samuel Beckett** used stream of consciousness to express the inner lives of characters. *Finnegan's Wake*, Joyce's unreadable 1939 epic, did not, despite predictions, signal the end of fiction.

Novelists continue to break new ground. **Truman Capote**'s *In Cold Blood* (1966) obsessively recounts the true story of a murderer. **Lawrence Durrell**'s *Alexandra Quartet* (1957) shows the same events from different viewpoints, echoing Einstein's theory of relativity. And **Martin Amis**'s *Time's Arrow* (1991) relates the Holocaust backwards, on the grounds that only in a world turned upside-down could such evil make any sense.

NATIONAL ANTHEMS

God save our ears: England rugby players Darren Garforth, Richard Cockerill and Jason Leonard make sweet music. Below: American sprinters Tommie Smith and John Carlos give a Black Power salute on the Olympic rostrum in 1968

As the United Kingdom devolves, its countries are returning to patriotic hymns more distinctively their own. The Scots, for instance, favour 'Flower of Scotland', though perhaps not at the dirge-like pace at which it was played before Scotland's 1999 Five Nations rugby match in Paris (a deliberate tactic by the French?).

Many anthems recount a defining episode in a nation's history: the 'Marseillaise' was written as a patriotic marching song during the initial, more peaceful stages of the French Revolution, while 'The Star-Spangled Banner' recounts an episode from the American War of Independence. As a result they often contain militaristic or imperialistic overtones that many today consider inappropriate.

There has never been a more potent demonstration of dissent than the Black Power salute made by US athletes on the medals rostrum at the 1968 Olympics, signalling their defiance of a national song which they considered did not represent their history.

NURSERY RHYMES

'HEY DIDDLE DIDDLE', 'MARY HAD A LITTLE LAMB', 'THREE BLIND MICE'... NURSERY RHYMES ARE A FORM OF FOLK LITERATURE AND A PLAYFUL WAY FOR CHILDREN TO DEVELOP LANGUAGE AND COUNTING SKILLS THROUGH MUSICAL REPETITION. BUT OFTEN, THERE'S A LOT MORE TO THEM: 'RING A RING O' ROSES', FOR INSTANCE, ALLUDES TO THE BUBONIC PLAGUE EPIDEMIC OF THE 17TH CENTURY. THE POSIES WERE THOUGHT TO WARD OFF DISEASE, WHILE THE MEANING OF "WE ALL FALL DOWN" IS ALL TOO TRAGICALLY OBVIOUS.

LIFELINES

SIR ISAAC NEWTON was the first scientist to be buried in Westminster Abbey – a pointer to the importance of his achievements. Born in 1642, he discovered the law of gravity, the three standard laws of motion still in use, and the fact that white light is actually made up of many colours. Inventor of the reflecting telescope, Newton was also the mathematician responsible for the creation of calculus, a Member of Parliament and, in 1699, the Master of the Royal Mint. Phew! He died, no doubt exhausted, in 1727.

MARTINA NAVRATILOVA, the most athletic female tennis player of her era, won Wimbledon nine times. Born in Communist Czechoslovakia in 1956, Navratilova defected to the US, becoming a citizen in 1981. A gay rights activist, she also loves animals and once made an advert against eating turkeys.

1936
THE KING ABDICATES
Edward VIII was the only British monarch ever to give up the throne voluntarily. He did it for the love of American divorcee Wallis Warfield Simpson. They became the Duke and Duchess of Windsor and spent the rest of their lives in exile in Paris. Edward's abdication forced his shy, stuttering brother Bertie to reluctantly take the Crown and become King George VI.

1939
THE SECOND WORLD WAR
On September 1, 1939, Hitler invaded Poland, the final straw which triggered the Second World War. By far the bloodiest conflict in history, it is estimated to have caused 54,800,000 civilian and military deaths.

1939
THE ATOM IS SPLIT
German chemist Otto Hahn learned how to split the atom, a discovery that would later lead the world – mercifully too late for Adolf Hitler – into the nuclear age.

PAUL NEWMAN

The eyes have it. Paul Newman's baby blues have brought him some of Hollywood's best roles, from the 1958 classic *Cat on a Hot Tin Roof* with Elizabeth Taylor (above) to 1969's superstarry *Butch Cassidy and the Sundance Kid*, with Robert Redford and Katharine Ross (left). He won an Oscar at 61 in *The Color of Money* (1986), but these days he's up to his neck in his Newman's Own Salad Dressings – which it is said he used to mix up in his bathtub. Since 1982 they've been the sauce of $100 million for charity.

NEWSPAPERS

THEN In the 15th century, newsletters for bankers were published in Europe. In 16th-century Venice, you paid money to read notices pinned on a wall. The weekly *Frankfurter Journal* (1615) is thought to be the first real newspaper, while the oldest paper in existence is the Viennese *Wiener Zeitung* (1703). *The Times* was founded in 1785, while the *Daily Mail* was the first British paper to top a million sales, in 1900.

NOW There are 60,000 newspapers in the world. Britain's papers have the highest circulations in Europe: The *News of the World* has a best circulation of 4.3 million, while the *Sun* is the top daily, at around four million. Britain has the highest proportion of newspaper readers in the world, while India has the most newspapers (4,235 in 1995). Japan probably has the world's highest circulations – Tokyo's *Yomiuri Shimbum* sells 14.5 million daily.

THE NOBEL PRIZE

Notable Peace Prize recipients

Jody Williams 1997
For the campaign to ban landmines

Joseph Rotblat 1995
British scientist, the only man to quit the Allies' atom bomb programme when it was learned that Germany wasn't working on a nuclear weapon

Lech Walesa 1983
Fought for workers' rights in communist Poland

Menachem Begin & Anwar Sadat 1978
For improving Arab-Israeli relations

Mother Teresa 1979
For helping India's poor

John Hume & David Trimble 1998
For efforts towards peace in Northern Ireland

The Dalai Lama 1989
For non-violent Tibetan resistance to China

Sir Winston Churchill 1953
Actually, although Churchill saw off Hitler, he didn't win a Peace Prize – but he did win the Nobel Prize for Literature, for his histories

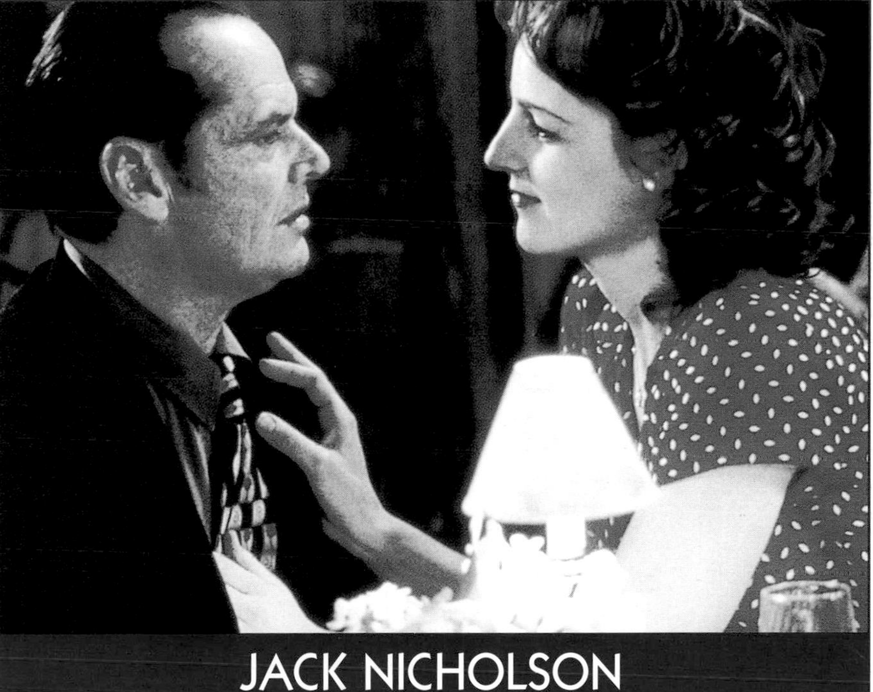

JACK NICHOLSON

It looked all over for Jack the lad. All the fiery promise of Five Easy Pieces (1970) and his Oscar-winning One Flew Over the Cuckoo's Nest (1975) was being squandered in lazy send-ups such as Batman (Jack the Joker) and The Witches of Eastwick (Jack the Devil). But lo and behold, in 1997 Hollywood's most charismatic actor walked away with the Best Actor Oscar for a great dramatic performance in As Good As It Gets, with Helen Hunt (above). Jack's back!

1939 Farewell Freud
The founder of psychoanalysis and modern psychology died in Hampstead, London, aged 83. Born in Vienna, Freud, a Jew, fled to London from the Nazis in 1938. His controversial theories – he believed that people were driven by a mixture of their sex drive and survival instinct – still face criticism, but his following stretches around the globe.

1940 Trotsky Assassinated
Russian revolutionary Leon Trotsky was assassinated on August 20, 1940, by a Spanish communist working for Russian dictator Stalin. Trotsky had been forced into exile by Stalin in 1928.

1940 World's Oldest Paintings Discovered
Wall paintings dating back to 18,000BC were discovered in a cave at Lascaux in southern France. It was closed to the public in 1963 because the paintings of buffaloes, horses and deer were deteriorating. But a replica of the cave and paintings built nearby attracts 300,000 visitors a year.

WILFRED OWEN

Wilfred Owen was a soldier and a poet. Most people today would say he was a poet and a soldier, but in fact only four of his poems were published in his lifetime – and not the ones we now know as the most moving epitaph for the millions of young men pointlessly slaughtered in the First World War.

Owen was not a healthy man, but he volunteered in 1915 and found himself in the long winter of the Somme, drowning in the mud, surrounded by the nightmarish scenes of death and degradation that his fellow men of both sides were going through in the name of patriotism.

Invalided out with shell shock in 1917, he wrote the brilliant *Strange Meeting* (in which he chats to an 'enemy' soldier in God's waiting room), *Dulce et Decorum Est* and *Anthem for Doomed Youth.* He bravely returned to the trenches in 1918 and was killed one week before the war ended.

'My subject is War, and the pity of War. The Poetry is in the pity'

WILFRED OWEN

ROY ORBISON

With his dark glasses, crying vocal style and hits such as 'Only The Lonely', 'It's Over' and 'Oh Pretty Woman', Texan Roy Orbison was an almost permanent fixture in the charts in the Sixties. He made a comeback with the superstar Traveling Wilburys, but died of a heart attack in 1988, aged 52.

OASIS

Described as the Sex Pistols meet the Beatles, Manchester band Oasis were the pioneers of Nineties Britpop, as renowned for their petulant, often violent, behaviour as for their expertly crafted pop anthems such as 'Wonderwall' and 'Don't Look Back in Anger'.

The Manchester band's singer Liam Gallagher and his songwriter-guitarist brother Noel are rock's new royalty and – as is the duty of rock royalty – they love to scandalise the populace.

It has all been done before, maybe, but Mick Jagger never sat in a theatre box watching Keith Richard do the singing for him, as Liam has done, simply because he said he wasn't up to it. Mind you, Johnny Rotten did that sort of thing all the time. Plus ça change…

1940
BATTLE OF BRITAIN
Between July and November 1940 the German Luftwaffe (air force) attacked Britain, starting with coastal targets before moving inland and finally bombing London (the Blitz). Heavily outnumbered, the RAF emerged victorious. Churchill said: "Never in the history of human conflict was so much owed by so many to so few."

1941
PEARL HARBOR
Japan's surprise bombing of the American Pacific Fleet in Hawaii's Pearl Harbor brought the United States into the Second World War. Japan wanted to cripple the American fleet and gain control of the eastern Pacific.

1942
THE HOLOCAUST
The Nazis, looking for a 'Final Solution to the Jewish problem', began building death camps in Poland and Germany where Jews and other 'undesirables' were sent. Millions were either worked to death or killed in gas chambers. The final death toll of the Holocaust was nearly six million.

LIFELINES

George Orwell, *born in 1903, realised that political messages were often more potent when placed in a setting that even a child could understand – a format he applied to Animal Farm, his great satire of Stalin's USSR. His hatred of state control over the individual also surfaced in the prophetic 1984, set in a then-future world dominated by the all-seeing Big Brother. Orwell, whose Keep The Aspidistra Flying was filmed in 1997 with Richard E Grant in the lead, died in 1950.*

John Osborne *created the Angry Young Man prototype in the ranting Jimmy Porter in his 1956 play Look Back In Anger. Born in 1929, Osborne was one of the writers who brought a mixture of realism and idealism to the era and kicked Britain into the post-imperial world.*

THE OSCARS

The first Academy Awards ceremony was in May 1929 at the Hollywood Roosevelt Hotel. Tickets cost $10 and 250 attended. ***The first ceremony wasn't broadcast on TV or radio, but it proved so popular that it was covered by radio every year after that. It was first televised in 1953.***

At the first ceremony, all of the 15 Oscars awarded went to men – apart from Janet Gaynor, who won Best Actress.

Two special awards were made at the first ceremony, one for the first 'talking picture', The Jazz Singer, the other to Charlie Chaplin for producing, directing, writing and starring in The Circus.

The first Oscar for Special Effects was awarded in 1939, for *The Rains Came*, which centred around an earthquake and starred Myrna Loy and Tyrone Power.

The ceremony has had to be postponed three times since its inception. The first was in 1938, when it was put back a week due to severe flooding in Los Angeles; the second in 1968 when it was moved back two days following the assassination of Martin Luther King; the third in 1981 when it was postponed 24 hours due to the assassination attempt on President Ronald Reagan.

Dame Judi Dench in 1999, picking up her second Oscar in a row – this one's for Shakespeare in Love. Right: The night of 1000 stars, and 20,000 photographers' flashguns

Raquel Welch

Famous actors who were never nominated for an Oscar

Al Jolson	Boris Karloff	Peter Cushing
Tallulah Bankhead	Veronica Lake	Brigitte Bardot
Errol Flynn	Olivia Hussey	Roger Moore
Hedy Lamarr	Glenn Ford	Jane Russell
Sir Dirk Bogarde	Jacqueline Bisset	Harry Belafonte
Raquel Welch	Dorothy Lamour	Martin Sheen

Martin Sheen

LAURENCE OLIVIER

Lord Olivier, born in 1907, was generally considered to be Britain's greatest actor – an intense performer with the ability to convincingly portray a third-rate comic in Osborne's The Entertainer (1960) or lead England to glory as Henry V. He died in 1989, but the South Bank's Olivier Theatre is an apt memorial.

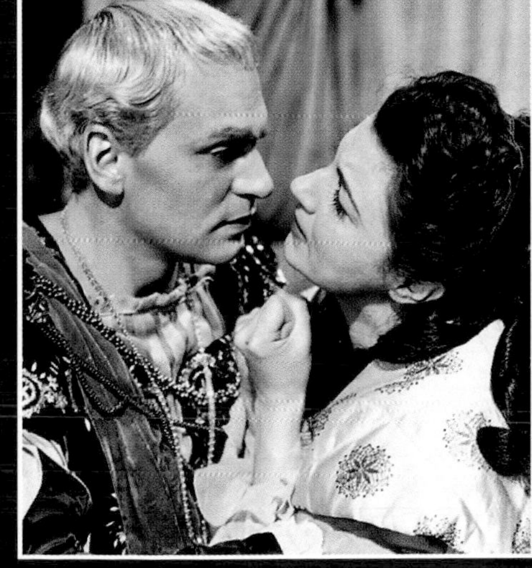

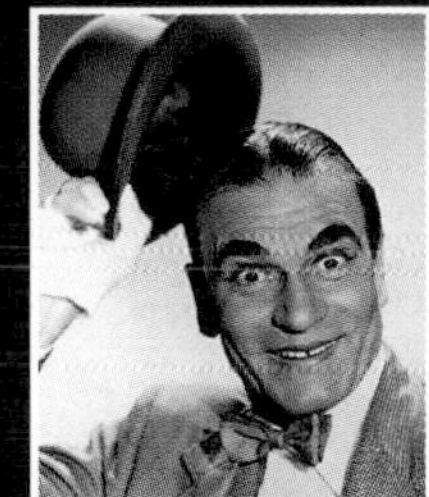

Left: Laurence Olivier in The Entertainer. Right: With Marilyn Monroe, his co-star in The Prince and the Showgirl (1957). Far left: Hamlet with Eileen Herlie (1948)

1942 Battle of Stalingrad
One of the most famous land battles in history, in which the Germans tried to wrest control of Stalingrad (now Volgograd). It lasted from July 1942 until February 1943, when the Germans were defeated.

1943 Hitler's First Big Defeat
The Battle of Stalingrad was Hitler's first big defeat of the Second World War. Commander Friedrich von Paulus, who had been captured along with 90,000 of his men, became the first German field marshal ever to surrender. More than 160,000 Germans were killed. The prisoners were forced to march to Siberia, most never to be seen again.

1943 Death of Mussolini
Fascist leader Benito Mussolini and his mistress, Clara Petacci, were shot by Italian partisans and their bodies hung upside down on lamp-posts in a Milan square.

THE OLYMPIC GAMES

The Olympic Games are the sport soap opera of the 20th century. Originally staged in ancient Greece, the Games were revived by Pierre de Coubertin (1863-1937), a young French nobleman. At the first modern Games, in Athens in 1896, 13 countries competed in nine sports – athletics, cycling, fencing, gymnastics, lawn tennis, shooting, swimming, weightlifting and wrestling. (The USA dominated the athletics, as it has done for most of the century.) The Winter Olympics began in 1924.

The finest athlete of the early days was Jim Thorpe, an American Indian, who won both the decathlon and pentathlon at Stockholm in 1912. Long-distance runner Paavo Nurmi, the 'Flying Finn', won six gold medals in his career, while Jesse Owens, a black American, won four golds in 1936, when Hitler had planned a show of Aryan supremacy. The record haul at one Games is the seven golds won by American swimmer Mark Spitz in 1972 at Munich. Sadly, his achievement was overshadowed by the terrorist massacre of Israeli athletes.

The greatest Olympian of recent years must be the American sprinter and long-jumper Carl Lewis, who won nine gold medals, but British rower Steven Redgrave runs him close with four gold medals at four Games. These days the Games often seem overblown, and a bribes scandal has undermined the Olympic ideal. The Olympics could yet go the way of the original Games, which were killed off in 394AD because the charioteers had turned professional and were being treated like gods.

This was the crowning moment of Linford Christie's career, as he won the 100 metres in 9.96 seconds at Barcelona in 1992. Christie had taken the silver behind Carl Lewis at the previous Games when 'winner' Ben Johnson was disqualified. The British sprinter's victory in '92 at the age of 32 was testimony to sheer will-power

Death came to the Olympics at dawn on September 5, 1972. 'Black September' Arab guerrillas broke into the Israeli building in the Olympic village in Munich with machine guns blazing. Wrestling coach Moshe Weinberg and weightlifter Yosef Romano were shot, and nine athletes were taken hostage. The terrorists were granted safe passage and flown to a nearby airport, but German police opened fire and all the hostages were killed.

Olympic darlings

Few of us had ever watched the Olympic gymnastics before 17-year-old Olga Korbut of Russia (below) won the world's hearts in Munich in 1972 with her cheeky smile and superb athleticism. But at Montreal in 1976 she was upstaged by 14-year-old Nadia Comaneci of Romania (left), whose ice-queen infallibility created the phrase 'Perfect 10'.

1943
ABOUT-FACE BY ITALY
A new government was formed in Italy after the downfall of Mussolini and his Fascists. Its first act was to declare war on former Axis partner Germany.

1943
CORSICA FREED
Free French troops liberated the city of Bastia on the island of Corsica, making it the first French territory in Europe to be taken back from the Nazis.

1944
D-DAY
On June 6, 1944, British and American forces successfully fought the Germans on the beaches of Normandy. The invasion involved 1,200 fighting ships, 4,126 landing craft, 10,000 aircraft, 804 transport ships, hundreds of tanks, and 156,000 troops.

1944
BATTLE OF LEYTE GULF
The Japanese fleet was massively damaged when the biggest naval battle in history was fought between the United States and Japan, near Leyte Gulf in the Philippines, in October 1944.

Great British Olympians

Sally Gunnell

Steve Redgrave

Anita Lonsbrough

Don Thompson

Mary Rand

Lynn Davies

David Wilkie

Chris Boardman

Mary Peters

Steve Ovett, Steve Cram and Sebastian Coe

Britain's Sebastian Coe (right), Steve Ovett (left) and Steve Cram were middle-distance marvels. In 1980, the Coe-Ovett Olympic showdown ended with Ovett taking the 800m, but Coe then won at 1500m. In 1984 Coe won the 1500m (above) with Cram second

Fanny Blankers-Koen of Holland won four golds in 1948 – without entering the long jump and high jump, in which she was world record-holder!

Sports not included in the first modern Olympics of 1896

- Rowing
- Hockey
- Equestrianism
- Football
- Yachting
- Boxing
- Archery
- Basketball
- Modern Pentathlon

JESSE OWENS

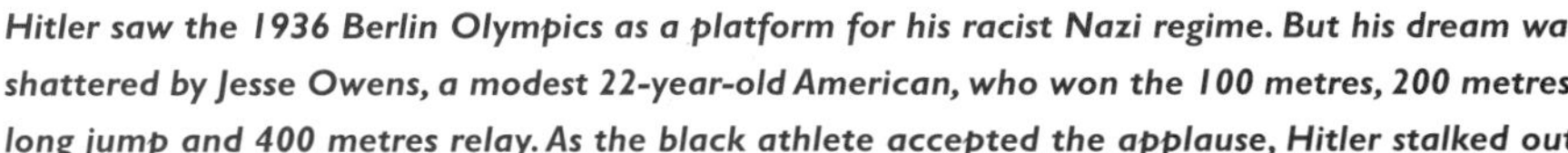

Hitler saw the 1936 Berlin Olympics as a platform for his racist Nazi regime. But his dream was shattered by Jesse Owens, a modest 22-year-old American, who won the 100 metres, 200 metres, long jump and 400 metres relay. As the black athlete accepted the applause, Hitler stalked out

1945 Second World War Ends
On May 7, German chief of staff General Alfred Jodl signed an unconditional surrender and delivered his nation, as he put it, "into the victors' hands, for better or worse". Hitler had committed suicide in his Berlin bunker a week earlier.

1945 Horror of Auschwitz
The Auschwitz death camp near Krakow in Poland was liberated by Soviet troops and the full horror of what the Nazis had been doing was revealed. At just this one camp the Germans had systematically murdered an estimated two million people, including 1.5 million Jews.

1945 The Atomic Bomb
The United States tested an atomic bomb in the New Mexico desert in July, 1945. Then on August 6, they dropped a uranium atomic bomb on Hiroshima, Japan, leaving 66,000 people dead or seriously hurt. And on August 9, they dropped a plutonium bomb on Nagasaki, which killed 39,000 people and injured 25,000.

PARLIAMENT

SOME NOTABLE SPEECHES FROM THE RECENT PAST

● "It may be my imagination, but I am under the impression that questions and answers have been longer today, and I cannot understand the reason why."
Speaker of the House George Thomas (later Lord Tonypandy) on the day Parliament was first broadcast (April 3, 1978)

● "Mr Speaker, now that the House of Commons has declared itself, we shall take our case to the country."
Prime Minister Jim Callaghan concedes defeat on a vote of no confidence (by one vote) and calls a general election (March 28, 1979)

● "It's rather like sending your opening batsmen to the crease, only for them to find, the moment the first balls are bowled, that their bats have been broken before the game by the team captain."
Sir Geoffrey Howe resigns in exasperation at Mrs Thatcher's views on Europe, a move which marked the beginning of her end (November 13, 1990)

● "You can wipe the floor with these people!"
Tory MP Michael Cartiss on Margaret Thatcher's bravura final speech (November 22, 1990)

● "Last night, he spoke at a gala dinner in London. He spoke, not from a text, but from notes, and when he sat down I congratulated him, especially on his final sentence. Spoken as it was, off the cuff and from the heart, they were almost the last words I heard him say. He looked at the assembled gathering and he said: 'The opportunity to serve our country, that is all we ask.' Let it stand as his epitaph."
Deputy leader Margaret Beckett on the death of Labour leader John Smith (May 12, 1994)

PEOPLE WHO STOOD UNSUCCESSFULLY FOR PARLIAMENT

SIR ROBIN DAY (LIBERAL)
TED DEXTER (CONSERVATIVE)
JONATHAN KING (ROYALIST)
PAMELA STEPHENSON (BLANCMANGE THROWER)
ERIC MORLEY (CONSERVATIVE)
VANESSA REDGRAVE (WORKERS' REVOLUTIONARY)
DENNIS POTTER (LABOUR)
CYNTHIA PAYNE (PAYNE AND PLEASURE)
JOHN ARLOTT (LIBERAL)
LINDI ST CLAIR (CORRECTIVE)

CYNTHIA PAYNE

PAMELA STEPHENSON

PILTDOWN MAN

THE MILLENNIUM'S GREATEST HOAX, PILTDOWN MAN WAS THE 'MISSING LINK' FROM APES TO MAN. ALLEGEDLY DISCOVERED IN KENT IN 1912 BY CHARLES DAWSON, IT WASN'T UNTIL 1953 THAT ALVAN MARSTON (ABOVE) PROVED IT WAS A HUMAN SKULL WITH AN ORANG-UTAN'S JAW.

PRISON

THEN Before the 18th century, prisons were largely for people awaiting trial or punishment, rather than the punishment itself – which might range from branding to execution. English and French rulers imprisoned political enemies in such notorious strongholds as the Tower of London and the Bastille. The first prisons were dark, highly insanitary and overcrowded. Men, women, children, dangerous criminals and debtors were all thrown in together. The first attempts at reform followed John Howard's book *The State of the Prisons in England and Wales* (1777). The new prisons became known as 'penitentiaries' because they tried to make prisoners feel remorse.

NOW Overcrowding remains a serious problem for prisons today, but is by no means the only one. Two serious miscarriages of justice – the imprisonment of the so-called 'Birmingham Six' (convicted 1974, released 1991) and the 'Guildford Four' (convicted 1975, released 1985) for terrorist bomb attacks – seriously shook confidence in British justice. Under the last Conservative Government some prisons, and other security duties, were given over to private companies, resulting in a series of embarrassing slip-ups. And as recently as 1999, 25 officers at Wormwood Scrubs were suspended after allegations of systematic violence against prisoners.

POLICE

THEN Novelist and magistrate Henry Fielding founded the Bow Street Patrols to police London's streets. Then came the Bow Street Runners – the first paid detectives – who ran to crime scenes and launched investigations. Statesman Sir Robert Peel founded the Royal Irish Constabulary in 1814, and the London Metropolitan Police in 1829, nicknamed 'bobbies' or 'peelers' after Peel himself. The first modern professional force, it was organised along military lines. Interpol was founded in Vienna in 1923 to link police forces from different countries.

NOW The UK has 150,000 policemen and women. In England and Wales they are organised into 41 county forces; Scotland has eight regional forces. The largest is the London Metropolitan police, which is often criticised. They were accused, for example, of 'institutionalised racism' in their murder investigation of black teenager Stephen Lawrence in south London in 1993. People still yearn for the bobby on the beat (above).

1945 CHURCHILL DEFEATED
In the post-war general election, Labour leader Clement Attlee ousted Prime Minister Winston Churchill with a landslide victory that gave Britain its first full-blooded socialist government. Attlee nationalised the railways, the mines and other industries. He also set up the National Health Service and the Welfare State.

1945 NUREMBERG TRIALS
A number of Nazi leaders were tried for war crimes before an international military tribunal in Nuremberg. The trials lasted a year and of the 24 leaders accused, 12 were condemned to death. The most prominent, Hermann Göring, second only to Hitler, committed suicide hours before he was to be hanged.

1946 THE FIRST BIRO PEN
A Biro ballpoint pen, invented by Hungarian Laslo Biro and manufactured by a British firm, went on sale for the first time.

THE PEASANTS' REVOLT

The Peasants' Revolt of 1381 was the closest England came to a revolution during the Millennium. The peasants were demanding not a minimum wage, but the repeal of the maximum wage. When a poll tax of a shilling a head was imposed on top of that, widespread violence broke out. The Kent peasants' leader Wat Tyler met King Richard II – aged just 14 – who granted their demands. But when Tyler was killed by the mayor of London, the rebels fled and the status quo was restored.

PUNK ROCK

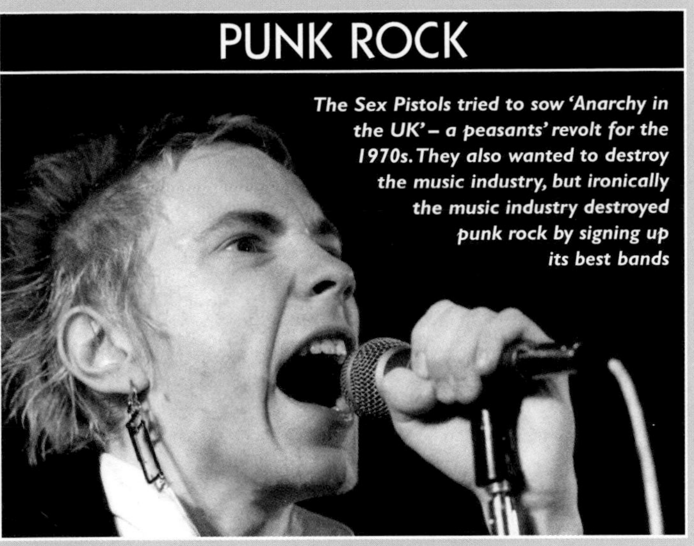

The Sex Pistols tried to sow 'Anarchy in the UK' – a peasants' revolt for the 1970s. They also wanted to destroy the music industry, but ironically the music industry destroyed punk rock by signing up its best bands

EMMELINE PANKHURST

We all owe a debt to Emmeline Pankhurst, the great campaigner for votes for women. She founded the Women's Social and Political Union in 1903 and – along with her daughters Sylvia and Christabel – was often arrested as the suffragettes became militant: Parliament was invaded, churches burnt, and Emily Davison was killed while trying to disrupt the 1913 Derby.

Women got the vote in 1918 but, ironically, the first woman MP did not take her seat – she was a Sinn Fein MP who refused to vow allegiance to the King.

> **'We have been patient too long. We can be patient no longer'**
>
> **EMMELINE PANKHURST, ADDRESSING A WOMEN'S RALLY IN TRAFALGAR SQUARE, 1906**

While Sylvia Pankhurst (1882-1960) became a revolutionary socialist and was jailed in 1920 for sedition, Emmeline ran for Parliament in 1928 as a Tory. She died before the election, aged 69. Christabel (1880-1958), an evangelist, became a Dame.

P

PRESIDENTS OF THE USA

GERALD FORD (1974-77) was the only President never to have been elected as either President or Vice-President. (He got the job as a result of Richard Nixon's resignation.)

JAMES GARFIELD 1880

JAMES GARFIELD (1881) could simultaneously write in Greek with one hand whilst writing in Latin with the other.

CALVIN COOLIDGE (1923-29) was famous for being a man of few words. At a White House dinner, a gushing female guest told him that her father had bet her that she wouldn't be able to get more than two words out of the President. "You lose," was his reply.

When FRANKLIN D ROOSEVELT (1933-45) was five years old, he visited the White House and was told by the then President, GROVER CLEVELAND (1885-89), "My little man, I am making a strange wish for you: it is that you may never be President of the United States." It is also worth noting that Franklin Roosevelt's mother dressed him exclusively in dresses until he reached the age of five.

Another example of a President meeting a future President came in 1963 when BILL CLINTON (1992-) shook hands with John F Kennedy (1961-63) at a White House reception for members of Boys' Nation.

The mother of RICHARD NIXON (1969-74) named her son after King Richard The Lionheart, and originally wanted him to be a Quaker missionary.

GERALD FORD 1975

JIMMY CARTER (1977-81) could speed-read. He was once tested and found to have a 95 per cent comprehension rate reading at 2,000 words a minute.

HERBERT HOOVER (1929-33) and his wife both spoke fluent Chinese. Hoover was the first President to have a telephone on his desk in the White House.

PRESIDENT TAFT 1912

At nearly 24 stones, WILLIAM TAFT (1909-13) was the heaviest President and once got stuck in the White House bath tub.

At just over seven stones, JAMES MADISON (1809-17) was the lightest President.

GEORGE WASHINGTON (1789-97) had wooden false teeth.

When CALVIN COOLIDGE (1923-29) was being driven in a car, he would always insist that the driver didn't exceed 16mph.

RONALD REAGAN (1981-89) was the first – and so far only – President to have been divorced.

JAMES BUCHANAN (1857-61) was the first – and so far only – bachelor to become President.

ANDREW JACKSON (1829-37) once killed a man in a duel because he had insulted his wife.

1946 FIRST TV LICENCES
Television licences were issued for the first time in Britain. They cost £2, but part of the money covered radio services.

1946 LORD HAW-HAW HANGED
William Joyce was hanged for treason in 1946. Throughout the Second World War Englishman Joyce, announcing "Germany calling", had broadcast Nazi propaganda over the radio to Britain.

1946 THE IRON CURTAIN
The Soviet Union imposed a policy of isolation involving strict censorship and restrictions on travel. In a speech on March 5, 1946, Winston Churchill declared that "an iron curtain has descended across the continent".

1946 U.N. MEETS
The first meeting of the United Nations' General Assembly took place in London.

POP MUSIC

The term 'Pop Music' evolved from Popular Music. But that included the likes of Barbra Streisand, Frank Sinatra, Vera Lynn even. To give a younger generation something they could identify with, the word 'pop' was increasingly used from the close of the Fifties, after rock 'n' roll gave teenagers something that was totally their own. Something with which their parents couldn't – and didn't wish to – identify.

Difficult to nail, 'pop' covers music made by Fifties icons like Cliff Richard and Billy Fury, through to that produced by the late-Nineties boy bands and their female equivalents who have flourished in the wake of Take That. Michael Jackson has proclaimed himself King Of Pop and Madonna may well be its queen, but Boyzone and The Spice Girls made the British pop scene much their own as the century spun to an end.

The main characteristic of pop is its transience – each generation ditches its elder sisters and brothers' idols. If you are under 50, the chances are that you once swooned over one of the teen idols pictured on this page. But could you swoon for them now…?

p

TAKE THAT

DURAN DURAN

NEW KIDS ON THE BLOCK

ADAM ANT

BILLY FURY

KYLIE MINOGUE

THE OSMONDS

BROS

BAY CITY ROLLERS

1946
ENTER JUAN PERÓN
Juan Perón became president of Argentina in 1946, instituting a Fascist government. He was ousted in 1955 and fled the country, but was reinstated in 1973. His wife, the beautiful and charismatic Eva Perón, who died in 1952, was immortalised in the musical *Evita*.

1947
DEATH OF AL CAPONE
Al Capone, one of the most notorious gangsters of the 20th century, died in Miami, Florida, from syphilis. He was 48. For more than a decade, Capone was the leader of organised crime in Chicago.

1947
FASTER THAN SOUND
US Air Force pilot Charles ('Chuck') Yeager became the first man to break the sound barrier. He travelled at 760mph (Mach 1.015) in a rocket-powered Bell X-1 research plane.

MICKIE MOST WAS THE BRITISH POP PRODUCER OF THE SIXTIES. HE MADE THE ANIMALS' CLASSIC 'HOUSE OF THE RISING SUN' AND PRODUCED A STREAM OF HITS FOR DONOVAN AND HERMAN'S HERMITS. SO IT'S NO SURPRISE THAT HE CHOOSES ONE OF THE BEST POP PRODUCTIONS OF ALL TIME...

'You've Lost That Lovin' Feelin''

"The Righteous Brothers' 1964 hit 'You've Lost That Lovin' Feelin'' is the best record ever, as it combines four magical ingredients. Lyrically and melodically the song has the maximum emotion you can get in a pop tune, it has fantastic vocal performances by Bill Medley (right) and Bobby Hatfield, the most incredible, dramatic arrangement and a superb Phil Spector production."

PIRATE RADIO

IT WAS PIRATE RADIO THAT MADE 'YOU'VE LOST THAT LOVIN' FEELIN'' A HIT. COMMMERCIAL RADIO REALLY BEGAN ON SATURDAY MARCH 28, 1964, WITH THE LAUNCH OF THE FLOATING RADIO CAROLINE – A DANISH PASSENGER FERRY RENTED BY IRISHMAN RONAN O'RAHILLY.

PIRATE RADIO SUBVERTED THE BBC MONOPOLY OF THE AIRWAVES AND WAS A HUGE HIT WITH TEENAGERS. OTHER STATIONS SOON FOLLOWED, INCLUDING RADIO SUTCH, RUN BY THE LATE SCREAMING LORD. CAROLINE'S DJS INCLUDED MANY OF TODAY'S BEST-KNOWN BROADCASTERS, AMONG THEM TONY BLACKBURN AND JOHN PEEL.

ELVIS PRESLEY

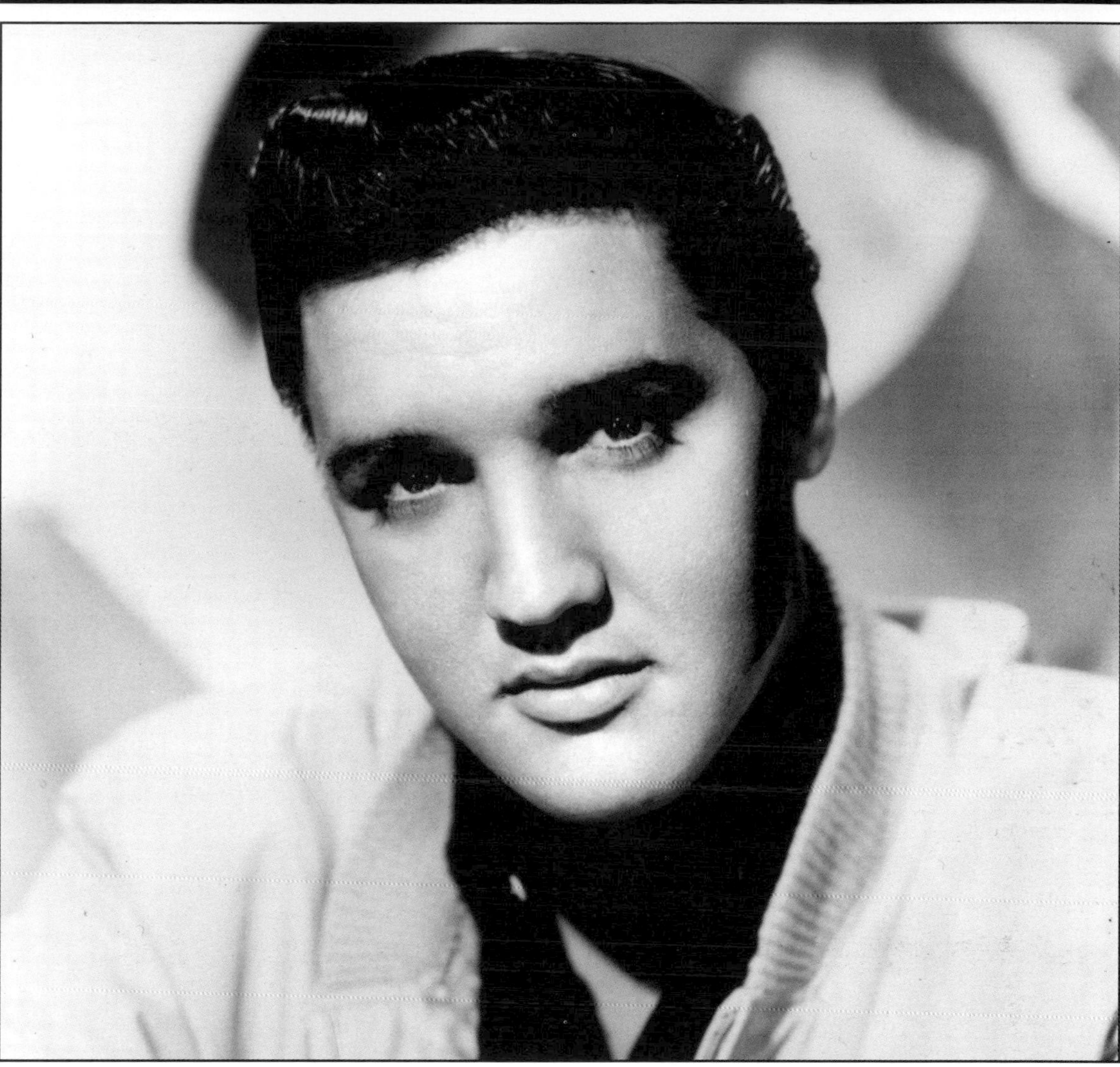

Elvis Presley proved that even if low-born American kids couldn't make it to President, they could become King, with subjects all over the world. A country boy, born in 1935, he listened to blues, gospel and country music, added sex appeal and then delivered his Southern-cooked amalgam in devastating style. After 'Heartbreak Hotel' sold a couple of million straight off, there was no holding him.

All grease and sneer, he represented teenage rebellion, yet had enough charm to woo the older generation, winning over his sternest critics by not evading the draft and spending two years as an ordinary GI Joe. Back in civilian life, he continued as a money-making machine, cutting many classic records and making bad, but punter-pulling, movies. He died in 1977, aged 44, a virtual pharmacy on legs, leaving rumours about his continued existence as a jump-suited chip-shop worker or supermarket employee.

Presley's top chart-toppers

Elvis had 17 British No I's, equalling The Beatles. Here are the ten that stayed at the top longest

1. IT'S NOW OR NEVER	1960	8 weeks
2. ALL SHOOK UP	1957	7 weeks
3. WOODEN HEART	1961	6 weeks
3. THE WONDER OF YOU	1970	6 weeks
5. A FOOL SUCH AS I	1959	5 weeks
5. GOOD LUCK CHARM	1962	5 weeks
7. ARE YOU LONESOME TONIGHT?	1961	4 weeks
7. SURRENDER	1961	4 weeks
7. HIS LATEST FLAME/LITTLE SISTER	1961	4 weeks
7. CAN'T HELP FALLING IN LOVE	1962	4 weeks

1947 DEAD SEA SCROLLS Manuscripts dating back to 100BC were discovered by a Bedouin shepherd in a cave near the Dead Sea in Jordan. Apparently written by the Essenes, a Jewish sect, they provided much insight into ancient Judaism.

1948 FIRST HOLOGRAPH Hungarian physicist Dennis Gabor developed a technique to create three-dimensional images on film.

1948 STATE OF ISRAEL CREATED The United Nations-approved State of Israel came into being and was almost immediately invaded by forces from Egypt, Iraq, Jordan, Syria and Lebanon. Israel defeated its enemies but was to face unending hostility from Arab nations.

1948 BERLIN BLOCKADE The Soviet Union, seeking total control of Berlin, imposed a blockade on all links between the city and the West. Britain, France and the United States responded by airlifting-in supplies. The blockade was lifted later in the year but tensions between East and West Berlin remained for 40 years.

LIFELINES

__Gregory Peck__, California-born in 1916, shocked the film world by playing a Nazi doctor in The Boys From Brazil (1978). Usually the good guy, he won an Oscar as a lawyer defending a black man in To Kill A Mockingbird.

__Sir Robert Peel__, born in 1788, founded the modern police force, hence the term 'bobbies'. A politician, he reformed the Tory Party as the Conservatives and twice became Prime Minister before his death in 1850.

__Dennis Potter__ – the most inventive, controversial and influential British TV playwright – found fame in 1978 with Pennies From Heaven, a mix of Thirties music and overt sexuality. He died in 1994, aged 59, from 'Rupert' – a cancer he had named after Rupert Murdoch.

P

ANNA PAVLOVA

Anna Pavlova was ballet's first superstar. A Russian born in poverty in 1881, she toured the world, became rich and famous, but died aged 49

LUCIANO PAVAROTTI

The BBC 1990 World Cup theme Nessun Dorma made Italian tenor Pavarotti a household name. The 'Three Tenors' roadshow has made him millions, and Princess Diana watched him in the rain in Hyde Park. A giant of a man, he had hip and knee replacements in 1998.

GIACOMO PUCCINI

With operas such as Tosca, La Bohème and Madame Butterfly, Giacomo Puccini (1858-1924) took up Giuseppe Verdi's baton as Italy's greatest composer, and set the seal on Italian mastery of colour, melody and drama.

PRE-RAPHAELITE ART

All the world loves the dreamily sensual art of the Victorian rebels called the Pre-Raphaelites ... and all the Pre-Raphaelites loved The Lady of Shalott. The heroine of Tennyson's Arthurian poem (1832) was painted by Rosetti, Holman Hunt, Millais and others. But the best-known image of the Lady doomed by her love for Sir Lancelot is this one – created a few years later, in 1888, by John W Waterhouse. She may wear more clothes than most of Waterhouse's nymphs, but no visit to the Tate Gallery is complete without a glimpse of her ethereal beauty

THE POPE

THEN At the turn of the Millennium the papacy was at an all-time low, fought over by Italian aristocrats whose corruption often stretched to murder. Reform came with Gregory VII, Pope from 1073-85 and known as 'the Great', who fought to restore credibility. He re-imposed celibacy on all members of the clergy and put a stop to the buying of church appointments by influential figures – an offence for which he made Emperor Henry IV of Germany do public penance.

NOW Pope John Paul II came to the Vatican in 1978 – the 'year of the three Popes', following the deaths of the moderniser Paul VI and John Paul I, whose mysterious death provoked conspiracy theories. Modern Popes have often exercised an authority beyond any political leader's. John Paul II will be best remembered as the towering influence behind the disappearance of communism in eastern Europe, beginning with Poland in 1989. He has declared the year 2000 a 'Holy Year'.

1982: Archbishop of Canterbury Robert Runcie prays with John Paul II – the first Pope to visit Britain for 450 years

1948
Birth of Apartheid
The apartheid system of racial segregation against non-whites – 'apartness' – was introduced by South Africa's National Party. The detested policy was condemned by much of the world and resulted in the country's near-isolation in politics, trade and sport for 50 years.

1948
Gandhi Assassinated
Indian leader Mahatma Gandhi, who had been instrumental in ending British rule in his country, was assassinated in New Delhi by a religious fanatic. Gandhi advocated non-violent resistance. He once said: "Non-violence is not a garment to be put on and off at will. It must be an inseparable part of our very being."

1950
Tibet Annexed
The year after it became a Communist state in 1949, China invaded and annexed Tibet. Although Tibet was promised self-rule it has remained under China's control. Tibetan leader the Dalai Lama was forced into exile in 1959.

PABLO PICASSO

1937 ***Guernica is often cited as the masterpiece of the century. Using Spanish symbols such as the horse and the bull, Picasso rails against the slaughter of civilians by German bombers in the Spanish Civil War***

1881-1973

Pablo Picasso was *the* artist of the 20th century. Ever inventive, equally at home in paint, sculpture and ceramics, the Malaga-born Spaniard changed the way we see the world.

His 'blue period' (1901-4), where his pictures use melancholy blue shades to represent the downcast, was followed by the jauntier 'rose period': gay pink and grey portrayals of the acrobats and dancers of Montparnasse in Paris.

His interest in African and primitive art led to *Les Demoiselles d'Avignon* (1907) which, with its radically distorted and simplified view of the human form, prefigured cubism, and generated that *frisson* that always attends the shock of the truly new.

Picasso developed cubism – basically an attempt to paint in 3D – with Georges Braque and Juan Gris, moving from exploded violins and fruit bowls to works that made no attempt to mirror the external world. And by incorporating 'real' objects in their work, they invented the future of art.

Later, his pictures became more anguished, culminating in *Guernica* (1937), a vast, emotive tableau which depicts the bombing of a Basque town by fascist forces during the Spanish Civil War. It is still displayed behind bullet-proof glass in a separate building attached to Madrid's Prado gallery.

With his demonic energy, Picasso terrified and enthralled women in equal measure – a larger-than-life artist for whom the normal rules did not apply.

PRIESTS

THEN After centuries of dispute, the eastern and western arms of the Christian church split for good in 1054. The Pope's authority was a major bone of contention; other arguments involved priestly celibacy and beards, which the eastern church made compulsory for priests (in emulation of Christ). Celibacy was a central issue of the 16th-century Reformation, when Protestants split from Catholics. Martin Luther, the first Protestant, married a former nun, as did Archbishop of Canterbury Thomas Cranmer, who reputedly defied Henry VIII by smuggling his wife into Lambeth Palace.

NOW Pope John Paul II has faced many priestly difficulties including celibacy, which he is determined to keep compulsory, and the ordination of women priests. When the Church of England synod voted for women in 1994, many Anglicans rejoiced, but a number of traditionalists (including the Duchess of Kent, the Bishop of London, and shadow home secretary Anne Widdecombe) defected to Rome. In recent years Catholics have been rocked by revelations of child abuse, but they applauded the 1994 film *Priest*, which sensitively explored celibacy and homosexuality.

LEANING TOWER OF PISA

1173 ***The Torre Pendente in Pisa, Italy, is a one-off. The foundations began sinking, so they went on building at an angle – no wonder it took 177 years (until 1350). It leans more each year, but work has begun to return it to how it was 300 years ago and remove the unsightly cables and girdle that hold it up. If the money runs out, it may yet fall down.***

1950
KOREAN WAR
Communist North Korea's attack on democratic South Korea triggered an immediate United States-sponsored UN resolution calling for military sanctions against North Korea. The ensuing war, with North Korea and China fighting forces from 19 nations, led by the United States, lasted three years and left nearly three million dead.

1950
DUM DE DUM DE DUM DE DUM...
Radio serial *The Archers*, an everyday story of country folk, was broadcast for the first time.

1950
McCARTHY'S WITCH-HUNT
Senator Joseph McCarthy launched a witch-hunt against influential figures he believed to be communist sympathisers. The reputations and careers of scores of people, especially in Hollywood, were ruined or destroyed before the Senate admitted McCarthy's four-year campaign had gone too far and he was formally censured.

1952
US H-BOMB
The United States exploded its first hydrogen bomb at the Elugelab Atoll in the Pacific Marshall Islands.

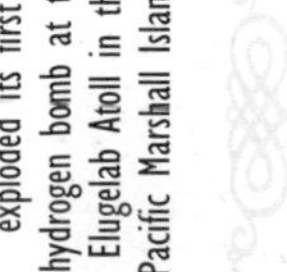

LIFELINES

OSCAR PETERSON *has been one of the most popular jazz artists ever since he took New York's Carnegie Hall by storm in 1949. A gifted pianist, he was born in Canada in 1925 – hence his Canadiana Suite, written in 1964.*

KIM PHILBY *was the most famous spy of the Cold War. Philby, born in 1912, was a British intelligence officer working for Russia. The 'Third Man' in the 1963 scandal with Burgess and MacLean, he fled to the USSR, where he died in 1988.*

WILLIAM PITT THE YOUNGER *was, at 24, Britain's youngest Prime Minister – and a contradictory one. A peace-maker, he became embroiled in a long war with France. He united Britain and Ireland but pressed for Catholics' rights. Born in 1759, he died in office, aged just 46.*

PELE

Pelé – Edson Arantes do Nascimento – was the greatest player of the world's favourite sport. Indeed, it was Pelé above all others who *made* football the world's favourite sport. Pelé called football 'the beautiful game'. The term has become soccer's greatest cliché – and its greatest lie, because Pelé was one of the few footballers who could make the game look beautiful.

An attacking midfielder or left-sided forward, Pelé played 1,363 matches for club and country, scoring 1,281 goals – an incredible average of 0.93 per game. In 1959 he scored 126 goals in one season (the British record is 60, by Everton's Dixie Dean in 1927/8). But his greatest achievements were in the World Cup, as the only man to have played in three winning teams – with Brazil in 1958, 1962 (when he was injured before the Final) and 1970.

Pelé made his debut for the Brazilian giants Santos in 1956 at the age of 15 – he scored four goals in his first match – and stayed with Santos until he retired in 1974. His only other club was New York Cosmos: he came out of retirement for $1.25 million (£750,000) a season in 1975 to kick-start soccer in the USA.

'Too many players think of a football as something to kick. They should be taught to caress it and to treat it as a precious gem'
PELÉ

Pelé burst on to the World Cup stage in Sweden in 1958, aged 17, scoring six goals including a hat-trick in the semi-final and two in the Final. But it was in Mexico in 1970 that Pelé truly left his mark. Brazil won every match on their way to the Final, where they registered a stunning 4-1 victory against the 'impregnable' man-for-man defence of Italy. Pelé scored one goal and made two others. In a team that oozed quality from top to bottom, he was the master.

Today, Pelé is Brazil's Minister for Sport and is still worshipped by millions. Such is his fame that when he played an exhibition match in Nigeria in the late 1960s, the ongoing civil war actually stopped for the duration of his visit so that the opposing sides could watch the great man in action.

Pelé and Bobby Moore swap shirts after Brazil's thrilling 1-0 win over England in the 1970 World Cup. It was a symbolic moment: Moore lifted the trophy in 1966, but he was only keeping it warm for Pelé

1952
THE FIRST POLIO VACCINE
American doctor Jonas Salk developed a vaccine against the potentially fatal disease poliomyelitis (polio). The vaccine, licensed for use in 1954, was made from a killed polio virus.

1953
ELIZABETH II CROWNED
Princess Elizabeth Alexandra Mary was crowned Queen Elizabeth II of Great Britain and Ireland at Westminster Abbey on June 2, 1953. It was a cold, wet day, but that did not stop hundreds of thousands lining the processional route in London. It was the first coronation to be televised live.

1953
THE GREAT FLOODS
Large parts of Kent and Essex were flooded when the Thames estuary burst its banks. A total of 307 people lost their lives. At the same time, other areas of the Continent were flooded, especially Holland. In all, more than 2,000 people died.

LESTER PIGGOTT

Lester Piggott was the greatest jockey of all time. He won his first race at 12, was champion 11 times, won the Derby nine times – but he couldn't beat the taxman. In 1987 he was jailed for three years for a £2.8 million tax evasion. He served 12 months but made a stunning comeback to racing before retiring at 59.

FRED PERRY

Fred Perry (1909-95) was the last British man to win Wimbledon – three times in a row, 1934-36 – and the first man to win all four Grand Slam titles. The most stylish of sportsmen, his brand-name shirts became a must-have for Mods and skinheads.

POPULATION

THEN In 1650, there were about 550 million people in the world. The population doubled between then and 1850, and has multiplied by a factor of five between 1850 and now. The population growth was due to advances in transportation, agriculture, medicine and communications, which did much to improve living conditions. But birth rates fell with the migration of workers to the cities in the wake of the Industrial Revolution.

NOW The population of the world rose to 5,812 million in 1996; China alone accounts for 22 per cent of this figure. The current rate of growth is estimated at 1.6 per cent a year. Asia is the most populous continent (and the most densely populated), Africa the fastest growing (2.8 per cent). In western Europe the declining birth rate means that the population is steadily ageing: already 18 per cent of us are above retirement age.

PUBS

Britain's Ten Most Common Names

1. The Red Lion
2. The Crown
3. The Royal Oak
4. The White Hart
5. The King's Head
6. The Bull
7. The Coach And Horses
8. The George
9. The Plough
10. The Swan

THE PARALYMPICS

Stephen Welch and Vance Parmelli of the USA celebrate winning the gold medal in the men's doubles tennis at the 1996 Atlanta Games

The Paralympic Games were founded and first hosted by Stoke Mandeville Hospital, where a fully-equipped sports stadium was opened in 1969.

The Games grew out of post-war interest in the importance of physical activity for people who were partially paralysed, and an archery competition was held at the hospital in 1948. Gradually other sports were included, such as fencing, weightlifting and basketball, and the Games gained international impetus when they began to be attached to the summer Olympic Games, starting with Rome in 1960.

At the 1996 Atlanta Paralympics, some 4000 disabled athletes from 27 countries competed in 18 events. New sports for Sydney 2000 will include rugby and sailing.

1953 DNA Code Cracked
In one of history's most important medical discoveries, British scientist Francis Crick and American biologist James Watson established the structure and function of DNA (deoxyribonucleic acid).

1953 Mount Everest Conquered
Sir Edmund Hillary from New Zealand and Sherpa Tenzing from Nepal are in the record books as being the first to reach the summit of the world's highest mountain. But did George Mallory get there first? (See 1999).

1955 Let's Rock...
Bill Haley and the Comets launched the rock 'n' roll era with the multi-million selling worldwide hit 'Rock Around The Clock'. Elvis Presley would soon emerge as 'the King' of the genre alongside stars such as Jerry Lee Lewis, Fats Domino, Eddie Cochran and Buddy Holly.

1955 Ruth Ellis Hanged
Nightclub hostess Ruth Ellis was executed at Holloway Prison in London. Found guilty of murdering her lover, she was the last woman to be hanged in Britain.

BEATRIX POTTER

"Once upon a time there were four little Rabbits, and their names were Flopsy, Mopsy, Cotton-tail, and Peter..." Thus began the world's love affair with Beatrix Potter. The tale of Peter Rabbit appeared in 1902, and was followed by a stream of other animal stories, at a rate of two books a year. The tales have even been turned into dance, performed by the Royal Ballet in 1993 (right). Later in life, Beatrix Potter became more interested in farming and the preservation of land in the Lake District. She died in 1943, leaving 4000 acres of land and 15 farms to the nation.

PUBLISHING

Novels originally rejected by publishers

Catch-22 *(Joseph Heller)*
The War of The Worlds *(H G Wells)*
Animal Farm *(George Orwell)*
A Time To Kill *(John Grisham)*
The Time Machine *(H G Wells)*
Lord of The Flies *(William Golding)*
The Rainbow *(D H Lawrence)*
The Wind In The Willows *(Kenneth Grahame)*
The Spy Who Came In From The Cold *(John Le Carré)*
Tess of The D'Urbervilles *(Thomas Hardy)*
The Mysterious Affair At Styles *(Agatha Christie)*
A River Runs Through It *(Norman MacLean)*
Barchester Towers *(Anthony Trollope)*
The Picture of Dorian Gray *(Oscar Wilde)*
The Naked And The Dead *(Norman Mailer)*
Moby Dick *(Herman Melville)*
The Razor's Edge *(W Somerset Maugham)*
Northanger Abbey *(Jane Austen)*
The Good Earth *(Pearl Buck)*
The Ginger Man *(J P Donleavy)*

POETRY

Once, society looked to its poets to entertain and amuse, and to pen lyrics that would place the great events of the day in their proper epic perspective. The appointment of Andrew Motion as Poet Laureate, to succeed the late Ted Hughes, shows that poetry at least retains some vestige of its public role. In keeping with the times, Motion's lines on the wedding of Prince Edward and Sophie Rhys-Jones focused on their private bonds rather than royal pomp.

Although poetry's position in the literary firmament has been usurped by the novel, poetry can still be influential. T S Eliot's *The Waste Land* (1922) was seen as experimental, but it soon became known as the definitive modern poem, not only for its form and complexity, but for its expression of a pessimistic world bruised by war.

Leading British poets have included W H Auden, whose *Stop All The Clocks* became a best seller after its recital in the hit romantic comedy *Four Weddings and a Funeral*, and Philip Larkin, whose melancholy evocations of thwarted emotions pointed up poetry's increasingly private role.

The definition of what constitutes poetry has widened too, with Beatles lyrics finding their way into anthologies, and the rising vogue for slam nights – a fast and furious free-for-all where poets rant and rap competitively.

Andrew Motion's Best of the Millennium Poets

Andrew Motion was appointed Poet Laureate for the new Millennium in 1999. Professor of Creative Writing at the University of East Anglia, his biography of Philip Larkin won the 1994 Whitbread Prize for Biography

William Wordsworth

"Wordsworth is my Millennium Poet – for the matchless delicacy of his lyrics, the emotional wisdom of his thinking and the great, grave architecture of his longer poems. Of course, he wrote some dud things. But at the height of his powers he combined beauty with truth like nobody else."

POET LAUREATE

Andrew Motion follows in a noble tradition. The first Poet Laureate was Shakespeare's contemporary Ben Jonson, who began life as a bricklayer and killed an actor in a duel. The first 'official' Laureate, John Dryden, secured the post with a poem about the 1666 Great Fire of London, *Annus Mirabilis*. After Nahum Tate it became a 'job for life'. Here are Andrew Motion's predecessors and dates of office:

John Betjeman's Collected Poems sold nearly a million copies

John Dryden (1668-89)
Thomas Shadwell (1689-92)
Nahum Tate (1692-1715)
Nicholas Rowe (1715-18)
Laurence Eusden (1718-30)
Colley Cibber (1730-57)
William Whitehead (1757-85)
Thomas Warton (1785-90)
Henry James Pye (1790-1813)
Robert Southey (1813-43)
William Wordsworth (1843-50)
Alfred, Lord Tennyson (1850-92)
Alfred Austin (1896-1913)
Robert Bridges (1913-1930)
John Masefield (1930-67)
Cecil Day Lewis (1968-72)
Sir John Betjeman (1972-84)
Ted Hughes (1984-1998)

1955
Warsaw Pact
The Warsaw Pact was signed by the Soviet Union, East Germany, Czechoslovakia, Poland, Hungary, Bulgaria, Romania and Albania. The main objective was to preserve Soviet military bases in those countries. The pact was dissolved in 1991 following the collapse of communism in 1989.

1955
The First Theme Park
Disneyland in California was the first themed amusement park, or 'theme park', in the world. In 1971, Disney followed the success with Florida's Disney World. Then came Disneyland in Japan in 1983 and Disneyland, Paris in 1992.

1955
Tears of a Princess
Princess Margaret, who was in love with Group Captain Peter Townsend, bowed to pressure and announced she would not marry him because of "constitutional problems". Townsend was a divorced man and therefore, in the eyes of the Establishment, an unacceptable suitor.

PLASTIC SURGERY

Pamela Anderson

Nowadays plastic surgery for cosmetic purposes is the norm among American film and TV stars, and many others besides. Cosmetic surgery is used to slim down noses, enhance breasts and lips, take weight of waists and thighs, and smooth out wrinkles. Marilyn Monroe used it, as have Jane Fonda, Dolly Parton, Pamela Anderson and Cher – though not, she says, to the extent the media claims. In 1992, Michael Jackson sued the *Daily Mirror* after it printed an unflattering picture of his face, claiming it had been ravaged by surgery.

The techniques are not new: in Britain, plastic surgery has been used since the 19th century for skin grafts for burns victims, and to mend facial features damaged in accidents. Cosmetic surgery was used 6000 years ago by the ancient Eygptians on the face, feet and arms. In the sixth century, Indians used it to correct noses that had been cut off as a punishment for adultery, and in 1597 the 'nose job' was brought to Europe by Italian surgeon Gasparo Tagliacozzi.

Jane Fonda

Now men, too, are turning to the knife to feel better about themselves, especially for liposuction and penis enlargement. Some commentators point to a worrying trend in society towards a kind of Hollywood ideal of permanent youth. And it's starting younger: facelifts, once the province of over-forties, are increasingly being requested by twenty-somethings, too.

Dolly Parton

PETER PAN

Peter Pan was invented by Scottish dramatist Sir James M Barrie in a 1902 novel called *The Little White Bird*.

Barrie's play 'Peter Pan or The Boy Who Would Not Grow Up' opened at the Duke of York's Theatre, London, in 1904. It became a Christmas favourite, usually with a female Peter.

Disney's animated *Peter Pan* (1953) took three years and $4 million to make. Walt Disney had played Peter Pan in his school play.

Legend has it that Disney based Tinker Bell on Marilyn Monroe – but since he had bought the film rights in 1939, she may have been based on wartime pin-ups such as Betty Grable. In the play, Tinker Bell was just a beam of light.

Barrie assigned the royalties from his play to the Great Ormond Street Hospital for Sick Children. The copyright was due to expire in 1989, 50 years after his death, but Lord Callaghan intervened to re-assign royalties to the hospital.

In Steven Spielberg's 1991 film Hook (left), Peter Pan was a grown-up, played by Robin Williams, with Dustin Hoffman as the evil Captain Hook.

LIFELINES

Samuel Pepys *wrote the world's most famous diary. Born in 1633, Pepys, who spent time imprisoned in the Tower, documented the Plague and the Great Fire during his decade of diary-keeping. He died in 1703.*

Edith Piaf, *who died in 1963, was the most popular singer to emerge from France. Born in 1915, she was tiny, but had a big voice that echoed with the heartbreak in her life. Her personalised songs include La Vie En Rose and the defiant No Regrets.*

Marcel Proust, *born in 1871, wrote probably the greatest novel of the 20th century. Written over 15 years (1913-27), Remembrance Of Things Past explores the subconscious via childhood memories. An obsessive and reclusive writer, the French novelist died in 1922.*

P

1955 First Nuclear Submarine
The first nuclear submarine, *USS Nautilus*, was launched in 1955. Powered by small quantities of uranium, it could stay under water for much longer periods than traditional diesel submarines.

1955 First TV Ad
Commercial television went on the air for the first time. The first advert was for Gibbs SR toothpaste.

1956 Hungarian Uprising
Students protesting against Soviet rule led a revolt in Hungary, calling for free elections and political independence. It led to a new liberal government which announced plans to withdraw from the Warsaw Pact. Soviet forces immediately invaded, their tanks remaining on the streets of Budapest until the rebellion was crushed.

1956 First Angry Young Man
Playwright John Osborne's *Look Back in Anger* opened at the Royal Court Theatre, London. It starred Alan Bates and launched an era of "angry young men".

LIFELINES

PHOTOGRAPHY

Louis Pasteur *gave the world pasteurisation, which kills the germs in milk. Born in 1822, he pioneered micro-biology and found a vaccine for rabies. France's greatest chemist died in 1895.*

Mervyn Peake *(1911-68) created a world of dreams and nightmares in his trilogy of Titus Groan novels. A master of the fantastic, the artist and author said he wished to conduct readers "to amazing climates of the mind".*

Niccolo Paganini, *born in 1782, was the greatest violinist of his time, and possibly ever. The Italian genius played his first concert at 11 years old, and revolutionised violin technique. He died in 1840 but is remembered in the Ella Fitzgerald song Mr Paganini.*

***May 4, 1967:** the picture millions of women never wanted to see – Elvis Presley eating wedding cake with his bride Priscilla Beaulieu at the Aladdin Hotel, Las Vegas*

The first true photograph was a grainy image taken in 1826 by French physicist Joseph Nicéphore Niepce. It involved exposing a light-sensitive metal plate for eight hours. Other technical advances, from Fox Talbot's invention of light-sensitive paper (1839), to George Eastman's 1888 Kodak box camera – the first mass-produced camera – refined the technique.

Part art, part science, photography has fundamentally changed the way in which we see the world. It showed us images of ourselves with a clinical clarity and precision we had never known before. It contributed to a new spirit of self-consciousness which continues to manifest itself in myriad ways, from eating disorders to anti-ageing creams, body building to plastic surgery.

In art, photography challenged painting's hold on direct representation, pushing it towards new directions such as cubism and abstraction.

Photography has left no facet of life untouched. It captured the atrocities of war, the motion of horses, the first man on the Moon and the human infant in its embryonic state, and will continue into the future, taking us to places where the unassisted eye cannot.

MILLENNIUM TIME LINE

1956
First Nuclear Power Plant
The first nuclear power plant, used to produce electricity, was opened at Calder Hall – now part of the Sellafield complex in Cumbria.

1957
Britain's H-bomb
Britain's first hydrogen bomb was dropped on Christmas Island in the Indian Ocean.

1957
Africa Breaks its Chains
The Gold Coast was the first British colony in Africa to gain independence. It became Ghana. Decolonisation then swept across the continent and was finally completed in the 1980s.

1957
Space Age Begins
On the 40th anniversary of the Russian Revolution, the Soviet Union ushered in the Space Age by launching the first satellite. *Sputnik I* stayed in orbit for 21 days. By the late 1990s, there were nearly 500 man-made satellites orbiting the Earth.

July 30, 1908: Dorando Pietri of Italy staggers to the line in the Olympic marathon. Pietri entered London's White City stadium well in the lead but then collapsed. Stewards rushed to help him – so he sadly had to be disqualified

July 7, 1946: A Casino de Paris dancer models the new 'Bikini' swimsuit, which had caused a sensation at a Paris beauty contest

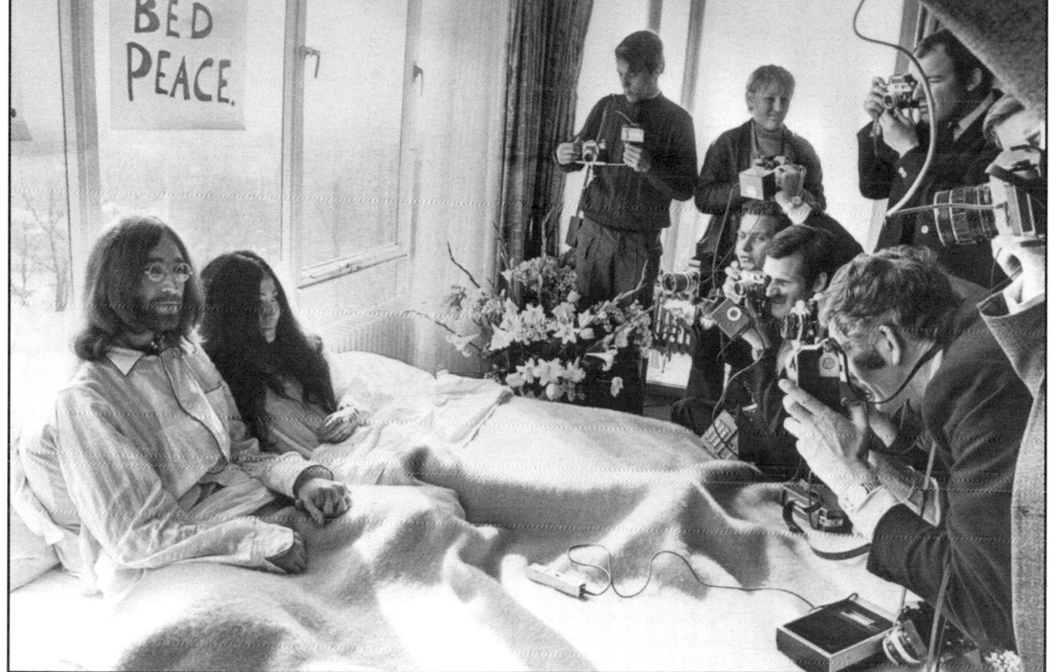

March 27, 1969: John Lennon and his wife Yoko Ono welcome the world's press to the Presidential Suite of the Hilton Hotel, Amsterdam, where they stayed in bed for seven days "as a protest against war and violence in the world"

October 1936: Two hundred unemployed men from the Tyneside town of Jarrow march to London to demand the right to work

1958
Manchester United Disaster
Eight soccer players, five of them internationals, were among those killed when Manchester United's plane crashed in snow trying to take off at Munich airport. Manager Matt Busby survived.

1958
Let's Ban the Bomb
The Campaign for Nuclear Disarmament (CND) was formed in London with veteran peace campaigner Bertrand Russell as its president, and "Ban the Bomb" as its slogan. The group wanted Britain to lead the way in stopping the arms race and to abandon its own nuclear weapons. In the Easter of 1958, 9,000 people took part in CND's four-day-long London-to-Aldermaston march where a protest was held at the Berkshire Atomic Weapons Research Establishment.

1958
The First Parking Meters
Parking meters were installed on the streets of London for the first time. The experiment began in the Mayfair area. Annoyed drivers just ignored them and parked their cars in un-metered streets nearby.

1982 *Countdown was the first programme on Channel 4. It's still going strong, even without £1 million prizes*

QUIZ SHOWS

Cheap and relentlessly cheerful, quiz shows were made for American TV – and they soon handed out big-money prizes. In 1959, the US Congress heard that the quiz show *Twenty-One* had told its star contestant Herbert Stempel to "grimace as if struggling" for answers he had already been fed. Robert Redford dramatised the scandal in his 1994 film *Quiz Show.*

Over here, early favourites were Hughie Green's *Double Your Money,* Michael Miles' *Take Your Pick* and Eamon Andrews' *What's My Line?* At the highbrow end of the scale, there was *Ask the Family, University Challenge,* and perhaps the ultimate cerebral quiz, Magnus Magnusson's *Mastermind.*

Countdown was the first programme broadcast by Channel 4 (1982), but the quiz that put quizzes back in the news was Chris Tarrant's *Who Wants to be a Millionaire?* with its promise of an instant million for a handful of correctly answered questions. Funny thing is, no one has done it yet…

'I have been trained since childhood never to show emotion in public'

THE QUEEN

Her Majesty in close-up

Queen Elizabeth II was the first monarch to be born in a private house – 17 Bruton Street, London W1 – which is now the site of a bank.

She was born by Caesarean section on a Wednesday (April 21, 1926).

At birth she was third in line to the throne (after her Uncle David, later Edward VIII, and her father).

She learned to curtsey perfectly before the age of two and made her last curtsey in 1952, to her father's body in St George's Chapel, Windsor.

At the precise moment in 1952 when she acceded to the throne, she was wearing a shirt, a cardigan and slacks.

She and Prince Philip were related before they married. They are third cousins (by descent from Queen Victoria) and second cousins once removed (through King Christian IX of Denmark).

She's 5 ft 4 ins tall and weighs about eight stones.

She is superstitious: she throws salt over her left shoulder if she accidentally spills any, she won't have 13 people at the dinner table and she has been known to touch wood before her horses run.

Whenever she travels abroad she always takes with her a special white kid loo seat, specially formulated egg and lemon shampoo, and her feather pillow.

Her grandmother, Queen Mary, used to call her 'the bambino'.

The Queen has only once signed an autograph for a member of the public – in 1945, for Sergeant Pat Hayes.

THINGS THE QUEEN CAN DO

Drive without taking a driving test.

Disobey the law and refuse to give evidence in court (they are her laws and her courts). She also can't be sued.

Declare war on another country, disband the army and sell the Navy's ships (the armed forces are under her command).

Send letters without stamps (her letters carry the Royal cipher).

Give away as many peerages and knighthoods as she likes.

Declare a State of Emergency (which she once did, on May 31, 1955 because of the railway strike).

Dismiss the Government and the Civil Service.

'If you find you are to be presented to the Queen, do not rush up to her. She will eventually be brought around to you like a dessert trolley at a good restaurant'

LOS ANGELES TIMES

1958 THE FIRST MOTORWAY Britain's first section of motorway, the Preston by-pass, was opened by Harold Macmillan, the Prime Minister. It was to become part of the M6.

1959 FIRST MOTORWAY DEATHS Less than a week after the M1 was opened, two drivers were killed in a collision.

1959 THE FIRST POST CODE The post code, introduced to speed up the mechanical sorting of mail, started as an experiment in Norwich.

1959 CASTLE SOLD Lord Brooke sold Warwick Castle to Madame Tussauds, the waxworks company, for £1.5 million. The castle had been the ancestral seat of the Earls of Warwick since 1449.

1960 ENTER ENA SHARPLES The first episode of the ITV soap *Coronation Street* went out on December 9.

Princess Elizabeth waves to the crowd from the balcony of Buckingham Palace, following her father's coronation at Westminster Abbey on May 12, 1937. Standing alongside the 11-year-old Princess are her smiling mother, Queen Elizabeth (now the Queen Mother); her sister, Princess Margaret; and her father, the newly-crowned George VI

Ten things the Queen loves

1. *Music* People who go to the Palace to receive their honours are often surprised to find a band playing selections from Hollywood musicals.
2. *Champagne* She also enjoys sweet white wines.
3. *Crossword puzzles* She does the *Telegraph*'s.
4. *Dogs* She owns and breeds corgis but only keeps female ones – passing the male dogs on to others.
5. *Racing* She would love to own a Derby winner.
6. *Television* She enjoys watching telly with her supper on a tray. Her favourite programmes include *Dad's Army* and *The Good Life*.
7. *Impersonations* She can 'do' family and politicians.
8. *Charades* At royal parties, everyone has to join in.
9. *Fancy Dress* When first married, she went to a ball dressed as a maid. In 1962 she dressed up for a 'Come-As-A-Beatnik' party at Balmoral.
10. *Barley Water* She takes some with her on tour.

Ten things the Queen hates

1. *Garlic* It's banned from the Palace kitchens.
2. *Cats* Loves dogs, hates cats.
3. *The Cold* She takes her own hot-water bottle on trips abroad.
4. *Snails* She once asked Prince Philip: "How can you eat those beastly things?"
5. *Smoking* Prince Philip gave up the night before they got married.
6. *Maths* She was hopeless at the subject when she was a girl.
7. *Any mention of Edward VIII* His abdication made her father King. The Queen Mother believed the stress caused his early death.
8. *Pomposity* When a journalist once suggested Diana could send a footman to buy winegums, the Queen said: "What a pompous remark, if I may say so."
9. *Tennis* She leaves Wimbledon to the Duchess of Kent.
10. *Dictating letters*

QUOTATIONS

'Did I really say that?'

"I'm astounded by people who take 18 years to write something. That's how long it took that guy to write Madame Bovary and was that ever on the bestseller list?"
– Sylvester Stallone (right) giving his considered views on Flaubert's oeuvre

"My imagination refuses to see any sort of submarine doing anything but suffocating its crew."
– H G Wells

"Get rid of the lunatic who says he's got a machine for seeing by wireless."
– The Editor of the Daily Express, refusing to meet John Logie Baird, the man who invented television

"Ah yes, Mohammed: that's one of the most common Christian names in the world."
– David 'Kid' Jensen

"Iran is an island of stability in one of the most volatile parts of the world."
– President Jimmy Carter (below), just before the Shah was overthrown

"So, Carol, you're a housewife and a mother. And have you got any children?"
– Michael Barrymore

"Come, come – why, they couldn't hit an elephant at this dist...."
– John Sedgwick, American Civil War General, just before he was shot dead

"We will make them grovel."
– Tony Greig, the then captain of the England cricket team, on what he and his men were going to do to the West Indies in 1976. In the event, the West Indies won the series 3-0

"This picture is going to be one of the biggest white elephants of all time."
– Victor Fleming, the director of Gone With The Wind, assessing its likely prospects at the box office. It is, of course, the biggest-grossing film (with figures adjusted for inflation) of all time

'Smoking kills. If you're killed, you've lost a very important part of your life'

Brooke Shields

1960 Nile Dam Started Construction began of the Aswan High Dam across the River Nile. The dam, opened in 1971, created the 2,000-square-mile Lake Nasser, one of the world's largest reservoirs, irrigating 100,000 acres of Egyptian desert.

1960 Lady Chatterley Goes on Sale Penguin Books were prosecuted for obscenity after publishing an unexpurgated version of DH Lawrence's *Lady Chatterley's Lover*. But in a landmark verdict against censorship, a jury at the Old Bailey decided that the book was not obscene, nor liable to deprave or corrupt those who read it. After the verdict, queues formed at bookshops as Penguin rushed to put it on sale.

1961 Spy Jailed Former diplomat George Blake was jailed for 42 years for spying for Russia. He escaped from Wormwood Scrubs in 1966.

1964 *The Stones started out in small blues clubs in West London, bringing with them a casual style that shocked a world used to seeing groups dressed up in identical custom-made suits. From left: Bill Wyman, Mick Jagger, Brian Jones, Charlie Watts, Keith Richards*

THE ROLLING STONES

The most enduring of rock bands, the Rolling Stones have been rocking the world for nearly 40 years. Yet the success of their *Bridges to Babylon* tour in the last year of the Millennium proved that the public's appetite for rock's premier bad boys is undimmed, while early hits such as 'Satisfaction', 'Sympathy For The Devil' and 'Jumping Jack Flash' are still their most popular.

Memorable events in the Stones' colourful history include the 1967 drugs bust which prompted *The Times* to ask "Who breaks a butterfly on a wheel?"; the death of guitarist Brian Jones in 1969; the riotous Altamont Festival at which a member of the audience was knifed to death by Hell's Angels employed by the Stones; and Bill Wyman's affair with 14-year-old Mandy Smith (to whom he was later briefly married).

Mick Jagger's liaisons still fascinate the newspapers, which never tire of listing a host of women including Marianne Faithfull, actress Marsha Hunt (with whom he has a child), and first wife Bianca Perez Morena de Macias (who gave birth to his second child). He ends the Millennium a free man once more, having just reached a divorce settlement with his second wife, Jerry Hall, with whom he has four children.

'Every eight weeks you had to come up with a red-hot song that said it all in two minutes 30 seconds'
KEITH RICHARD ON WRITING ROLLING STONES SONGS IN THE SIXTIES

1999 *And then there were four – from left: Charlie Watts, Ron Wood, Keith Richards and Mick Jagger*

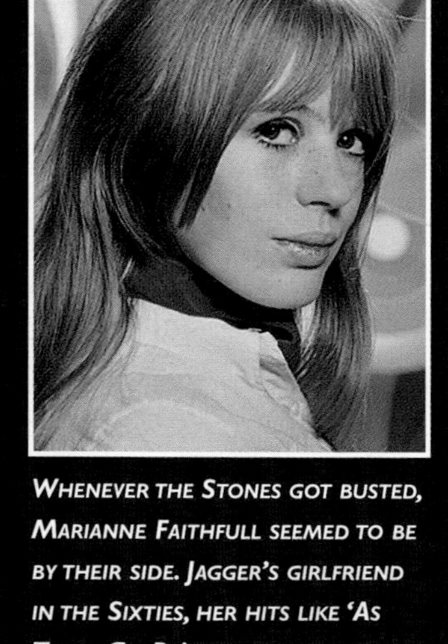

WHENEVER THE STONES GOT BUSTED, MARIANNE FAITHFULL SEEMED TO BE BY THEIR SIDE. JAGGER'S GIRLFRIEND IN THE SIXTIES, HER HITS LIKE 'AS TEARS GO BY' WERE WRITTEN BY THE STONES. BUT THERE WAS MORE TO MARIANNE THAN THAT. NOW A CULT SINGER/WRITER, HER VAGABOND WAYS ALBUM WAS ONE OF THE BEST IN THE FINAL YEAR OF THE MILLENNIUM.

MILLENNIUM TIME LINE

1961
FIRST MAN IN SPACE
On April 12, 27-year-old Russian pilot Yuri Gagarin became the first man in space after completing a 108-minute orbit of the Earth.

1962
CUBAN MISSILE CRISIS
The confrontation between the United States and the Soviet Union that nearly resulted in a third world war. Soviet nuclear missiles were installed on Cuba, just 140 miles (225km) from the US mainland. President Kennedy demanded their removal and blockaded the island. After seven tense days, with Soviet warships bearing down on the US Navy, Soviet leader Nikita Khrushchev backed down and took the missiles away.

1962
SELF-RULE FOR UGANDA
After nearly 70 years of British rule, Uganda became independent. Within a decade it would be under the control of Idi Amin, one of the bloodiest tyrants of the 20th century.

ROCK AND ROLL

Rock and roll developed from a fusion of R&B and country music, the term being popularised by DJ Alan Freed during the Fifties. Everything spiralled after Bill Haley's 'Rock Around The Clock' sparked cinema riots in *The Blackboard Jungle*. The film was about teenage rebellion – and Elvis Presley provided a hip-shakin' godhead for such a rebellion. The original form, now dubbed rockabilly, has since seen countless changes. Hardly a year passes without some media-touted offshoot such as progressive rock, punk rock, jazz-rock, folk-rock, psychedelic rock, new wave, garage, cowpunk… The labels change but as the Rolling Stones rightly proclaimed: It's only rock and roll.

CLIFF RICHARD

One of the most memorable moments in Cliff Richard's 40-year career has to be his impromptu performance at the Wimbledon tennis championships in 1996, when he sang 'Congratulations' backed by Virginia Wade, and 'Bachelor Boy' aided by Martina Navratilova (above). It seems strange now that Sir Cliff – knighted in 1995 – was ever a rebel, but in 1959, when 'Living Doll' gave him the first of his ten No 1's, he was a lip-curling, sullen sex symbol with screaming girls trying to rip his clothes off. Anyone for tennis?

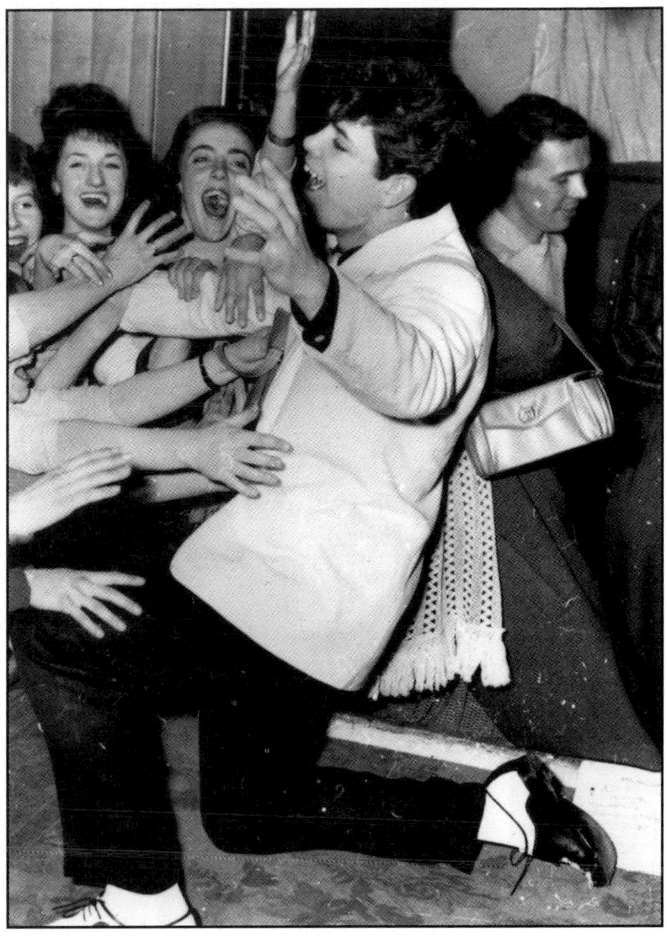

1959 ***Cliff Richard, the new teen sensation, is mobbed on his first headlining tour of Britain, supported by Wee Willie Harris***

SMOKEY ROBINSON

Smokey Robinson was one of pop's finest singers and writers. His group the Miracles were the first on Motown, and he is vice president of the company. He had a solo No 1 with 'Being With You' in 1981.

OTIS REDDING

Otis Redding recorded one of the greatest soul albums in Otis Blue. His many hits included the moving '(Sittin On) The Dock of the Bay', released after his death in a plane crash in 1967.

LOU REED

Lou Reed's Velvet Underground were Andy Warhol's 'house band' in the Sixties. Reed's first hit was 'Walk on the Wild Side' – for which bassist Herbie Flowers was paid £17! Reed also wrote 'Perfect Day'.

'When you're writing a song, you hope people are going to sing it forever and ever'

Smokey Robinson, composer of 'Tracks of my Tears', 'My Girl', 'Tears of a Clown' and many other Motown classics

LIFELINES

__Maurice Ravel__, born in France in 1875, brought the modern influences of Impressionist painting and jazz into classical music. His greatest hit – the show-stopping Bolero – was reworked in 1999 by Jacques Loussier. Ravel died in 1937.

__Django Reinhardt__ lost the use of two fingers in a caravan fire. Even so, the Belgian gypsy, born in 1910, became one of the best-loved guitarists in jazz, particularly when teamed with violinist Stephane Grappelli. He died in 1953.

__Robert Bruce__, born in 1274, freed Scotland from English rule. Crowned King Robert I in 1306, he was forced to flee by Edward I, but defeated Edward II's army at Bannockburn. Stricken by leprosy in later life, he died in 1329.

R

1963 Kennedy Assassinated President John F Kennedy was shot dead while being driven in a motorcade through the streets of Dallas, Texas. His alleged killer, Lee Harvey Oswald, was also shot dead while in police custody.

1963 The Profumo Scandal War Minister John Profumo resigned after admitting in the Commons he lied over his relationship with prostitute Christine Keeler. She was seeing a Soviet naval attaché at the same time, raising security fears. The scandal stunned Prime Minister Harold Macmillan and nearly ended his government.

1963 The Great Train Robbery Ronnie Biggs and Buster Edwards were among the armed robbers who took £2.6 million from the Glasgow-to-London Royal Mail train after bringing it to a halt in Buckinghamshire. Gang members were sentenced to a total of 307 years in jail.

ROCK MUSIC

Singles that went straight to Number One

In the first two decades of the singles chart, only four records debuted at No 1 – two by Elvis ('Jailhouse Rock' and 'It's Now Or Never') and one each by Cliff Richard and The Beatles. It was a landmark achievement. These days, with fewer singles being sold and record companies using greater marketing expertise, it happens a lot. Listed below are some notable records that have gone straight in at No 1 since the chart started in 1952…

Jailhouse Rock .... Elvis Presley
January 24, 1958

The Young Ones .... Cliff Richard
January 11, 1962

Get Back .... The Beatles
April 23, 1969

Cum On Feel The Noize .... Slade
March 3, 1973

I Love You Love Me Love .... Gary Glitter
November 17, 1973

Going Underground .... The Jam
March 22, 1980

Don't Stand So Close To Me .... The Police
September 27, 1980

Stand And Deliver .... Adam And The Ants
May 9, 1981

Is There Something I Should Know .... Duran Duran
March 26, 1983

Two Tribes .... Frankie Goes To Hollywood
June 16, 1984

Do They Know It's Christmas? .... Band Aid
December 15, 1984

Dancing In The Street .... David Bowie & Mick Jagger
September 7, 1985

Sealed With A Kiss .... Jason Donovan
June 10, 1989

Bring Your Daughter To The Slaughter Iron Maiden
January 5, 1991

The Fly U2
November 2, 1991

Saturday Night .... Whigfield
September 17, 1994

Some Might Say .... Oasis
May 6, 1995

Never Forget .... Take That
August 5, 1995

Fairground .... Simply Red
September 30, 1995

Jesus To A Child .... George Michael
January 20, 1996

Say You'll Be There .... The Spice Girls
October 26, 1996

Slade were the first artists to see three singles debut at No 1, starting with 'Cum On Feel The Noize'

'Going Underground' was the first of three singles by The Jam that went straight into the chart at No 1

Ten rock giants who never had a number one single in Britain

The Who
Billy Fury
Tina Turner
Bananarama
Elvis Costello
Kim Wilde
Prince
The Carpenters
Depeche Mode
Free

THE RENAISSANCE

The word Renaissance means rebirth, of course, and stands for a great cultural movement, an explosion of learning and art which began in Italy in the early 14th century and had spread to England, France, the Netherlands, Germany and Spain by the late 15th.

The architects of the movement were to be found among the ruling families (notably the Medicis) of the Italian city states of Milan and Venice and Florence, who encouraged the arts and emphasised people's duty to their society rather than the passive medieval focus on saving one's soul.

In this as in all things, the Renaissance harked back to the civilisations of Rome and Greece, studied and reappraised by scholars such as Petrarch and Boccaccio. Elegance and precision were encouraged, in emulation of the classical approach. Petrarch's maxim 'style is the man' implied a belief that careless expression reflected careless thought.

Renaissance artists – Leonardo da Vinci, Raphael, Donatello, Michelangelo – painted realistic figures that emphasised the beauty of the human form. Huge medieval cathedrals were replaced by smaller buildings designed to make people aware of their own power and dignity. And so the Renaissance helped develop the modern view of the world, based on a human scale rather than a godly one.

AUGUSTE RODIN

What's he thinking about? Frenchman Auguste Rodin's The Thinker has fascinated the world ever since it was first seen in 1880. Inspired by Michelangelo, Rodin brought a new realism to sculpture.

1963 'The Greatest' Fights On
Hopes were high when British boxing champion Henry Cooper floored Cassius Clay. But Cooper was soon badly cut and had to retire. Clay later changed his name to Muhammad Ali and went on to proclaim himself the greatest boxing champion of all time. Many agreed.

1964 Beatlemania hits US
Mass hysteria greeted The Beatles as they began their first tour of the United States. Police reported that there was a significant drop in the crime rate on the night that 73 million Americans stayed at home to watch the 'Fab Four' on television's *Ed Sullivan Show*. At one time in 1964, the top five records in the *Billboard* 100 singles chart were by The Beatles.

1964 Prize for Luther King
A year after delivering his famous "I have a Dream" speech, civil rights leader Dr Martin Luther King was awarded the Nobel Peace Prize. Aged 35, he was the youngest person ever to receive it and he donated the $54,000 prize money to the civil rights movement.

REMBRANDT

The 1999 exhibition of over 60 Rembrandt self-portraits at London's National Gallery is the first and most extensive autobiography in paint ever produced. "From smooth-faced student to bulb-nosed old master," said one critic, "Rembrandt recorded himself from first to last, a time-lapse scrutiny of change and decay unparalleled in the history of art."

Seen together, Rembrandt's portraits trace the narrative of his life. A Dutchman, born in 1606, Rembrandt Harmensz van Rijn came from a humble background in Leiden. As his work took off, he moved to Amsterdam, and self-portraits of his student days soon give way to a well-dressed, contented-looking husband and businessmen who thrived on portrait commissions. It was during this period that he created his epic-scale masterpiece *The Night Watch* (1642), packed with local dignitaries.

His later years were not so happy, and the self-portraits show a weary and increasingly lonely widower who outlived his children and was declared bankrupt. The final pictures, painted in his fifties and sixties, courageously confront his weakening mortality.

Rembrandt's pictorial sorcery stemmed from his mastery of the medium of paint. He used its texture realistically, as a way almost of sculpting what it represented: folds in the paint for eye-bags, loose hair depicted with lines etched in wet paint by the brush handle.

But, transcending the technique, there is the life that shines through his pictures, as if we are seeing into the soul of the subject.

The Shakespeare of visual art, Rembrandt died in 1669 – but his pictures will last as long as there is human life on Earth.

Rembrandt through the mirror of his own eyes. Left: A dandyish young man in his late twenties. Above: The world-weary master, aged about 60

LIFELINES

***Walter Raleigh** is an accidental villain of the Millennium, as he popularised tobacco. A poet, soldier and explorer, born around 1552, Raleigh strove to establish an English colony in America. He was a favourite with Elizabeth I – he named Virginia in the Virgin Queen's honour and famously laid down his cloak for her. But he was imprisoned for treason for 13 years by her successor, James I, and was executed in 1618.*

***Ronald Reagan** was America's oldest President. Born in 1911, the son of a bankrupt shoe salesman, he acted in over 50 films including Bedtime For Bonzo – co-starring with a chimp – before moving on to become governor of California. An extreme right-winger, he was America's most popular politician. Elected President in 1981, he won a landslide re-election victory in 1984.*

1964 THE GREAT ESCAPE A record 57 East Germans escaped to West Berlin after building a tunnel beneath the notorious Wall.

1964 FORTH BRIDGE The Forth Road Bridge in Scotland was opened, at the time the longest bridge in Europe.

1964 CHINA AND THE BOMB China detonated its first nuclear bomb at the Lop Nor test site in Sinkiang.

1964 CIGARETTES CONDEMNED The first official warning against cigarettes was issued in 1964 when the US Surgeon General declared that they "may be hazardous to health".

1964 JAMES BOND CREATOR DIES Ian Fleming, creator of 007, Britain's most celebrated secret agent, died, never to know that his books would be the inspiration for the most popular series of films in cinema history.

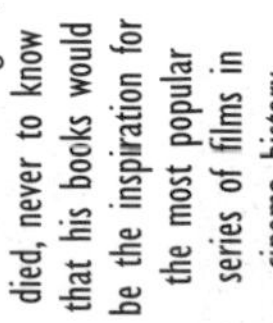

LIFELINES

MAXIMILIEN ROBESPIERRE, *born in 1758, was a French Revolution leader who helped force the execution of Louis XVI. A lawyer and politician known as 'The Incorruptible', he made numerous enemies and was guillotined in 1794.*

R

JEAN JACQUES ROUSSEAU *(1712-78) was a French writer and philosopher who greatly influenced the French Revolutionists. His Confessions, published in 1778, were a startling account of his libertarian life.*

MARGARET RUTHERFORD *was forever the very British eccentric in her film roles. Born in 1892, she played numerous formidable matrons, as well as a rather tongue-in-cheek Miss Marple in four films. She died in 1972.*

ROLLS-ROYCE

Car of the Millennium, surely. Ever since the Silver Ghost arrived in 1906, Rolls-Royce has meant style. The company began making aircraft engines in the First World War. It did it so well, the Government stepped in to save it in the 1970s. Rolls-Royce is now part of Volkswagen, but the stars still love the cars…

SHOWBIZ STARS WHO BOUGHT THE CARS

GARY GLITTER
MARVIN GAYE
NOEL GALLAGHER
SHANE RITCHIE
RUTH MADOC
SIR JIMMY SAVILE
MICHAEL CAINE
DONOVAN
CILLA BLACK
JOHN LENNON
MAE WEST
ELVIS PRESLEY

…AND SOME UNLIKELY ROLLS-ROYCE FANS

T E LAWRENCE (LAWRENCE OF ARABIA)
AUTHOR RUDYARD KIPLING
PLAYWRIGHT GEORGE BERNARD SHAW
UGANDAN DICTATOR IDI AMIN
RUSSIAN REVOLUTIONARY VLADIMIR LENIN
RUSSIAN MYSTIC GRIGORIY RASPUTIN
ITALIAN DICTATOR BENITO MUSSOLINI

***Top:** If you've got it, flaunt it – high rollers Tom Jones (left), Engelbert Humperdinck (right) and manager Gordon Mills. **Above:** A six-wheeled Rolls-Royce, as driven by Thunderbirds puppet Lady Penelope. **Left:** Mr Showbiz, Sammy Davis Jr*

LEONARD ROSSITER

LEONARD ROSSITER WAS THE MAN WE LOVED TO SEE GET HIS COME-UPPANCE AS THE WEASEL-LIKE LANDLORD RIGSBY IN THE TV SITCOM RISING DAMP. A BRILLIANT CHARACTER ACTOR, BORN IN 1926, HE PROVED EQUALLY MEMORABLE IN THE ZANY FALL AND RISE OF REGINALD PERRIN. HE DIED IN 1984 AND IS STILL SORELY MISSED.

RAILWAYS

THEN The first public railway to use a steam locomotive was the Stockton and Darlington. At its opening in 1825, George Stephenson powered his engine the Locomotion at 15 mph pulling wagons of passengers. In 1829, he and his son Robert won a competition when their Rocket drew a train weighing 20 tonnes 35 miles in under two hours. Their engine opened the Liverpool and Manchester Railway in 1830 – the real beginning of the railway age.

NOW The modern railway has seen many breakthroughs – monorails, high-speed trains, the Channel tunnel. Under the last Tory government, British Rail was broken up and sold off as private companies; the passenger railway, split into 25 franchises, was sold in 1997. Complaints are as common as ever. In 1998 the Virgin West Coast service was given a D grade by the rail watchdog, who noted that on 137 days of the year 'no effective service' was provided at all.

MILLENNIUM TIME LINE

1964 THE LAST EXECUTIONS
At dawn on August 13, John Walby was hanged at Strangeways prison in Manchester. At the same time, Peter Allen was executed at Walton jail, Liverpool. They were the last people to be hanged in Britain.

1965 ENTER THE MINI-SKIRT
The mini-skirt, a symbol of the freedom and culture of the Swinging Sixties, was designed in 1965 by Mary Quant and became an instant fashion sensation.

1965 DEATH OF CHURCHILL
A tear fell on England's cheek when it was announced that Winston Churchill, the great wartime Prime Minister, had died. He was 91 and his death came 70 years to the day after his father. An impressive state funeral in London, where at one stage Churchill's coffin was carried by boat along the Thames, was followed by burial at the parish church in Bladon, Oxfordshire.

ROMEO AND JULIET

BAZ LUHRMANN'S 1996 MOVIE WILLIAM SHAKESPEARE'S ROMEO AND JULIET BROUGHT SHAKESPEARE INTO THE MODERN WORLD OF THE ROCK VIDEO. STARRING CLAIRE DANES AND LEONARDO DICAPRIO, IT PORTRAYS ADOLESCENT LOVE IN THE HARD-EDGED WORLD OF TEENAGE GANGS. DICAPRIO'S POWERFUL PERFORMANCE CATAPULTED HIM INTO THE MAINSTREAM, WHERE HE WENT ON TO MAKE THE BOX-OFFICE SMASH TITANIC

'But, soft! what light through yonder window breaks? It is the East, and Juliet is the sun...'

It is still surely the world's best-known love story. At its heart it contains an element – the testing of love by the opposition of one's own family – that is entirely human and understandable. The circumstances, however, are rather less ordinary.

Romeo falls in love with Juliet while disguised at a ball, and can only marry her in secret because of the deadly feud between their respective families, the Montagues and Capulets. Forced to marry another against her will, Juliet takes a potion that enables her to simulate death.

Romeo, exiled after killing Juliet's cousin to avenge the murder of his best friend, hears of her death – but not the explanation. He drinks poison at her tomb, she awakens, realises the truth and stabs herself.

William Shakespeare's play – written in 1594-5 – has been served unusually well by the cinema. Franco Zeffirelli's 1968 version was followed by Leonard Bernstein's musical adaptation, *West Side Story*, which aptly relocated the action among rival immigrant gangs in inner-city New York.

More recently *William Shakespeare's Romeo and Juliet* made an icon of Leonardo DiCaprio, and won huge acclaim for its hip Venice Beach setting, sizzling soundtrack and brilliantly edited camera narration.

ROMANCE

THE LOWDOWN ON KISSING IN THE MOVIES

1. THE FIRST FILM KISS was in, appropriately enough, the 1896 movie *The Kiss.* The protagonists were the actors John C Rice and May Irwin.

2. THE FILM WITH THE MOST KISSES was the 1926 film *Don Juan*, in which John Barrymore performed 191 kisses with different women. This was before the 1930 Hays Code which banned "excessive and lustful kissing".

3. THE LONGEST KISS IN A FILM lasted three minutes, five seconds. The 1941 film was *You're In The Army Now* and the kissers were Jane Wyman (Ronald Reagan's first wife) and Regis Toomey.

4. STEVE MCQUEEN famously kissed Faye Dunaway for 55 seconds in the 1968 film *The Thomas Crown Affair.*

5. THE MOST FAMOUS KISS IN A HOLLYWOOD FILM is probably that between Burt Lancaster and Deborah Kerr in *From Here To Eternity.*

6. THE FIRST GENUINE FRENCH KISS IN A HOLLYWOOD MOVIE was between Warren Beatty – who else? – and Natalie Wood in the 1961 film *Splendor In The Grass.*

7. THE FIRST KISS IN AN INDIAN FILM didn't take place until the 1978 movie *Love Sublime* when Shashi Kapoor and Zeenat Aman embraced. An Indian minister called the kissing scenes "an insult" and called for a mass protest. Nepal bans films featuring kisses by Nepalese actors.

8. GRETA GARBO didn't relish kissing scenes with Fredric March, her co-star in *Anna Karenina*, so she ate garlic before every such scene. Diana Rigg did the same before kissing George Lazenby in *On Her Majesty's Secret Service.*

9. JULIA ROBERTS hated kissing Nick Nolte whilst making *I Love Trouble.* At one point she sent a memo to the producer saying: "If he puts his tongue in my mouth one more time I'm walking off the set."

10. VIVIEN LEIGH hated having to kiss Clark Gable in *Gone With The Wind.* Gable's bad breath wasn't improved by the whisky he regularly drank or the false teeth he wore.

1965 AMERICA IN VIETNAM
American troops went to help prop up the South Vietnam government. The US was to become more and more involved in a bitter and costly war until it finally pulled out, defeated, in 1973. In 1975, South Vietnam surrendered to Ho Chi Minh's forces.

1966 WORLD CUP VICTORY
"It's only 12 inches high, solid gold, and it means... England are the world champions." So announced BBC commentator Kenneth Wolstenholme to a breathtaken nation as captain Bobby Moore and his team-mates danced around Wembley with the World Cup trophy after beating West Germany 4-2 in the final.

1966 FIRST FOR US CABINET
Robert Clifton Weaver, Housing and Urban Development Secretary, was the first African-American member of a US Cabinet.

1966 ABERFAN DISASTER
A huge coal slag heap slid down like an avalanche after several days of rain, nearly burying the local school at the South Wales village of Aberfan. Of the 144 people killed in the shocking disaster, 116 were children.

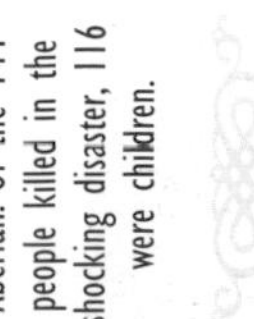

LIFELINES

Grigoriy Rasputin *was one of history's oddest figures. Born in 1871, he was a mystic with huge influence on Tsarina Alexandra (Boney M dubbed him 'Russia's greatest love machine'). In 1916, jealous nobles poisoned, shot and drowned him.*

Richard I, *known as the Lionheart (1157-1199), was hardly the hero portrayed in countless films. He spent virtually all his reign abroad, often fighting in the Crusades, leaving his brother John (cast as the villain) to rule England.*

Jackie Robinson, *born in 1919, was the first black player inducted into the Baseball Hall of Fame. The first black major league baseball star – he joined the Brooklyn Dodgers in 1947 – he died in 1972 after a life dogged by prejudice.*

VANESSA REDGRAVE

Vanessa Redgrave is one of the century's most fiery spirits. Born in 1937, she has enjoyed an enviable acting career since 1961, winning an Oscar in Julia (1977). But she has gained notoriety for supporting the Workers' Revolutionary Party, which she does with equal passion to her acting.

RADIO

The ten longest-running programmes on BBC Radio

- Daily Service (started in 1928)
- The Week in Westminster (1929)
- Desert Island Discs (1942)
- Saturday Night Theatre (1943)
- This Week's Composer (1943)
- From Our Own Correspondent (1946)
- Woman's Hour (1946)
- Choral Evensong (1946)
- Down Your Way (1946)
- Letter From America (1946)

RUDOLPH THE RED-NOSED REINDEER

Rudolph The Red-Nosed Reindeer was good for Hollywood's first singing cowboy, Gene Autry (above). As important to him as his wonder horse, Champion. For when Autry recorded 'Rudolph', it sold over eight million – the second biggest-selling Christmas record from the pre-rock period.

RICHARD RODGERS

Richard Rodgers was one of America's Big Five popular composers, along with George Gershwin, Cole Porter, Jerome Kern and Irving Berlin. Born in 1902, he proved his brilliance in two successful partnerships. First, with lyricist Lorenz Hart, he wrote many Broadway shows including Pal Joey. After Hart's death he teamed with Oscar Hammerstein II to write some of the world's most popular musicals including South Pacific, which spawned a soundtrack album that remained at the top of the British charts for 70 consecutive weeks in 1958-60. Rodgers died in 1979.

1966
Myra Hindley Jailed
'Moors murderers' Ian Brady, 28, and Myra Hindley, 23, were jailed for life after a stunned court heard how they had tortured and killed children, then buried their bodies on the Pennine Moors.

1966
Hydrogen Bomb Accident
An American Air Force B-52 jet carrying a hydrogen bomb collided with its refuelling plane over Palomares in Spain. Eight crewmen were killed in the near-disaster, but the pilot managed to release the bomb into the Atlantic.

1966
Mrs Gandhi Elected
Indira Gandhi was elected prime minister of India, serving until 1975. She was re-elected in the Eighties but in 1984 was assassinated by her bodyguards. Her son, Rajiv, became the next prime minister. In 1991, he also was assassinated.

SIR ALF RAMSEY

"They think it's all over… IT IS NOW!" Wembley 1966 was indubitably England's finest (sporting) hour. But the genius behind the triumph, coach Alf Ramsey, was almost out of a job as soon as he started: his first match in charge saw England knocked out of the European Championship by an out-of-form France.

Ramsey was born in 1922, in Dagenham (like Jimmy Greaves and Terry Venables). He played for Southampton and Spurs (who bought him in 1948 for £21,000, then a record signing for a full-back), and was capped for England 32 times. As a manager he took Ipswich from the Third Division to the League Championship, and took over the national team in 1962, immediately forecasting that England would win the World Cup.

Ramsey built up a national side that had the feel and spirit of a club team. He had an astute footballing brain and was popular with the players he selected, who were always given several matches to prove themselves.

After England were knocked out in the quarter-finals in 1970, they failed to qualify for the 1974 tournament, and Ramsey was sacked – a decision which hurt him deeply.

But he understood Kipling's line about dealing with triumph and disaster just the same. At the end of the 1966 final, he stood calmly outside the touchline, his face showing no emotion while all cheered and danced around him. Then, as Bobby Moore led his winning players towards the Royal Box to collect the trophy, Alf Ramsey quietly stepped forward and shook each of them by the hand.

WILMA RUDOLPH

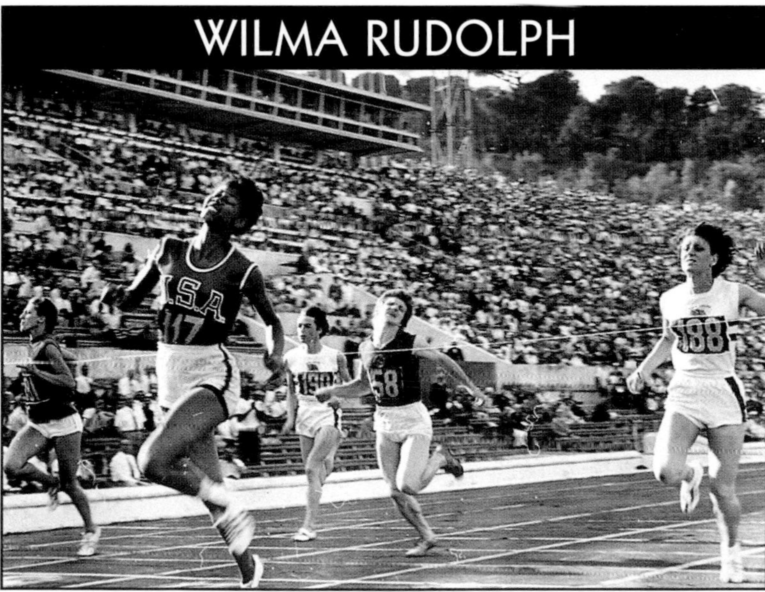

Wilma Rudolph's three gold medals in the Rome Olympics of 1960 were all the more remarkable because polio prevented her walking properly until she was eight. The US runner won the 100 metres, 200 metres and relay in the first Games televised worldwide

RED RUM

Red Rum, the only horse to win the Grand National three times, became a legend in his own lifetime. The world's best-loved horse won the world's toughest race in 1973 and '74, came second in '75 and '76, and won again in '77. A lifesize statue of Red Rum was unveiled at Aintree in 1988, and he died at the age of 30 in 1995.

1967 Colour Comes to TV BBC2 began transmitting in colour for the first time with viewers treated to nearly seven hours of the Wimbledon tennis championships.

1967 Astronauts Die Three American astronauts died when fire engulfed Apollo I during launch trials at Cape Kennedy, Florida.

1968 The End of a Dream US civil rights leader Dr Martin Luther King, famous for his "I have a Dream" speech, was shot dead at a motel in Memphis, Tennessee. His assassin, James Earl Ray, fled but was later caught in London. He was given a jail sentence of 99 years.

1968 My Lai Massacre Five hundred and four men, women, and children in the Vietnam village of My Lai were put to death by American troops. Twenty-five army officers were later charged with complicity in the massacre and subsequent cover-up. Only one was convicted, and he was pardoned by President Nixon.

ROYALTY

Kings and their Unfortunate Nicknames

King Louis the Fat *(Louis VI of France, 1108-37)*
King Rudolf the Sluggard *(Rudolf III of Burgundy, 993-1032)*
King Malcolm the Maiden *(Malcolm IV of Scotland, 1153-65)*
King Ferdinand the Fickle *(Ferdinand I of Portugal, 1367-83)*
King Charles the Mad *(Charles VI of France, 1380-1422)*
King Louis the Stubborn *(Louis X of France, 1314-16)*
King Charles the Bad *(Charles II of Navarre, 1349-87)*
King Henry the Impotent *(Henry IV of Castile, 1454-74)*
King Ethelred the Unready *(Ethelred II of England, 978-1016)*

Kings and their Fortunate Nicknames

King William the Good *(William II of Sicily, 1166-89)*
King Louis the Just *(Louis XIII of France, 1610-43)*
King Philip the Handsome *(Philip of Castile, 1506 – married Joan the Mad)*
King Charles the Victorious *(Charles VII of France, 1422-61)*
King Henry the Saint *(Henry II of Germany, 1014-24)*
King Richard the Lionheart *(Richard I of England, 1189-99)*
King Philip the Fair *(Philip IV of France, 1285-1314)*
King Ferdinand the Great *(Ferdinand I of Castile, 1035-65)*
King Charles the Wise *(Charles V of France, 1364-80)*
King Louis the Well-Beloved *(Louis XV of France, 1715-74)*

ROBINSON CRUSOE

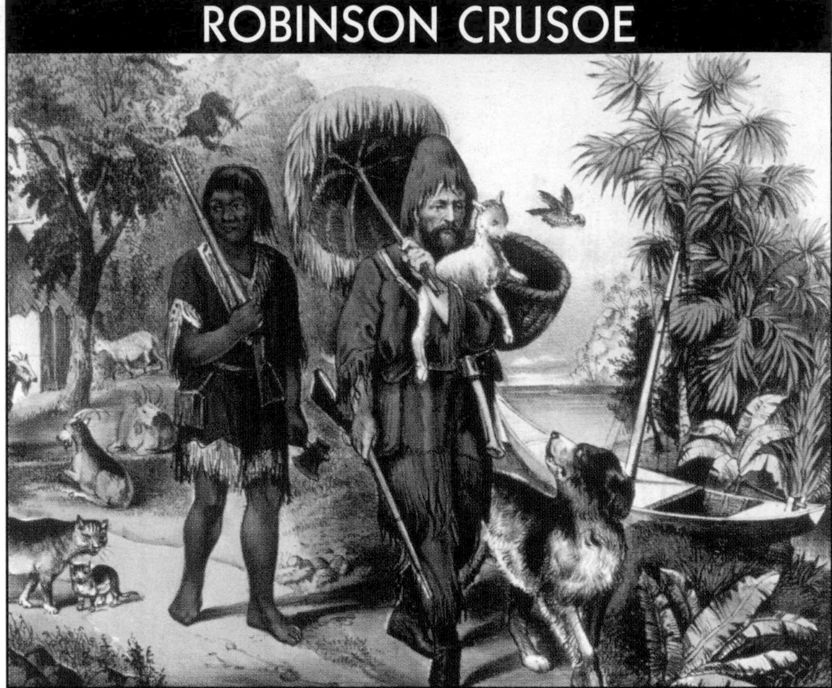

The story of marooned Scottish sailor Alexander Selkirk, Daniel Defoe's *Robinson Crusoe* created an enduring fantasy – the castaway robbed of his habitual comforts and habits who triumphantly survives by living off his own wits. Written in 1719, *Robinson Crusoe* is generally considered the first great English novel. Without it we might never have had *The Swiss Family Robinson, Lord of the Flies,* or *Desert Island Discs.*

RACE

THEN At the turn of the Millennium, England was already a society of ethnic diversity. Germanic tribes – Saxons, Jutes and Angles – had lived here for two centuries. The Romano-British had been pushed to the west, to Wales and Cornwall. Vikings were gradually being assimilated. King Canute (1016-35) was a successful immigrant – a Danish king who enjoyed a peaceful reign over the united Saxon kingdoms. But this fragile harmony was shattered by William the Conqueror in 1066. Norman French became the language of the upper classes.

NOW The Race Relations Act of 1965 made racial discrimination illegal. Since 1976 the Commission for Racial Equality has been able to take people to court. Such measures suggest that multi-ethnic Britain should be a haven of racial freedom. But in 1999 alone, nail bombs exploded in racist attacks on Brixton and Brick Lane; a black man was found to have been airbrushed from an advertisement; and London's police were accused of institutionalised racism.

The world's most famous rock face, Mount Rushmore in South Dakota was carved out over 14 years (1927-41) with the heads of four American Presidents, 60 feet high. From left: George Washington (representing the founding of the nation); Thomas Jefferson (the nation's philosophy); Theodore Roosevelt (expansion); and Abraham Lincoln (unity)

MOUNT RUSHMORE

1968
Jackie Remarries
Five years after the assassination of President John F Kennedy, his widow Jacqueline surprised the world by marrying multi-millionaire Greek tycoon Aristotle Onassis.

1968
New Kennedy Tragedy
Robert F Kennedy, brother of the assassinated President, was shot dead in a Los Angeles hotel where he had been celebrating his victory in a California presidential primary election. He was 42.

1968
The First Decimal Coins
Britain's first decimal coins were issued – the 5p and the 10p.

1968
Rise and Fall of Dubcek
Alexander Dubcek became first secretary of Czechoslovakia's Communist Party and began liberal reforms which he called "Communism with a human face". The revolution ended when Soviet troops invaded and Dubcek was later stripped of power.

LIFELINES

SALMAN RUSHDIE, *born in 1947, is the most noted recent victim of literary repression. He was forced into hiding when Iran's Ayatollah Khomeni declared a fatwah (death sentence) after taking offence at The Satanic Verses (1988).*

BERTRAND RUSSELL *(1872-1970), Britain's most famous philosopher, won the 1950 Nobel Prize for literature. A leading pacificist and nuclear disarmer, Earl Russell was jailed aged 89 for 'inciting a breach of the peace'.*

PAUL ROBESON'S *wonderful bass voice was immortalised by 'Ol' Man River'. Born in 1898, the singer and actor tried to find roles not usually reserved for blacks, seeking most of his film work outside his native USA. He died in 1976.*

ROBIN HOOD

All the world loves an outlaw, and Robin Hood is England's favourite – whether played by Errol Flynn in the 1938 movie, British actor Richard Greene in the Fifties TV series, or Kevin Costner (left) in the 1991 smash hit Robin Hood: Prince of Thieves. The Sherwood Forest freedom fighter who robbed from the rich and gave to the poor has been praised in ballads since the 13th century, along with his merry men – Little John, Friar Tuck, Alan a Dale – and his sweetheart Maid Marian. It's an idyllic fantasy of the rightful rebel's life, as long as your name's not the Sheriff of Nottingham.

ROB ROY

All the world loves an outlaw, and Rob Roy is Scotland's favourite – whether played by Richard Todd in the 1953 film or by Irishman Liam Neeson (left) in 1995. Rob Roy (1671-1734) was a Scottish outlaw who fought in the doomed Jacobite rebellion of 1715, trying to restore the Scottish house of Stuart to the British throne. Rob Roy – real name Robert MacGregor – was captured in 1722, sentenced to exile, then pardoned. Sir Walter Scott made him a romantic hero with his 1817 novel of the same name.

RED CROSS

The reassuring sight of Red Cross workers helping traumatised Kosovan refugees in 1999 was a reminder of the key role played by this humanitarian organisation founded by Swiss national Henri Dunant in 1863.

Dunant, appalled by the suffering at the Battle of Solferino, Italy, in 1859, set in train the International Red Cross and the Geneva Convention, to protect victims of war.

The everyday work of the British Red Cross (founded 1870) now includes first aid, therapeutic beauty care and work with the young and elderly. With its 160-odd sister organisations worldwide (in Moslem countries it's known as the Red Crescent), the organisation is ever on hand to dispense tea and sympathy, blankets and food in the wake of natural disasters. Henri Dunant

was awarded the Nobel Prize in 1901, and the Red Cross won it again in 1917 (for its work in the First World War, above), 1944 (Second World War) and 1963 (for alleviating world suffering).

RSPCA

It is a common jibe that the Brits love their animals more than their children. Certainly we love animal TV programmes, with RSPCA officers swooping to save ill-treated creatures.

The Royal Society for the Prevention of Cruelty to Animals has its origins in the 1822 anti-cruelty legislation backed by anti-slavery campaigner William Wilberforce which led to the first-ever UK law enforcement agency – an 'animal police' which pre-dated the first 'bobbies' by two years. The RSPCA gained royal recognition in 1840.

Today 309 officers investigate 100,000 complaints of animal cruelty every year. But its campaigns do not always go according to plan. A recent RSPCA vote on whether to campaign against hunting was defeated because the membership had been quietly infiltrated by pro-hunting activists.

1968 GOODBYE TO CENSORSHIP As a celebration of the Theatres Act abolishing censorship, 13 members of the cast of *Hair* in London's West End bared all to a bemused audience.

1968 TET OFFENSIVE BEGINS In a massive surprise offensive, North Vietnamese troops attacked 36 provincial capitals and five cities in South Vietnam. They also attacked the US embassy and the presidential palace in Saigon. The North Vietnamese were eventually beaten back, but graphic television reports of the fighting helped turn American public opinion against the war.

1969 JOHNSON QUITS President Lyndon Johnson, worn down by the pressures of the Vietnam War, announced that he would not stand for re-election. He died four years later.

1969 ENTER GADDAFI The Libyan government was overthrown in a military coup. Colonel Muammar Gaddafi seized control and established the Libyan Arab Republic.

SURGERY

THEN Until the mid-18th century, surgery was held in little esteem, and was frequently performed by barbers and wandering quacks. Slowly progress was made. Ambroise Pare, a 16th-century French military surgeon, put a stop to the practice of pouring boiling oil on wounds to sterilise them. Ephraim MacDowell of Kentucky performed the first successful removal of an ovarian tumour in 1809. Fellow American Crawford Long is thought to have been the first to use diethyl ether as an anaesthetic, in 1842.

NOW The first heart transplant operation was performed by Dr Christiaan Barnard in Cape Town, South Africa, in 1967. The heart of 53-year-old Louis Washkansky was replaced with that of a young woman killed in a car accident. The operation involved opening the patient's chest, splitting his breastbone and pulling the ribs aside, then attaching two thin electrodes to the new heart to restart it. The procedure remained rare until a new drug (cyclosporin) improved survival rates. In 1980 there were 105 heart transplants; in 1990, there were 3332.

ALBERT SCHWEITZER

Albert Schweitzer was one of the noblest figures of the 20th century. A renowned organist, born in 1875, he was also a respected philosopher, but opted to set up a missionary hospital in Gabon, Africa. His acclaimed works, expounding his philosophy of reverence for life, won him a Nobel Peace Prize before his death in 1965.

PETER SELLERS

Peter Sellers found fame in The Goon Show in the Fifties, but the world fell in love with him as the word-mangling Inspector Clouseau in The Pink Panther. One of Britain's first superstars, he married Britt Ekland (above) in 1964 and had a hit record with Sophia Loren. He died in 1980, aged 54, amid acclaim for his latest film, Being There.

SCOTLAND

Scotland can blow its own trumpet at last, since the long-awaited Scottish parliament began work in 1999

The final year of the Millennium was an auspicious one for Scotland, as 74 per cent of Scots voted for their own parliament – a measure of self-government Scotland had not enjoyed since the 17th century.

Prime Minister Tony Blair gave the Scottish assembly leeway to lower or raise the rate of income tax by three per cent, which may hasten a move towards full independence. The British Cabinet's three top officials were all educated (and two of them born) in Scotland, and now run a United Kingdom where English outnumber Scots by ten to one. But the Act of Union which bound England and Scotland together is now being loosened.

Despite all the symbolic resonances, the dawn of New Scotland has proved rather anti-climactic. Its first proceedings were less than earth-shattering. Minister for Scotland Donald Dewar proposed a mere eight Bills for the first year's work – not before the new parliament had voted itself annual leave of 17 weeks. Is this what *Braveheart* was all about?

1969
THE FIRST MAN ON THE MOON
On July 20, astronaut Neil Armstrong, Commander of the historic *Apollo II* space mission, manoeuvred the *Eagle* lunar module on to the surface of the Moon as millions of awestruck viewers watched his progress on television. As he stepped down to become the first man on the Moon, Armstrong said: "That's one small step for man, one giant leap for mankind."

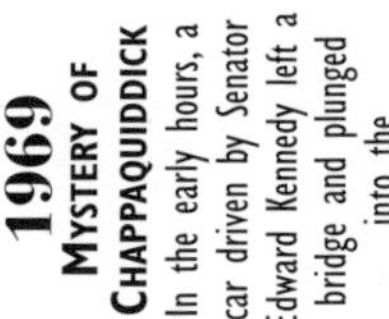

1969
MYSTERY OF CHAPPAQUIDDICK
In the early hours, a car driven by Senator Edward Kennedy left a bridge and plunged into the Chappaquiddick River in Massachusetts. His companion Mary Jo Kopechne drowned. Kennedy did not report the accident for ten hours and was later given a suspended sentence for leaving the scene of an accident. Kennedy denied doing anything wrong, but the incident dashed his hopes of one day becoming President.

WILLIAM SHAKESPEARE

The Bard, aged 41

Shakey is inescapable. He is watermarked on our money, hologrammed on our credit cards, and plastered all over the cinema, winning Oscars year in, year out. The 'Swan of Avon' has become the icon's icon, an international brand for the selling of England and the English language.

In his own day, Shakespeare was just one of a bevy of golden writers, some of whom were actually more popular – Francis Beaumont, John Fletcher, Christopher Marlowe, Ben Jonson… Born in 1564, Shakespeare was a jobbing actor as well as a playwright, and his works would have been subject to hasty revisions according to how they went down the night before. But this chaotic method somehow produced the greatest body of work in literature. He died aged just 51, but few would quibble with him being named as the Man of the Millennium.

Yet, for all Shakespeare's prominence, we know little about him, and his plays cover such a range of emotions and characters that one can scarcely trace him there. His works are open to almost any interpretation – from *Kiss Me Kate* to Olivier, *West Side Story* to *Shakespeare in Love*, Shakespeare is a personality cult with no personality of his own – but with something of everyone's.

Possibly the best of Laurence Olivier's four Shakespeare films was his ingenious Henry V, which he directed in 1944

SOAP OPERAS

Above: Original EastEnders stars Susan Tully, Wendy Richard, Anna Wing, Anita Dobson and Leslie Grantham. Left: Larry Hagman as Dallas's JR. Below: Dynasty with Joan Collins, left, and Linda Evans, right

The first soap operas were American radio programmes sponsored by washing powder manufacturers, but they soon became highly successful formats on television.

Britain's longest-running soap is *Coronation Street*, which began in 1960 and now does weekly battle at the top of the ratings with its BBC rival, *EastEnders*, which started in 1985. Since the late Eighties, along with *Brookside* and *Emmerdale*, they have also had to compete with the Australian soaps *Home and Away* and *Neighbours* (which launched the careers of pop stars Jason Donovan, Kylie Minogue and Natalie Imbruglia) and the glitzy escapism of American soaps *Dallas* and *Dynasty* and their often hilarious offspring *Sunset Beach* and *The Bold and the Beautiful*.

Corrie out-performs the other soaps because of its fine comic acting and less histrionic pace that mirrors real life. The quiet Liverpool close of *Brookside*, on the other hand, has had an armed siege, a bomb blast, rape, drug barons, at least three murders, and a fatal outbreak of a rare disease.

LIFELINES

GEORGE BERNARD SHAW, born in Dublin in 1856, wrote plays that often seemed like comedies at surface level, yet pricked the social conscience. He was a renowned music and drama critic, and a brilliant debater. But more famously he's remembered as the man who wrote Pygmalion. A great play in its own right, it was used by Lerner and Loewe as the basis of My Fair Lady. Their musical began a record-breaking run in 1956, six years after Shaw's death, and was made into a hit film in 1964.

MARQUIS DE SADE explored the idea of pain as part of sex – hence the word sadism. A French count born in 1740, he lived out the fantasies of his most famous book, Justine. Often imprisoned, he died in a lunatic asylum in 1814. His spirit lives on in modern writers such as Bret Easton Ellis.

1969 THE KRAYS ARE JAILED Gangland leaders Reggie and Ronnie Kray, 35-year-old twins, were convicted of murder and sentenced to serve a minimum of 30 years.

1969 WOMEN'S VOTES All women aged 18 and over finally enjoyed the right to vote, giving them equality with men.

1969 THE FIRST WOODSTOCK The Woodstock pop concert began in a field near New York. The three-day event featured 24 bands and drew a crowd of more than 400,000.

1970 STUDENTS SHOT DEAD After President Nixon decided to invade Cambodia, 1,000 students held a protest demonstration at Kent State University. National Guardsmen opened fire, leaving four students dead and 11 wounded. The shootings set off massive demonstrations across the country.

SCIENCE FICTION

Hugo Gernsback, editor of 1920s magazines like *Science Wonder Stories*, called sci-fi "a charming romance intermingled with scientific fact and prophetic vision". The appeal lies in trying to predict the future of technology and its impact on everyday lives.

Early masters were Jules Verne, who envisaged a train to the moon, and H G Wells, who wrote *The War of the Worlds* (1898) and *The Time Machine* (1908). The golden age of science fiction was the Sixties, before reality and the movies overtook the visions of Brian Aldiss, Arthur C Clarke and Philip K Dick.

Recent sci-fi has retreated into comedy in Douglas Adams' *A Hitchhiker's Guide to the Galaxy* and Terry Pratchett's *Discworld* novels.

Today science fiction belongs to the cinema. *Metropolis* (1926) imagined cities of the future, but it wasn't until Stanley Kubrick's *2001: A Space Odyssey* (1968) that films began to paint realistic visions of space.

Its special effects paved the way for Steven Spielberg's *Close Encounters of the Third Kind* and George Lucas' *Star Wars* saga. More chilling vistas were conjured up by Ridley Scott's *Blade Runner* (1987) and Sigourney Weaver's *Alien* series. Now movies are taking the comedy route, too, with *Mars Attacks!*, *Independence Day* and *Men in Black*.

STAR WARS

Even George Lucas cannot have imagined how the derring-do of his Star Wars trilogy (1977-83) would capture a generation. When The Phantom Menace came out in 1999, it took millions back to their childhood. Above: Mark Hamill, Carrie Fisher and Harrison Ford in Star Wars – but the real stars were the effects and robots R2D2 and C3PO.

GREG PROOPS' BEST OF THE MILLENNIUM

SCIENCE FICTION

COMIC AND SCI FI BUFF GREG PROOPS APPEARS ON WHOSE LINE IS IT ANYWAY?

THE MARTIAN CHRONICLES BY RAY BRADBURY

"Ray Bradbury is the most human science fiction writer: he is the least concerned with technology and the most concerned with how we as a species will deal emotionally with the future. He cares about us and for that I must love him.

"I particularly recommend *The Martian Chronicles.* Written in 1951 and set in 1999, it's about Americans conquering space and spending time taking potshots at ancient Martian temples. Some sci-fi is too true."

SUPERMAN

SUPERMAN WAS CREATED BY TWO OHIO STUDENTS IN 1934. BASED ON FILM STAR DOUGLAS FAIRBANKS JR, HE CAME FROM THE PLANET KRYPTON BUT WAS AS AMERICAN AS COCA-COLA. HE'D BECOME OLD HAT UNTIL SQUARE-JAWED CHRISTOPHER REEVE REVIVED HIM IN FOUR FILMS (1978-87) WITH MARGOT KIDDER AS LOIS LANE (LEFT). AND IN 1993 SUPERMAN FINALLY GOT SEXY AT 60 IN THE LOIS & CLARK TV SERIES.

STAR TREK

Star Trek is the most popular form of entertainment of all time. With its different TV series – including *Star Trek: The Next Generation* and a cartoon – and seven films, *Star Trek* is a billion-dollar industry, with more merchandise (books, comics, clothes, etc) sold than any other film or TV series.

An episode of Star Trek is transmitted somewhere on Earth 24 hours a day for 365 days of the year.

The original TV series wasn't a hit – every year, its future was in doubt – so there weren't many famous guest stars. One notable exception was Joan Collins, in 'City On The Edge of Forever'.

The captain in the pilot episode was played by Jeffrey Hunter, but when the series got the go-ahead, he said no (it's said his wife advised him against it!) and so William Shatner got the part.

'City On The Edge of Forever' and 'The Trouble With Tribbles' (the one with all the little furry animals) are said by most Trekkers to be the best episodes of *Star Trek.* It is generally accepted that 'Spock's Brain' – in which the great man has his brain stolen – is the most stupid episode.

Just as Bogart never said, "Play it again, Sam", so Captain Kirk never said, "Beam me up, Scottie."

Michelle Nichols (Uhura) broke new ground as a black actress on US TV equal on screen with white actors. She almost quit because she only got a couple of lines per show (eg "Getting no reply, Captain") but was persuaded to stay by civil rights leader Dr Martin Luther King.

1971
TATE KILLERS GUILTY
Charles Manson, leader of a macabre Californian cult called The Family, was sentenced to death for the ritual slaughter of Hollywood actress Sharon Tate and four others in 1969. Manson, obsessed with race war and Satanism, led a drug-ridden commune.

1971
AMIN HORROR BEGINS
Idi Amin seized control of Uganda after leading a military coup against President Milton Obote. Amin then ruled as dictator, ordering the execution of at least 300,000 people. He also expelled all Asians from Uganda. He was ousted from power in 1979.

1972
ELIZABETH SHIP ABLAZE
The *Queen Elizabeth*, Cunard's former trans-Atlantic liner, was destroyed by a mysterious blaze at Hong Kong harbour. The ship, which was launched in 1938, had become a floating university and had been moored in the harbour for some time.

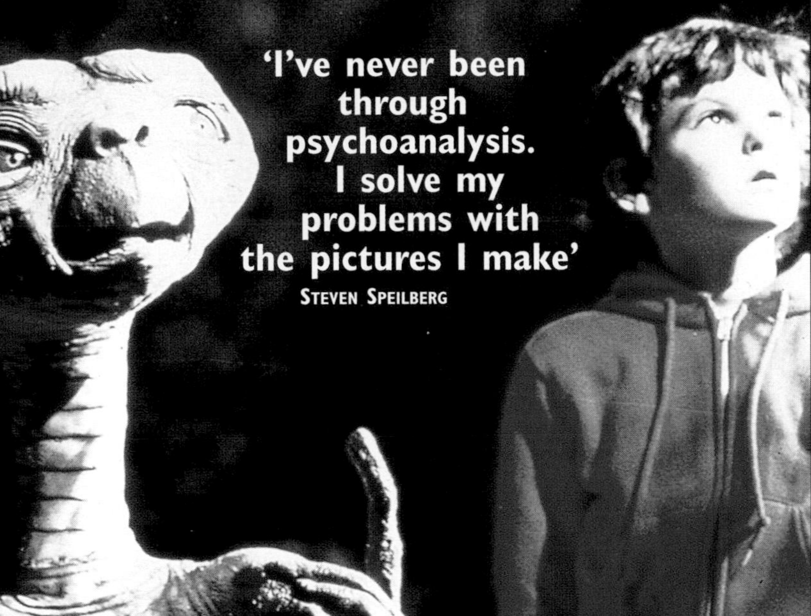

Every one's a winner... Steven Spielberg has made many of the most successful films of all time, including ET (above), Jaws (below left), Indiana Jones (below right) and Jurassic Park (above right).

STEVEN SPEILBERG

Hollywood's modern Midas made his name with a film about a shark described by one critic as a "semi-adult treatment of what once would have been comic-strip material for children".

It's an accusation (or tribute) you could level at any block-buster by Steven Spielberg, the man who almost single-handedly turned the past 25 years' cinema into a special-effects playground.

Jaws rewrote box-office records in 1975. Spielberg followed it up with more huge hits – *Close Encounters of the Third Kind* (1977); *ET* (1982), with its charming alien; the comic-book capers of *Indiana Jones* (1984); and the dinosaur disaster flick *Jurassic Park* (1993), which earned him $200 million.

But with *The Color Purple* (1985), based on Alice Walker's novel in praise of black women, he showed his other side.

He won a long-awaited director's Oscar for *Schindler's List* (1993), about the Holocaust. The film was not without its critics, but no one could fault his sincerity.

The trend continues with *Saving Private Ryan*, about the D-Day landings. Serious stuff – but, as ever, it's brilliant movie-making.

LIFELINES

***Charles Stewart** – Bonnie Prince Charlie – was James II's grandson, the Young Pretender to the British crown. Born in Rome in 1720, he landed in Scotland in 1745, invaded England, was defeated at Culloden and fled back to Italy, where he died in 1788.*

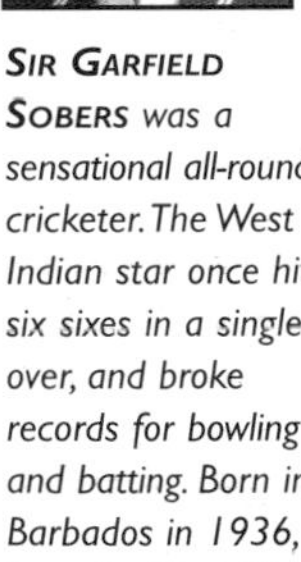

***Sir Garfield Sobers** was a sensational all-round cricketer. The West Indian star once hit six sixes in a single over, and broke records for bowling and batting. Born in Barbados in 1936, he retired in 1974.*

***Igor Stravinsky** set the tone for 20th-century music. Russian-born in 1882, he found fame in 1910 with The Firebird for Serge Diaghilev's Ballets Russes in Paris. The violent Rite of Spring (danced by Nijinsky) caused a riot. He died in 1971.*

SCIENCE

TEN SCIENTIFIC ADVANCES AND WHEN THEY TOOK PLACE

THE FIRST HEART PACEMAKER was fitted in 1952. The first internal pacemaker came in 1958. The first successful heart operation was in 1896, by Louis Rehn in Frankfurt, Germany.

THE FIRST COLOUR PHOTOGRAPHY – using three colours – was patented by William Morgan-Brown in 1876.

THE DUPLICATING MACHINE was patented by James Watt in 1780. The photo-copier wasn't invented until 1938.

LINOLEUM was patented in 1863 by Frederick Walton of London.

THE FIRST SCHEDULED PASSENGER AIR SERVICE started in Florida in 1914.

THE FIRST BRITISH TELEPHONE DIRECTORY was published in London in 1880. It listed 250 names and numbers.

THE FIRST ELECTRIC BURGLAR ALARM was installed in 1858 by one Edwin T Holmes of Boston, Massachusetts.

THE LONDON UNDERGOUND system was inaugurated in 1863.

THE FIRST ESCALATOR that was a commercial success was patented in 1892 by Jesse Reno of New York.

THE TYPEWRITER (right) was patented by Henry Mill in 1714 but he never managed to market his invention.

1972 THE START OF WATERGATE Five men were arrested as burglars after breaking into the Democratic party's headquarters in the Watergate building in Washington. Inquiries revealed that they were agents hired by the Committee for the Re-election of President Richard Nixon. Attempts by the White House to cover up the affair led to a chain of events over the next three years resulting in the jailing of Nixon's right-hand men and his own resignation to stem off impeachment.

1972 NIXON IN CHINA Richard Nixon became the first U.S. President to visit China. He held talks with Chairman Mao Tse-tung and Premier Chou En-lai.

1972 BLOODY SUNDAY Thirteen Roman Catholics were killed by British troops during a banned civil rights march In Londonderry. The event became known as Bloody Sunday.

1972 BATTLING ON Shoichi Yokoi, a Japanese soldier from the Second World War, was found on the Pacific island of Guam still hiding out. He didn't know the war ended 28 years earlier.

THE SPICE GIRLS

The Spice Girls follow in a long line of successful female singing groups that began with US recording stars The Boswell Sisters in the 1930s and continued through The Andrews Sisters in the swing-era Forties, Motown's Supremes in the Sixties, to Bananarama in the Eighties.

However, the Spices (above from left: Emma Bunton, Melanie Brown, Melanie Chisholm, Victoria Adams and Geri Halliwell) did everything bigger and in the glare of intense media coverage.

The best-known British group since The Beatles, the master stroke of adopting instantly memorable nicknames – Baby, Scary, Sporty, Posh and Ginger, respectively – meant that everyone could name the whole quintet.

Their first single, 'Wannabe' in 1996, gave birth to the line *"I'll tell you what I want, what I really, really want"* and sparked the Girl Power credo which implied that the Spices were the greatest blow for womanhood since the suffragettes. The glam five promptly notched up eight No 1's in less than three years.

Geri's sudden departure in 1998, and the birth of two baby Spices, did not dampen the group's popularity, while Victoria's marriage to footballer David Beckham in 1999's 'Wedding of the Decade' has only enhanced it.

STAMPS

PEOPLE WHO HAVE BEEN FEATURED ON STAMPS

IAN BOTHAM (St Vincent)
ARNOLD SCHWARZENEGGER (Mali)
CLIVE LLOYD (Guyana)
DOLLY PARTON (Grenada)
VIV RICHARDS (Antigua)
CHER (Grenada) (above)
DAVID PLATT (Lesotho)
JIMMY CONNORS (Lesotho)
CARL LEWIS (Niger)
EDDIE MURPHY (Tanzania)
MUHAMMAD ALI (Liberia)
BARONESS THATCHER (Kenya)
NICK FALDO (St Vincent)
STEVIE WONDER (Tanzania)
GLADYS KNIGHT (Tanzania)
BRUCE SPRINGSTEEN (Grenada)

LIFELINES

***SIR WALTER SCOTT** was the master of the tartan-clad historical novel. Born in Edinburgh in 1771, he made his name as a poet in 1805 with The Lay of the Last Minstrel, but turned down the post of Poet Laureate. He turned to novels in 1814, including Rob Roy and Ivanhoe. Sadly, book keeping was not his forte, and he spent his last years in debt. He died in 1832.*

***PERCY BYSSHE SHELLEY** was both a great romantic poet and the original angry young man. Born in 1792, he was called 'Mad Shelley' at Eton, and was expelled from Oxford for advocating atheism. He also expounded vegetarianism and pro-Irish politics. Though married, he ran off to Europe with Mary Wollstonecraft (who wrote Frankenstein), became friends with Lord Byron, and wrote Prometheus Unbound. Shelley drowned in a sailing accident, aged 29.*

DR SPOCK

Even today, many parents will know the name of American childcare expert Dr Benjamin Spock (left), even if they don't know his theories. Spock's *Commonsense Book of Baby & Child Care* (1946) has sold 30 million copies, second only to the Bible.

His radical approach urged parents to enjoy their babies, follow their instincts and forget the rigid ideas of earlier generations. A strong opponent of the arms race and the Vietnam War, Spock was accused of raising a "spineless and permissive" generation and jailed for helping conscripts dodge the draft, though he successfully appealed against his conviction.

Spock was also a rower in the 1924 Olympics, and stood for American President in 1972. In old age, however, he was less tolerant of the freedoms he had once advocated for young children.

DR SEUSS

GENERATIONS OF CHILDREN HAVE RELISHED THE ZANY DRAWINGS AND VERSES OF DR THEODORE SEUSS GEISEL. BOOKS SUCH AS 1957'S THE CAT IN THE HAT (LEFT) REVEL IN THE FUN OF WORDS, ABETTED BY THE COMIC ENERGY OF HIS ARTWORK (DESPITE ACCUSATIONS OF OCCASIONAL GRAPHIC VIOLENCE). BORN IN 1904, SEUSS WROTE MORE THAN 50 BOOKS BEFORE HIS DEATH IN 1991.

1972
THE MAN WHO WOULDN'T BE KING
The Duke of Windsor died in Paris. He had abdicated the throne in 1936 to marry Wallis Simpson, an American divorcee. The couple spent the rest of their lives exiled in Paris. The Duke was buried near Windsor Castle.

1973
BRITAIN JOINS EUROPE
Prime Minister Edward Heath took Britain into the European Economic Community, or Common Market, as it was known. Opinion polls showed that most people were against the move.

1973
GAME, SET AND MATCH
Self-styled male chauvinist Bobby Riggs was beaten in three straight sets by tennis player and women's rights activist Billie Jean King in a much-hailed "Battle of the Sexes" game at Houston, Texas. Riggs, a retired tennis champion, had constantly complained about the quality of the women's game.

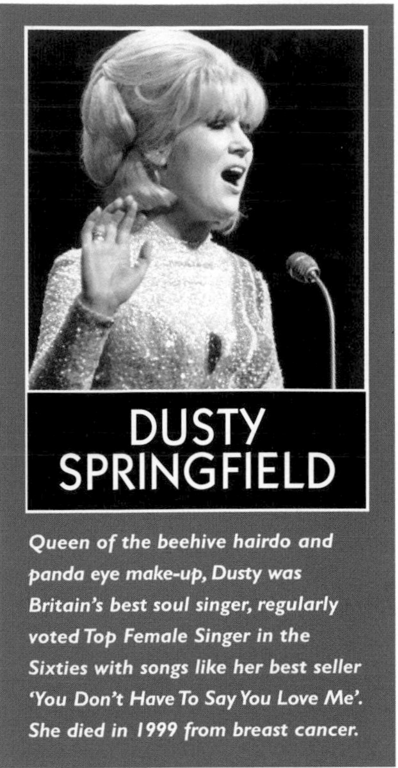

DUSTY SPRINGFIELD

Queen of the beehive hairdo and panda eye make-up, Dusty was Britain's best soul singer, regularly voted Top Female Singer in the Sixties with songs like her best seller 'You Don't Have To Say You Love Me'. She died in 1999 from breast cancer.

PHIL SPECTOR

Phil Spector and his 'Wall of Sound' made record production an art form. His classic hits include 'Be My Baby' by The Ronettes (below), and 'You've Lost That Lovin' Feelin''. But when his masterpiece, Ike and Tina Turner's 'River Deep Mountain High' (1966), wasn't a US hit, he became a recluse.

FRANK SINATRA

Frank Sinatra had hits in every decade from the Thirties to the Nineties. Rated by many as the singer of the century, he was also a magnet for the media as his life tumbled through rocky marriages to sex goddess Ava Gardner and waif-like Mia Farrow, and tales of Mafia involvement.

As a singer Sinatra was noted for his phrasing, which he said he picked up by studying the horn players in the dance bands he first worked for. When he went solo in 1942, US musicians were on strike – forcing Sinatra to make records without instrumental backing. But by 1943 he was a big star – the first singer girls screamed at. He was also a good enough actor to win an Oscar in *From Here To Eternity* (1953).

He had a No1 at 50 with 'Strangers In The Night', and 'My Way' – a song he said he hated – spent 124 weeks in the charts.

He had never been in the armed forces, but when he died in 1998 he was buried with full military honours.

SATURDAY NIGHT FEVER

Saturday Night Fever had all a Hollywood musical could have wanted in 1977: a sexy new star in John Travolta, who had been treading water in a US TV series; songs by The Bee Gees, who had just made a stunning comeback with hits in the new 'disco' style; and a new dance craze coming out of the clubs.

It was masterminded by rock impresario Robert Stigwood, who had wanted to call the film *Saturday Night* until vetoed by the Gibb brothers. *Saturday Night Fever* was not only a huge box-office success: it also sold records by the million. The best-selling film soundtrack of all time, the *Saturday Night Fever* double album contained four No1 singles.

Overnight it turned disco into the world's most in-demand music, capturing the spirit of the late Seventies and making every red-blooded male wish that he was Tony Manero, strutting down the avenue on his way to a place where working-class zeros could become dancefloor heroes.

S

1973
The Three-Day Week
Oil prices quadrupled after an Arab embargo against pro-Israeli countries. Then, as demand for coal to produce power soared, the miners went on strike for more pay. To conserve energy, Prime Minister Edward Heath put industry on a three-day working week and ordered power cuts across the nation. On the sidelines, Margaret Thatcher quietly fumed.

1973
Watergate Net Closes
As the Watergate scandal engulfed Richard Nixon's presidency in 1973, White House aides Gordon Liddy and James McCord were convicted of burglary, wire-tapping and attempted bugging of the Democratic Party headquarters at the Watergate building in Washington.

1973
Vietnam War is Over
The United States and North Vietnam signed a peace treaty in Paris and thus America ended the longest war in its history, defeated for the first time. Over 58,000 Americans were killed, 300,000 wounded and 2,500 declared missing.

LIFELINES

Robert Louis Stevenson's *novels spanned a huge range, from adventure stories such as Kidnapped (set in his native Scotland) and Treasure Island, to the horror of Dr Jekyll and Mr Hyde. He died from TB in 1894, aged just 44.*

Jock Stein *was the most successful manager ever in Scottish football. He turned Celtic into the first British team ever to win the European Cup and took Scotland to two World Cups. He died aged 62 in 1985, watching his team play Wales.*

Marie Stopes *(1880-1958) changed women's lives by promoting contraception. Author of the best-seller Married Love, the campaigner opened Britain's first birth control centre in London in 1921.*

SPORT

It was George Orwell who described serious sport as "war minus the shooting". His remark was echoed in rather more positive terms by Ernest Hemingway, who argued in *Death in the Afternoon*, his idiosyncratic manual on bullfighting, that with sport modern man has replaced the fear of death with the fear of defeat.

Sport, in other words, is a symbolic reminder of more primitive, pagan times, when everyday survival was a life-and-death struggle. For most of us this is a positive development, but Hemingway despised the civilising nature of sport and hymned the praises of the *corrida*, which he said returned us to those fiercer, more authentic times.

Sport today brings out the competitive instinct in more ways than one. Our top players and athletes are a breed apart, hot-housed from early childhood and militarily dedicated to their chosen sport with the aim of a few brief years of glory.

Sport is a pretext for fierce commercial battles, too, as sponsors vie for coverage and broadcasters negotiate astronomical figures for the rights to competitions such as Premier League football. Sport is Britain's 11th largest industry, and accounts for three per cent of world trade. Sport can unite a country in benevolent patriotism behind a team or player, and bring together countries which, in political terms, are poles apart.

In Britain, poor showings in football and cricket provoke regular press inquests. Now the Government has got in on the act, announcing £600 million of lottery money to build better links between schools and clubs, in a bid to produce a 'play to win' culture.

PETE SAMPRAS

Pistol Pete is starting to stake a convincing claim as the best tennis player of them all. His unhistrionic efficiency may not be good box-office, but his record brooks no argument. The most successful man at Wimbledon this century (six wins including 1999), with four US Open and two Australian Open titles, he needs one Grand Slam title to overtake Roy Emerson. He dominated the 1990s and won't be 30 until the new Millennium. Scary.

INGEMAR STENMARK

Who's the greatest skier – Italy's Alberto Tomba or his idol, Ingemar Stenmark? The Swede, born in 1956, was overall World Cup winner three times, and won two Olympic gold medals in 1980, in giant slalom and slalom. His record of 86 World Cup wins in 16 years may never be beaten, but if anyone does it, it will be Tomba.

AYRTON SENNA

"With Ayrton, racing isn't a sport, it's war." The words of his great rival Alain Prost make a sombre epitaph to the man most people believe was the best racing driver of modern times. Ayrton Senna died on May 1, 1994, on the seventh lap of the Imola Grand Prix. He was 34 – but in the eyes of his fellow Brazilians, already immortal.

1974 Pub Bombs Outrage
Two pubs in Birmingham were bombed by the IRA in one of the worst terrorist attacks on mainland Britain. Twenty-one people were killed and 182 injured. The attack prompted the Prevention of Terrorism Act in an attempt to combat the IRA. Six people jailed for the bombing – 'the Birmingham Six' were freed in 1991 when the Appeal Court ruled that police evidence against them was unsatisfactory.

1974 Nixon Resigns
Richard Nixon, facing impeachment for trying to cover up the Watergate break-in scandal, became the first President to resign in office.

1974 Lord Lucan Disappears
After the murder of nanny Sandra Rivett at the Lucan family's Mayfair home, Lord Lucan, widely believed to be the killer, drove away from the house and was never seen again. Speculation over his whereabouts has continued ever since.

MARK SPITZ

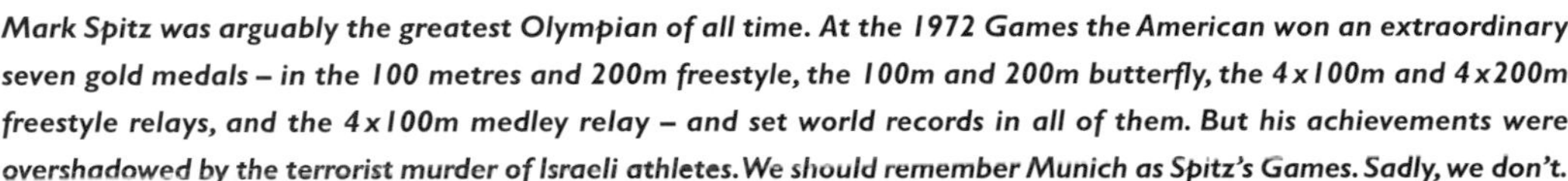

Mark Spitz was arguably the greatest Olympian of all time. At the 1972 Games the American won an extraordinary seven gold medals – in the 100 metres and 200m freestyle, the 100m and 200m butterfly, the 4x100m and 4x200m freestyle relays, and the 4x100m medley relay – and set world records in all of them. But his achievements were overshadowed by the terrorist murder of Israeli athletes. We should remember Munich as Spitz's Games. Sadly, we don't.

ALAN SHEARER

England striker Alan Shearer set a world transfer record when he moved from Blackburn Rovers to Newcastle United in 1996 for £15 million, but within three years that was peanuts as Italian striker Christian Vieri left Lazio for Internazionale of Milan for £30 million.

SHERGAR

The name Shergar is most likely to be heard these days as a joke about how Elvis or Lord Lucan has been spotted … riding Shergar. But the Shergar story is actually one of sport's greatest tragedies.

This picture shows Shergar winning the 1981 Derby. There's Shergar and then the rest. He won by a record ten lengths at a canter, added the Irish Derby and the King George VI and Queen Elizabeth Stakes to his trophy cabinet, and was then retired to stud, worth £10 million.

But on February 9, 1983 this great horse was snatched by an armed gang – thought to be the IRA. His owner, the Aga Khan, refused to pay a £2 million ransom. Shergar was never seen again.

JACKIE STEWART

SCOTSMAN JACKIE STEWART TURNED DOWN £1 MILLION TO RETURN TO RACING AFTER HE QUIT IN 1973, FOLLOWING THE DEATH OF HIS TYRRELL TEAM-MATE FRANÇOIS CEVERT. STEWART HAD JUST WON THE WORLD TITLE FOR THE THIRD TIME. HE IS NOW PRESIDENT OF THE STEWART-FORD FORMULA ONE TEAM.

1974
McDONALD'S ARRIVES
The first McDonald's restaurant opened in South London.

1975
TUBE TRAIN HORROR
In one of the worst London Tube disasters, a morning rush-hour Northern Line train crashed through buffers at Moorgate Station and hit a wall. Forty-one people, including the driver, were killed and 50 others were seriously hurt. The rescue operation took three days.

1975
NIXON AIDES GUILTY
President Nixon's former top aides, Attorney General John Mitchell, Domestic Affairs Advisor John Erlichman and Chief of Staff HR Haldeman, were all found guilty of obstructing justice.

1975
THATCHER'S RISE TO POWER
After his battle with the unions, Edward Heath called a "Who Rules?" general election in 1974. He lost – narrowly – to Harold Wilson. Heath's humiliation was complete in 1975 when Margaret Thatcher challenged him for leadership of the Conservative Party – and won. He never forgave her.

LIFELINES

Josef Stalin, *born in 1879, was presented as a man of the people. It later transpired that this Soviet leader was vicious, tyrannical and as anti-semitic as Hitler. After his death, in 1953, he was denounced by Russia's leaders.*

Aleksandr Solzhenitsyn *was imprisoned in his native Russia from 1945-53 because of his anti-Stalinist beliefs. Born in 1918, he was expelled from his homeland in 1974 for writing books graphically describing life in Soviet labour camps.*

Stephen Sondheim *is the most creative Broadway musical writer of our times. A New Yorker, born in 1930, he is both composer and lyricist. His work includes West Side Story (lyrics) and A Little Night Music.*

SPACE TRAVEL

It was Johannes Kepler, the 17th-century German astronomer and mathematician, who first wrote about the scientific possibilities of travelling to other worlds. The dream did not move much closer to reality until the first two decades of this century, when the principles of rocket technology were developed.

In 1957, the USSR beat America by launching the first satellite, *Sputnik*, into orbit round the Earth. A week later, Russia sent up a dog.

As the space race hotted up, the superpowers' first goal was to put a man in space. Russia won again: Yuri Gagarin completed an orbit of Earth in 1961, and in 1965 Aleksei Leonov was the first human to walk in space.

The Americans soon caught up. In March 1966, two US craft achieved the first docking in orbit. And, of course, in 1969 Americans were the first on the Moon.

But the US space programme was set back years by the *Challenger* space shuttle disaster of 1986. Millions watched live as, 73 seconds after lift-off, the craft exploded in mid-air.

By then, unmanned probes were exploring the vastness of space. *Voyager* was launched in 1977, reaching Jupiter in 1979, Saturn in 1981, Uranus in 1986 and Neptune in 1989. Probes have also landed on and explored Mars.

No one has been to the Moon since 1972, but space stations have allowed more people into space. *Salyut* was launched by the Soviet Union in 1971. Three cosmonauts spent 23 days aboard, performing experiments, but an air leak led to their death on the return journey.

America sent up the reusable *Skylab* station in 1973, and in 1986 the Soviet Union's *Mir* ('peace') began its virtually non-stop lodging of cosmonauts, often for a year at a time. Disaster was narrowly averted in June 1997 when a supply craft crashed into the *Mir* station.

In 1991, Helen Sharman became the first Briton in space, on a Russian mission. In 1995, Briton Michael Foale walked in space from America's *Discovery* space shuttle. In 1999, American Eileen Collins became the first female space commander, aboard the *Columbia* shuttle.

The oldest person in space was American John Glenn, who first orbited Earth in 1962 and found himself back up there on a space shuttle in 1998 – at the age of 76.

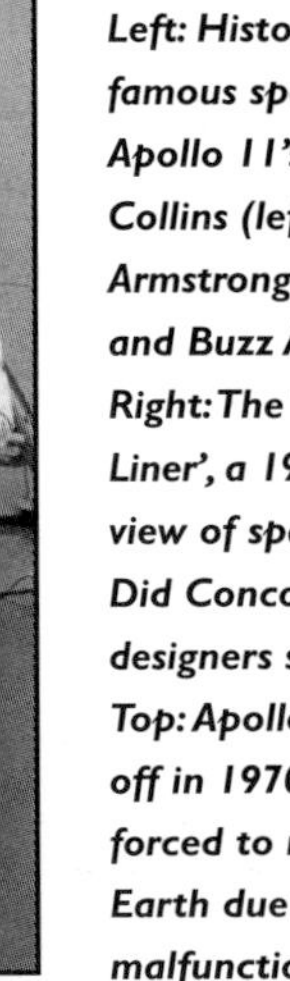

Left: History's most famous spacemen – Apollo 11's Michael Collins (left), Neil Armstrong (centre) and Buzz Aldrin. Right: The 'Lunar Liner', a 1958 artist's view of space travel. Did Concorde's designers see this? Top: Apollo 13 takes off in 1970. It was forced to return to Earth due to a malfunction.

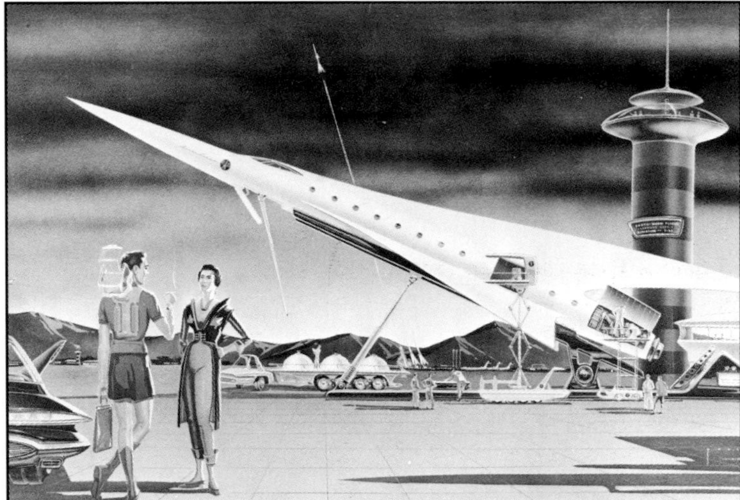

MILLENNIUM TIME LINE

1976
Concorde Takes Off
The Concorde supersonic jet went into service with flights from London to Bahrain and Paris to Rio de Janeiro. Concorde cruises at twice the speed of sound (Mach 2) and flies at an altitude up to 60,000 feet.

1976
Killing Fields of Pol Pot
Pol Pot and his Khmer Rouge followers seized control of Cambodia and began a three-year reign of terror. Over a million people died in 'the killing fields' as he forced people out of cities and into the countryside to create what Pol Pot proclaimed would be an idyllic agrarian society. Educated and professional people were almost completely wiped out.

1977
Just Champion, Virginia
The Queen's Silver Jubilee year was enhanced when British hopeful Virginia Wade beat Dutch Betty Stove to win the women's singles title at the Wimbledon tennis championships.

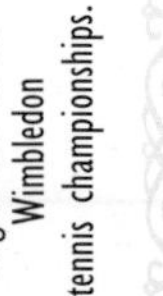

SCANDAL

We are naturally suspicious of our leaders, so any sign of hypocrisy can seem like a gleeful confirmation of our worst fears. Britain's biggest post-war scandal was the Profumo Affair of 1963, when Secretary of State for War John Profumo (right) lied to Parliament about his sexual involvement with Christine Keeler, a prostitute who had also been sleeping with a Russian naval attaché. Fears for national security almost brought down the Conservative Government.

These days, scandals come at an ever-faster rate. In 1998 Peter Mandelson, the architect of New Labour, quit the Cabinet when he was found to have borrowed money to buy a grand house from Treasury minister Geoffrey Robinson. And in 1999 former Tory defence minister Jonathan Aitken was jailed for perjury after he lost a libel case against Granada TV and *The Guardian.* The aristocratic Aitken is now in a London prison, whence he issued a poem, *A Ballad from Belmarsh Gaol,* apparently in emulation of Oscar Wilde's *The Ballad of Reading Gaol.* Parliament's loss is poetry's gain…

Christine Keeler, 21, became a celebrity when her affair with John Profumo was revealed

SONGS

The Top Ten Songs of the Century

Compiled by Paul Gambaccini for Radio 2 from listeners' votes, experts' views, music sales and radio plays

1 Yesterday	*Paul McCartney (credited Lennon/McCartney)*	*1965*
2 Stardust	*music Hoagy Carmichael, wds Mitchell Parrish*	*1929*
3 Bridge Over Troubled Water	*Paul Simon*	*1970*
4 White Christmas	*Irving Berlin*	*1942*
5 Unchained Melody	*music Alex North, words Hy Zaret*	*1955*
6 Imagine	*John Lennon*	*1971*
7 My Way	*music François/Revaux/Thibaut, wds Paul Anka*	*1969*
8 Summertime	*music George Gershwin, wds DuBose Heyward*	*1935*
9 Over The Rainbow	*music Harold Arlen, words E Y Harburg*	*1939*
10 As Time Goes By	*Herman Hupfeld*	*1931*

SEX

The Ten Sexiest Women in the World

Hollywood princess Grace Kelly

1959

Voted by the readers of Reveille magazine

1. Marilyn Monroe
2. Brigitte Bardot
3. Jayne Mansfield
4. Gina Lollobrigida
5. Grace Kelly
6. Jane Russell
7. Diana Dors
8. Ava Gardner
9. Kim Novak
10. Doris Day

1999

Voted by the readers of FHM magazine

1. Sarah Michelle Gellar
2. Louise Nurding
3. Kelly Brook
4. Catherine Zeta Jones
5. Jenny McCarthy
6. Jennifer Aniston
7. Cameron Diaz
8. Gail Porter
9. Cat Deeley
10. Melanie Sykes

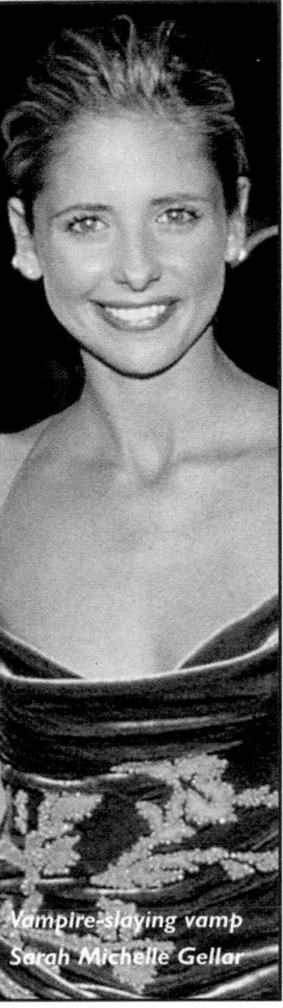

Vampire-slaying vamp Sarah Michelle Gellar

Ten Famous Sayings About Sex

"I believe sex is a beautiful thing between two people. Between five, it's fantastic..." –Woody Allen

"When women go wrong, men go right after them." – Mae West

"My father told me all about the birds and the bees. The liar. I went steady with a woodpecker till I was 21." – Bob Hope

"I honestly prefer chocolate to sex." – Dale Winton

"Sex is about as important as a cheese sandwich. But a cheese sandwich, if you ain't got one to put in your belly, is extremely important." – Ian Dury

"The only unnatural sexual behaviour is none at all." – Sigmund Freud

"All this fuss about sleeping together; for physical pleasure I'd sooner go to my dentist any day." – Evelyn Waugh

"I know it does make people happy but to me it is just like having a cup of tea." – Cynthia Payne

"It's been so long since I made love, I can't remember who gets tied up." – Joan Rivers

"Sex appeal is 50 per cent what you've got and 50 per cent what people think you've got." – Sophia Loren

1977 Worst Plane Disaster
Two Boeing 747 jets collided on the ground in the Canary Islands, killing 570 people. It was the worst accident in civil aviation history.

1977 Farewell Elvis
Rock 'n' roll king Elvis Presley was found dead in his Graceland mansion at Memphis, Tennessee, apparently from a heart attack. He was 42. Presley began his career as a lean, raw and exciting rocker, and ended it, after a string of mediocre film musicals, bloated, drug-dependent and sometimes almost incoherent on stage. But he remains the biggest-selling solo artist ever.

1978 First Test-tube Baby
Louise Brown, the world's first test-tube baby, was born at Oldham hospital in Lancashire. Her birth followed pioneering research and trials by gynaecologist Patrick Steptoe and Cambridge physiologist Dr Robert Edwards.

1978 Ayatollah Out
Religious leader Ayatollah Khomeini, expelled by the Shah from Iran, was given asylum in France.

TOP OF THE POPS

The Hollies (from left: Allan Clarke, Bobby Elliott, Graham Nash, Tony Hicks, Eric Haydock) reached No 8 with 'Stay'

Top of the Pops went on air on July 1, 1964 – and, while Ready Steady Go!, Juke Box Jury and Thank Your Lucky Stars are just memories, it's still going strong. These are the first ten records presented by disc jockey Alan Freeman:

1. **I Only Want To Be With You** *Dusty Springfield*
2. **I Wanna Be Your Man** *The Rolling Stones*
3. **Glad All Over** *The Dave Clark Five*
4. **Stay** *The Hollies*
5. **Hippy Hippy Shake** *The Swinging Blue Jeans*
6. **Don't Talk To Him** *Cliff Richard And The Shadows*
7. **You Were Made For Me** *Freddie And The Dreamers*
8. **Twenty Four Hours From Tulsa** *Gene Pitney*
9. **She Loves You** *The Beatles*
10. **I Want To Hold Your Hand** *The Beatles*

ELIZABETH TAYLOR

Elizabeth Taylor is regarded by many as the most beautiful woman to ever grace a cinema screen. But it came as a shock when she also proved a brilliant actress, the winner of two Oscars for her powerful performances in *Butterfield 8* (1960) and *Who's Afraid of Virginia Woolf?* (1966).

Born in London in 1932, she made her film debut at the age of ten. Since then, she has been married eight times – twice to the great Welsh actor Richard Burton, whom she met while filming *Cleopatra* – and has famously battled against alcoholism and enough ailments to fill a good-sized medical volume, nearly dying from pneumonia in 1990.

A true survivor, she has worked hard on behalf of various charities and in 1993 won a Humanitarian Award for her AIDS crusades.

***Left:* Taylor as Cleopatra – the role that made her a superstar in 1962 – and with her Cleopatra co-star Richard Burton in 1964, the year they were first married. They divorced in 1974, remarried in 1975 and redivorced in 1976. *Right:* Liz in 1954**

1978
Year of the Three Popes
After the death of Pope Paul VI, Italian Cardinal Albino Luciani was elected Pope and became John Paul I. But he died less than five weeks later. Cardinal Karol Wojtyla of Poland was then elected, the first non-Italian Pope for 456 years. He took the name John Paul II.

1978
Thorpe Goes On Trial
In one of the most sensational trials of the century, charismatic Liberal leader Jeremy Thorpe was accused of conspiring to murder male model Norman Scott. Thorpe was acquitted, but his political career lay in ruins.

1979
Return of the Ayatollah
Islamic fundamentalists led by Ayatollah Ruhollah Khomeini forced the Shah of Iran to flee the country. They objected to the Shah's attempts to westernise the culture of Iran. Khomeini took over as leader, imposing an iron Islamic religious discipline.

TEENAGERS

Until the last half of this century, teenagers were merely adolescents – smaller and younger versions of the adults they would inevitably become. They would dress like their parents and learn the same skills and roles.

Teenagers 'began' with post-war prosperity, as consumerist lifestyles bred relative affluence but stifling conformity. Young people ached for a sense that their own lives would be different, that for perhaps the first time in history, they would not grow up to be like their parents.

Rock 'n' roll and cinema were the prime influences. Marlon Brando's exchange – "What are you rebelling against?" "What have you got?" – in *The Wild One* (1954) gave the world the teenager as a separate entity. When Elvis appeared on Johnny Carson's TV show, his host made a point of telling America what a decent young man he was, in response to adults' fears about the new rebellious younger generation.

But it was too late. From then on, the job of every teenager was to find out what their parents wouldn't do, or wouldn't like – and make sure they were doing it and liking it. Invariably, this meant sex and drugs, and still does: every weekend in Britain today, an estimated three million Ecstasy tablets are sold.

The teenagers who shocked their parents in the Sixties are now parents themselves. Yet that hasn't stopped them being just as worried about teenagers as their parents were. Funny, that…

Leonardo DiCaprio and Kate Winslet in Titanic and, below, the real thing

TITANIC

The 1997 blockbuster Titanic proved the world's love affair with Leonardo DiCaprio, but also its enduring fascination with the loss of that 'unsinkable' luxury liner off Newfoundland in 1912, with 1515 deaths. The ship's double-bottomed hull compartments were designed to be iceberg-proof, but five of the 16 were breached – one too many to avoid calamity. Many questions remain unanswered. Why were there only 1178 lifeboat places for 2224 passengers? Did the ship's ambition for a record Atlantic crossing preclude slowing down for known icebergs? The hull found in 1985 in two pieces, two miles underwater, showed no gash. Heroes and cowards emerged from that terrible night (many passengers and crew voluntarily sacrificed their lives for others), but the full story remains buried at sea.

THE TWIST

"Come on, let's twist again…" The Twist was pop's funniest dance craze. An offshoot of the rock 'n' roll jive, it was so easy that anyone could do it. And, fired by Chubby Checker's 1961 hit, the whole world did.

TELEVISION

In 1925, penniless Scottish inventor John Logie Baird became the first person to transmit live moving images to a remote receiver. The first provider of regular programmes was Hitler's Germany in 1935, followed next year by Britain's state-run BBC. Commercial television, born in the United States, began in Britain in 1955.

Since then, television has made the world a 'global village'. The first mass TV audience in Britain was for the Queen's coronation (1953). More recently, millions were moved by Michael Buerk's reports of famine in Ethiopia. Telly highlights are many and varied. There are the great live broadcasts, from the Moon landing to Live Aid. High comedy, from *Steptoe and Son* to *Friends*. Intimate revelations, such as Martin Bashir's *Panorama* interview with Princess Diana; or the irresistible trash of *The Jerry Springer Show* and *Blind Date*. And that's not to mention the adverts…

But in this era of health scares, TV has been blamed for causing obesity and diabetes – and with hundreds of channels available to all, it's said that a child born now will spend seven years of its life in front of the box.

LIFELINES

***PIOTR ILYICH TCHAIKOVSKY**, born in 1893, put the fireworks into classical music. A 19th-century Russian giant, his work included the ballets Swan Lake, Sleeping Beauty and The Nutcracker as well as the all-guns-blazing 1812 Overture. His death in 1893 may have been suicide after a threat to reveal his homosexual affair with a young nobleman.*

***LEO TOLSTOY** wrote War And Peace, probably the world's greatest novel. Born near Moscow in 1828, Tolstoy began writing in the army. It was after settling down to family life that he produced War And Peace (1869) and Anna Karenina (1877). He later became a pacifist, admired by Gandhi, but he was excommunicated by the Orthodox Church and his books were banned. In 1910, disillusioned with life, he left home and died soon after from pneumonia.*

1979
THREE MILE ISLAND
Uranium in a reactor core overheated due to a cooling valve failure at the Three Mile Island nuclear power plant in Pennsylvania, USA. A catastrophic nuclear meltdown was threatened, causing worldwide concern about the safety of such plants.

1979
LET'S BE FRIENDS
Encouraged by President Jimmy Carter, Prime Minister Menachem Begin of Israel and Egyptian President Anwar Sadat went to America and signed a treaty of mutual recognition and peace. It ended 30 years of hostilities between the two nations.

1979
THATCHER COMES TO POWER
The Conservatives won the General Election by 50 seats and Margaret Thatcher became Britain's first female Prime Minister. She became known – affectionately or disparagingly – as the Iron Lady.

MIKE TYSON

Mike Tyson, twice imprisoned for violent crimes, is as notorious out of the boxing ring as in. Tyson became the youngest world heavyweight champion in 1986, aged 20 years and 144 days, and rapidly won all three boxing organisations' titles to become the undisputed champion. A squat, menacing figure whose raw power and unflashy look harked back to the old-time fighters he admired, it looked like he would reign for as long as he wanted. But his chaotic private life began to undermine his talent, and he lost to the unknown Buster Douglas in 1990. Still a huge draw, he is the sportsman with the highest earnings in one year: in 1996, he made £50 million from three bouts. But despite his achievements, he will be remembered mainly for biting a chunk out of Evander Holyfield's ear in a 1997 title fight – a moment of madness that cost him £2 million and the last vestiges of his reputation.

TOUR DE FRANCE

First staged in 1903, the Tour de France is the world's greatest cycle race. Every year in France, entire towns and villages gather to follow the gruelling mountainous route, which often spills over into other countries – Britain in 1994, for instance. Though rocked by a huge drugs scandal in 1998, the race goes on, and its mountain sprints, yellow jerseys and climactic dash up the Champs-Elysées in Paris are the stuff of folklore.

FRED TRUEMAN

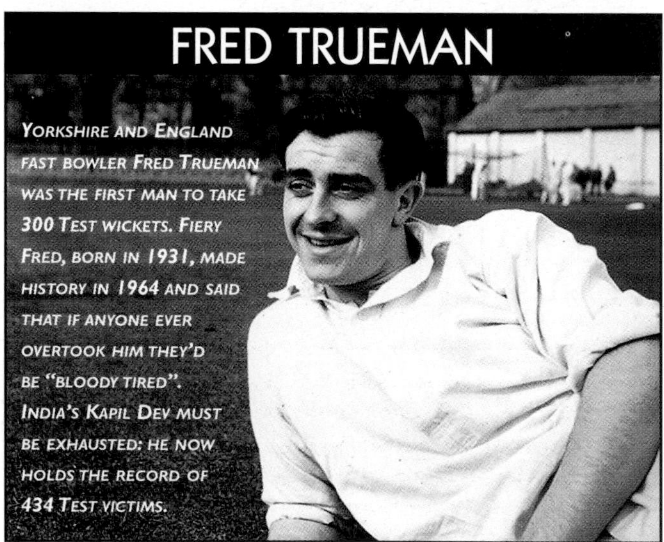

YORKSHIRE AND ENGLAND FAST BOWLER FRED TRUEMAN WAS THE FIRST MAN TO TAKE 300 TEST WICKETS. FIERY FRED, BORN IN 1931, MADE HISTORY IN 1964 AND SAID THAT IF ANYONE EVER OVERTOOK HIM THEY'D BE "BLOODY TIRED". INDIA'S KAPIL DEV MUST BE EXHAUSTED: HE NOW HOLDS THE RECORD OF 434 TEST VICTIMS.

MILLENNIUM TIME LINE

1980
JOHN LENNON MURDERED
John Lennon, 40, was murdered outside the Dakota building in New York where he lived. Supposed fan Mark Chapman, who earlier had asked the former Beatle for his autograph, shot Lennon five times.

1980
YUGOSLAVIA IN MELTING POT
The death of Marshal Tito, who had ruled Yugoslavia for 35 years, plunged the country into uncertainty. Ancient enmity between Serbs, Croats and Muslims would resurface in the next two decades, causing conflicts and wars that would culminate in the Nato bombing and invasion of Kosovo in 1999.

1981
THE POPE IS SHOT
Pope John Paul II was shot four times at close range while riding in an open vehicle in St Peter's Square. The Pope later had a private meeting with the man who had tried to kill him. He forgave him.

DALEY THOMPSON

Daley Thompson – born in London in 1958 to a Scottish mother and Nigerian father – dominated the decathlon in the 1980s. His prowess at the supreme test in athletics (ten events including 100 metres, 400 metres, 1500 metres, hurdles, discus, shot, javelin, pole vault, long jump and high jump) gave him the aura of Superman. His eight major gold medals included the 1980 and 1984 Olympics.

TORVILL & DEAN

It was not only winning the World, Olympic and European ice-dance titles in 1984 that turned British ice skaters Jayne Torvill and Christopher Dean into media darlings, but also speculation over their personal relationship. To the newspapers' chagrin, it was eventually revealed to be platonic.

TENNIS

The only ten countries to win the Wimbledon men's singles

1. Britain	35 wins	Most recent: Fred Perry, 1936
2. USA	32 wins	Most recent: Pete Sampras, 1999
3. Australia	20 wins	Most recent: Pat Cash, 1987
4. Sweden	7 wins	Most recent: Stefan Edberg, 1990
5. France	7 wins	Most recent: Yvon Petra, 1946
6. New Zealand	4 wins	Most recent: Tony Wilding, 1913
7. Germany	4 wins	Most recent: Michael Stich, 1991
8. Spain	1 win	Manuel Santana, 1966
9. Czechoslovakia	1 win	Jan Kodes, 1973
10. Holland	1 win	Richard Krajicek, 1996

In addition, Jaroslav Drobny won in 1954 representing Egypt, though he was in fact a Czech. He later became British.

LIFELINES

***William Tell** may not have existed, but he is a hero in Switzerland. An archer forced by Bailiff Gessler to shoot an apple off his son's head in 1307, he then led a rebellion. A symbol of independence, he inspired a Rossini opera and a TV series.*

***Alfred, Lord Tennyson**, born in 1809, became Poet Laureate in 1850. His body of work includes The Lady Of Shalott and The Charge Of The Light Brigade, with its unforgettable "Into the valley of death" references. He died in 1892.*

***Harry S Truman**, born in 1884, was the US President who sanctioned the use of the atom bomb against Japan and sent troops into South Korea. A popular leader who helped create NATO in 1949, he died in 1972.*

1981
Life for the Ripper
Lorry driver Peter Sutcliffe, the infamous Yorkshire Ripper, was jailed for life. He had murdered 13 women over four years.

1981
Reagan Forgets To Duck
At the age of 69, Ronald Reagan, who had spent 30 years as an actor in TV and films, specialising in cowboy movies, became the oldest President to take office in America in 1980. A year later he was wounded in an assassination attempt, telling his wife later: "Honey, I forgot to duck" – a line from one of his films.

1981
Royal Wedding
Prince Charles married Lady Diana Frances Spencer at St Paul's Cathedral. The event was televised across the world and watched by an estimated 750 million people.

1982
Princess Grace Dies in Crash
Princess Grace of Monaco died after her car plunged off a road in Monte Carlo. Her daughter Stephanie survived the crash. The Princess, formerly Hollywood actress Grace Kelly, met Prince Rainier while making a film in Monaco. She married him in 1956.

LIFELINES

William Makepeace Thackeray *(1811-63) was one of the greatest Victorian novelists. Vanity Fair – the tale of amoral Becky Sharp – has been filmed three times, while Barry Lyndon became a stunning Stanley Kubrick picture.*

Dylan Thomas *(1914-53) is the one Welsh poet and author whose name is familiar to everyone. His best-known work, the radio play Under Milk Wood, was turned into a George Martin-produced musical in 1988.*

Anthony Trollope, *born in 1815, invented the town of Barchester as a setting for a series of novels delineating English middle class life in the early 19th century. Also a distinguished political novelist, he died in 1882.*

TRIVIA

Ten amazing facts to share with friends

Florence Nightingale used to keep a pet owl in her pocket.

The Bible is the most shoplifted book in the USA.

Just 1,000 words make up 90 per cent of all writing.

Disney World, Florida, is bigger than the world's five smallest countries.

Shakespeare invented more than 1700 words.

There are three American towns named Santa Claus.

If a 20-a-day smoker inhaled a week's worth of nicotine in one go they would die instantly.

Six out of seven gynaecologists are men.

Twenty per cent of the people in the whole history of mankind who have lived beyond the age of 65 are alive today.

Volleyball is the most popular sport at nudist camps.

MARGARET THATCHER

Margaret Thatcher, born in 1925, was Britain's first woman Prime Minister – and one of the most remarkable. A lover of controversy, she was both hated and admired for her iron will. The first Prime Minister in 160 years to be elected three times, she reduced inflation, went to war over the Falkland Islands, set out to end Communism in Europe, and divided Britain by almost destroying the trade unions. But it was the Poll Tax that fatally dented her popularity. Along with the authoritarian style which made enemies in the Conservative Party, it triggered her resignation in 1990. Even so, Baroness Thatcher remains a politician of influence, particularly abroad. The lady is still "not for turning".

MARK TWAIN

Mark Twain was one of the 19th century's great humorists. Born Samuel Clemens in 1835, he was a Mississippi riverboat pilot before becoming a travel writer and novelist. The author of Tom Sawyer and the American masterpiece Huckleberry Finn (1885) died in 1910.

The sayings of Mark Twain

- 'When angry, count to four. When very angry, swear.'
- 'Familiarity breeds contempt ... and children.'
- 'Such is the human race, often it seems a pity that Noah didn't miss the boat.'
- 'It is better to deserve honours and not have them than to have them and not deserve them.'
- 'Confession may be good for my soul, but it sure plays hell with my reputation.'
- 'There are several good protections against temptation, but the surest is cowardice'
- 'Always do right. This will gratify some people and astonish the rest.'
- 'Man is the only animal that blushes – or needs to.'

1983
Nazi Butcher Captured
Former Gestapo official Klaus Barbie was arrested in Bolivia. Known as the 'Butcher of Lyon', he organised the deporting of Jewish children from Lyon to Auschwitz where they were gassed. He was also responsible for the murder and torture of members of the French Resistance. Convicted by the French in 1987, he died in prison.

1984
The Thames Barrier
The Thames Barrier was opened. It was designed to prevent serious flooding in central London.

1984
Miners' Last Stand
Government plans to shut 21 coal pits with a loss of 20,000 jobs prompted union leader Arthur Scargill to call a national strike. It would last a year and be marked with ugly violence as pickets and police clashed. In the end the miners gave in. Mrs Thatcher claimed 'a famous victory'.

THE TOWER OF LONDON

Today's babble of schoolchildren, tourists and decorative Beefeaters seems a long way from the Tower of London's bloody history.

A royal fortress-residence built by William the Conqueror (atop Roman ruins) in 1078, his White Tower was extended by successors, notably Richard III, and rebuilt in 1638. In 1377, Richard II added the Bloody Tower, so-called for the young princes who were murdered there.

Royal heads fell on the block, too, most famously Ann Boleyn's, while the Tower's dank prisons have held umpteen traitors and religious dissenters, especially in Tudor times. St Thomas More, Sir Walter Raleigh and Judge Jeffreys were prominent inmates. Death was often welcome after long incarceration and torture.

Irish nationalist Sir Roger Casement was imprisoned here in 1916 (he was later hanged), and later Rudolf Hess, on his abortive 1941 mission to win Britain over to the Nazis. Now the Crown Jewels and the ravens are the Tower's sole charges.

Once a place to be feared, the Tower is now one of Britain's foremost tourist attractions

TOURISM

THEN The first mass tourists were pilgrims. Christians travelled to cathedral towns and religious centres such as Rome, Canterbury, the Holy Land and Santiago de Compostela in Spain, where the remains of St James the Apostle are supposedly buried. In an age when ordinary people rarely ventured far from home, their faith provoked these incredibly arduous journeys. The pilgrims on St James Way made their way along one of three well-trudged routes through France and Spain – a tradition that continues today.

NOW Modern mass tourism began on July 5, 1841, when Thomas Cook's first supervised excursion left Leicester railway station. Cook, who organised rides for temperance groups and children, began commercial tours in 1845 – visits to the World Fair in Paris (1855) and walking tours of the Swiss Alps. Cook's invention, the Circular Note, was the forerunner of the traveller's cheque. After the Second World War, the cheap package holiday took off: between 1970 and 1990, world tourism grew by 260 per cent.

THE TAJ MAHAL

It was built as a monument to love, but the most famous photograph of the Taj Mahal is a monument to love lost. The greatest masterpiece of Mogul architecture, the Taj Mahal was built by Shah Jahan in 1631-48 as a mausoleum for his favourite wife, Mumtaz Mahal. Princess Diana visited it on her own during a tour of India with Prince Charles in 1992. A lone, beautiful woman seated before one of the world's most beautiful buildings, the pictures sent out a powerful and poignant message to the world about her disintegrating marriage.

1984
FRIENDS AGAIN
The Vatican and the United States established full diplomatic relations after a break of 116 years.

1984
GRAND HOTEL BOMBING
The IRA planted a bomb at the Grand Hotel in Brighton where Mrs Thatcher and several members of the Cabinet were staying for the Conservative Party conference. The Prime Minister escaped unhurt, but four died and many were hurt.

1985
LIVE AID CONCERT
Shocked by starvation and deaths from famine in Ethiopia, rock star Bob Geldof masterminded the Live Aid concerts. The world's top stars appeared for nothing at two simultaneous 17-hour concerts, one at Wembley Stadium and the other in Philadelphia, linked by satellite. They raised about £50 million for famine relief.

1985
VIOLENCE AGAINST GREENPEACE
Rainbow Warrior, flagship of Greenpeace, the environmental activist group, sank after two explosions in Auckland, New Zealand. France later admitted responsibility.

TOILETS

● ***It's Sir John Harington (1561-1612) we have to thank for the flush toilet. He invented the toilet for Elizabeth I after she had banned him from her court for circulating smutty stories. It did the trick and she let him return.***

● Victorian plumber Thomas Crapper perfected the hygienic flush system which we all know and use.

● ***The air-freshener, that indispensable toilet accessory, started life as a pomegranate stuffed with cloves.***

● *Psycho* was the first Hollywood film to show a toilet flushing – thereby generating many complaints.

● ***Cheltenham council once voted to replace the words Women and Men on their public toilets with Ladies and Gentlemen in order to "attract a better class of person".***

● In 1992, British public toilets were voted among the worst in the world – just ahead of those in Thailand, Greece and France.

● ***Before toilet paper was invented, people used shells, stones, or bunches of herbs – or, at best, a bit of sponge attached to a stick which they rinsed with cold water.***

● When Queen Victoria visited Cambridge, she looked down at the River Cam – which was basically an open sewer – and, seeing the toilet paper, asked Dr Whewell, the Master of Trinity College: "What are all those pieces of paper floating down the river?" He replied: "Those, ma'am, are notices that bathing is forbidden."

● ***In 1986, Nathan Hicks of Missouri shot his brother Herbert because he used six toilet rolls in two days.***

Nicole Kidman caused a sensation in The Blue Room in London

THEATRE

Theatre was people's main entertainment from Shakespeare's time until films and TV took over – and even in Hollywood's heyday, British actors tended to treat the movies as a pale imitation of the real thing.

Now the trend has reversed. American actors such as Dustin Hoffman, Kevin Spacey and Nicole Kidman – as well as home-grown stars like Ewan McGregor – seem increasingly eager to tread the boards on the London stage. The impression lingers that live theatre is the ultimate test of acting credibility.

Yet the theatre is not in the best of health. The West End is dominated by tourist-attraction musicals, and even though the subsidised theatres such as the RSC and the National still showcase new talent, they are often criticised for being too commercial. The risk-taking is largely relegated to pub theatres, although amateur drama still flourishes.

The way forward might be shown by *Art*, which has enjoyed a long West End run by dispensing with the usual formula whereby a play's original star cast is replaced by lesser lights. Instead, *Art* keeps recruiting celebs, and the announcement of a new cast is now an event in itself.

TAX EVASION

CELEBRITIES SENT TO JAIL FOR DODGING THE TAXMAN

Steffi's father **PETER GRAF** *(3 years, 9 months; 1997)*
Former Beatles manager **ALLEN KLEIN** *(2 months; 1979)*
Divorce lawyer **MARVIN MITCHELSON** *(30 months; 1993)*
The Reverend **SUN MYUNG MOON** *(14 months in 1984)*
US presidential artist **PETER MAX** *(2 months; 1998)*
Hotelier **LEONA HELMSLEY** *(4 years; 1990)*
Jockey **LESTER PIGGOTT** *(1 year; 1987)*
Gangster **AL CAPONE** *(11 years; 1931)*
Fashion boss **ALDO GUCCI** *(1 year; 1986)*
Actress **SOPHIA LOREN** *(17 days; 1982) (left)*

THE THREE MUSKETEERS

All for one and one for all! Alexandre Dumas' novel The Three Musketeers (1844) tells the swashbuckling adventures of four royalist swordsmen – Porthos, Athos, Aramis and D'Artagnan – in France before the Revolution. The story has been filmed at least six times; the 1973 version starred Michael York, Oliver Reed, Richard Chamberlain, Charlton Heston and Faye Dunaway. There have been cartoons, too, and even, in the 1930s, a Three Musketeers candy bar.

MILLENNIUM TIME LINE

1986 KILLER VOLCANO
A volcanic eruption under Lake Nios in Cameroon produced deadly fumes that killed more than 1,500 people.

1986 PREMIER ASSASSINATED
Swedish Prime Minister Olof Palme was shot dead as he came out of a Stockholm cinema with his wife.

1986 CHALLENGER DISASTER
Tragedy struck the Nasa space programme in 1986 when the US space shuttle *Challenger* exploded 74 seconds after lift-off. All seven aboard were killed, including teacher Christa McAuliffe who was to have been the first ordinary citizen in space.

1986 GOODBYE FLEET STREET
Entrepreneur Eddy Shah launched the *Today* newspaper. It was the first in colour, the first to be produced on computers and the first to be printed without union labour. It paved the way for the smashing of the print unions and the great exodus from Fleet Street.

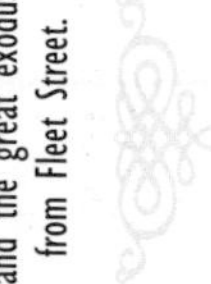

J R R TOLKIEN

John Ronald Reuel Tolkien's door-stopper tales of good and evil in a mythical kingdom occupy a unique place in literature. At the end of the Millennium, *The Hobbit* (1937) and *The Lord of the Rings* (1954-55) keep being voted Britain's best-loved books.

The *Lord of the Rings* characters – from dwarfish, beer-and-tobacco Bilbo Baggins to the spiritual elves – were based on Tolkien's comrades in the First World War trenches. It was that experience, and his study of Old English and Norse at Oxford, that sparked his love of fantasy.

He died in 1973, aged 81, just as the Tolkien cult was really taking off.

TRAINSPOTTING

IRVINE WELSH'S *TRAINSPOTTING* WAS THE ONLY NINETIES NOVEL VOTED INTO WATERSTONE'S TOP TEN BOOKS OF THE CENTURY – AND WHEN WELSH'S HILARIOUS ACCOUNT OF THE EDINBURGH DRUGS SCENE BECAME A FILM IN **1996,** IT ROCKETED EWAN MCGREGOR TO HOLLYWOOD STARDOM AND MADE UNDERWORLD'S THUNDEROUS 'BORN SLIPPY' THE CULT HIT OF THE DECADE.

LIFELINES

TITIAN *(circa 1488-1576) argued that "it is not bright colours but good drawing that makes a figure beautiful". A surprising statement from one of Italy's most influential painters – a Venice Renaissance master famed for his richly coloured artworks.*

TITO *(real name Josip Broz) held Yugoslavia together for 35 years. The Communist leader of the partisans in the Second World War became leader of a federal republic in 1945, ruling until his death, aged 87, in 1980.*

DICK TURPIN, *born in 1706 and the best-known highwayman, was not the courageous and generous character depicted in legend. He is said to have been hanged in York in 1739 for horse-stealing and murder.*

J M W TURNER

Joseph Mallord William Turner (1775-1851) was one of England's finest painters, noted for his spectacular seascapes such as *The Fighting Temeraire* (left). He lived his last years as a recluse in Chelsea, under a false name, and bequeathed the nation some 40,000 works, many of which are in the Tate Gallery. The annual Turner Prize – a showcase for cutting-edge art – is named after him.

TRAFFIC

THE TEN EUROPEAN CITIES WITH THE WORST JAMS

1. LISBON (AVERAGE SPEED: 5.8 MPH)
2. PARIS (8.5 MPH)
3. LONDON (10.4 MPH)
4. ISTANBUL (11.2 MPH)
5. ATHENS (12.4 MPH)
6. MADRID (14.9 MPH)
7. BUDAPEST (16.5 MPH)
8. BERLIN (18.2 MPH)
9. ROME (22.4 MPH)
10. WARSAW (23 MPH)

1986
CHERNOBYL DISASTER
The Chernobyl nuclear reactor in the Soviet Union exploded, causing the biggest nuclear disaster in history. Fall out from the Ukraine plant travelled across northern Europe, including Britain.

1987
MARCH OF THE DOW
On January 8, 1987 the Dow Jones industrial average topped the 2,000 mark for the first time. Such has been the rise of the American economy that by the end of the 1990s it was nudging the 12,000 mark.

1987
BLACK MONDAY
On October 19, the Dow Jones Index on Wall Street plunged a record 508 points. The 22.6 per cent fall was the biggest one-day drop ever and became known as 'Black Monday'.

1987
HERALD OF FREE ENTERPRISE SINKS
Cross-Channel ferry *The Herald of Free Enterprise* sank within minutes of leaving Zeebrugge harbour in Belgium. The bow doors, through which cars boarded, were left open, causing the tragedy. More than 200 people died.

THE VIETNAM WAR

The Vietnam War caused political rifts around the world, left a deep scar in America's psyche, and reduced Vietnam itself to ruins. It all began in 1957 as a battle for control of South Vietnam between the non-communist government and a mix of Indo-Chinese communists, nationalists and reformers with Chinese and Soviet support. By the mid-Sixties, US President Johnson had committed hundreds of thousands of troops to defend the government.

The average age of these soldiers – as a pop song later reminded us – was just 19. As opposition to US involvement in Vietnam escalated, anti-war demonstrations were staged in Britain as well as America. GIs wore peace badges and deserted in droves.

Richard Nixon finally removed the last ground troops in 1973. The US had been defeated by a tiny, technologically inferior country – albeit with superpower help – at a cost of 57,000 American deaths and a generation of traumatised young men. (Nixon's bombing of Vietnam and Cambodia, however, accounted for a great many more dead.) Today, US foreign policy is still influenced by a keen desire to avoid 'another Vietnam'.

Vietnam has been the subject of many films, including Platoon (1986, right), Apocalypse Now and Born On The Fourth Of July (1989). Most show great disillusionment with the war

VINCENT VAN GOGH

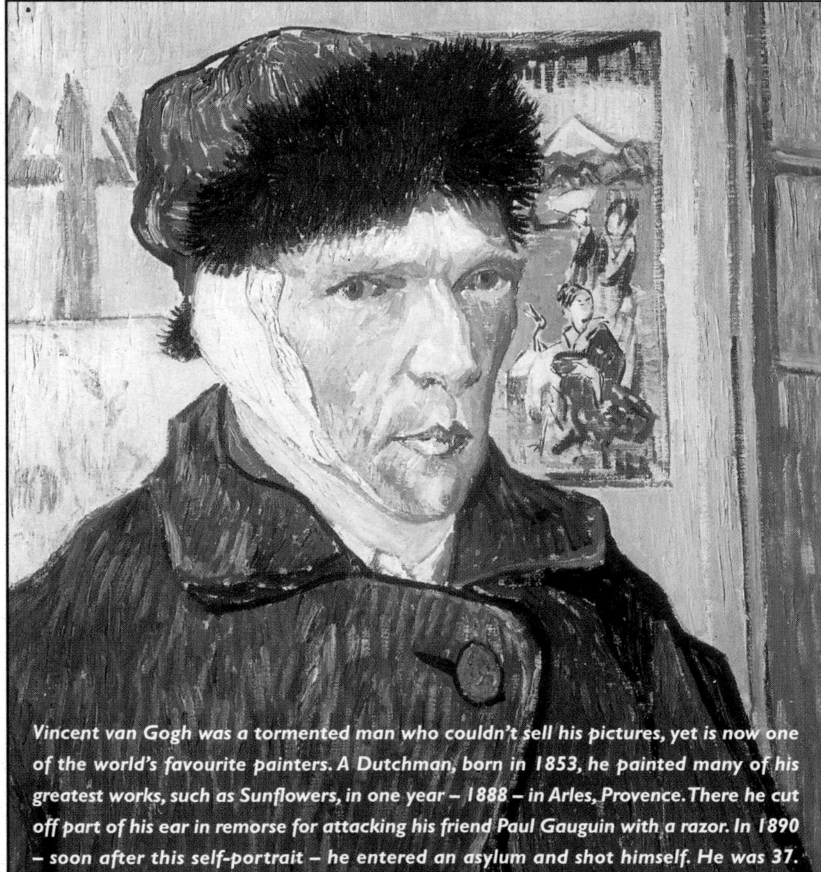

Vincent van Gogh was a tormented man who couldn't sell his pictures, yet is now one of the world's favourite painters. A Dutchman, born in 1853, he painted many of his greatest works, such as Sunflowers, in one year – 1888 – in Arles, Provence. There he cut off part of his ear in remorse for attacking his friend Paul Gauguin with a razor. In 1890 – soon after this self-portrait – he entered an asylum and shot himself. He was 37.

THE UNITED STATES

THEN Vikings from Greenland, led by Leif Eriksson, were probably the first white people to reach the North American mainland around 1000AD. But they did not settle permanently, and the existence of the Western hemisphere was unknown to Europeans until Columbus' voyages, beginning in 1492. At the time of his arrival, what is now Canada and the US was already inhabited by up to 15 million native Americans.

NOW The USA is the third largest country in the world by population, and fourth largest by area. Economically, however, it is the strongest, the world leader in the production of goods and services, with one of the highest standards of living anywhere. Its population has grown from three million people (not counting the native Americans) in 1776 to 260 million today.

LIFELINES

***Diego Velazquez** was the outstanding Spanish painter of the 17th century. Born in 1599, he was able to define subjects in a few sure strokes and was the master of contrast and texture. Mainly a court painter, he died in 1660.*

***Jules Verne**, born in 1828, wrote of fantastic journeys to the Earth's centre and lands below the sea. A man ahead of his time, he foresaw submarines and space travel. Around The World In 80 Days is his best-known work. He died in 1905.*

***Voltaire**, born François Arouet in 1694, was sent to prison and exiled for his often satirical writings on tolerance and human rights – a basis for later existentialism. He died in his native France in 1778.*

1987 England's Hurricane The worst storm since 1703 hit the south of England. It caused 17 deaths, destroyed 15 million trees and left a trail of damage costing £100 million. Weather forecasters had failed to predict the hurricane.

1987 King's Cross Tube Fire A cigarette discarded on a wooden escalator at London's King's Cross Tube station caused a massive fire that led to 31 deaths. Smoking has since been banned on the Underground network.

1988 The Lockerbie Disaster A Pan-Am jumbo jet exploded and crashed over the Scottish town of Lockerbie, killing 270 passengers and 11 residents of the town. Terrorists had planted a bomb in the luggage.

1989 Oil Tanker Disaster The oil tanker *Exxon Valdez* ran aground in Prince William Sound off Alaska, and spilled 11 million gallons of oil. The slick stretched for 45 miles.

QUEEN VICTORIA

Victoria ruled Britain for 64 years – longer than any other monarch – and continues to reign as one of the most important Britons of the Millennium. This was her life:

- *1819* Born in Kensington Palace, London, an only child.
- *1837* Became Queen at 18, crowned a year later.
- *1840* Married her German cousin Prince Albert of Saxe-Coburg and Gotha, to whom she proposed.
- *1841* Gave birth to her first son, later to become Edward VII. He was one of four sons and five daughters born to the woman who, because of her many family ties, became known as 'the grandmother of Europe'.
- *1856* Instituted the Victoria Cross, Britain's highest decoration for bravery.
- *1857* Had the title Prince Consort conferred on Prince Albert. She was deeply in love with Albert, and her era's straitlaced 'Victorian values' came as much from him as her.
- *1861* Went into long-term seclusion following the death of Prince Albert.
- *1876* Was proclaimed Empress of India by the imperialist Prime Minister Benjamin Disraeli, whom she adored. He flattered her shamelessly.
- *1887* Celebrated her Golden Jubilee.
- *1897* Celebrated her Diamond Jubilee.
- *1901* Died at Osborne House on the Isle Of Wight.

Victoria's legacy was the greatest empire the world has known. During her reign, Britain benefited from political changes that made the country more democratic; gained control of the Suez Canal; set up self-ruling colonies; and led the world in science and industry.

THE VICTORIA CROSS

- ***The Victoria Cross – our highest military decoration, awarded to British and Commonwealth forces for bravery – was instituted by Queen Victoria in 1856.***
- ***There have been 1354 VCs awarded, including 634 in the First World War and 182 in the Second. The last two VCs were won during the Falklands War in 1982.***
- ***Andrew Fitzgibbon, 15 at the time of action, is the youngest recipient. The oldest was William Raynor, 61.***
- ***Three VC winners lived in one street – Pine Street, later renamed Valour Road, in Winnipeg, Canada.***
- ***When Queen Victoria gave the VC to Commander Raby, one of the first 62 recipients, she is said to have inadvertently pinned it to his flesh. He didn't flinch.***

THE UNITED NATIONS

ESTABLISHED ON OCTOBER 24, 1945, THE UN'S CHARTER WAS INITIALLY SIGNED BY 51 COUNTRIES, ALL PLEDGING TO UPHOLD PEACE AND HUMAN DIGNITY IN A BID TO AVOID ANOTHER WORLD WAR. THE UN'S WORK COVERS COMMUNICATIONS, EDUCATION, FOOD, AGRICULTURE, HEALTH AND LABOUR. IT HAS AN INTERNATIONAL COURT OF JUSTICE, AND A SECURITY COUNCIL WHICH MONITORS AREAS OF TENSION IN THE WORLD. TODAY, THE UN HAS 187 MEMBERS.

THE UNIVERSE

THEN Until the 18th century, astronomers knew of only six planets – Mercury, Venus, Earth, Mars, Jupiter and Saturn. In 1781, British astronomer William Herschel discovered Uranus, and in 1841 the German Johann Galle added Neptune to our cosmology. The epic search for a body which appeared to affect the paths of these two ended in 1930 when American Clyde Tombaugh realised that a faint image on his photographic plates was, in fact, a planet – Pluto.

NOW Today's map of the cosmos is far more detailed. In our own solar system, manned space probes have discovered moons belonging to the most distant planets, and scientists speculate about the feasibility of life – either self-generated, or one day imported from Earth – existing there. It is thought that Jupiter's moon, Europa, may already support some form of primitive life, while Saturn's moon Titan, is considered the most conducive to human life.

WHAT A TEN-STONE PERSON WOULD WEIGH ON OTHER PLANETS

Pluto 7 lb • The Moon 1st 10 lb • Mercury 3st 11 lb • Mars 3st 11 lb • Uranus 9st 1 lb • Venus 9st 11 lb Saturn 10st 11 lb • Neptune 11st 12 lb • Jupiter 25st 5 lb • The Sun 280st

RUDOLPH VALENTINO

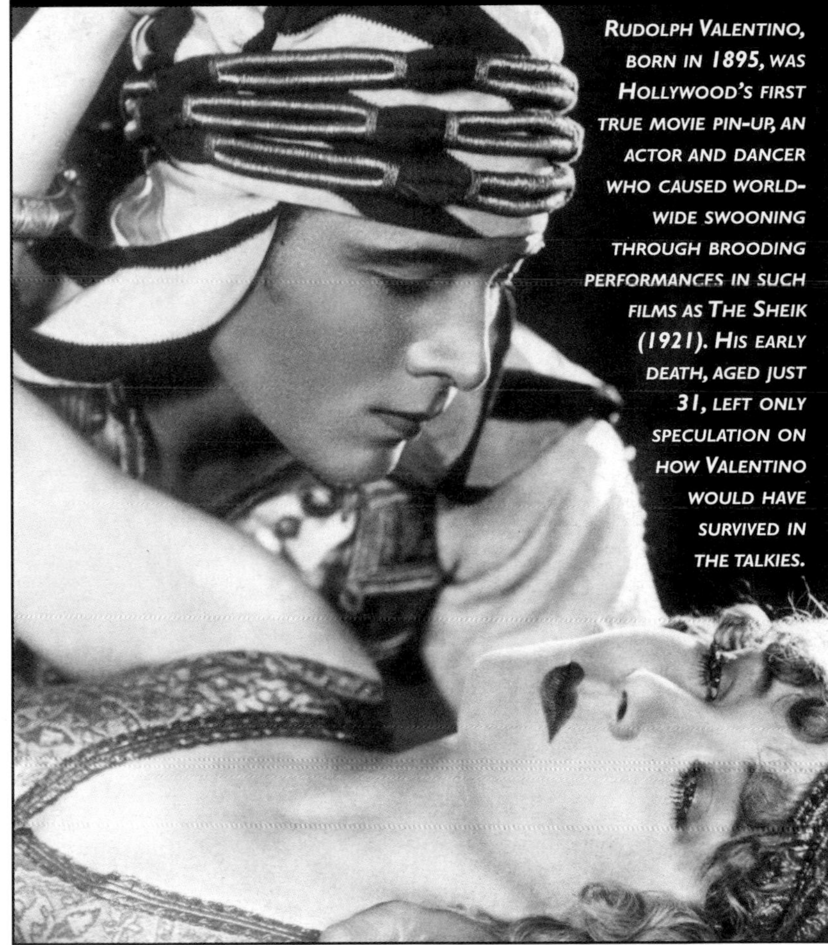

RUDOLPH VALENTINO, BORN IN 1895, WAS HOLLYWOOD'S FIRST TRUE MOVIE PIN-UP, AN ACTOR AND DANCER WHO CAUSED WORLD-WIDE SWOONING THROUGH BROODING PERFORMANCES IN SUCH FILMS AS THE SHEIK (1921). HIS EARLY DEATH, AGED JUST 31, LEFT ONLY SPECULATION ON HOW VALENTINO WOULD HAVE SURVIVED IN THE TALKIES.

1989
SOVIETS QUIT AFGHANISTAN
Soviet forces pulled out of Afghanistan after nearly 10 years of occupation. The civil war between Muslim rebel groups and the Soviet-backed government resulted in more than 15,000 Soviet troops being killed.

1989
COLD WAR IS OVER
Soviet leader Mikhail Gorbachev met US President George Bush for a summit which signalled the end of the Cold War. Gorbachev came to power in 1985 and his Russian revolution was as great as the one in 1917. He introduced *perestroika* (reconstruction) and *glasnost* (openness). It led to independence and democracy behind what Churchill had called the Iron Curtain.

1989
FREEDOM AT LAST
Thirty-three years after the uprising (see 1956) against communist rule, Hungary declared itself an independent republic.

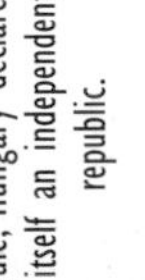

THE WORLD

WALES

For most of the Millennium, Wales has been considered a principality of England. It lost its independence in 1282, when Edward I's troops killed Llywelyn, Prince of Wales. The Welsh fought in the armies of English kings (gaining special renown for their archery) but there were outbreaks of rebellion, notably the uprising led by Owain Glyn Dwr (1400-10). He set up a Welsh parliament, but was eventually crushed by Henry V. The Act of Union (1536) banned the Welsh language for official purposes.

The Welsh Methodist movement began in the 1730s, around the same time as the 'Welsh renaissance', when literacy expanded, In the late 19th century, Wales produced a quarter of the world's coal, but mining and other heavy industries are now in decline.

By 1981, only one in five Welsh people spoke Welsh, but steps were taken to reverse the trend, including S4C, the first Welsh-language TV channel (1982). In 1999, the Welsh set up their own parliamentary Assembly (above) and hosted the Rugby World Cup.

The Ten Largest Countries in the World

1. Russia (6.59 million square miles)
2. Canada (3.85 m)
3. China (3.71 m)
4. USA (3.54 m)
5. Brazil (3.29 m)
6. Australia (2.97 m)
7. India (1.22 m)
8. Argentina (1.07 m)
9. Kazakhstan (1.05 m)
10. Sudan (0.97 m)

The Ten Wealthiest Countries in the World

1. USA
2. Japan
3. Germany
4. France
5. United Kingdom
6. Brazil
7. Canada
8. China
9. Spain
10. South Korea

1989
Missile Attack 'From Stress'
Two hundred and ninety passengers aboard Iran Air Flight 655 died when the US Navy warship Vincennes fired two surface-to-air missiles at the plane as it flew over the Persian Gulf. A military inquiry said the civilian plane was mistaken for an enemy F-14 fighter through "stress-related human failure".

1989
The Hillsborough Tragedy
Ninety-five football fans were crushed to death and 200 hurt at Hillsborough stadium, Sheffield, where Liverpool were to play Nottingham Forest in an FA Cup semi-final. It was Britain's worst sports disaster.

1989
Tiananmen Square Massacre
Students staged a pro-democracy rally in Tiananmen Square, Beijing, to which the Chinese authorities responded by sending in tanks and troops. After they had opened fire, some 2,000 demonstrators lay dead.

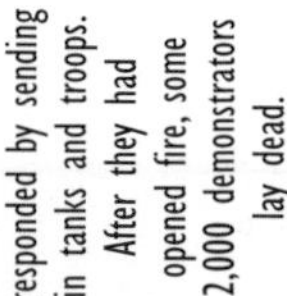

TEN COUNTRIES WHERE THERE ARE MORE MEN THAN WOMEN

1. VATICAN CITY
2. THE FALKLAND ISLANDS
3. KUWAIT
4. LIBYA
5. PAKISTAN
6. SRI LANKA
7. GREENLAND
8. SINGAPORE
9. ALBANIA
10. CUBA

TEN COUNTRIES WHERE THERE ARE MORE WOMEN THAN MEN

1. MONACO
2. RUSSIA
3. PORTUGAL
4. AUSTRIA
5. GERMANY
6. UNITED KINGDOM
7. JAMAICA
8. HUNGARY
9. CAYMAN ISLANDS
10. ITALY

TEN COUNTRIES AND THEIR PREDICTED POPULATION FOR THE YEARS 2000 AND 2050

COUNTRY	YEAR 2000	YEAR 2050
UNITED KINGDOM	57 MILLION	51 MILLION
UNITED STATES	268 MILLION	299 MILLION
FRANCE	57 MILLION	52 MILLION
CHINA	1212 MILLION	1555 MILLION
INDIA	1013 MILLION	1591 MILLION
PAKISTAN	145 MILLION	424 MILLION
AUSTRALIA	19 MILLION	24 MILLION
BRAZIL	179 MILLION	368 MILLION
IRAN	74 MILLION	252 MILLION
JAPAN	130 MILLION	115 MILLION

THE WORLD CUP

In the Nineties, the football World Cup overtook the Olympic Games to become the world's top sporting event. The first World Cup of the next millennium will be held in Japan and Korea. Here's the story of the World Cup Final winners and losers so far…

1930	**URUGUAY** 4 Argentina 2	Montevideo, Uruguay
1934	**ITALY** 2 Czechoslovakia 1*	Rome, Italy
1938	**ITALY** 4 Hungary 2	Paris, France
1950	**URUGUAY** 2 Brazil 1	Rio de Janeiro, Brazil
1954	**WEST GERMANY** 3 Hungary 2	Berne, Switzerland
1958	**BRAZIL** 5 Sweden 2	Stockholm, Sweden
1962	**BRAZIL** 3 Czechoslovakia 1	Santiago, Chile
1966	**ENGLAND** 4 West Germany 2*	Wembley, England
1970	**BRAZIL** 4 Italy 1	Mexico City, Mexico
1974	**WEST GERMANY** 2 Holland 1	Munich, West Germany
1978	**ARGENTINA** 3 Holland 1*	Buenos Aires, Argentina
1982	**ITALY** 3 West Germany 1	Madrid, Spain
1986	**ARGENTINA** 3 West Germany 2	Mexico City, Mexico
1990	**WEST GERMANY** 1 Argentina 0	Rome, Italy
1994	**BRAZIL** 0 Italy 0 (pens: 3-2)	Pasadena, USA
1998	**FRANCE** 3 Brazil 0	Paris, France

(* = after extra time)

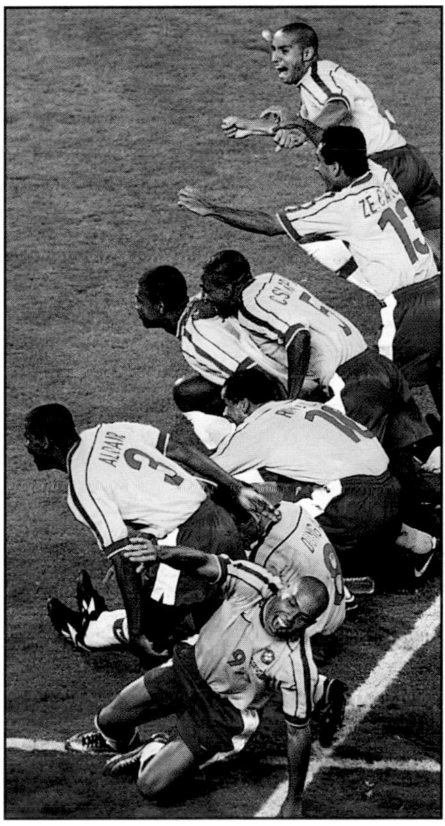

The Brazilian team celebrate during the 1998 World Cup. They reached the Final but did not play well – partly because their star striker Ronaldo (front) was not well. Brazil and West Germany have been the major forces in the World Cup, with each appearing in six finals – but Brazil are the only team to have won the Cup away from their own continent.

LIFELINES

WILLIAM WILBERFORCE, *born in 1759, was the Millennium's most famous reformer. An MP and evangelical Christian, he abolished the British slave trade in 1807. Slaves were freed in 1833, the year he died.*

DICK WHITTINGTON *(circa 1358-1423) is the most famous mayor of London. Though many think of him as a fictional cat-lover, he was actually mayor four times between 1397 and 1420. The son of a knight, he died in 1423.*

MUDDY WATERS *was the blues giant whose song 'Rollin' Stone' gave the Rolling Stones their name. Born McKinley Morganfield in 1915, he bossed the post-war Chicago electric blues scene that inspired many famous rock stars. He died in 1983.*

1990 GERMANY REUNITED East and West Germany were reunited as the Federal Republic of Germany. After the fall of Hitler, Germany had been divided for 45 years by the Cold War.

1990 ANC BAN IS LIFTED South African President FW de Klerk lifted a 30-year-old ban on the African National Congress. He also promised to free Nelson Mandela and drop restrictions on political opposition.

1990 CEAUSESCU OVERTHROWN Dictator Nicolae Ceausescu was overthrown in Romania where he had ruled for 24 years. The Communist Party was then outlawed in the country.

1990 CHANNEL TUNNEL IS COMPLETED The Channel Tunnel linking England and France between Folkestone and Calais was completed.

WEST SIDE STORY

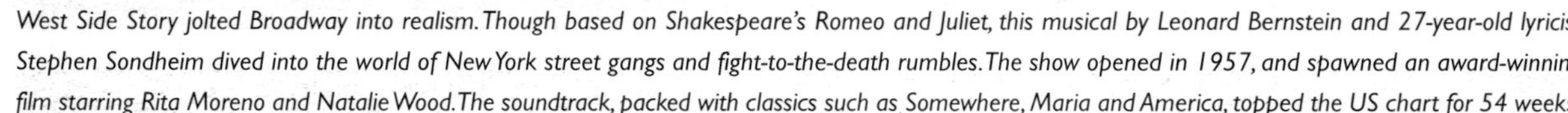

West Side Story jolted Broadway into realism. Though based on Shakespeare's Romeo and Juliet, this musical by Leonard Bernstein and 27-year-old lyricist Stephen Sondheim dived into the world of New York street gangs and fight-to-the-death rumbles. The show opened in 1957, and spawned an award-winning film starring Rita Moreno and Natalie Wood. The soundtrack, packed with classics such as Somewhere, Maria and America, topped the US chart for 54 weeks.

OSCAR WILDE

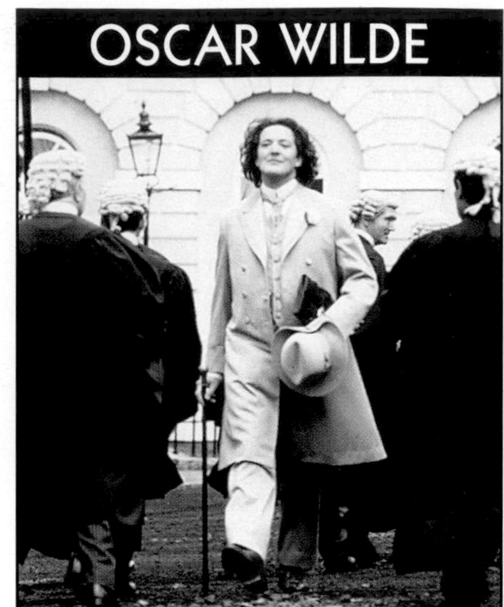

Oscar Wilde, was one of the Millennium's great wits – and a tragic genius to boot. Born in Dublin in 1854, he found fame in London with his novel *The Picture Of Dorian Gray* and witty plays such as *The Importance Of Being Earnest.* A flamboyant homosexual, he was sentenced to two years' hard labour for what his friend Lord Alfred Douglas called "the Love that dare not speak its name". The subject of several films – he was brilliantly played by Stephen Fry (above) in 1997 – Wilde died in France in 1900.

JOHN WAYNE

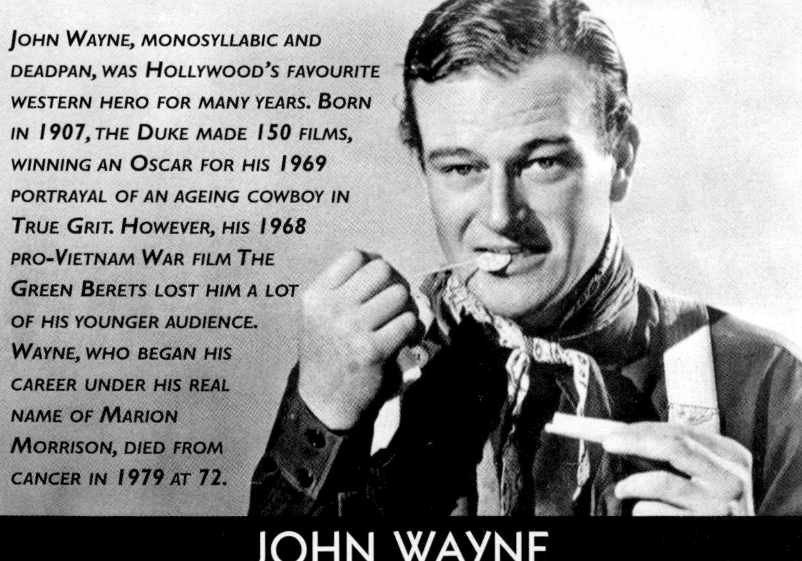

John Wayne, monosyllabic and deadpan, was Hollywood's favourite western hero for many years. Born in 1907, the Duke made 150 films, winning an Oscar for his 1969 portrayal of an ageing cowboy in True Grit. However, his 1968 pro-Vietnam War film The Green Berets lost him a lot of his younger audience. Wayne, who began his career under his real name of Marion Morrison, died from cancer in 1979 at 72.

EVELYN WAUGH

Evelyn Waugh wrote Brideshead Revisited, the novel on which the classic 1981 TV series was based. Brideshead, and similarly serious later works, were a departure from the comic novels that made Waugh famous, such as Scoop (1938), which turned his experiences as a Fleet Street war reporter into high farce. He died in 1966, aged 62.

Millennium Time Line

1990
The People's Voice is Heard
As the collapse of communism spread, Ukrainian Prime Minister Vitaly Masol resigned. He had faced massive student-led unrest and was the first Soviet official of such status to quit because of public pressure.

1990
War Against Saddam
Iraqi troops, on orders from President Saddam Hussein, invaded and occupied neighbouring Kuwait. An international force, led by the United States and Britain, then launched an invasion to drive out the Iraqis and restore Kuwait's independence. The battle was called Operation Desert Storm.

1990
Russian Church is Back
A Russian Orthodox service was held in St Basil's Cathedral, next to the Kremlin, in Red Square, Moscow. It was the first of its kind for over 70 years.

LIFELINES

William Wordsworth *(1770-1850) was Poet Laureate from 1843. His work included the influential collection Lyrical Ballads (with his friend Samuel Coleridge) and the famous 'daffodils' poem, 'I wandered lonely as a cloud'.*

Virginia Woolf, *born in 1882, was a fine, stream-of-consciousness author and mainstay of the famous Bloomsbury set of writers. She died in 1941 and is remembered in the title of an Edward Albee play, later turned into a film.*

James Watt *made a vital contribution to the Industrial Revolution. The Scottish engineer did not invent the steam engine, as often believed, but greatly improved an existing design. Born in 1736, he died in 1819.*

WOODSTOCK

Woodstock was the high point of the hippies. Held on farmland in Bethel, New York in August 1969, it is remembered as much for its peaceful atmosphere as its killer line-up of artists including Jimi Hendrix, The Who and Janis Joplin. The festival was turned into a free event when 400,000 people turned up, mostly without tickets, and the chaos made it news. Woodstock coincided with two landmark shows in Britain – the Rolling Stones' free concert in Hyde Park and Bob Dylan's comeback at the Isle of Wight Festival – but Woodstock had a better film crew, who made it into a classic movie.

H G WELLS

The 1953 film of The War of the Worlds

Herbert George Wells wrote made-for-movies sci-fi novels before Hollywood existed. And if *The Time Machine* (1895) and *War Of The Worlds* (1898) proved he was a master of fiction, then his *Shape Of Things To Come* showed him to be a prophet. A great humorist about ordinary life in novels such as *Mr Polly*, Wells died in 1946, aged 79.

ORSON WELLES

Citizen Kane – the greatest movie ever?

Orson Welles made what many consider the best film ever: *Citizen Kane*, released in 1941 when he was 25. He was a rule-breaker as actor and director in films such as *Touch of Evil* (1958). But to many he remains the man who panicked America in 1938 with a radio version of *The War Of The Worlds* so realistic that people really believed the Martians had landed. He died in 1985.

ANDY WARHOL

Andy Warhol – who correctly predicted that "In the future, everyone will be famous for 15 minutes" – made celebrity an art form. Born in 1928, the blond-haired icon was the leader of Pop Art in the 1960s. His most familiar works are his silkscreen prints of American consumer objects – Campbell's soup – and stars such as Marilyn Monroe (right). He added to his notoriety with deliberately trashy films such as Chelsea Girls (1966) that cried out to be banned. He launched the Velvet Underground, survived a 1968 shooting, and died in 1987.

1990
Russia's About-Turn
Soviet President Mikhail Gorbachev, faced with monumental financial problems, persuaded the Soviet parliament to adopt a market economy.

1990
Major Change at No 10
Challenged for the Tory Party leadership, a disbelieving Margaret Thatcher resigned after being advised that she could not win. She later left Downing Street in tears. John Major fought off Michael Heseltine and Douglas Hurd to become Prime Minister.

1991
The Start of 'Ethnic Cleansing'
After Soviet rule collapsed across Eastern Europe, the republics of Croatia and Slovenia declared themselves independent of Yugoslavia. As a result, simmering ethnic rivalries between Serbs and Croats came to the surface. In Bosnia-Herzegovina, fighting broke out between Serbs and Muslims, with the Serbs launching a programme of 'ethnic cleansing' – a euphemism for a campaign of terrorism and genocide. There were soon about two million refugees, and about 200,000 Muslims were missing, presumed dead.

WAR

THEN A millennium ago, wars were about land. Territory was under constant foreign attack. As one historian put it: "Outbreaks of peace punctuated war." Apart from the Crusades – where thousands lost their lives trying to help the Pope win back the Holy Lands from Islam – fighting was a job for the rich and powerful. Battles revolved around sieges of castles, and rape, looting and pillaging were soldiers' fringe benefits. The development of stirrups allowed knights to stand on their horses to throw their lances, increasing their kill rate. Bloodier still was the invention of gunpowder in the 14th century.

NOW On August 6, 1945, America dropped the first of two atomic bombs on Japan. Instantly, 80,000 people died, and the city of Hiroshima simply vanished. "People near ground zero were vaporised," one report put it, "leaving only charred shadows." The Second World War was a 'total war', in which entire populations were mobilised. Subsequent conflicts, such as the Gulf War, have been 'limited wars' centred on specific regions and issues. Another total war would be totally it for all of us, so while the specialists slug it out, we watch the highlights on TV…

FIRST WORLD WAR

It wasn't 'all over by Christmas', not by a long way. After four years, eight million soldiers had died – and few really knew what for.

The Great War began in a domino effect of overlapping conflicts and loyalties. The Austro-Hungarian Empire felt threatened by Serbia, while Britain was worried by Germany's growing naval power. The trigger was the 1914 assassination of Austrian archduke Franz Ferdinand by a Serb terrorist in Sarajevo.

Britain entered the war on August 4, 1914 after Germany invaded Belgium, whose independence both had guaranteed. The Allies – Russia, France, Britain and Serbia (plus, later, Japan, Italy and USA) – lined up against the Central powers: Germany and Austro-Hungary (plus Turkey and Bulgaria).

Trench warfare led to a machine-gun and barbed-wire stand-off all the way from the English Channel to Switzerland, a Western front which did not move more than ten miles in three years.

Losses were horrific. Poison gas, tanks and submarines all played a part. America's entry into the war in December 1917 saw off the final German offensive, and an armistice was signed on November 11, 1918. What a waste.

THE WORLD WAR DEAD

It is estimated that around 10 million people were killed during the First World War, and around 55 million during the Second World War. The ten countries with the biggest losses are listed below. Statistics vary from source to source, particularly for the First World War.

First World War fatalities

Country	Military killed
Germany	1,718,250
Russia	1,700,000
France (inc. colonial territories)	1,385,250
Austria-Hungary	1,200,000
UK	702,500
Italy	460,000
Turkey*	335,750
Romania	200,000
Serbia	127,500
USA	116,750
Rest of the World	2,000,000

** No official records for Turkish fatalities*

Second World War fatalities

Country	Military	Civilian	Total
USSR	13,600,000	7,720,000	21, 320, 000
Germany	3,300,000	3,063,000	6,363,000
Poland	320,000	6,028,000	6,348,000
China	1,324,500	Unknown*	Unknown
Japan	1,140,500	953,000	2,093,500
Yugoslavia	305,000	1,355,000	1,660,000
Austria	380,000	145,000	525,000
Romania	325,000	145,000	470,000
USA	348,000	None	405,000
UK	264,500	60,500	325,000
Rest of the World			14,000,000

** Estimates of Chinese civilian dead vary from 700,000 to 10,000,000*

***Sir Dirk Bogarde** (actor), a Queen's Royal Regiment captain, saw action in the Far East, France and Germany and helped liberate the Belsen concentration camp.*

***Kirk Douglas** (actor) was a US Navy lieutenant in the Pacific. Internal injuries from combat led to an early discharge.*

***Sir Edward Heath** (former Prime Minister) served as a major in the Royal Artillery. He was mentioned in despatches and was also awarded a military MBE.*

TONY CURTIS

***Tony Curtis** (actor) served in the US Navy in the Pacific and witnessed the Japanese surrender.*

1991 GORBACHEV HELD
Hard-line communists took Soviet leader Mikhail Gorbachev prisoner and tried to stage a coup. It failed within 72 hours as Boris Yeltsin rose to the occasion and rallied the people against the plotters. Yeltsin was to become the Russian leader and the Communist Party, which had ruled the Soviet Union for nearly 75 years, was suspended. By the end of the year the Soviet Union itself was falling apart.

1991 A FIRST FOR RUSSIA
Boris Yeltsin was inaugurated President of the Russian republic – the country's first freely-elected leader.

1991 MAXWELL SCANDAL
Robert Maxwell, the tycoon who owned Mirror Group Newspapers, was found drowned after falling – or jumping – from his yacht. Auditors later discovered that his companies owed more than £1 billion and that 68-year-old Maxwell had stolen at least £400 million from pension funds.

SECOND WORLD WAR

Adolf Hitler's rise to power in Germany was fuelled by a resurgent nationalism that seeked to restore the country's pride after the humiliation of defeat in the First World War and the crippling reparation demands that followed it.

Hitler began occupying territory where Germans already lived, such as Sudetenland in Czechoslovakia. Prime Minister Neville Chamberlain thought Hitler's ambitions had been appeased, but on September 1, 1939 the Germans invaded Poland. Britain and France declared war.

With the US and Russia still neutral, there was little the Allies could do as Germany invaded Denmark, Norway, Holland, Belgium and France in 1940. Soon after Winston Churchill became Prime Minister, 338,000 Allied troops were evacuated from Dunkirk in an armada of small boats.

The Battle of Britain was Hitler's first reverse, and in December 1941 Germany's ally Japan attacked Pearl Harbor, bringing the Americans into the war. By the end of 1942, after Hitler's failed attempt to invade Russia, the tide turned. Montgomery defeated Rommel in the African desert and the Allies conquered Germany's ally, Italy.

The D-Day invasion in June 1944 finally brought victory in Europe in May 1945. In August, the US dropped two atom bombs on Japan, and Emperor Hirohito surrendered.

The shocked liberators of the concentration camps discovered that Germany had tried to murder the entire Jewish race. The war left nearly all of Europe devastated.

WAR AND PEACE

Leo Tolstoy's War and Peace, written between 1865 and 1869, may be the greatest novel of the Millennium. This vast chronicle of 19th-century Russian life – all balls, battles, duels, troika rides and philosophical speculations – brought realistic fiction into the ranks of great art. King Vidor's 1956 film version, starring Audrey Hepburn and Henry Fonda, was lavish and respectful, while Sergei Bondarchuk's 1967 Russian epic lasted 8½ hours and used 20,000 extras in scenes such as Napoleon's retreat from Moscow in 1812 (above).

SOME FAMOUS SECOND WORLD WAR VETERANS

ROBERT RUNCIE

Lord Robert Runcie (former Archbishop of Canterbury) served with the Scots Guards and was a tank officer, seeing action in Normandy and being awarded the Military Cross.

Patrick Moore (astronomer) was an RAF navigator with Bomber Command, reaching the rank of flight lieutenant.

Tony Benn (politician) joined the RAF in 1943 aged 18. He got his wings just as Germany surrendered, so he switched to the Fleet Air Arm to fight against Japan.

Richard Todd (Dam Busters actor) served with the Light Infantry, the Parachute Regiment and the 6th Airborne Division, seeing action on D-Day and in the Battle of the Bulge.

Patrick Macnee (actor who played John Steed in The Avengers) was a Royal Navy lieutenant and won the Atlantic Medal.

ROD STEIGER

Rod Steiger (actor) lied about his age to join the US Navy as a torpedoman on a destroyer in the South Pacific and saw action at Iwo Jima.

Lord Roy Jenkins (politician) served in the Royal Artillery and as a captain in special intelligence.

Sir Alec Guinness (actor) captained a ship in the Royal Navy.

DENIS HEALEY

Lord Denis Healey (politician) was an Army major, and Beachmaster at the Anzio landings in Italy. Mentioned in despatches, he was given a military MBE.

Christopher Lee (actor), an RAF flight lieutenant, served with Intelligence and Special Forces in the Western Desert and Europe. He was mentioned in despatches.

WAR TALK

"History is littered with wars everybody 'knew' would never happen." – Enoch Powell

"Men love war because it allows them to look serious. Because it is the one thing that stops women laughing at them." – John Fowles, British novelist

"One murder makes a villain; millions a hero. Numbers sanctify." – Charles Chaplin

"This war, like the next war, is a war to end war." – David Lloyd George, Britain's Prime Minister during the First World War

"Wars make for better reading than peace does." – A J P Taylor, historian

"War is like love – it always finds a way." – Bertolt Brecht, playwright

"In starting and waging a war, it is not right that matters but victory." – Adolf Hitler

"There never was a good war, or a bad peace." – Benjamin Franklin, US statesman

1991
TOO MUCH, TOO SOON
Georgia, birthplace of Joseph Stalin, voted for independence from the Soviet Union in 1991. Similar votes had already been carried in Lithuania, Estonia and Latvia. It was all too much for Moscow. A state of emergency was declared and troops despatched.

1991
IRA ATTACK DOWNING STREET
An explosive device was launched from a van parked near Downing Street while the Cabinet was in session. Windows were shattered but no one was hurt. An appalled John Major said it was an IRA attempt to kill the Cabinet.

1992
ANNUS HORRIBILIS
A fire caused extensive damage to Windsor Castle, destroying St George's Hall, the Waterloo Chamber and the private chapel. The blaze contributed, with squabbling children, to what the Queen would call an 'annus horribilis'.

1992
MANDELA RELEASED
Watched by millions of television viewers all over the world, Nelson Mandela walked to freedom from a jail near Cape Town. He had been a political prisoner for 27 years.

OPRAH WINFREY

One of a wave of American afternoon chat-show hosts serving up true confessions, Oprah won out with a style that was never patronising but almost embarrassingly personal. Like a best friend, she spilled out revelations about her own sexual history and weight problems.

With the rise of Jerry Springer, Oprah has steered her show away from the prurient to the educational. It still attracts 15-20 million viewers a day, making it the highest-rated in history. Only the third woman ever to own a major studio, she was named 'highest-paid entertainer' by Forbes magazine, and is well on her way to becoming America's first black billionaire.

WEDDINGS

THEN For centuries, weddings were exclusively religious affairs. Ceremonies would be avoided during Lent and Advent, when the Church banned sexual relations. Traditionally, too, most marriages took place between harvest and Christmas – when supplies for wedding feasts would be most plentiful. The two tunes heard at every wedding today were both composed in the 1840s. Mendelssohn's 'Wedding March' (the one like a peal of bells) comes from his setting of Shakespeare's *A Midsummer Night's Dream*, while Wagner's 'Bridal March' (*"Here comes the bride"*) is part of the opera *Lohengrin*.

NOW There is much less pressure on couples to get married, so marriage can be seen as a statement of intent. Marriage remains modish, and its appeal has been boosted by some big celebrity weddings, including those of two of the Spice Girls. The most famous wedding of century – that of Prince Charles and Lady Diana Spencer (above left) – took place in 1981 but ended in dovorce in 1996. By the time Prince Edward married Sophie Rhys-Jones (above), all of his siblings were divorced, leading *Private Eye* to depict Edward asking his two brothers: "What's it like being married, chaps?" Andrew replies: "You tell us."

JUNE WHITFIELD AND BARBARA WINDSOR

Two of Britain's favourite female comedy troupers, Barbara Windsor and June Whitfield both appeared in the ever-popular Carry On films of the late Fifties and Sixties, and are now enjoying a renaissance that gives the lie to the idea that there are no good parts for actresses of a certain age. June Whitfield (left) – star of the naff Seventies sitcom Terry And June – proved she was still very much a contender with her brilliant role as Jennifer Saunders' mother in the pioneering Absolutely Fabulous. Barbara Windsor is as upfront as ever as Peggy Mitchell, the landlady of the Queen Vic in EastEnders.

1993 SANCTIONS LIFTED United Nations economic sanctions, which had been in force against South Africa for 30 years, were lifted after the ending of apartheid.

1994 THE WRITER RETURNS Russian author Aleksandr Solzhenitsyn returned to his homeland after 20 years in exile. He had been expelled in 1974 for exposing the Soviet prison camp system in a book that was published in the West.

1994 NATO IN COMBAT For the first time in its 45-year history, Nato forces went into action. Four Bosnian Serb jets were shot down by American fighters in a no-fly zone.

1994 WOMEN PRIESTS The Church of England ordained 32 women priests. The move is believed to have resulted in thousands of church members switching to Roman Catholicism.

VIRGINIA WADE

In recent decades Britain has had little to cheer about come Finals Day at Wimbledon, but Virginia Wade changed all that with her victory in the ladies' singles. Her timing was impeccable, too. The year was 1977 – the Queen's Silver Jubilee – leaving some cynics to wonder if the whole thing hadn't been fixed!

WOMEN

THEN Women are surely the most persecuted group in all history. Throughout the Millennium, aristocratic women were expected to breed continually to ensure the line (and keep property in the male-dominated family) – look no further than Henry VIII, who disposed of wives when they failed to produce heirs. Unattached women were often accused of witchcraft by men suspicious of their mysterious biology. Religion tended to see women either as 'Eve-like' temptresses or exemplary virgins. In India, Hindu wives were expected to throw themselves on their husband's funeral pyre.

NOW The early 1900s witnessed the first suffragette marches, leading to the imprisonment of women campaigning for the vote. Votes for all were granted in 1928, though some women were still against the idea. Two World Wars propelled women from domesticity to employment in the war effort. The real advance has been in women gaining control over their fertility, first through such birth-control pioneers as Dr Marie Stopes in the 1930s, and then the Pill in the 1960s. Since the 1950s, divorce and employment laws have improved, but complaints persist of a glass ceiling at the top of the job ladder.

WOMEN IN SPORT

THE ONLY TEN WOMEN TO HAVE WON THE BBC SPORTS PERSONALITY OF THE YEAR AWARD

Anita Lonsborough 1962 swimmer
Dorothy Hyman 1963 sprinter
Mary Rand 1964 long jump/pentathlon/relay
Ann Jones 1969 tennis player
Princess Anne 1971 equestrian
Mary Peters 1972 pentathlon
Virginia Wade 1977 tennis player
Jayne Torvill (with Christopher Dean) 1984 ice dancer
Fatima Whitbread 1987 (above) javelin thrower
Liz McColgan 1991 long-distance runner

1994
Germans Back In Paris
German troops were back on the streets of Paris for the first time since the Second World War – taking part in Bastille Day celebrations. Germany's Constitutional Court had ended the ban on sending troops to fight outside the country which had been in effect since 1945.

1994
America's New Friend
The United States ended its long-standing trade embargo with Vietnam. Full diplomatic relations were restored in 1995.

1994
Romania Joins Nato
Romania became the first former Cold War opponent to join the North Atlantic Treaty Organization (Nato) following the collapse of the Soviet Union.

1994
Peace At Last In Londonderry
There were no British troops on the streets of Londonderry for the first time in 25 years. The pullout came after ceasefires by the IRA and Loyalist paramilitary forces.

LIFELINES

RICHARD WAGNER *(1813-1883) revolutionised opera. He turned it into an art form of epic proportions, his masterpiece being The Ring Of The Nibelung, an amalgam of four operas. But his most played piece is the Bridal March.*

SHANE WARNE *is cricket's biggest star. The Australian leg-spin bowler, born in 1969, played his first Test in 1991. In a fast bowlers' era, his famous first ball in England in 1993 to bamboozle Mike Gatting showed that slow bowling could be just as lethal.*

GEORGE WASHINGTON, *the American War of Independence general who became the first President, was born in 1732. His split with Thomas Jefferson led to two-party politics. He died in 1799.*

WORDS

WORDS WHICH DEFINE EACH YEAR OF THE 20TH CENTURY

ACCORDING TO THE TIMES AND COLLINS DICTIONARIES (WE'VE ADDED OUR OWN CHOICES FOR 1998 AND 1999)

1900 **LABOUR PARTY** *1901* **FINGERPRINT** *1902* **TEDDY BEAR** *1903* **TARMAC** *1904* **FIFA** *1905* **SINN FEIN** *1906* **SUFFRAGETTE** *1907* **ALLERGY** *1908* **BORSTAL** *1909* **JAZZ** *1910* **GIRL GUIDE** *1911* **AIR RAID** *1912* **SCHIZOPHRENIA** *1913* **ISOTOPE** *1914* **VORTICISM** *1915* **TANK** *1916* **DADA** *1917* **CHEKA** *1918* **BOLSHY** *1919* **FASCISM** *1920* **ROBOT** *1921* **CHAPLINESQUE** *1922* **GIGOLO** *1923* **SPOONERISM** *1924* **SURREALISM** *1925* **BRITISH SUMMER TIME** *1926* **TELEVISION** *1927* **TALKIE** *1928* **PENICILLIN** *1929* **MAGINOT LINE** *1930* **PLUTO** *1931* **OSCAR** *1932* **NEUTRON** *1933* **GESTAPO** *1934* **BELISHA** *1935* **ALCOHOLICS ANONYMOUS** *1936* **MICKEY MOUSE** *1937* **SURREAL** *1938* **NYLON** *1939* **WALTER MITTY** *1940* **JEEP** *1941* **RADAR** *1942* **ROBOTICS** *1943* **DAM BUSTERS** *1944* **DOODLEBUG** *1945* **TUPPERWARE** *1946* **BIKINI** *1947* **FLYING SAUCER** *1948* **SCRABBLE** *1949* **BIG BROTHER** *1950* **NATO** *1951* **DISCOTHEQUE** *1952* **STONED** *1953* **ROCK 'N' ROLL** *1954* **TEDDY BOY** *1955* **LEGO** *1956* **ANGRY YOUNG MAN** *1957* **PSYCHEDELIC** *1958* **SILICON CHIP** *1959* **HOVERCRAFT** *1960* **LASER** *1961* **CATCH-22** *1962* **MONTEZUMA'S REVENGE** *1963* **RACHMANISM** *1964* **MOOG SYNTHESISER** *1965* **MINISKIRT** *1966* **CULTURAL REVOLUTION** *1967* **PULSAR** *1968* **FOSBURY FLOP** *1969* **MOON BUGGY** *1970* **BUTTERFLY EFFECT** *1971* **WORKAHOLIC** *1972* **WATERGATE** *1973* **VAT** *1974* **CEEFAX** *1975* **FRACTAL** *1976* **PUNK ROCK** *1977* **ERM** *1978* **TEST-TUBE BABY** *1979* **RUBIK CUBE** *1980* **SOLIDARITY** *1981* **SDP** *1982* **CD** *1983* **AIDS** *1984* **YUPPIE** *1985* **GLASNOST** *1986* **MEXICAN WAVE** *1987* **PEP** *1988* **ACID HOUSE** *1989* **VELVET REVOLUTION** *1990* **CROP CIRCLE** *1991* **ETHNIC CLEANSING** *1992* **CLONE** *1993* **INFORMATION SUPERHIGHWAY** *1994* **NATIONAL LOTTERY** *1995* **ROAD RAGE** *1996* **ALCOPOP** *1997* **BLAIRITE** *1998* **GIRL POWER** *1999* **MILLENNIUM**

They became words of the century: pioneering American high jumper Dick Fosbury and a trio of British youth fashions – punks, Teddy boys and the miniskirt

WILDLIFE

THEN A thousand years ago, Britain's native wildlife included the brown bear, the grey wolf, the wild boar, the black rat (recently rediscovered) and the great auk – which is now extinct globally. The animals men worked with were no different from ours, however: no new animals have been domesticated for 4000 years.

NOW In the last 400 years, over 600 species have been recorded as becoming extinct worldwide, the biggest group among these being rodents and bats. Although this is partly a natural process – the average lifetime of a species is an estimated 5-10 million years – extinctions are now accelerating at a rate which alarms conservationists. Today there are over 5200 threatened species on the planet.

VICTORIA WOOD

Victoria Wood is the only British comedian to sell out 15 consecutive nights at the Royal Albert Hall. Born in 1953, she has written her own sitcom – dinnerladies – and won awards as a playwright. But she is best-loved for the series As Seen on TV (co-starring Julie Walters, Duncan Preston, Celia Imrie and Susie Blake) and its immortal Crossroads send-up Acorn Antiques.

1994
CHANNEL TUNNEL OPENS
The Channel Tunnel between Folkestone and Calais was opened on May 6, 1994. One of the greatest civil engineering projects of the century, it was originally estimated to cost £4.8 billion. The final bill was £10.5 billion.

1994
MANDELA ELECTED
Multi-racial elections were held in South Africa and 18 million blacks were able to vote for the first time. Nelson Mandela was elected President.

1994
ROYAL ADULTERY
Prince Charles admitted in a 1994 TV interview that he had committed adultery with Camilla Parker-Bowles, with whom he had been in love for several years. Six months later, Princess Diana also admitted on TV that she had been to bed with Life Guards officer James Hewitt. Charles and Diana were divorced in 1996.

1995
GAS ATTACK
Twelve people were killed and 5,000 injured in a nerve gas attack on the Tokyo subway system.

THE WIND IN THE WILLOWS

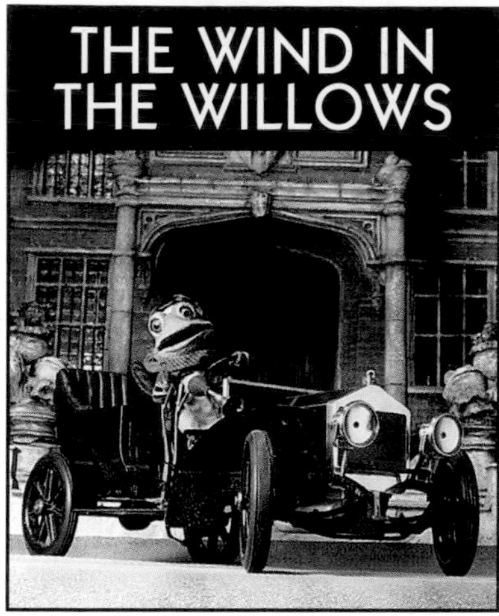

Ratty, Mole, Badger and Toad star in Kenneth Grahame's affectionate woodland soap opera of British wildlife, written in 1908. Grahame, a Scotsman who worked for the Bank of England, only wrote four books, but his riverbank story – written for his son Alastair – continues to delight. It has been filmed with actors, Disney cartoon characters and puppets (above).

WINNIE-THE-POOH

A A Milne's *Winnie-The-Pooh* (1926) centred on a whimsical teddy bear who led Christopher Robin (the author's son) into a series of funny adventures with his friend Piglet, drawn by E H Shepard – who also illustrated *The Wind in the Willows*. Pooh's endless search for 'hunny' became a Disney film (above) in 1966 with a new, rather un-English character called Gopher.

THE WIZARD OF OZ

"Follow the yellow brick road…" This magical 1939 film would surely have won a Best Film Oscar had it not been for *Gone With the Wind*, released in the same year.

But 16-year-old Judy Garland did win an Oscar for her rendition of 'Somewhere Over the Rainbow', while *The Wizard of Oz* won a place in the hearts of all who saw it, with its story of brave young Dorothy seeing off a wicked witch in her bid to get back to Kansas and help her friends the cowardly lion, the brainless scarecrow, and the heart-less tin man. Meanwhile, the wizard – well, we're sure you know the rest…

Sidney Lumet made a disco version in 1978 called *The Wiz*, set in New York, with Michael Jackson and Diana Ross.

1995
OJ Simpson is Acquitted
Former American movie star and football player OJ Simpson was found not guilty of murder in one of America's most sensational trials, watched live on TV by millions. He was accused of stabbing to death his ex-wife Nicole Brown and her male friend.

1995
Harold Wilson Dies
Former Labour Prime Minister Harold Wilson, who became Lord Wilson, died in 1995 after a long illness and was buried on his beloved Scilly Isles. Wilson will long be remembered for his television speech, after devaluation, when he assured the British public: "This, of course, does not affect the pound in your pocket…"

1996
Serbs Named as War Criminals
Radovan Karadzic, leader of the Bosnian Serbs, was indicted as a war criminal by the International Court at The Hague. Karadzic resigned after international pressure but is believed to be active behind the scenes. In 1999, Slobodan Milosevic, president of Yugoslavia, was also indicted as a war criminal.

CHRISTOPHER WREN

Christopher Wren is the man who gave life to London in the wake of the Great Fire of 1666. Born in 1632, he began his adult life as a mathematician who became a professor of astronomy at Oxford University, and displayed little interest in being an architect until he was almost 30. His early work included the Sheldonian Theatre, Oxford.

An undoubted genius who could have been anything he wanted to be, Wren submitted plans for the complete rebuilding of London in the wake of the fire. His design had broad avenues, a series of large squares and wonderful vistas.

When this was rejected due to property disputes, Wren concentrated on designing St Paul's Cathedral (below) and an amazing 52 churches in the city. Those still standing include St Bride's, St Lawrence and St Stephen's. The inventiveness and beauty of these buildings, plus his work for Chelsea Hospital, Greenwich Hospital and Greenwich Observatory, show what might have been had the grand plan been accepted.

An MP, inventor and biologist, Wren died in 1723 and was buried in St Paul's. His epitaph reads: "If you seek his monument, look about you."

WESTMINSTER ABBEY

For centuries Westminster Abbey has been the church of royalist Britain. Built by Edward the Confessor in the 11th century, all but two monarchs have been crowned here since William the Conqueror – and many of them buried too. In 1998 it witnessed a wave of grief unprecedented even in this ancient church: the funeral of Diana, Princess of Wales

LECH WALESA

LECH WALESA LIT THE FIRST SPARK IN THE FIRE THAT FREED EASTERN EUROPE FROM THE DEAD HAND OF SOVIET COMMUNISM. BORN IN 1943, HE WAS A SHIPYARD EMPLOYEE UNTIL POOR CONDITIONS FORCED HIM TO BECOME A REAL WORKING-CLASS HERO. HE FORMED THE SOLIDARITY UNION IN 1980 (LEFT), AND WAS THROWN IN PRISON IN 1981. BUT IN 1983 HE WON THE NOBEL PEACE PRIZE FOR HELPING TO START DEMOCRACY IN POLAND. WHEN FREE ELECTIONS WERE HELD IN 1990, HE BECAME PRESIDENT BY A LANDSLIDE.

1997
LABOUR LANDSLIDE
Tony Blair, who became Labour leader in 1994 after the death of John Smith, dragged the party from its traditional roots and dogmas and presented 'New Labour' to the electorate. The result was a landslide victory, ending 18 years of Tory rule.

1997
TENNIS UPS AND DOWNS
Sixteen-year-old tennis player Martina Hingis, of Switzerland, became the youngest player in 100 years to win the women's singles championship at Wimbledon. Two years later, in 1999, Martina was knocked out in the first round by Jelena Dokic of Australia – also 16.

1997
GOODBYE HONG KONG
Hong Kong, under British control since 1842, reverted to Chinese rule on July 1 under the terms of a century-old treaty. Prince Charles was there as pomp, ceremony, fireworks – and tears – marked the transition.

HAROLD WILSON

Harold Wilson was the first Prime Minister to understand TV appeal. Pipe-smoking, soccer-loving and ever-affable on screen, the Labour politician was able to connect directly with ordinary people, regardless of his warring party. Shades of Tony Blair, who inherited Wilson's mantle of the youngest PM of the century – Wilson was 48, Blair 43. Britain's leader twice, in 1964-70 and 1974-76, Wilson was knighted in 1976 and became Baron Wilson of Rievaulx in 1983.

THE WEATHER FORECAST

THEN Modern weather forecasting began in the 16th century, when Galileo developed a thermometer in 1593. A pupil of his, Evangelista Torricelli, developed a simple barometer in 1643. The first weather map appeared in 1686, a chart of the trade winds by English astronomer Edmond Halley. Until the 20th century, weather forecasting was almost exclusively about predicting the movement of areas of high and low pressure.

NOW Our ability to anticipate the weather was boosted by Vilhelm Bjerknes, who in the early part of the century showed that the movement of enormous masses of air greatly influenced weather conditions. When a warm and cold mass meet, an area of rapidly changing weather occurs, which Bjerknes called a 'front'. Radar was first used for weather observation in the 1940s, and the first successful computerised forecast took place in 1950. In 1959, America launched the first satellite equipped to report back from space with weather data.

THE WALL STREET CRASH

On Black Thursday, October 24, 1929, the world's biggest financial disaster hit the New York Stock Exchange (left). Fears of 'insecure' securities sparked panic selling – 16 million shares changed hands in a day. Bank failures led to 17 million unemployed worldwide and the Great Depression, which lasted until the Second World War. The crash was caused by speculators creating an artificial boom. On the first day alone, 11 investors killed themselves.

WEALTH

There are said to be 42,000 millionaires in Britain today, though they are not rich by some standards. Billionaires are on the rise, and Britain's richest 200 people own two per cent of the country's wealth. According to a trades union survey in 1997, the average salary of the highest-paid director at Britain's top 100 companies was £970,000 a year.

THE PEOPLE SAID TO BE THE RICHEST IN BRITAIN

(THOUGH, AS ROBERT MAXWELL'S PRESENCE IN THE LIST SHOWS, THE FIGURES CAN LIE!)

1989

1. DUKE OF WESTMINSTER £3 billion+
London landowner

2. ROBERT MAXWELL £3 billion
Daily Mirror owner (when he died two years later he was found to owe £2bn)

2. DAVID SAINSBURY £3 billion
Owner of Sainsbury's supermarkets

3. LORD SAMUEL VESTEY AND EDMUND VESTEY £2 billion+ Meat producers

1999

1. DUKE OF WESTMINSTER £3.3 billion
The Duke – Gerald Cavendish Grosvenor – owns 300 acres in London's West End

2. RICHARD BRANSON £2.6 billion
Record, video and airline company owner

3. GARRY WESTON £1.6 billion
Chairman of British Associated Foods, maker of Twinings Tea, Silver Spoon Sugar etc

Richard Branson, seen at home, has managed to be both rich and popular. Born in 1950, he set up the Virgin mail-order record shop in 1969 and turned it into a record label, megastore, airline and pensions company. He is also an adventurer, having made the fastest Atlantic sea crossing and the first crossings of the Atlantic and Pacific by balloon.

LIFELINES

JOHN WESLEY *(1703-91) founded the Methodist Church. Although a Church of England minister, he rode around the country for 50 years preaching to all comers. His brother Charles wrote 5000 hymns including 'Hark, the Herald Angels Sing'.*

TENNESSEE WILLIAMS *(1911-83) wrote steamy plays about America's South. A Streetcar Named Desire and Cat On A Hot Tin Roof created vivid, sexually-charged film roles for Marlon Brando and Elizabeth Taylor. He died in 1983.*

P G WODEHOUSE *introduced the quintessential English toff, Bertie Wooster, in his Jeeves tales. But Wodehouse (1881-1975) later became an American citizen, writing lyrics for some of Broadway's biggest hits.*

1997 DEATH OF A PRINCESS
Diana, Princess of Wales, was killed in a car crash on August 31. With her lover Dodi al-Fayed, she was in a Mercedes being driven at high speed through the streets of Paris, pursued by photographers. Her driver, who had taken drugs and alcohol, lost control in a tunnel. The death of Diana, 36, caused mourning across the world.

1998 THE RISE OF BILL GATES
In August 1998, Microsoft, the computer software company founded and run by Bill Gates, overtook General Electric to become the most valuable company in the United States. By the time he was 31 in 1986, Gates had made his first million. He rapidly moved on to become the richest person in the world.

1998 IRELAND PEACE
After 22 months of gruelling negotiations, the warring parties in Northern Ireland sat down on April 10 – Good Friday – and signed an historic peace agreement. Knowing there was still a long way to go, an elated but cautious Tony Blair said: "It is a beginning. But it will only work if people want to make it work."

ZOOS

THEN Man has collected animals since time immemorial. Menageries and aquariums – the forerunners of the modern zoo – have long existed in Europe. The Tower of London housed beasts as early as the reign of Henry I, who had lions and leopards there in the 12th century. Later, a white bear and elephant were added, and by the 18th century the Tower sheltered a large collection. These animals were transferred to St Marylebone – later Regent's – Park in 1834 by the Royal Zoological Society (founded in 1826). It survives today, in the form of the frequently beleaguered London Zoo.

NOW In 1907 Carl Hagenback, a campaigner against cruel techniques in training wild animals, opened the first true modern zoo near Hamburg, Germany. Until then, animals tended to be displayed in cramped, heavily armoured cages. Hagenback's enclosures reflected the animals' natural habitats, with animals and audience separated by pits which created a sense of freedom. London Zoo incorporated his approach in 1913. More recently, many zoos have seen a fall in the number of visitors – and revenue – due to public concern over the caging of wild animals.

THE YALTA CONFERENCE

The shape of the post-war world was decided at the Yalta Conference, towards the end of the Second World War. The leaders of the 'Big Three' Allies – Britain's Winston Churchill (far left), Franklin D Roosevelt of the US (centre) and Russia's Josef Stalin – met in February 1945 at Yalta, in the Crimea.

They decided that when Germany was defeated it would be split into four zones (the fourth under French control), and its military industry dismantled.

Stalin's pledge to join the war against Japan earned him territories lost to that country, and he agreed to guarantee democracy for countries freed from Nazi occupation.

But with the Red Army already holding Eastern Europe, one occupying force merely supplanted another.

A baby vicuna – a South American camel – born in London Zoo by Caesarean section

1998
MICROSOFT IN THE DOCK
The biggest anti-trust lawsuit of the 20th century began when software giant Microsoft Corporation was sued by the US government and 20 state governments. The company, led by billionaire Bill Gates, was accused of using unfair tactics to crush competition and restrict choice for consumers.

1999
CLINTON GOES ON TRIAL
President Clinton was found not guilty of perjury and obstruction of justice in the first presidential impeachment trial in 130 years. The two articles of impeachment stemmed from his relationship with former White House intern Monica Lewinsky.

1999
ENTER THE EURO
The Euro, a single European currency, was introduced on January 1, 1999. Eleven nations, not including Britain, began using it for financial and business transactions. Actual Euro coins and notes would not be issued until January, 2002.

BABE ZAHARIAS

'Babe' Zaharias was one of the great sporting heroines. Born Mildred Didrikson in 1914, she won two gold medals at the 1932 Olympics – javelin and 80 metres hurdles – and also excelled at high jump, tennis, basketball, baseball, swimming and rifle-shooting. After taking up golf, she won the US Women's Open three times, under her married name, the last only a year after a cancer operation. Had she not died in 1956, who knows which sport 'Babe' would have dominated next?

X-RATED FILMS

Before X, there was H. Originally, the British Board of Film Classification (or Censors, as it was then called) classed films as U and A (no under-16s). From 1933, 'A' became 'H' as in 'horrific', and in 1951, with cinema getting ever sexier, 'H' became 'X', meaning 'sex and horror'. By the Sixties, the X simply meant 'over-18s only', like its '18' equivalent today.

The history of film censorship is the story of a strict moral stranglehold becoming gradually loosened and replaced by a liberal tolerance that is sensitive both to market forces and artistic freedom.

In 1930, themes that could get a film banned included 'travesties of religious rites', 'too much shooting', 'free love', and 'British officers shown in an unflattering light'. Today, none of these would raise a flicker; films may be toned down, but it seems almost impossible to get one banned.

Recent films shown in Britain include a new version of *Lolita*, Nabokov's tale of a man who has sex with an under-age girl in his care; *Crash*, based on J G Ballard's story of a group of people who get turned on by car accidents; and *Boogie Nights*, an everyday tale of porn industry workers.

In America, however, the X-rating equivalent ('NC-17') is still likely to discourage distributors. It was rumoured that Stanley Kubrick's *Eyes Wide Shut* had been edited after his death so that it would be rated more accessibly.

Burt Reynolds in a role he never expected to play – that of a porn movie director, in 1997's Boogie Nights. Reynolds is seen making XXX films in a movie released with an 18 certificate – today's equivalent of the old 'X'.

X-RAYS

THE X-RAY IS AN ESSENTIAL OF MODERN LIFE, WHETHER DETECTING FAULTS IN STEEL OR BONE, OR SCANNING TISSUE FOR THE TUMOUR-PRODUCING ACTIVITY OF CANCER CELLS. THE GERMAN WILHELM RÖNTGEN WON THE FIRST-EVER NOBEL PRIZE FOR PHYSICS WITH HIS 1895 DISCOVERY THAT A BEAM OF ELECTRONS HITTING A SOLID TARGET PRODUCES ELECTROMAGNETIC RAYS OF SHORTER WAVELENGTH THAN VISIBLE LIGHT. THEY WERE DUBBED X-RAYS BECAUSE OF THEIR MYSTERIOUS NATURE RATHER THAN POTENTIAL SIDE EFFECTS, WHICH INCLUDE HAIR LOSS, SKIN ULCERATION AND GENETIC MUTATIONS.

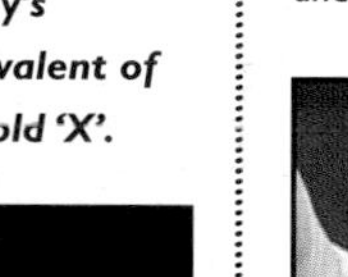

EMIL ZATOPEK

EMIL ZATOPEK'S RUNNING STYLE WAS UNGAINLY BUT HIS RECORD WAS UNMATCHED. HE WON THE 1948 OLYMPIC 10,000 METRES, BUT HIS CROWNING GLORY WAS THE 1952 GAMES. HE WON BOTH THE 10,000 METRES AND 5,000 METRES, THEN ENTERED THE MARATHON FOR THE FIRST TIME IN HIS LIFE – AND WON.

LIFELINES

EMILE ZOLA *(1840-1902) was the crusading author of Germinal. He split France by publishing J'Accuse, championing Alfred Dreyfus, an army officer falsely jailed for spying. Zola was sentenced to prison but fled, and became a hero.*

W B YEATS, *born in 1865, was one of Ireland's foremost writers. A leader of celtic revivalism, his work also included the occult. Yeats served in the Irish Senate from 1922 to 1928, received a Nobel Prize for Literature in 1923, and died in 1939.*

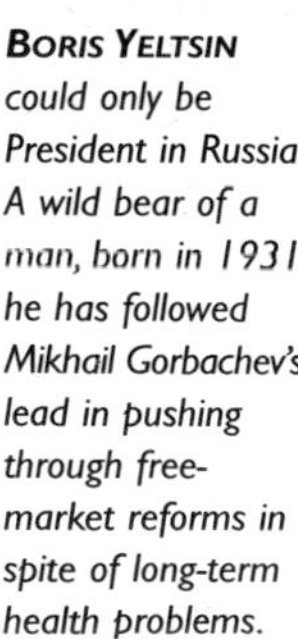

BORIS YELTSIN *could only be President in Russia. A wild bear of a man, born in 1931, he has followed Mikhail Gorbachev's lead in pushing through free-market reforms in spite of long-term health problems.*

X Y Z

1999 NEW POET LAUREATE Following the death of Ted Hughes, Professor Andrew Motion, 47, began a 10-year appointment as Poet Laureate. Hailed as a "people's poet", his first work commemorated the Royal Wedding of Prince Edward and Sophie Rhys-Jones.

1999 MALLORY PUZZLE When asked why he wanted to climb Everest, George Mallory famously replied: "Because it's there." He was last seen climbing up it on June 8, 1924. Almost exactly 75 years later, the Briton's body, preserved by snow, was found just 600 metres (2,030 feet) from the summit. The intriguing question remains: Was he on his way back down?

1999 MILLENNIUM DOME As the world entered the excitement and uncertainty of the new Millennium, the Dome to commemorate mankind's hopes and achievements was built in London.

PHOTOGRAPHIC CREDITS

The publishers would like to thank all those who have supplied photographs for use in this book and apologise to any whose contribution may have been inadvertently omitted from these acknowledgements. We are particularly grateful to Colin Finlay, Caroline Theakstone and their colleagues at Hulton Getty, and to Lee Martin and Rob Harborne at Allsport.

The majority of the photographs in this book are from Hulton Getty, London. Other sources are as follows:

The Advertising Archives, London 15tl, 15tr, 15cl, 15cc, 15cr, 30tr, 33b, 39tl, 47tl, 59cl, 74br, 84bl, 97b; Allsport, London 12r, 18tc, 18tr, 21cr, 24cl, 40bl, 56r, 57bl, 61tl, 61tc, 66 (all), 67tc, 69bl, 82bl, 89tr, 94tc, 95t, 95br, 98tl, 103bc, 104tl, 104br, 108t, 108bc, 108br, 109 (all), 116c, 116r, 117tl, 117r, 121tl, 125tl, 131(all), 140c, 140cr, 140br, 141(all), 146(all), 147l, 147c, 155bl, 161(all), 162 extreme cl, 162cl, 167tl, 167bl; Associated Press, London 6, 7; Bridgeman Art Library, London 10bl, 42bl, 61bl, 64tl, 73tl, 81bc, 88tr, 100tr, 135br, 152bl; Corbis, London 85tr, 125cr; E.T. Archive, London 10br, 25t, 33tl, 42tr, 68tr, 77tr, 80tr, 80b, 81tc, 88cr, 100tl, 101tl, 114tr, 115tl, 126br, 127tl, 127bl, 151bl, 157br; The Kobal Collection, London 23br, 40tr, 92r, 129, 159tr; Popperfoto, Northampton 16br, 27bcl, 35bc, 36b, 45l, 74tl, 90tr, 90b, 107tl, 130tr, 134br, 148c, 154bl, 166br; Rex Features, London 14bl, 17tl, 17tcr, 17bl, 19tcl, 19tcr, 19br, 21ccl, 21ccr, 21bl, 21bc, 24tr, 25b, 26tr, 26br, 28bl, 32cl, 33br, 35tc, 35bl, 36tr, 37r, 41bl, 41br, 44r, 46t, 46bl, 48tr, 49tl, 49c, 50t, 51l, 51c, 52tl, 52bl, 53cl, 54bl, 54br, 55l, 55br, 56l, 58bc, 58br, 59tl, 59cr, 59bc, 60bl, 62l, 62c, 64tl, 64bl, 67tl, 68br, 69br, 70tl, 72br, 75tr, 75b, 76tr, 79br, 82tc, 82bc, 83tl, 85tcl, 85tcc, 85bcl, 85bcc, 85bl, 86bl, 87br, 89br, 93tl, 96bc, 97t, 97cl, 97cr, 99tr, 100br, 102br, 105 (all), 106tr, 107tc, 107tr, 107bcl, 107bcr, 110tc, 110tr, 112 (all), 113tl, 113bl, 114c, 115r, 118tl, 118bl, 119tl, 119tcl, 119tcr, 119bl, 124tr, 124bl, 124br, 126tl, 126bl, 128bl, 133tl, 133tc, 133tr, 135tc, 135cl, 135cc, 136 (all), 137tl, 137tc, 137cl, 137bl, 137bcl, 138tl, 138tc, 138bc, 139r, 143tc, 143tr, 149r, 150t, 151tc, 152c, 156tr, 157tcl, 158b, 159br, 160tl, 160bl, 160bc, 162c, 162r, 162br, 164bl, 165bl, 167c, 167br; The Ronald Grant Archive, London 112tr, 145tl, 163tl, 163r, 163bl.

Pictured above: One of the first professional photographers, at work on Clapham Common in 1873

Past meets future as fireworks explode over Tower Bridge to usher in the year 2000. The historic bridge, completed in 1894, provided a picturesque focus for London's celebrations

INTO THE THIRD MILLENNIUM

KIRIBATI

Dawn of a new era for Earth

The first sun of the third Millennium rose over a tiny volcanic Pacific atoll called … Millennium. One of a group of islands that make up Kiribati, it was previously known as Caroline Island, but had been specially renamed. It is also normally uninhabited, but on January 1, 2000 it came under the spotlight as the first speck of land on the International Date Line.

The Kiribati government had brought in 60 singers and dancers to celebrate the Millennium – along with the world's media. President Teberuro Tito took a lighted torch from an old man and passed it to a young boy in a symbol of time passing into the hands of a new generation, saying: "Take this torch of hope and peace from Kiribati so that it may light up the whole world."

The irony is that Millennium island, just three feet above sea level, will almost certainly disappear beneath the waves as global warming raises the sea level over the next few decades. According to BBC reporter John Simpson, ten days of human occupation have already wrought havoc with the precious wildlife.

As Kiribati's torch-bearers sailed into the west in a dugout canoe, the new Millennium began to ripple round the world. Minutes later, it was the turn of New Zealand's Chatham Islands to celebrate, with Monique Croom becoming the first bride of the Millennium. Out at sea, the American nuclear submarine *USS Topeka* straddled the Date Line, so its sailors were able to stroll from the 20th century into the 21st – and back.

'Let all the world be joined with us to greet the new Millennium. Let us put aside all divisions. Let us unite in love and peace.'

– SONG BY THE PEOPLE OF KIRIBATI
A new vow for the 21st century, sung on the beach at Millennium Island

Right: A dancer greets the dawn on Millennium Island in the South Pacific, where local people in traditional grass skirts put on a celebration that inspired the whole world

AUSTRALIA

It's a real whizz-bang in Oz

Sydney Harbour in Australia was the beautiful setting for the first fireworks extravaganza of Millennium night, enjoyed by a million people on the waterfront. Thousands more, including Hollywood stars Nicole Kidman and Tom Cruise, watched from a packed flotilla of boats as the famous Harbour Bridge erupted in a dazzling waterfall of light. On another boat, singer Dannii Minogue married motor racing driver Jacques Villeneuve at midnight.

With the clocks in Britain still reading 1pm on December 31, the world watched on television as £3 million worth of fireworks spelt out the message 'Eternity', then left a huge grinning face hanging over the surreal armadillo curves of the Opera House.

The year 2000 will be very special in Sydney, with the Olympics taking place there in September, and this was a celebration of a country whose time has come. Australia is already riding high with world trophies in cricket, rugby, rugby league and the tennis Davis Cup.

But it wasn't all peace and light in Oceania. In the Philippines, two people – including a 12-year-old boy – were killed by stray bullets fired off by revellers in the capital, Manila, and another nine died in fires started by fireworks.

Meanwhile in Antarctica scientists greeted the new century 24 times over, because the Amundsen-Scott reasearch base at the South Pole sits astride all the world's time zones. A foolhardy few wore Hawaiian shorts in sub-zero temperatures, proving that people in the 21st century will be just as mad as their 20th-century ancestors.

'This is the greatest party in the world. This is the place to be.'

– JAMES CRUICKSHANK
Tourist from Bristol, who had travelled from England to see the Millennium dawn in Australia

Right: Fireworks over Sydney Harbour Bridge, with the famous Opera House in the foreground. Australia's Millennium show was seen by many as the world's best

MILLENNIUM FIRSTS

The first wedding of the Millennium took place in the Chatham Islands, New Zealand – the first populated area on Earth to see in the Millennium. The local hardware store owners Monique Croom, 33, and Dean Braid, 27, exchanged vows on television just seconds after midnight.

The first wedding of the Millennium in England was at Liverpool Town Hall. David Hollingdrake, 47, and Alison Bully, 31, had to wait until 8 am, the earliest time permitted under English law, to exchange their vows. In Scotland, many couples took advantage of the more relaxed laws to wed at the stroke of midnight. Darren Cornelius and Amanda Barr, both 23, were married in Motherwell. "It was a bit strange getting married when it was pitch black outside," she said, "but it's definitely the best day of my life."

The first cricket match of the Millennium took place in the Hampshire village of Hambledon, where the game first came to maturity in the 19th century. The Englishmen ensured their place in the record books when bowler Dick Orders sent down one ball to batsman Andy Smith under the glare of car headlights. Play was then stopped for bad light. Sadly, there was no such let-off for the England team. The conditions in Cape Town, South Africa, were perfect on January 5, when England lost their first Test match of the Millennium by an innings and 37 runs.

THE FIRST CENTENARIAN OF THE MILLENNIUM WAS VIOLET DICKSON, WHO WAS BORN IN AN AUSTRALIAN PUB THREE MINUTES AFTER MIDNIGHT ON JANUARY 1, 1900. SHE CELEBRATED HER 100TH BIRTHDAY IN HOSPITAL NEAR SYDNEY. THE FIRST BRITISH CENTENARIAN WAS ELSIE RHODES, WHO RECEIVED HER TELEGRAM FROM THE QUEEN IN LINCOLNSHIRE ON JANUARY 1.

Britain's first conviction of the Millennium was a £200 fine handed out to a Polish tourist on New Year's Day at Horseferry Road court, London, for throwing a champagne bottle.

The first English Premiership goal of the Millennium was a sign of the times – it was scored by a foreign player. Derby County's Belgian striker Branko Strupar registered his first Premiership goal two minutes into the game against Watford on January 3, and went on to score the second in a 2-0 victory. The first team to top the Premiership in the Millennium were Leeds United, whose manager David O'Leary said: "It is unbelievable being top of the table for the new Millennium. In a few years' to come I'm sure there'll be a few quizzes on that one."

The first No 1 hit single of the Millennium was by Irish boy band Westlife, who also had the last Christmas No 1 of the 20th century with their double A-side 'I Have A Dream'/'Seasons In The Sun'. Band member Kian Egan said: "After the New Year celebrations, being No 1 at such a historic time has lifted our hangovers."

CHINA

Midnight on the great wall of fire

The term 'Wall of Fire' took on a literal meaning in China, where the Millennium was greeted with flames along the entire 2,150 miles of the Great Wall. Even though their New Year was not due until February 5, the Chinese were determined to put on a bravura show on the eve of a century in which they hope to become the world's dominant superpower. Lighting a ceremonial 'eternal flame' at the specially built China Centenary Altar in Beijing, President Jiang Zemin expressed the wish that China would soon be reunited with Taiwan – the island which opted out of China's Communist revolution in 1949.

On a more romantic note, Beijing went Millennium wedding crazy, with 2,000 couples tying the knot in a mass ceremony – including two sets of identical twins who married each other. In Bangkok, Thailand, 4,000 newlyweds shared a 72-tier, 30ft-high wedding cake.

For 60,000 people in Hong Kong, the Millennium started at the Happy Valley race track, where punters went home with an £80 million hangover.

In Muslim countries such as Indonesia, Iran and Pakistan, the Millennium was largely ignored, but India celebrated in style – especially in Goa, where 200,000 visitors held a massive beach party.

In Moscow, fireworks lit up Red Square and the Kremlin, but Russia's new acting president Vladimir Putin was not there to see them. He spent the first day of the 21st century – and his first day since taking over from Boris Yeltsin – visiting troops fighting in Chechnya.

'I ask your forgiveness, because many of our hopes have not come true, because what we thought would be easy turned out to be painfully difficult.'

– BORIS YELTSIN
Resigning as President of Russia on New Year's Eve

***Right:** It's 2,000 miles long, 2,000 years old, and it's still standing in the year 2000. Chinese people celebrate the third Christian Millennium on the Great Wall of China*

ISRAEL

A new star rises over Bethlehem

Of all the apocalyptic predictions about the Millennium, most centred on Jerusalem. Thousands of Christians flocked to Israel in the hope of witnessing the Second Coming of the Messiah, or simply to celebrate Christ's 2,000th birthday where He lived and died. Police had already arrested dozens of American 'fanatics' who they feared would commit mass suicide, but in the event the hymn-singing pilgrims, tourists and cult members clustering on the Mount of Olives were outweighed by TV crews.

At Manger Square in Bethlehem, at midnight, the Palestinian authorities released 2,000 'doves of peace' (actually pigeons), accompanied by the 21st-century sound of a Pink Floyd record. Middle East watchers hoped that the happy mix of religions was an omen of things to come – though if there was a star in the east, it was blotted out by the inevitable fireworks.

In many places, historic monuments built before Christ formed the backdrop to thoroughly modern spectaculars. In Egypt, the 4,500-year-old pyramids at Giza were lit up by a rock laser show as Frenchman Jean Michel Jarre entertained 50,000 people with an electronic music extravaganza. In Athens, blue and white light gave the Acropolis a new look after 2,500 years.

In Germany, at the Brandenburg Gate linking East and West Berlin, two million people enjoyed yet more futuristic rock – this time by English hippie Mike Oldfield. A dramatic laser show shot beams of light 18 miles into the sky; it was seen from 50 miles away.

'Christians and Muslims have been here in Bethlehem for centuries. We're brothers. There's no difference between us. Everyone was laughing, dancing, having fun.'

– FATHI KANAN
Muslim bank worker in Bethlehem

Right: Fireworks over Bethlehem, where Jesus was born, seen from nearby Jerusalem with the Dome of the Rock in the foreground. Inset: Nuns hold a candle-lit vigil

MILLENNIUM POLLS

PERSONALITY OF THE MILLENNIUM

(Chosen by BBC Radio 4's Today Programme)

1 ***William Shakespeare***
2 ***Winston Churchill***
3 ***William Caxton***
4 ***Charles Darwin***
5 ***Isaac Newton***
6 ***Oliver Cromwell***

PERSON OF THE CENTURY

(Chosen by politicians and journalists for Time magazine)

1 ***Albert Einstein***
2 ***Franklin D Roosevelt***
3 ***Mahatma Gandhi***

PRIME MINISTERS OF THE CENTURY

(Chosen by historians, politicians and commentators on BBC Radio 4's The Westminster Hour. There were 19 PMs in the 20th century; Tony Blair was not included)

1 ***Winston Churchill***
2 ***David Lloyd George***
3 ***Clement Attlee***
4 ***Herbert Asquith***
5 ***Margaret Thatcher***
6 ***Harold Macmillan***
7 ***Marquess of Salisbury***
8 ***Stanley Baldwin***
9 ***Sir Henry Campbell-Bannerman***
10 ***Harold Wilson***

BRITISH SPEECH OF THE CENTURY

(Chosen by 137 experts for two American universities)

Winston Churchill "Let us brace ourselves to our duties and so bear ourselves that, if the British Empire and its Commonwealth last for a thousand years, men will say, 'This was their finest hour'."

AMERICAN SPEECH OF THE CENTURY

Martin Luther King "I have a dream that my four little children will one day live in a nation where they will not be judged by the colour of their skin."

SONG LYRICS OF THE CENTURY

(Voted by the public on National Poetry Day)

1	***Imagine***	John Lennon
2	***Angels***	Robbie Williams
3	***Bohemian Rhapsody***	Queen
4	***I Am The Walrus***	The Beatles
5	***Millennium***	Robbie Williams

SOUTH AFRICA

Mandela's smile lights the world

Probably only one man could have transcended all the fireworks with a simple act of humanity. Nelson Mandela, a beacon of peace and freedom throughout the Nineties, made a personal journey back to the dark days of his incarceration and shone a light into a better, more humane future.

The first president of democratic, post-apartheid South Africa returned to the prison at Robben Island, just off Cape Town, where he had been held captive for 18 years. Now retired, Mandela showed he had lost none of his power to move the world as he revisited the tiny cell that was his 'home' for so long.

At midnight, smiling as ever, he stood behind the bars in what is now a museum of reconciliation and lit a Millennium "flame of freedom", which he passed on to his successor, President Thabo Mbeki. He, in turn, passed it to a child, symbolising what Mandela optimistically called "the dawn of the African century".

Across the water, fireworks exploded and laser beams lit up Table Mountain as three million locals and 200,000 tourists defied the bombers who had blasted Cape Town three times in the previous two months, dancing, drinking at the world's longest bar, and then watching the dawn from the famous flat-topped mountain.

Meanwhile in Britain, there was further proof of Mandela's almost saintly status when *Daily Mirror* readers voted him their 'man of the millennium', just ahead of British war hero Sir Winston Churchill.

'I have been fortunate to live through most of the century. It brought such great hope and at other times such disappointment.'

– NELSON MANDELA
Speaking at Robben Island, near Cape Town

***Right:** Nelson Mandela, the prisoner who became President, revisits his jail cell at Robben Island and lights a flame of freedom to celebrate 'the dawn of the African century'*

FRANCE

Eiffel Tower becomes a giant sparkler

Paris was the undisputed winner of the fireworks war. Its display cost less than most – £450,000 to London's £4 million – but was so beautifully staged that it gave us the most breathtaking image of all: the Eiffel Tower as a gigantic child's sparkler.

Not everyone in France enjoyed the Millennium. The country had been hit by a 120mph hurricane on Christmas Day, and 500,000 homes were still without electricity. But the 1.5 million who ventured out in Paris saw a sight that will stay with them forever.

The show centred on Alexandre Eiffel's mighty tower – the tallest building of the 19th century, now put to glorious use to see in the 21st. The pyrotechnics began with an amazing, shimmering effect, achieved by 20,000 flash bulbs which had been strung along the ironwork by a team of rock-climbers over a period of four months.

Then, to the amazement of television viewers around the world, 12,000 fireworks shot out vertically and horizontally from 80 racks placed within the Tower.

The only hitch was that the huge digital clock which had been counting down to the Millennium for 1,000 days chose 6.45pm on December 31 to seize up – and the fireworks were due to be triggered by the clock. Technicians tried in vain to restart the clock and finally installed a new timer with just two hours to spare.

After the fireworks, 11 Ferris wheels covered in lights began turning in the Champs-Elysées, where the crowds were entertained by musicians and dancers.

'The clock of history strikes an important hour. For believers this is the year of the Great Jubilee. As He did 2,000 years ago, Christ comes with his saving gospel.'

– POPE JOHN PAUL
Addressing 150,000 tourists and pilgrims in St Peter's Square, Rome

***Right:* The spectacular view of the Eiffel Tower from the right bank of the River Seine. The seven-minute fairytale display involved 20,000 lights and some 12,000 fireworks**

MILLENNIUM POLLS

BEST ALBUM OF ALL TIME

(Chosen by 600,000 people in a Channel 4/HMV poll)

1	***Sgt Pepper***	The Beatles
2	***Thriller***	Michael Jackson
3	***Revolver***	The Beatles
4	***Aloha From Hawaii***	Elvis Presley
5	***Nevermind***	Nirvana
6	***The Stone Roses***	The Stone Roses
7	***Morning Glory***	Oasis
8	***Dark Side Of The Moon***	Pink Floyd
9	***I've Been Expecting You***	Robbie Williams
10	***The Bends***	Radiohead

BEST MALE AND FEMALE VOCALISTS

(Chosen by 600,000 people in a Channel 4/HMV poll)

1	***Elvis Presley***	1	***Madonna***
2	***Robbie Williams***	2	***Aretha Franklin***
3	***Michael Jackson***	3	***Celine Dion***
4	***Frank Sinatra***	4	***Ella Fitzgerald***
5	***George Michael***	5	***Mariah Carey***
6	***Freddie Mercury***	6	***Whitney Houston***
7	***David Bowie***	7	***Alanis Morissette***
8	***John Lennon***	8	***Annie Lennox***
9	***Thom Yorke***	9	***Kate Bush***
10	***Kurt Cobain***	10	***Björk***

BEST VIDEOS OF ALL TIME

(Chosen by MTV viewers)

1	***Thriller***	Michael Jackson
2	***Vogue***	Madonna
3	***Smells Like Teen Spirit***	Nirvana
4	***Sledgehammer***	Peter Gabriel
5	***Walk This Way***	Run DMC/Aerosmith
6	***Sweet Child O' Mine***	Guns 'N Roses
7	***Sabotage***	Beastie Boys
8	***Addicted to Love***	Robert Palmer
9	***California Love***	Tupac/Dr Dre
10	***Express Yourself***	Madonna

GREATEST ROCK SONGS OF ALL TIME

(Chosen by 700 music industry people for VH1)

1	***Satisfaction***	The Rolling Stones
2	***Respect***	Aretha Franklin
3	***Stairway To Heaven***	Led Zeppelin
4	***Like A Rolling Stone***	Bob Dylan
5	***Born To Run***	Bruce Springsteen
6	***Hotel California***	The Eagles
7	***Light My Fire***	The Doors
8	***Good Vibrations***	The Beach Boys
9	***Hey Jude***	The Beatles
10	***Imagine***	John Lennon

LONDON

Spotlight on the biggest party ever

London was determined to put on the biggest party of all time, and it certainly succeeded. Three million people thronged the funfairs along a three-mile stretch of the River Thames, strained their ears to hear the 12 o'clock chimes of the world's most famous clock, Big Ben, and then gasped as £4 million worth of fireworks lit up the sky and sent thunder crashes booming off the side of the Royal Festival Hall.

The night was not without disappointments. The giant 'Millennium Eye' Ferris wheel on the south bank, which had taken seven years to plan and £35 million to build, was due to start up on New Year's Eve. But with 24 hours to go, a problem with one of the cars meant it would have to turn without passengers – and by the time Prime Minister Tony Blair sent a laser beam whizzing across the river to set the wheel in motion, a new problem meant that even that did not happen. Still, it looked wonderful…

The most eagerly anticipated event was the midnight River of Fire, a 200-metres-high sheet of flame which ran down the river from Tower Bridge to Lambeth at 775 mph – the speed of the Earth's rotation. But the whole thing came and went so quickly that it left most spectators mystified.

Earlier, the Queen had ignited the world's largest beacon on the river at the Tower. The old fortress has seen many colourful sights in its 1,000-year history, but none as dramatic as the firework show that exploded over its head on January 1, 2000.

'As we enter the 21st century there can be no pride in the fact that millions in our country still can't read, and so many children live in poverty. But I believe we can meet these challenges.'

– PRIME MINISTER TONY BLAIR

***Right:** The Millennium Eye is lit up by a laser beam fired from the opposite bank by Tony Blair. Though the wheel failed to turn, it is a majestic addition to London's skyline*

MILLENNIUM DOME

Welcome to the Pleasure Dome...

The £750 million Dome opened its doors to the public on the eve of the Millennium – to mixed reactions. The Party of the Millennium was preceded by the Queue of the Apocalypse, as one critic put it, as guests waited for up to six hours to get in.

But the show, which included pop stars Mick Hucknall and The Corrs, the orchestra of the English National Opera, and awe-inspiring displays from teams of acrobats, trapeze artists, jugglers and aerial ballet dancers, went down a storm.

The Dome's 13-zone exhibition, which will remain in place throughout the year 2000, comprises:

- **Learning Zone** A new world of learning.
- **Body Zone** A 27-metre-high 'sculpture' of entwined bodies, entered through a 'vein' full of artificial blood.
- **Play Zone** Unusual children's games.
- **Journey Zone** Driving a futuristic car which turns into an airplane is just one of the experiences here.
- **Shared Ground Zone** Our changing way of life.
- **Living Island Zone** A beach with deckchairs, seagulls and lifeguard tower made from household items.
- **Home Planet Zone** Virtual reality tour of the Universe.
- **Self-Portrait Zone** A celebration of British life.
- **Talk Zone** Two buildings which 'talk' to each other.
- **Faith Zone** The different religions in Britain.
- **Mind Zone** Your 3-D image changes sex or age.
- **Rest Zone** Chill out in a mental flotation tank.
- **Money Zone** An opportunity to spend £1 million in a computer-generated department store.

'Someone once said that history is written by the victors, but I believe God keeps an alternative record – a chronicle of the unsung heroes of history.'

– *Dr GEORGE CAREY*
Archbishop of Canterbury, in his New Year's address

***Right:* Exotically-dressed dancers entertain the 10,000 guests at the opening night of the Dome. *Inset:* The Queen sings Auld Lang Syne with Tony and Cherie Blair**

MILLENNIUM POLLS

SPORTSMEN AND SPORTSWOMEN OF THE CENTURY

(According to a poll of sports writers on The Independent)

1 ***Muhammad Ali***
2 ***Pele***
3 ***Donald Bradman***
4 ***Jack Nicklaus***
5 ***Jesse Owens***
6 ***Rod Laver***
7 ***Juan Manuel Fangio***
8 ***Emil Zatopek***
9 ***Carl Lewis***
10 ***Babe Zaharias (Mildred Didrikson)***

TOY OF THE MILLENNIUM

(Daily Mirror readers' poll)

1 ***The teddy bear***

FILMS OF THE MILLENNIUM

(Voted by viewers of BBC TV's Film '99)

1 ***Star Wars***
2 ***Blade Runner***
3 ***Casablanca***
4 ***Alien***
5 ***Star Wars: The Phantom Menace***
6 ***The Shawshank Redemption***
7 ***Star Wars: The Empire Strikes Back***
8 ***Schindler's List***
9 ***Saving Private Ryan***
10 ***Pulp Fiction***

THE 50 WILDEST WOMEN OF THE CENTURY

(Chosen by National Enquirer magazine)

Ava Gardner Billie Jean King ***Bonnie Parker*** Bette Davis ***Clara Bow*** Courtney Love ***Drew Barrymore*** Donna Rice ***Diana Ross*** Dolly Parton ***Elizabeth Taylor*** Farrah Fawcett ***Fanne Foxe*** Gypsy Rose Lee ***Gloria Swanson*** Grace Slick ***Hedy Lamarr*** Heidi Fleiss ***Ida Lupino*** Isadora Duncan ***Joan Crawford*** Josephine Baker ***Jane Fonda*** Katharine Hepburn ***Lena Horne*** Lorena Bobbitt ***Lucille Ball*** Marilyn Monroe ***Maria Callas*** Madonna ***Marlene Dietrich*** Mata Hari ***Monica Lewinsky*** Mae West ***Natalie Wood*** Oksana Baiul Pamela Anderson Lee ***Queen Latifah*** ***Rita Hayworth*** Roseanne ***Shirley Maclaine*** Stevie Nicks ***Tonya Harding*** Tallulah Bankhead ***Ursula Andress*** Virginia Hill ***Whoopi Goldberg*** Xaviera Hollander ***Yoko Ono*** Zsa Zsa Gabor

BRITAIN & IRELAND

Hopes for a future with no Troubles

The worldwide wishes for a peaceful Millennium carried extra meaning in Northern Ireland, where Protestants and Catholics celebrated together. In Londonderry, 2,000 voices united in a rousing rendition of 'Danny Boy', and torch-bearers formed a Circle of Light on the city's 17th-century walls. Belfast held an inter-denominational church service, while in the Irish Republic, President Mary McAleese lit the first of 1.3 million candles to welcome "the dawn of peace in Northern Ireland".

By contrast, the big news in Manchester was David and Victoria Beckham going to the United footballers' party. Liverpool's River of Light featured 30-mile-long laser beams, while in Birmingham Sir Cliff Richard lit a Flame of Hope. In Norwich, 2,000 candles floated poetically down the River Wensum. Newcastle pulled off the feat of suspending a string quartet above the crowds, and Bristol was lit by a swaying lantern parade.

Beacons created a ring of fire on Plymouth Sound, Druids danced round the stones at Stonehenge, and Southampton launched 50,000 rockets and spelled out the number 2000 in the sky. In Coventry, Ramon Kelvink from Bordeaux walked a tightrope from the Holy Trinity Church to the Old Cathedral.

Pop fans flocked to Cardiff, where 57,000 saw the Manic Street Preachers at the Millennium Stadium, and Edinburgh, where Texas and the Bay City Rollers played at the world's biggest Hogmanay party. But Britain on this New Year's Eve was one humungous Hogmanay party.

'We stand on the brink of a momentous benchmark in history. With new understanding on this island, we may act as a beacon to other countries.'

– *BERTIE AHERN*
Prime Minister of the Republic of Ireland

***Right:** Having chimed in the new Millennium, Big Ben disappears in a red mist as £1 billion goes up in smoke around Britain. Inset: A brief glimpse of the River of Fire*

USA

We're going to party like it's 1999

New York waved goodbye to the American Century in the American way – with showers of confetti, clouds of balloons, dazzling fireworks, lights playing on the Empire State Building, two million people kissing and hugging beneath the neon signs on Times Square … and no alcohol.

Fearful of terrorism, Seattle had cancelled its celebrations. New York went ahead, but with strict precautions such as sealing all the manholes in Midtown Manhattan. Throughout the day, as other countries entered the new Millennium, huge carnival floats paraded, representing the country concerned (in Britain's case, it was Old Father Time). At midnight, strangers kissed one another as if it was VE Day.

In Washington, President Bill Clinton hosted a grand dinner attended by Hollywood stars Elizabeth Taylor, Jack Nicholson and Sophia Loren, along with Muhammad Ali and astronaut John Glenn. The Clintons and their guests then joined the thousands in the Mall – site of Martin Luther King's "I have a dream" speech – for a pop concert hosted by rapper/actor Will Smith, with performers including Tom Jones.

Finally, the President lit the fuse on a fireworks show that ran up the Washington monument, echoing the pyrotechnics at the Eiffel Tower.

The hot spot in South America was Rio de Janeiro, where three million Brazilians on Copacabana Beach saw a £1 million fireworks show, and cast white flowers into the waves for the Brazilian sea goddess Iemanja.

'(In the new Millennium) when we see threats to peace and human dignity abroad, we can choose not to speak; we can choose not to act; but we can no longer choose not to know.'
– *U.S. PRESIDENT BILL CLINTON*

***Right:** A no-alcohol rule didn't stop New Yorkers going wild after the annual New Year 'ball drop', in which a crystal globe descends a 77 ft flagpole atop No. I Times Square*

WHATEVER NEXT...

The way of the world in the new Millennium

Where will we be living, what will we be eating, and will virtual reality sex be our most popular recreational pursuit in the third Millennium? Experts have made the following predictions...

HOME COMFORTS

Boring household chores will be a thing of the past

- *Robots that can learn and make choices will take over many domestic duties.*
- *Computerised homes will enable you to run a bath, make a cup of tea, and adjust heating, lighting and decor by voice command.*
- *Kitchen cupboards and fridges will notify you when food is approaching its sell-by date and re-order your favourite foods and essential items as required.*
- *Inventor James Dyson says washing machines will sort clothing by barcode, select the right temperature and cycle.*

DRIVE TIME

Travelling by car will be quicker, easier and safer

- *Gerald Celente, director of New York's Trends Research Institute, says cars will fly by magnetic levitation.*
- *They'll operate by autopilot – you'll simply log in your destination, sit back and enjoy the view.*
- *Accidents will be reduced by collision-avoiding radar.*
- *Cars will be powered by a new, clean energy source.*
- *Car sharing may be run along the same lines as time-sharing holidays.*

FOOD FACTS

Our diet will change for the better

- *Microchips inserted under the skin, or worn in a belt or wristband, will monitor our nutritional status and suggest foods for optimum health maintenance.*
- *Fast food will still be popular, but it'll all be freshly prepared organic fare.*
- *Your fridge will suggest recipes based on its contents.*
- *According to inventor James Dyson, cookers will make your favourite meal by voice command.*

HEALTH

We may not totally eradicate ill health, but new drugs and techniques will make prevention and treatment more effective

- *Genetic testing will help stop many diseases developing.*
- *Drugs will be produced on a personal basis, eliminating many of the side effects associated with mass-produced medicines.*
- *Ovary transplants will enable women to have children at any age.*
- *Tissue engineering will ensure a regular supply of replacement organs and other body parts.*

MILLENNIUM BABIES

Unto us a child is born

The first documented baby of the third Millennium was born at ten past midnight on January 1, 2000 in Auckland, New Zealand *(inset)*. Mother Milika and father Sifoni Fetuani named their daughter Tupou and, as she is their seventh child, probably breathed a sigh of relief at the thought of all the lucrative sponsorship deals and free nappies heading their way.

Around 350,000 babies were born as dawn rolled around the world, and Britain didn't have long to wait for its first Millennium baby. At 15 seconds past midnight, Alison Webb, 28, gave birth to a 7lb 2oz girl with her partner Mark Heafield, 40, at her side. "The baby's head was visible at 11.59pm, and as the last chime of Big Ben could be heard the baby was born. It was a wonderful moment," said a spokesman for Birmingham Women's Hospital, which claimed a unique hat-trick, having also delivered babies during the total eclipse in August 1999, and at 9.09 on 9.9.99.

Other special Millennium babes included twins born in different Millennia. Julie Wallman of Indianapolis, USA, accomplished the remarkable feat of giving birth to baby Jacob, weighing 5lbs 6oz, at one minute before midnight on December 31, 1999, swiftly followed by Jordan, 5lbs, at one minute past midnight on January 1, 2000 *(main picture)*.

However, no baby was more precisely timed than Rupa Pandya's daughter, born in Bombay on the cusp of the second and third Millennia at exactly midnight.

'Computers' speed and complexity double every 18 months. This will probably continue until computers have a similar complexity to the human brain.'

– *PROFESSOR STEPHEN HAWKING*
Author of A Brief History Of Time

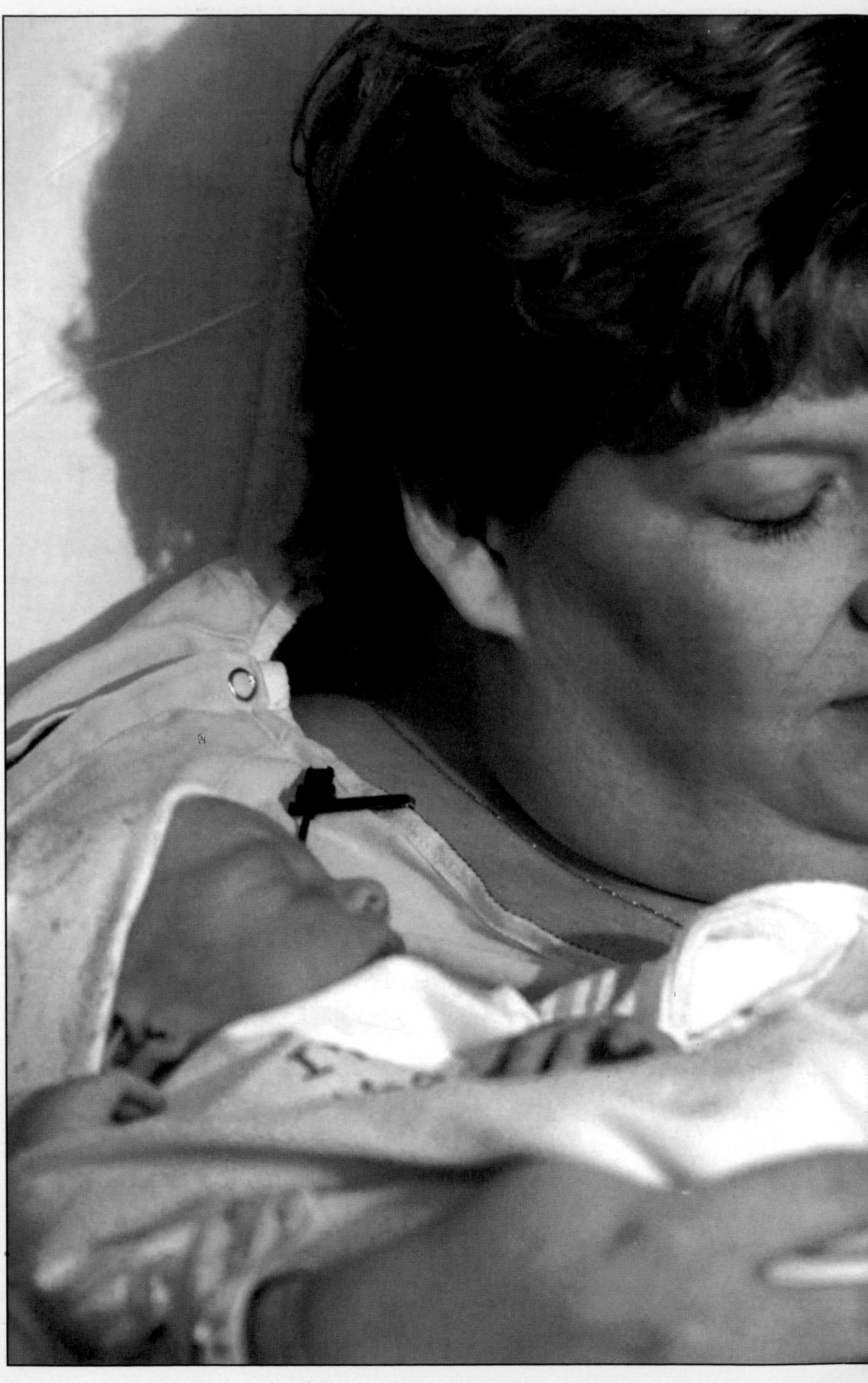

***Right:** Julie Wallman with twins Jacob and Jordan, born in different Millennia. **Inset:** Milika and Sifoni Fetuani with daughter Tupou, the first baby of the third Millennium*

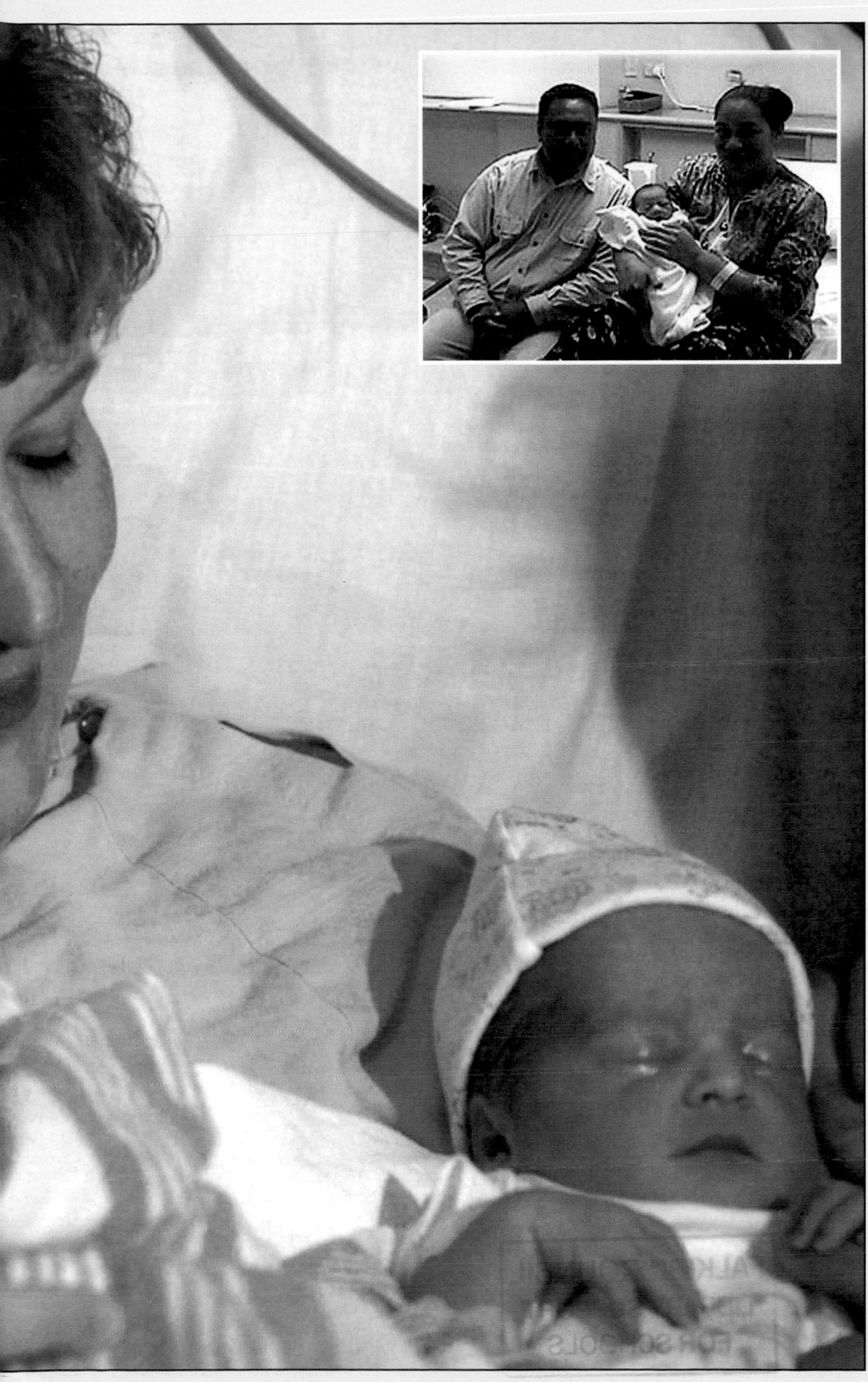

WHATEVER NEXT...

EDUCATION

We'll probably still all need to attend school, but teaching methods will be very different

- *Children will spend some of their time being taught at home, via online interactive programmes and 3-D holograms of teachers.*
- *A universal language and voice-activated translators will provide easy access to libraries and other educational institutions around the world.*

FUN TIME

With more leisure time, here's how we'll fill it

- *Holographic images will turn our front rooms into stadiums for live concerts and sports events.*
- *Films and video games will be interactive, so you can direct the storyline yourself, or superimpose your own image on to one of the characters.*
- *Stimulating body suits and computer links will allow you to have virtual reality sex with whoever you want, without the risk of disappointment or disease.*

FERTILITY RITES

Making babies may be very different to today

- *Designer babies based on physical and intellectual attributes will be commonplace through genetic engineering and test tube techniques.*
- *Animals may be used to grow the sperm of sterile men.*
- *Women may gestate their babies in artificial wombs.*

ENVIRONMENTAL ISSUES

This is one of the most controversial areas of discussion among world experts, who predict:

- *Toxic emissions will increase six-fold in 100 years.*
- *If we continue to pollute and over fish the sea, seafood will be off the menu in a mere 25 years' time.*
- *If global warming goes on, world temperatures will rise 11°C by 3000, making the planet uninhabitable.*
- *Windmills and solar panels will be our main sources of power and the saviours of the environment.*

HOME SECURITY

Life will become much more difficult for burglars

- *Fingerprinting, retina scanning, DNA profiling and voice activation entry systems will foil unwanted visitors.*
- *Security cameras will link every home with police surveillance units.*
- *Pressure pads in and around the home will detect intruders and notify you wherever you are.*
- *Remote-control central locking devices and electrified exits will help you apprehend intruders.*

BUSINESS MATTERS

Working life will also change beyond recognition

- *Genetic screening will be part of every job interview.*
- *There will be a single global currency.*
- *Coins and notes will become obsolete, replaced by credit and debit cards.*
- *Most people will work from home, with only a few working in centralised business locations.*

FIRST JOB OF THE NEW MILLENNIUM: CLEARING UP AFTER THE LAST!

It's a dirty job, but someone's got to do it. The morning after the Millennium before, workers in New York's Times Square sweep up several tons of confetti. Welcome to the year 2000

Apocalypse now? No – the outlook for tomorrow's world looks positively rosy

Not everyone predicts doom, gloom and apocalypse for the Millennium ahead. Peter Schwartz, a former oil industry analyst in California, firmly believes in what he calls the Long Boom theory.

Schwartz forecasts that our quality of life will increase enormously over the century and that we will be healthier, happier and more humanitarian. He says that crime and violence will be almost non-existent and that, due to the creation of a global village, there will be no more wars. He also insists that during the third Millennium it will become possible to prevent illness, ageing and even death.

"At the start of the 20th century, the average life expectancy in the West was around 47 years," he says. "Now it is 75. That is a 60 per cent increase in the course of one century.

"Today we have – or will soon have – the life science to go much, much further. My eight-year-old son has a good chance of seeing in the 30th century."

'We will realise that we have trashed our planet, but there's still time to repair the damage'

John Simpson – the BBC's World Affairs Editor and our man in Kiribati – reflects on the mistakes and the achievements of the 20th century, and the possible new directions for the next 100 years and beyond...

'No one, a century ago, foresaw the extraordinary changes of the 20th century. We're unlikely to do better now. Still, there are trends. The nation-state is coming to an end. Because we're better at dealing with conflict, there are fewer wars now than throughout history. Crime, though, is beyond our control; our future problems will be internal, not external. We will quickly realise how we have trashed our planet, and will have time to repair the damage. But the diversity of human life will be a thing of the past. For better and for worse, we will all be the same.'

PICTURES IN THIS SECTION COURTESY OF ASSOCIATED PRESS; JOHN SIMPSON PHOTO COURTESY OF BBC; ORIGINATION BY TARN PRINT LTD.